A *Practitioner's* Guide to Financial Crime Typologies and Investigative Techniques

Financial Crime Investigation

DR IAN MESSENGER

Financial Crime Investigation

Interior Design and Formatting: Nonon Tech & Design

ISBN: 978-1-998376-09-4 (Hardback)

Financial Crime Investigation

TABLE OF CONTENTS

Introduction 1

PART I
FOUNDATIONS OF FINANCIAL CRIME

Chapter 1: Introduction to Financial Crime 7

Chapter 2: The Financial Crime Ecosystem 37

Chapter 3: Global Legal and Regulatory Frameworks 69

PART II
CORE FINANCIAL CRIME TYPES

Chapter 4: Money Laundering 103

Chapter 5: Fraud 135

Chapter 6: Bribery and Corruption 163

Chapter 7: Terrorist Financing 189

Chapter 8: Sanctions Evasion and Trade-Based Crime 215

Chapter 9: Cyber-Enabled Financial Crime 241

PART III
INVESTIGATION METHODOLOGIES

Chapter 10: Planning a Financial Crime Investigation 267

Chapter 11: Gathering and Analyzing Evidence 293

Chapter 12: Interviewing and Human Intelligence 317

Chapter 13: Digital and Open-Source Intelligence............. 343

Chapter 14: Forensic Technology and Data Analytics......... 369

Chapter 15: Following the Money 391

PART IV
SECTOR-SPECIFIC FINANCIAL CRIME RISKS

Chapter 16: Financial Institutions 413

Chapter 17: Public Sector and Procurement....................... 431

Chapter 18: Real Estate and Luxury Goods 451

Chapter 19: Casinos and Gaming Environments 471

Chapter 20: Cryptocurrency and Digital Assets 487

Chapter 21: Non-Financial Businesses and Professions....... 505

Chapter 22: Charities and Non-Profits 523

Conclusion 543

INTRODUCTION

Financial crime has expanded in scale, complexity, and impact, affecting economies, institutions, and communities in ways that demand a more sophisticated response than ever before. It is no longer limited to discreet acts carried out by isolated individuals. It has become a global industry in which organized networks, corrupt professionals, technology-enabled offenders, and opportunistic insiders exploit weaknesses across financial systems. This advancement has placed significant pressure on investigators, compliance professionals, regulators, and decision-makers who must detect, understand, and prevent conduct that is constantly evolving. The purpose of this book is to provide a clear and authoritative guide for practitioners who require practical knowledge, structured methodologies, and reliable insights to address financial crime in a world where both the stakes and complexities continue to rise.

Professionals working in this field face the combined challenge of fast-moving criminal innovation and increasingly stringent regulatory expectations. Traditional investigative experience, although valuable, is not sufficient on its own. Criminals adopt new techniques rapidly, often supported by technology, professional enablers, or global networks that conceal assets and identities. Investigators must therefore understand not only how crimes are committed, but also how evidence is created, obscured, stored, and transferred across digital and financial environments.

Despite the abundance of academic material available on financial crime, practitioners often struggle to find resources that explain concepts in plain, functional terms while maintaining technical accuracy. This book seeks to bridge that gap. It emphasizes clarity without oversimplifying essential details, and it presents complex ideas in a manner that is accessible, precise, and directly relevant to operational work.

A Modern View of Financial Crime

Financial crime today encompasses a broad spectrum of misconduct, from laundering illicit proceeds to executing sophisticated fraud schemes, manipulating procurement channels, abusing digital assets, and misusing philanthropic structures. Criminal activity spans multiple jurisdictions, uses legitimate institutions as conduits, and relies on loopholes created by fragmented regulatory frameworks. In many cases, the financial system becomes a tool for exploitation rather than protection.

The modern offender is not defined by any single profile. Organized criminal groups employ accountants, lawyers, and technology specialists. Insiders misuse trusted positions. Cybercriminals hide behind anonymizing technologies. Corrupt officials manipulate public systems. Even small operators can cause extensive damage when equipped with the right digital infrastructure. Understanding these actors, how they behave, and the systemic weaknesses they exploit is crucial for developing effective investigative strategies.

Purpose and Scope of This Book

This book offers a structured and comprehensive reference that covers fundamental concepts, major crime types, investigative techniques, and sector-specific risks. It is arranged into four interconnected parts: *Foundations of Financial Crime, Core Financial Crime Types, Investigation Methodologies,* and *Sector-Specific Risks.* Each chapter outlines practical knowledge required to recognize, analyze, and address the unique challenges associated with different forms of financial crime. While the material reflects global concepts, it also acknowledges that legal frameworks vary, and investigators must always consider local obligations and constraints.

The aim is not to provide theoretical commentary but to equip the reader with applicable understanding. Every chapter is designed to support practical tasks such as recognizing suspicious behavior, tracing funds, analyzing documents, interviewing individuals, interpreting digital footprints, and assessing organizational vulnerabilities. The content also emphasizes the importance of ethics, accountability, and objectivity, all of which are essential for credible and defensible investigative outcomes.

An essential component of financial crime investigation is maintaining a high standard of professional conduct. Misinterpreting evidence, approaching inquiries with bias, or overlooking procedural obligations can compromise both investigations and institutions. For this reason, investigative work must be grounded in impartiality, discretion, and respect for legal boundaries.

This book reinforces these principles throughout its chapters. The goal is to encourage a disciplined approach that aligns investigative effectiveness with ethical responsibility. Readers are reminded that uncovering wrongdoing is only one part of their role; ensuring that processes remain lawful, transparent, and justifiable is equally important.

Audience and Practical Value

This guide is written for investigators, compliance officers, auditors, analysts, regulators, and professionals in sectors exposed to financial crime risks. It is also suitable for students entering the field and managers responsible for oversight or policy development. Regardless of background, readers will find structured explanations that support day-to-day responsibilities as well as strategic decision-making.

The content prioritizes practical application. It highlights the indicators professionals should watch for, the questions they should ask, the mistakes that frequently occur, and the methods that produce the most reliable results. Whether the reader is tracing layered transactions, conducting interviews, reviewing procurement anomalies, or assessing crypto asset flows, the information aims to strengthen both technical competence and investigative confidence.

The chapters ahead will equip readers with the clarity needed to understand how financial crime operates and how it can be addressed using evidence-based techniques. Each section introduces essential concepts, progresses logically through related ideas, and concludes with insights that support stronger investigative judgment. The tone remains objective, direct, and grounded in professional practice, avoiding sensationalism while recognizing the seriousness of the subject matter.

While no single resource can capture every nuance of global financial crime, this book offers a framework that readers can adapt to their contexts and regulatory environments. Its purpose is to serve as a reliable companion - one that provides structured guidance, enhances analytical abilities, and supports the development of sound investigative practice.

PART I

FOUNDATIONS OF FINANCIAL CRIME

CHAPTER 1

INTRODUCTION TO FINANCIAL CRIME

DEFINING FINANCIAL CRIME

FINANCIAL CRIME refers to conduct that uses financial systems, economic structures, or access to assets to obtain an illegal benefit, conceal illicit proceeds, or inflict economic harm. It covers a wide range of activities, yet all forms share a core characteristic: an intent to misuse financial or commercial channels to gain something that is not legitimately earned. The concept is sometimes misunderstood as a narrow field limited to money laundering or fraud, but in reality, it is far broader, encompassing both overtly criminal acts and abuses of authority that distort financial integrity. Understanding what qualifies as financial crime is essential because investigative decisions, legal interpretations, and regulatory obligations depend heavily on the clarity of this definition.

At its most fundamental level, financial crime involves the movement, acquisition, concealment, or manipulation of value. The value may be monetary, physical, digital, contractual, or proprietary, and the methods used to access it may be simple or highly sophisticated. What distinguishes financial crime from other forms of unlawful behavior is that the financial component is not incidental; it is central to how the misconduct is planned, executed, or concealed. A traditional theft, for example, involves an unlawful taking of property, but financial crime focuses more on actions that exploit the trust, systems, and controls that govern economic interactions. This distinction explains why financial crime often causes widespread repercussions that extend beyond direct financial loss.

The Evolution of the Concept

Historically, financial crime was viewed primarily through the lens of fraud or embezzlement. These offenses were understood as breaches of trust within commercial settings or institutions. Over time, however, changes in global finance, digitization, and cross-border commerce reshaped the nature of misconduct. As financial markets expanded and technology introduced new ways to move and disguise value, criminal activity adapted rapidly. What once consisted of isolated schemes carried out by individuals is now a complex environment involving networks, professional intermediaries, and sophisticated tools designed to bypass detection.

Regulators and enforcement agencies also broadened their understanding of financial crime as new risks emerged. Money laundering, sanctions evasion, market manipulation, bribery, terrorist financing, and cyber-enabled schemes gradually became recognized as part of the same landscape because they rely on the misuse of financial channels to achieve unlawful objectives. This shift emphasized that financial crime is not simply about theft or deception; it is about undermining economic order, exploiting regulatory gaps, and manipulating institutional processes in ways that damage the stability and reliability of financial systems.

As the definition expanded, so did the professional responsibilities of those responsible for detecting and investigating misconduct. Financial institutions, law enforcement agencies, auditors, regulators, and specialized investigators must now understand a wide set of behaviors that interact with one another, often across jurisdictions. A clear and modern definition therefore matters not only for academic precision but as the foundation for practical work in risk assessment, investigation, and compliance.

Core Elements of Financial Crime

While financial crime takes many forms, several elements are consistently present. First, there is an intention to gain an unlawful benefit or to assist someone else in doing so. This benefit may be direct, such as acquiring stolen funds, or indirect, such as helping a sanctioned entity conduct otherwise prohibited transactions. Criminal intent distinguishes wrongdoing from operational errors or procedural failures.

Second, financial crime relies on the misuse of systems that are designed to support legitimate economic activity. These systems include banking platforms, corporate structures, trade mechanisms, payment channels, regulatory filings, technological interfaces, and administrative processes. The crime succeeds when controls are circumvented or when opportunities created by weak oversight are exploited. In more advanced schemes, offenders take advantage of the very features that make financial systems efficient - such as speed, global reach, or automation -to obscure their activities.

Third, financial crime often involves concealment. Offenders try to hide either the origin of the funds, the identity of the individuals involved, or the nature of the transaction. Even crimes that appear simple at first glance frequently contain layers of obfuscation designed to frustrate detection. Concealment may involve laundering methods, falsified documentation, use of intermediaries, manipulation of digital tools, or exploitation of regulatory blind spots.

Finally, financial crime interferes with trust. Financial systems operate on the assumption that participants act with honesty and transparency. When individuals, corporations, or networks violate that expectation, the integrity of transactions and institutions becomes compromised. The resulting damage can be severe even when the monetary value of the crime is comparatively small, because the harm extends to confidence in the system itself.

Legal and Practical Definitions

Different jurisdictions define financial crime in slightly different ways, often shaped by local law, enforcement priorities, and regulatory structures. Some countries categorize it under economic crime or white-collar crime, while others treat it as a subset of corruption, organized crime, or market misconduct. Despite these variations, several types of behavior consistently fall under the umbrella of financial crime: fraud, money laundering, bribery, corruption, market abuse, sanctions evasion, terrorist financing, theft involving financial channels, cyber-enabled financial offenses, and the misuse of corporate or professional services for illegal purposes.

From an investigator's perspective, however, legal labels matter less than understanding how the conduct operates in practice. Investigations require clarity on mechanisms, motivations, and the pathways through which value is moved or concealed. A statutory definition may describe bribery as an improper transfer of value in exchange for influence, but an investigator must understand how that payment was arranged, disguised, processed through accounts, justified internally, and connected to a specific decision. The practical nature of financial crime means the definition must be sufficiently broad to encompass real-world behavior without losing the precision required for legal action.

The Role of Intent and Deception

Financial crime frequently involves deception, although the form of deception varies depending on the scheme. In fraud, deception is explicit, used to convince a victim to part with assets or information. In money laundering, deception focuses on disguising the origin of proceeds rather than misleading a specific individual. In bribery, deception may be implicit, concealed through falsified invoices, consulting arrangements, or inflated contracting. In sanctions evasion, the deception is aimed at bypassing restrictions through shell companies, misdeclared goods, or falsified documentation.

Intent plays a critical role in distinguishing misconduct from poor judgment or administrative weakness. A financial transaction may appear suspicious, but without intent it may be a legitimate activity carried out inadequately or without proper controls. Investigators must therefore examine patterns, context, and supporting evidence to establish whether the actions were deliberate. Intent can be inferred from behaviors such as structured transactions, use of shadow intermediaries, destruction of records, deliberate silence when questions arise, or reliance on methods commonly associated with concealment.

Economic Crime vs. Financial Crime

The terms "economic crime" and "financial crime" are sometimes used interchangeably, but they have different meanings. Economic crime is a broader concept that includes any offense affecting the economy or economic institutions, such as tax evasion, price-fixing, antitrust violations, or illegal trade practices. Financial crime focuses more directly on the financial system and the movement of value. While there is overlap, the distinction matters for investigative work. Many economic crimes do not involve financial systems directly, whereas nearly all financial crimes depend on them.

For example, tax evasion becomes relevant to financial crime investigations when offenders use corporate structures, banking channels, or financial intermediaries to hide income. Market manipulation, although fundamentally about influencing prices, remains a financial crime because it distorts the functioning of regulated financial markets. Understanding these distinctions allows investigators to identify which crimes fall squarely within the financial crime mandate and which require cooperation with specialists in related fields.

Institutional Responsibilities

An accurate definition of financial crime influences institutional responsibilities. Banks, payment platforms, insurers, investment firms, money service businesses, and other regulated entities have obligations to identify, report, and mitigate financial crime risks. These obligations are not limited to customer transactions; they extend to the behavior of employees, third-party partners, and anyone who uses institutional systems. A broad and well-grounded definition helps institutions determine which activities require monitoring controls, escalation procedures, or specialist review.

For regulators and policymakers, defining financial crime establishes the boundaries for supervision and enforcement. It allows them to set expectations, issue guidance, and shape rules that prevent actors from exploiting regulatory gaps. For law enforcement agencies, the definition determines jurisdiction, investigative powers, and the types of cases they are authorized to pursue. For investigators, clarity supports consistent analysis and reduces the risk of misinterpreting conduct that may appear suspicious but does not meet the threshold for criminal or regulatory action.

Financial Crime as an Adaptive Threat

A defining feature of financial crime is its ability to adapt. As soon as a method becomes widely recognized or countered, offenders shift tactics. This adaptability requires definitions that are both precise and flexible. Overly prescriptive definitions risk becoming obsolete as technology evolves. Overly broad definitions can dilute meaning and complicate enforcement. A balanced approach recognizes the essential elements - intent, misuse of systems, concealment, and unlawful gain - while allowing space to address new behaviors.

This adaptability is evident in areas such as digital assets, online fraud, ransomware, synthetic identities, and complex cross-border corporate structures. These developments challenge traditional investigative methods because they blur the line between financial activity and digital activity. A clear definition of financial crime ensures that investigators remain focused on the core objective: identifying and addressing behavior that uses financial channels to commit or conceal unlawful acts, regardless of how the underlying technology changes.

Why a Clear Definition Matters

A precise definition of financial crime influences every stage of investigative and compliance work. Risk assessments rely on it to determine where institutions are vulnerable. Controls and monitoring systems depend on it to identify what constitutes suspicious activity. Investigations hinge on it to establish whether conduct is illegal and whether evidence is sufficient. Training programs use it to ensure staff understand their responsibilities. Policies and procedures are built around it to maintain consistent standards across organizations.

When definitions are vague, institutions may either over-report or fail to report relevant activity. Over-reporting burdens regulators and weakens investigative focus. Under-reporting exposes institutions to legal, financial, and reputational consequences. A clear and practical definition, grounded in real-world behavior, enables balanced, defensible, and effective action.

MAJOR CATEGORIES AND TYPOLOGIES

Financial crime encompasses a wide spectrum of misconduct, and understanding its principal categories is essential for recognizing how criminals exploit financial systems. While each type of crime has its own mechanics, they often share structural similarities, rely on overlapping vulnerabilities, and involve multiple actors working in coordinated or opportunistic ways. Typologies help practitioners interpret patterns of behavior that may not be obvious in individual transactions but become clearer when understood in a broader context. This section outlines the major categories of financial crime and the typological patterns most relevant to investigative and compliance work.

Money Laundering

Money laundering is one of the most recognized forms of financial crime because it supports a wide range of illegal activities. Its purpose is to make criminal proceeds appear legitimate so offenders can use them without attracting scrutiny. Although the traditional description divides the process into placement, layering, and integration, real-world laundering often varies considerably in complexity. Criminals use diverse techniques such as structured deposits, cash smuggling, false invoicing, trade manipulation, professional intermediaries, and digital assets. Some rely on networks of shell companies to obscure true ownership, while others employ informal value transfer systems that leave minimal documentation.

Typologies in this area frequently involve rapid movement of funds, routing transactions through accounts with limited due-diligence oversight, using jurisdictions with permissive regulations, or mixing illicit funds with legitimate commercial flow. Laundering is rarely a standalone act; it is typically the financial expression of another underlying offense. Understanding it therefore requires the ability to identify behaviors that indicate concealment rather than merely unusual financial activity.

Fraud

Fraud covers a broad spectrum of schemes in which offenders obtain value through deception. Fraud typologies range from simple misrepresentations to highly structured schemes involving multiple actors. Investment fraud, for example, relies on false promises of returns, fabricated credentials, or manipulation of investor trust. Mortgage fraud may involve inflated property valuations, falsified income, and collusion among borrowers, brokers, and appraisers. Pension fraud often exploits complex administrative systems and long-term investment structures, making irregularities difficult to detect until losses accumulate.

Business Email Compromise (BEC), a prominent contemporary typology, uses social engineering rather than technical intrusion. Offenders impersonate senior executives, suppliers, or trusted partners to persuade victims to transfer funds. It is effective because it exploits organizational processes rather than technological weaknesses.

Internal fraud, committed by employees or insiders, takes many forms including unauthorized transactions, manipulation of customer accounts, and misappropriation of assets. It is particularly harmful because it occurs within an environment of trust and may remain undetected for extended periods. Fraud typologies evolve rapidly, and investigators must be alert to behavioral indicators as much as financial anomalies.

Bribery and Corruption

Bribery involves offering, giving, receiving, or soliciting something of value to influence the actions of an individual in a position of authority. Corruption encompasses a wider range of behaviors including abuse of office, conflict of interest, extortion, and improper influence. Typologies vary significantly depending on the sector involved. In public procurement, bribes may be disguised as consulting fees, marketing payments, or inflated contract values. In private-sector environments, bribery can occur through preferential pricing, undisclosed commissions, or incentives hidden within complex commercial arrangements.

Corruption often relies on intermediaries who create separation between the bribe payer and the official. These intermediaries may be law firms, accounting practices, corporate service providers, or local agents with access to decision-makers. Payments are frequently routed through offshore jurisdictions, non-transparent corporate structures, or obscure service contracts. The financial component is critical because it provides the means through which influence is bought, sustained, or rewarded.

Terrorist Financing

Terrorist financing differs from many other forms of financial crime because the underlying motivation is ideological rather than profit-driven. Funds may be raised through criminal activity, legitimate income, charitable donations, informal transfers, or community fundraising. The amounts involved may be relatively small, but the impact is significant. Typologies often involve using personal accounts, remittance services, or nonprofit organizations to move funds discreetly. Some groups rely on trade-based methods or cash-intensive businesses to mask activity.

Unlike money laundering, where offenders try to obscure the origin of funds, terrorist financing frequently attempts to conceal the destination. Investigators must therefore look for patterns that indicate funds are being directed toward high-risk individuals, regions, or entities rather than analyzing the legitimacy of source alone. The diversity of funding structures challenges standard detection systems because transactions may appear routine.

Sanctions Evasion

Sanctions are intended to restrict certain individuals, entities, or jurisdictions from accessing financial and commercial systems. Evasion occurs when parties attempt to bypass these restrictions through indirect or concealed transactions. Common typologies include using shell companies, front businesses, or third-country intermediaries; falsifying information on trade documents; using vessels that disable tracking systems; and routing payments through banks that lack strong compliance oversight.

Dual-use goods pose a particular challenge because they have both civilian and military applications. Offenders may conceal the true nature of the goods or manipulate shipping documents to obscure the involvement of sanctioned actors. Sanctions evasion often overlaps with trade-based money laundering, which adds another layer of complexity for investigators.

Trade-Based Crime

Trade-based financial crime exploits international trade mechanisms to move value illicitly. This may occur through over-invoicing, under-invoicing, phantom shipments, multiple invoicing, or falsified descriptions of goods. The purpose may be to launder proceeds, evade taxes, move capital, or finance prohibited activities. Because trade transactions typically involve multiple parties, jurisdictions, and intermediaries, the opportunities for manipulation are significant.

Typologies frequently include discrepancies between shipping documents, inconsistencies in pricing relative to market values, mismatched cargo descriptions, or routing goods through unnecessary transit points. The physical movement of goods often creates a veneer of legitimacy, making detection difficult without specialized trade knowledge.

Cyber-Enabled Financial Crime

Technology has introduced numerous opportunities for offenders to commit financial crime remotely, rapidly, and at scale. Cyber-enabled crime includes ransomware, identity theft, credential compromise, online fraud, and illicit use of digital platforms. Ransomware typologies involve encrypting an organization's data and demanding payment—often in cryptocurrency—to restore access. Identity theft uses stolen personal information to open accounts, obtain credit, or conduct fraudulent transactions.

Criminals also exploit dark web markets that sell compromised credentials, malware kits, or stolen financial information. These platforms offer anonymity and sophisticated support services that allow offenders with limited technical knowledge to conduct complex schemes. Digital laundering typologies use mixers, tumblers, and decentralized financial applications to obscure cryptocurrency flows. The rapid evolution of technology requires investigators to maintain awareness of both the technical tools and behavioral patterns used by offenders.

Market Abuse and Securities Crime

Market abuse includes insider trading, market manipulation, and false or misleading statements intended to distort the price or perception of securities. These crimes undermine market integrity and erode investor confidence. Insider trading typologies involve trading based on confidential information or tipping others who then trade on behalf of the insider. Market manipulation schemes may include pump-and-dump operations, spoofing, layering, or creating artificial demand through coordinated trading.

Securities crimes often rely on sophisticated networks that mask beneficial ownership, enabling offenders to profit while concealing their involvement. Some schemes make use of offshore brokerages, opaque custodial arrangements, and complex corporate structures. Detection typically requires advanced analytics, market surveillance tools, and an understanding of trading behavior in context.

Tax Crime and Illicit Tax Schemes

Tax crime encompasses intentional acts designed to evade legal tax obligations. Offenders may conceal income, inflate deductions, shift profits to low-tax jurisdictions, or use offshore structures to hide assets. Although tax crime is sometimes viewed separately from financial crime, it frequently overlaps with money laundering, fraud, and corruption. Typologies include shell companies used to obscure beneficial ownership, artificial transactions creating false expenses, and aggressive schemes facilitated by professionals who exploit technical loopholes.

These offenses can have significant consequences for public finances, and they often coexist with other criminal behavior. Effective investigation requires understanding both the financial flows and the legal mechanisms used to disguise them.

Asset Misappropriation

Asset misappropriation refers to stealing or misusing property or funds entrusted to an individual or organization. It includes embezzlement, unauthorized transfers, procurement manipulation, payroll fraud, and misuse of corporate credit facilities. Although sometimes viewed as less complex than other forms of financial crime, misappropriation can be highly sophisticated when offenders understand internal controls and exploit weaknesses to avoid detection.

Typologies may involve creating fictitious vendors, misdirecting payments, altering account records, or using personal relationships to circumvent oversight. In some environments, collusion among employees or between employees and external suppliers increases the complexity and scale of the misconduct.

Professional Facilitation and Abuse of Gatekeepers

Professionals such as lawyers, accountants, corporate service providers, and financial advisors can become facilitators of financial crime when they assist clients in structuring transactions or entities for illicit purposes. This facilitation may be intentional or may occur because of inadequate oversight or insufficient due-diligence procedures. Typologies include creating shell companies with concealed ownership, establishing trust structures to hide assets, drafting falsified contracts, or helping clients move funds through complex arrangements designed to obscure origin and control.

The involvement of professionals is particularly concerning because it provides legitimacy to illicit activity. When a transaction is supported by legal documentation or professional advice, institutions may overlook indicators of misconduct.

Nonprofit and Charitable Abuse

Criminals sometimes misuse nonprofit organizations to raise, move, or disguise funds. These organizations often receive donations from numerous sources, operate in high-risk regions, and manage activities that involve cash, cross-border transfers, or humanitarian projects. Typologies include diversion of funds by insiders, using charities as fronts for terrorist financing, and funneling money through programs that lack adequate oversight. Because many nonprofit transactions appear benevolent, they may not attract the same level of scrutiny as commercial transactions.

Typologies as Analytical Tools

Typologies serve as reference points for understanding how financial crime manifests in practice. They are not rigid categories but patterns that help investigators interpret behavior. A single case may involve multiple typologies overlapping across sectors and jurisdictions. For example, a corruption case may involve money laundering, use of shell companies, falsified trade documents, and cyber-enabled communication between facilitators.

Investigators must recognize that typologies guide analysis rather than limit it. They provide context, highlight risks, and inform the selection of investigative techniques. Effective use of typologies requires staying current with criminal innovation, monitoring shifts in regulatory environments, and understanding how economic and technological developments influence offender behavior.

IMPACT ON SOCIETY, MARKETS, AND INSTITUTIONS

Financial crime is often discussed in technical terms, yet its consequences extend far beyond the immediate loss of funds. It affects how societies function, how markets operate, and how institutions maintain stability and trust. Its impact rarely stays confined to the parties directly involved. Instead, it influences public confidence, economic development, regulatory priorities, and the overall integrity of financial systems. Understanding these broader effects is essential because the significance of financial crime is not measured only by the value of stolen assets, laundered proceeds, or fraudulent transactions. It is measured by how it weakens the frameworks that allow economies to function reliably.

Social Impact

Financial crime disrupts societies in ways that are often overlooked because the harm is not always immediate or visible. While some offenses cause direct losses to individuals—such as fraud targeting consumers, pension abuse, or theft from vulnerable populations—others affect society indirectly by reducing public resources, eroding trust in institutions, or enabling harmful activity that affects communities.

Fraud against individuals can undermine personal financial security, leaving victims with long-term consequences such as damaged credit, lost savings, and emotional distress. Identity theft, unauthorized transactions, and investment scams often target those with limited financial literacy or access to support, amplifying inequalities. In many cases, victims struggle to recover because the systems designed to protect them may not move quickly enough or may require evidence that is difficult to obtain.

At a broader level, financial crime reduces public funds that are necessary for education, healthcare, infrastructure, and social programs. Tax evasion and corruption divert resources away from essential services, creating structural disadvantages that persist across generations. In countries with weak governance, corruption can severely impair development by distorting how public money is allocated. Instead of supporting long-term investment, funds may be channeled toward private benefit, resulting in poor-quality public services, limited economic opportunity, and widespread distrust.

Financial crime also strengthens organized criminal networks that use illicit proceeds to expand their influence. When money laundering succeeds, it enables criminals to reinvest earnings into activities such as drug trafficking, human exploitation, illegal mining, or arms trading. These activities directly harm communities, fuel violence, and undermine public safety. The damage is therefore not abstract; it manifests in concrete social costs that affect the everyday lives of citizens.

Terrorist financing presents another layer of impact, as even small amounts of money can support actions that threaten public security. Funds directed to extremist groups facilitate recruitment, propaganda, training, and operations. The social implications extend beyond the immediate acts of violence. A climate of fear can develop, affecting public behavior, community interactions, and social cohesion.

Impact on Markets

Financial markets depend on transparency, fairness, and consistency. When financial crime occurs within these systems, the consequences ripple through market behavior, pricing mechanisms, and investor confidence. Markets operate efficiently only when participants trust that information is accurate and that rules are applied consistently.

Fraud, market manipulation, insider trading, and false disclosures distort the signals markets rely on to set prices. Investors may allocate capital based on inaccurate information, leading to mispricing of assets, inefficient investment decisions, and in some cases, significant losses when misconduct is eventually uncovered. These distortions can dissuade both domestic and foreign investment, especially in markets perceived as vulnerable to manipulation or inadequate oversight.

In financial institutions, money laundering and sanctions evasion present risks that extend beyond the individual transaction. When illicit funds pass through banks undetected, they create exposure to regulatory penalties, loss of correspondent banking relationships, and reputational damage. Markets rely heavily on the stability of major financial institutions. When a bank suffers reputational harm due to weak controls, market participants may reassess the institution's reliability, potentially affecting liquidity, share prices, or credit ratings.

Corruption in procurement, licensing, and contracting can distort competitive markets, allowing resources to flow not to the most capable or efficient businesses, but to those with illicit access or influence. This discourages legitimate companies from operating in environments where misconduct provides unfair advantage. Over time, market quality declines, innovation slows, and prices may increase because competitive pressure is weakened.

Trade-based financial crime also harms market integrity. Manipulation of invoices, misrepresentation of goods, and misuse of shipping documents can undermine legitimate commerce. When trade flows include significant volumes of illicit or mispriced goods, markets lose their ability to reflect true supply and demand. Legitimate businesses may find themselves unable to compete with artificially subsidized or illicitly financed counterparts.

Financial crime in the digital asset sector also creates market instability. Cryptocurrency fraud, exchange manipulation, and pump-and-dump schemes cause volatility that discourages legitimate adoption and institutional investment. Without confidence in the integrity of these markets, regulatory scrutiny intensifies and the sector's long-term growth prospects become uncertain.

Impact on Institutions

Financial institutions sit at the center of most financial crime risks. Banks, insurers, payment companies, investment service providers, and fintech platforms all face pressure to maintain strong defenses while still facilitating smooth customer transactions. When financial crime infiltrates these institutions, the consequences can be severe and long-lasting.

Weak controls can result in fines, criminal liability, and loss of authorization to operate. Regulators impose significant penalties not only for direct misconduct but for inadequate systems that allow illicit activity to occur. Institutions may be required to conduct costly remediation programs, overhaul compliance frameworks, or limit certain business activities until improvements are made. These interventions drain resources, divert management attention, and sometimes trigger organizational restructuring.

Reputational damage is particularly difficult to recover from. Once an institution is associated with financial crime - whether through internal misconduct or external actors using its services - customers, counterparties, and investors may lose trust. Rebuilding credibility requires sustained effort, transparency, and proven improvements in governance and compliance. In severe cases, reputational harm can affect market capitalization, funding costs, and strategic partnerships.

Operational impact is another important consideration. Investigating financial crime within an institution can strain internal resources, disrupt normal business functions, and expose deficiencies in processes that were previously overlooked. Staff may require extensive retraining, systems may require redesign, and data management practices may need revision. These operational burdens can persist for years, especially if systemic failures are uncovered during investigations or regulatory reviews.

Institutions also face internal cultural consequences. If financial crime is committed by employees or facilitated by insiders, it signals failures in governance, oversight, and ethical standards. Such failures can create distrust within the organization and hamper efforts to build a culture of accountability. A strong compliance environment depends not only on procedures but on staff who understand and respect their responsibilities. When internal misconduct occurs, institutions must reassess how they communicate expectations, conduct monitoring, and manage conflicts of interest.

Government institutions are equally affected by financial crime. Corruption erodes the credibility of public bodies, undermines democratic processes, and discourages international cooperation. When public procurement is manipulated or licensing decisions are influenced by improper payments, institutions lose legitimacy. Citizens may become less willing to comply with laws or pay taxes if they believe public officials misuse resources. This erosion of trust has long-term consequences for public governance and social cohesion.

Economic Impact

The cumulative economic impact of financial crime is significant, although difficult to measure accurately due to its concealed nature. Economic losses arise from direct theft, fraud, and misappropriation, but also from lost investment, reduced tax revenues, higher costs of compliance, and inefficiencies caused by corruption. These costs are carried not only by victims or institutions but by entire economies.

Corruption, for example, can depress growth by deterring investment and reducing productivity. When businesses spend resources managing corrupt demands instead of improving operations, the overall efficiency of the economy declines. Investors may avoid countries with persistent financial crime risks, further limiting economic expansion.

Money laundering enables criminal enterprises to expand, which perpetuates illegal sectors that harm legitimate competition. Capital flight facilitated by illicit financial flows weakens local economies by reducing funds available for productive investment. Tax crimes directly reduce government revenues, affecting a country's ability to meet public obligations.

The cost of compliance, while necessary, is substantial. Financial institutions must invest heavily in monitoring systems, staff training, reporting obligations, and audits. These costs are eventually passed to consumers or absorbed as operational overhead, influencing product pricing and business strategy.

Global Impact and Systemic Risks

Many financial crimes operate across borders, linking actors in multiple jurisdictions. This interconnectedness creates systemic risks that threaten the stability of global financial markets. When illicit funds move freely across regions, they exploit mismatches in regulation, enforcement capability, and political will. Criminals often channel activity through less regulated regions before re-entering major markets, complicating compliance and investigative efforts.

Large-scale money laundering and corruption can distort foreign exchange markets, damage a country's financial reputation, and create vulnerabilities in international banking networks. The withdrawal of correspondent banking relationships due to financial crime concerns can isolate regions from global financial systems, harming trade, remittances, and economic development.

Globalization of financial crime also increases the burden on regulatory authorities and law enforcement agencies. Effective oversight requires cross-border cooperation, information sharing, and synchronized standards - tasks that remain challenging despite international frameworks.

Impact on Public Confidence

Across all environments - social, economic, institutional, or cross-border - financial crime ultimately erodes confidence. Trust is essential for any financial system to function. Consumers must believe their savings are safe; investors must trust that markets operate fairly; citizens must have confidence that public institutions act in the collective interest.

Every major financial crime scandal, whether involving a bank, a government agency, a corporation, or a nonprofit organization, diminishes this confidence. Restoring it requires transparency, accountability, and sustained action to strengthen systems and prevent recurrence. Without these efforts, financial crime becomes normalized, and the credibility of institutions deteriorates.

WHY FINANCIAL CRIME PERSISTS

Financial crime continues to grow in scale and complexity despite advances in regulation, technology, and enforcement. Its persistence cannot be attributed to a single cause. Instead, it arises from a combination of strong incentives for offenders and systemic vulnerabilities that create opportunities. Even well-structured financial systems contain weaknesses that can be exploited by determined individuals, organized groups, and professional facilitators. Understanding why financial crime remains a persistent threat is essential for designing effective investigative strategies and developing preventive frameworks that reflect real-world conditions rather than theoretical assumptions.

Attractive Rewards and Perceived Low Risk

One of the primary reasons financial crime persists is the imbalance between potential gains and perceived consequences. Many forms of financial crime offer high financial rewards with relatively limited physical risk. Unlike violent crime, financial misconduct can be committed remotely, discreetly, and with minimal personal exposure. This creates a powerful incentive for offenders seeking profit without the dangers associated with other criminal activities.

In many jurisdictions, enforcement resources are limited, and only a fraction of financial crime is ever detected. Even when cases are identified, investigations may take years, during which evidence can degrade and offenders may move assets beyond reach. Some crimes, such as corruption or sophisticated laundering schemes, require substantial time and resources to investigate. Offenders understand this gap between monitoring capacity and criminal innovation, and they take advantage of it.

The perception of low risk is reinforced by the fact that many financial crimes are nonviolent and often appear administrative in nature. Offenders may rationalize their actions as technical maneuvers rather than wrongdoing, especially when facilitated by complex structures or intermediaries. When penalties are inconsistent or enforcement is uneven across jurisdictions, the deterrent effect diminishes further.

Complexity of Financial Systems

Modern financial systems are intricate and interconnected, providing a wide range of instruments, technologies, and channels through which value can be transferred. These systems are designed for efficiency, speed, and accessibility, but these same qualities provide opportunities for abuse. A transaction may pass through several intermediaries, jurisdictions, and technologies in a matter of seconds. This complexity makes oversight challenging, particularly when institutions must balance stringent controls with customer convenience.

Offenders exploit this environment by using methods that blend illicit activity with legitimate commercial flow. For example, money laundering schemes may be embedded within real trade transactions, investment structures, or routine business operations. Digital platforms, payment processors, and decentralized financial networks add additional layers of complexity. The sheer volume of global financial transactions makes comprehensive monitoring impossible, creating spaces where suspicious behavior can be concealed within normal activity.

Complexity also benefits offenders who use professional support to construct intricate schemes. Lawyers, accountants, and corporate service providers may design structures that appear legitimate but can be used to disguise ownership, move funds covertly, or manipulate documentation. These structures can be difficult for investigators to interpret, particularly when they involve multiple legal systems or specialized financial instruments.

Regulatory Gaps and Inconsistent Oversight

Financial crime thrives where regulatory oversight is fragmented or inconsistent. Jurisdictions vary significantly in their legal frameworks, enforcement priorities, and supervisory capacity. Offenders exploit these differences by routing activity through countries with weaker controls, less transparency, or limited cooperation with international authorities.

Some sectors operate with fewer regulatory expectations than traditional banking. Non-financial businesses, payment intermediaries, crypto asset firms, and professional service providers may not be subject to the same level of scrutiny. This disparity allows offenders to move between regulated and less regulated environments to avoid detection. Even within regulated sectors, regulatory gaps may arise due to outdated rules that do not account for technological developments or emerging business models.

The pace of regulatory reform often lags behind criminal innovation. New financial technologies can enter markets faster than regulators can adapt, creating periods during which oversight is inadequate. Offenders exploit these windows to test methods, establish channels, and embed illicit activity before controls are strengthened.

Globalization and Cross-Border Movement of Funds

Globalization has enabled financial markets to operate across borders with unprecedented efficiency. Capital can move instantly between countries, and digital platforms allow individuals to engage in economic activities without geographical limitations. While this has facilitated economic growth, it has also created vulnerabilities.

Cross-border transactions complicate investigations because they require cooperation between jurisdictions with different legal systems, languages, standards, and enforcement capacities. Mutual legal assistance processes are often slow, and some countries may be unwilling or unable to provide meaningful cooperation. Offenders rely on these barriers to fragment evidence, disperse assets, and create legal uncertainty. Once funds have moved through several countries, tracing them becomes significantly more difficult.

The global nature of commerce also increases opportunities for trade-based financial crime. Offenders can disguise illicit transfers within legitimate supply chains that span multiple countries. Manipulated invoices, falsified documentation, and phantom shipments often go undetected because no single authority maintains oversight over the entire transaction.

Technological Innovation

Technology has transformed financial crime in ways that previous generations of investigators could not have anticipated. Cyber-enabled crime, digital assets, encrypted communication channels, and anonymizing technologies provide offenders with tools that increase both efficiency and anonymity. These tools are accessible not only to organized criminal groups but also to individuals with modest technical knowledge, thanks to the availability of criminal services on darknet markets.

Technological innovation also accelerates the speed at which financial crime occurs. Fraud schemes can target thousands of victims simultaneously through automated phishing campaigns. Ransomware attacks can paralyze institutions within minutes. Cryptocurrency transactions can move across borders without reliance on traditional banks. This speed limits the time investigators have to respond and reduces opportunities for real-time intervention.

Moreover, digital systems generate immense volumes of data. While data can support investigations, its scale can be overwhelming without advanced analytical tools. The ability of offenders to conceal activity within encrypted networks, decentralized platforms, or anonymized services further challenges traditional investigative methods.

Socioeconomic Drivers

Financial crime is influenced not only by opportunity but by socioeconomic conditions that increase its attractiveness. In environments with limited formal employment opportunities, weak governance, or pervasive corruption, financial crime may become normalized or seen as necessary for economic survival. In such settings, citizens may have little trust in public institutions, making them more susceptible to bribery, fraud, or participation in informal value transfer systems.

Even in stable economies, financial pressure can motivate employees to commit internal fraud, misuse organizational assets, or manipulate financial records. Personal debt, addiction, and family obligations can contribute to rationalization, especially when controls are weak or oversight appears ineffective.

At the organizational level, aggressive profit expectations may encourage employees to bypass procedures or take unethical shortcuts. A culture that focuses heavily on performance without adequate emphasis on compliance can create implicit incentives for misconduct. Offenders often exploit these cultural weaknesses by aligning their actions with perceived organizational goals, even when those actions violate policy.

Corruption and Collusion

Corruption enables financial crime by lowering the barriers that should prevent illicit activity. When officials, gatekeepers, or insiders participate in misconduct, they provide access to information, influence, or systems that criminals cannot obtain externally. Corruption undermines enforcement, weakens regulatory frameworks, and creates environments where financial crime can flourish.

Collusion among multiple actors—whether within an institution, between institutions, or across public and private sectors—further compounds the problem. Many sophisticated schemes rely on cooperation among insiders who manipulate records, approve transactions, or suppress red flags. Collusion significantly reduces the likelihood of detection because internal controls rely heavily on the assumption that staff act independently and in good faith.

Ease of Concealment and Obfuscation

Financial crime persists because offenders have access to effective methods for concealing activity. These methods include the use of shell companies, complex corporate structures, offshore jurisdictions, falsified documents, intermediaries, and digital anonymization tools. When these methods are combined, the resulting opacity can frustrate even well-resourced investigations.

Beneficial ownership concealment is particularly problematic. When true owners are hidden behind multiple layers of entities, trusts, or nominees, tracing responsibility becomes challenging. Offenders can transfer assets rapidly, change structures frequently, and exploit legal protections that shield corporate information from public view. This opacity allows crimes to continue for long periods without detection and complicates efforts to recover stolen or misappropriated funds.

Human Behavior and Cognitive Biases

Financial crime continues partly because individuals underestimate the likelihood of being caught or overestimate their ability to manage risk. Offenders often rely on optimism bias, believing that their method is unique or that controls are too weak to identify them. Some commit financial crime incrementally—a small act that escalates over time as they gain confidence or become accustomed to misconduct.

Cognitive biases also affect investigators and institutions. Confirmation bias can lead investigators to interpret evidence in ways that support initial assumptions rather than exploring alternative explanations. Familiarity bias may cause staff to overlook suspicious behavior by long-standing customers or colleagues. These biases create blind spots that offenders can exploit.

Institutional Weaknesses

Financial crime thrives in environments where controls, governance, or oversight are inadequate. Institutions may lack trained staff, modern technology, or clear policies. High employee turnover, insufficient segregation of duties, and inadequate monitoring procedures create weaknesses that offenders can exploit. Some institutions prioritize customer growth or market expansion over compliance, resulting in controls that lag behind business operations.

In many cases, institutions underestimate their exposure to financial crime because they rely on outdated risk assessments or incomplete data. Without accurate understanding of risks, preventive measures may be misaligned with actual threats. Offenders recognize these weaknesses and adjust their methods accordingly.

International Barriers to Enforcement

Even when crimes are detected, enforcement is impeded by jurisdictional barriers, resource constraints, and procedural requirements. Gathering evidence across borders can take significant time. Some jurisdictions may lack the capacity or willingness to cooperate. Offenders exploit these challenges by dispersing funds across countries with varying legal frameworks, making enforcement costly and time-consuming.

These delays provide offenders with opportunities to move assets further, dismantle structures, or claim legal protections. As a result, even well-coordinated investigations may struggle to achieve timely outcomes.

CHAPTER 2

THE FINANCIAL CRIME ECOSYSTEM

FINANCIAL CRIME is rarely the result of a single individual acting in isolation. Instead, it arises from an ecosystem of participants who each play a distinct role. Some individuals initiate and control the wrongdoing, others provide access or legitimacy, and others become victims of deception, exploitation, or systemic failure. Understanding the characteristics and behaviors of these actors is essential for investigations because their roles shape the structure, complexity, and detectability of misconduct. A clear view of this ecosystem allows investigators to anticipate how schemes unfold, identify weak points, and assess how various actions contribute to the overall pattern of offending.

Criminals

Criminals engaged in financial wrongdoing range from opportunistic individuals to highly organized networks. Their sophistication varies widely. Some rely on simple tactics, such as submitting falsified documents or stealing customer credentials. Others operate complex schemes involving coordinated activity across multiple jurisdictions, technological infrastructure, and professional assistance. Regardless of scale, the distinguishing feature of financial criminals is their intent to exploit financial systems for illicit gain.

There is no single profile of a financial criminal. They may be business owners, professional fraudsters, cybercriminals, corrupt officials, or individuals driven by personal financial pressures. Some offenders specialize in particular crime types, such as investment fraud or sanctions evasion, while others operate broadly across multiple activities. Organized criminal groups often incorporate financial crime as a core revenue stream because it offers high profits with comparatively limited exposure to physical risk.

Many criminals study institutional procedures closely. They learn how due-diligence systems work, identify automated monitoring blind spots, and exploit processes that rely heavily on trust or documentation rather than verification. Some criminals use technology to automate or scale their activity, relying on malware, credential harvesting, or fraudulent online platforms. Others exploit regulatory weaknesses by shifting activity to jurisdictions with limited oversight.

What unites these actors is their deliberate misuse of financial and commercial structures to obtain or conceal value. Their actions may be motivated by financial gain, ideological objectives, or a desire to support broader criminal enterprises. Understanding their tactics requires investigators to examine not only financial behavior but the strategic thinking behind it.

Insiders

Insiders pose unique risks because they operate from within organizations that rely on their judgment and integrity. Insiders include employees, contractors, executives, board members, or individuals with privileged access to systems, sensitive information, or decision-making authority. Unlike external criminals, insiders are positioned to bypass controls that would otherwise prevent or detect wrongdoing.

Insider misconduct takes many forms. Some may abuse their access to steal funds, manipulate accounts, or approve fraudulent transactions. Others may provide sensitive information to external criminals, helping them bypass verification processes or identify weak points in controls. In some cases, insiders do not commit the crime directly but assist by ignoring suspicious behaviors, approving questionable documentation, or adjusting records to conceal evidence.

Insider misconduct is particularly damaging because it undermines institutional trust. Organizations rely on their staff to uphold standards and apply controls consistently. When insiders misuse their position, they not only cause financial loss but jeopardize the credibility of internal processes. Detecting insider wrongdoing is challenging because offenders understand how monitoring systems function and may intentionally structure their activity to avoid triggering alerts.

Insiders may commit misconduct for personal gain, under pressure from external actors, or due to ideological alignment with criminal networks. Financial distress, dissatisfaction at work, or weak organizational culture can also contribute. Some insiders rationalize misconduct as temporary or justified by perceived grievances. Effective prevention therefore requires not only strong technical controls but an environment that encourages accountability, ethical judgment, and internal transparency.

Facilitators

Facilitators are individuals or entities that provide the structures, services, or expertise that allow financial crime to succeed. Some facilitators operate knowingly, while others may claim ignorance or fail to apply due-diligence obligations that would have exposed illicit activity. Both groups play a significant role in enabling misconduct.

Professional facilitators include lawyers, accountants, corporate service providers, financial advisors, and fiduciaries who create or manage entities used for concealment. They may establish shell companies, prepare contracts, structure trusts, or provide nominee services that obscure the identities of beneficial owners. While many professionals operate legitimately, their services can be exploited when oversight is weak, fees are prioritized over integrity, or compliance obligations are treated as administrative formalities rather than safeguards.

Other facilitators include technology providers, brokers, traders, escrow agents, and individuals who sell access to compromised credentials or digital infrastructure. In cyber-enabled crime, facilitators may operate darknet platforms, provide malware kits, or offer data-laundering services. These individuals may not participate in the underlying criminal conduct but provide tools that make it possible.

At the transactional level, facilitators may act as intermediaries who move funds through accounts, execute trades, or route payments through jurisdictions designed to obscure source or destination. Some operate money remittance businesses with limited oversight, allowing criminals to transfer funds with minimal traceability. Others serve as "fixers" who arrange introductions, manage negotiations, or influence decision-makers in corruption schemes.

Professional facilitators are particularly challenging for investigators because their involvement gives illicit activity an appearance of legitimacy. Transactions supported by legal agreements or conducted through reputable service providers are less likely to raise suspicion. Understanding the role of facilitators therefore requires careful scrutiny of the economic purpose of arrangements, the transparency of ownership, and the consistency between documentation and actual behavior.

Victims

Victims of financial crime include individuals, corporations, governments, and even entire communities. Their experiences vary widely depending on the nature of the crime, the scale of the loss, and the systems involved. Despite this diversity, a common theme is that victims often face consequences that extend beyond financial harm.

Individual victims may suffer from fraud, identity theft, unauthorized transactions, or investment scams. These crimes can deplete savings, damage credit profiles, and cause long-term psychological stress. Victims frequently feel ashamed or hesitant to report, particularly in cases where deception relied on emotional trust or manipulation. Elderly individuals, recent immigrants, and individuals with limited financial literacy are especially vulnerable.

Corporate victims experience financial crime in ways that compromise operations, governance, and reputation. Internal fraud, cyberattacks, procurement manipulation, and third-party misconduct can cause significant disruption. Losses may include stolen funds, corrupted data, contractual disputes, or loss of market confidence. Institutions also face regulatory and legal consequences if they fail to detect or prevent misconduct affecting customers or stakeholders.

Government institutions suffer when corruption, tax evasion, and procurement fraud divert public resources. These crimes reduce the quality of public services and undermine public confidence. In some jurisdictions, systemic corruption erodes the integrity of institutions to the point where enforcement becomes ineffective, allowing financial crime to flourish unchecked.

Communities and societies are indirect victims when financial crime funds broader criminal activity, distorts markets, or contributes to economic instability. Money laundering enables criminal enterprises to expand; corruption limits development; and large-scale fraud can destabilize entire sectors. The cumulative effect impacts economic opportunity, public safety, and social trust.

Overlapping Roles and Fluid Boundaries

While financial crime actors can be categorized, their roles often overlap. A criminal may also be an insider if they work within an institution. A facilitator may simultaneously become a victim if they unknowingly assist a scheme that later implicates them. A victimized corporation may employ an insider whose misconduct contributed to the loss. These overlaps complicate investigations because relationships between actors may be concealed, misrepresented, or misunderstood.

In organized crime, criminals, facilitators, and insiders often operate in coordinated networks. These networks may include professionals who provide services, insiders who provide access, and external criminals who control operations. Some networks treat financial crime as a business, complete with hierarchies, division of labor, and strategic planning. Their structure may resemble legitimate enterprises, making them difficult to identify.

Even individual actors may move between roles over time. A low-level insider may become a facilitator after gaining experience. A facilitator may transition into direct criminal activity once they recognize the profitability of schemes. A victim of a fraud scheme may later participate in a different scheme after being coerced or financially pressured. These transitions highlight the dynamic nature of the financial crime ecosystem.

Human Factors and Behavioral Characteristics

Understanding the human factors behind each actor is essential. Criminals often exhibit traits such as opportunism, adaptability, and strategic thinking. They learn from failed attempts, shift methods quickly, and exploit emerging technologies with minimal hesitation. Some are motivated by greed or ambition, while others operate under coercion or ideological alignment.

Insiders may display behavioral indicators such as withdrawal from colleagues, unexplained lifestyle changes, frustration with management, or attempts to control processes beyond their role. Their familiarity with internal systems enables them to manipulate procedures subtly, making detection difficult until significant damage has occurred.

Facilitators often have professional sophistication. Their misconduct may be disguised within legitimate activities, making it difficult to separate legal actions from illicit facilitation. Some operate with plausible deniability, relying on ambiguity or gaps in regulation to avoid accountability.

Victims may demonstrate patterns that assist investigators in understanding offender behavior. Their experiences, when analyzed collectively, often reveal strategies used by criminals to exploit vulnerabilities. Victim analysis therefore plays a crucial role in identifying typologies, emerging risks, and systemic weaknesses.

Institutional and Environmental Influence

The broader environment in which these actors operate significantly shapes their behavior. Weak governance, limited oversight, inadequate compliance functions, and cultural normalization of misconduct all contribute to financial crime. Institutions with poor controls inadvertently encourage insider and facilitator activity by making opportunities accessible and lowering the perceived likelihood of detection.

Environments with extensive bureaucracy and limited transparency provide opportunities for corruption. Jurisdictions with permissive regulations create attractive channels for laundering and concealment. Markets with volatile digital assets attract cybercriminals seeking anonymity. Each actor responds to environmental conditions, refining their behavior based on perceived opportunity and risk.

Interdependence of Actors

Financial crime functions because these actors rely on one another. A criminal may initiate the scheme, but without insiders to provide access, facilitators to disguise transactions, and victims whose funds or systems are exploited, the scheme cannot succeed. This interdependence explains why dismantling financial crime requires a holistic approach. Isolating one actor may disrupt the immediate activity, but unless broader vulnerabilities are addressed, others will fill the role.

Investigators must therefore understand relationships as much as individual actions. Networks, communication channels, patterns of cooperation, and transactional links all reveal how actors coordinate. A single suspicious transaction may not be meaningful alone, but when analyzed within a network of actors, it becomes part of a larger pattern.

MOTIVATIONS AND BEHAVIORAL DRIVERS

Financial crime is not a random or spontaneous act. It is shaped by motivations that influence how offenders think, plan, and execute misconduct. These motivations vary considerably across individuals, organizations, and networks, but they share certain underlying themes that explain why people engage in illegal financial activity despite the risks. Understanding these drivers allows investigators to interpret behavior more accurately, anticipate methods, and assess how future developments may influence criminal evolution. Motivation is not merely about intent; it reflects psychological, economic, cultural, and situational factors that converge to make certain actions more attractive or more likely.

The Pursuit of Financial Gain

The most common motivator behind financial crime is the pursuit of monetary reward. Unlike crimes of passion or impulse, financial crimes are often calculated efforts to obtain assets, increase wealth, or improve financial standing. For some offenders, the motive is straightforward: they want money, and financial crime offers access to large sums with minimal physical confrontation. This attraction is especially strong in environments where opportunities for legitimate economic advancement are limited, or where illegal gains appear more efficient or profitable than lawful alternatives.

Financial gain also motivates offenders who already have access to resources. Some individuals commit financial crime not out of need but out of ambition or greed. Their misconduct reflects a desire to enhance status, achieve rapid financial growth, or fund lifestyles that exceed legitimate income. These offenders may rationalize their behavior by viewing illegal profit as a reward for perceived skill or intelligence, particularly in sectors where success is measured by financial outcomes.

Sophisticated criminals often treat financial crime as a business model. They analyze costs, risks, and returns, seeking methods that generate high profit with minimal exposure. Organized networks invest in corrupting insiders, building infrastructure, and testing weaknesses because the expected financial gain justifies the effort. In these environments, profit is not an incidental benefit—it is the foundation of decision-making and operational strategy.

Pressure and Financial Stress

Many offenders are influenced by financial pressures. These pressures may arise from personal debt, failing businesses, medical expenses, or other financial hardships. In such circumstances, individuals who would not normally consider misconduct may view illegal activity as a temporary solution or last resort. Some justify their actions as a means to bridge a difficult period, intending to "fix" the situation before detection occurs. This mindset often leads to escalated misconduct when initial actions fail to resolve underlying problems.

Internal fraud is frequently linked to financial stress. Employees with unrestricted access to funds or financial records may misuse their position to cover personal expenses, repay debts, or meet family obligations. The misconduct may begin with small acts that escalate as the offender becomes desensitized to risk. Rationalization plays a critical role here; employees may convince themselves that they are only "borrowing" funds or that the organization will not suffer significant harm.

Financial pressure also affects small business owners who manipulate invoices, falsify financial statements, or misuse loan applications to sustain their operations. These actions may initially appear pragmatic, but they create patterns of deception that evolve into larger criminal schemes.

Opportunity and Rationalization

Financial crime requires opportunity, and opportunity shapes motivation. Individuals who perceive that controls are weak, oversight is inconsistent, or detection is unlikely are more inclined to rationalize misconduct. Opportunity can exist in many forms: inadequate segregation of duties, ineffective monitoring systems, permissive compliance cultures, or reliance on documentation without verification.

Once an opportunity is recognized, rationalization becomes a powerful behavioral driver. Offenders often justify their actions through internal reasoning such as:

- believing they deserve the money
- assuming the institution can absorb the loss
- considering the act harmless because no physical harm occurs
- viewing misconduct as temporary or reversible

These rationalizations reduce internal resistance and allow offenders to commit actions that conflict with their ethical values. Investigators frequently observe that rationalization precedes misconduct and intensifies as crimes continue.

Organizations with weak leadership or unclear accountability structures unintentionally strengthen rationalization. When employees see others violating policies without consequence or observe management prioritizing profits over ethics, they may interpret misconduct as acceptable or even expected.

Greed and Moral Disengagement

Some offenders are driven by greed rather than necessity. Greed reflects a desire to accumulate wealth beyond any practical need and is often accompanied by a belief that rules apply only to others. These offenders may display traits such as entitlement, arrogance, or a belief that they can outsmart the system. Their decision-making focuses on maximizing personal benefit without regard for victims or consequences.

Moral disengagement allows individuals to distance themselves from the harm they cause. Offenders may minimize the impact of their actions, transfer responsibility to external conditions, or dehumanize victims. In corporate or institutional settings, offenders may claim that misconduct is "part of how the industry works," allowing them to commit crimes without feelings of guilt. This psychological detachment strengthens motivation and reduces hesitation.

Ideological and Political Objectives

Financial crime is sometimes motivated by ideology rather than personal gain. Terrorist financing is the most prominent example, but ideology also plays a role in fraud, cybercrime, and corruption. Offenders motivated by ideology believe their actions serve a higher purpose that justifies illegal conduct. They may view financial crime as a tool to promote political objectives, support extremist causes, or challenge systems they perceive as unjust.

Ideologically motivated offenders often prioritize secrecy and loyalty to their cause, making them difficult to identify through traditional financial indicators alone. Their motivations allow them to endure personal sacrifice, operate with discipline, and exploit vulnerabilities strategically. These characteristics distinguish them from profit-driven criminals and require investigators to consider behavioral patterns that extend beyond financial incentives.

Revenge, Resentment, and Personal Grievances

Some financial crimes are motivated by emotion rather than financial calculation. Employees who feel mistreated, undervalued, or unfairly disciplined may engage in misconduct as an act of retaliation. Their actions may aim to cause financial loss, disrupt operations, or undermine the institution's reputation. Such offenders often justify their actions by framing themselves as victims seeking justice or revenge.

These motivations may lead to destructive behavior, including unauthorized transfers, data manipulation, or cooperation with external criminals. Emotional drivers create unpredictable behavior because decisions are influenced by personal grievances rather than logical assessment of risk and reward. While financial gain may still occur, it is not the primary motive.

Influence of Organizational Culture

Organizational culture significantly shapes motivations. In environments where ethical standards are strong, transparency is valued, and misconduct is addressed promptly, motivation to commit financial crime decreases. By contrast, environments that tolerate misconduct, reward aggressive performance, or provide ambiguous guidance create fertile ground for criminal behavior.

Employees may feel pressured to meet unrealistic targets, leading them to manipulate data or falsify reports. Leaders who disregard compliance obligations or dismiss concerns encourage a perception that rules are flexible. In such environments, employees may believe misconduct is a legitimate method to achieve organizational goals.

Culture also influences facilitators who provide professional services. When firms prioritize revenue over compliance, professionals may overlook red flags, accept suspicious clients, or design structures that support concealment. Their motivation becomes financial success rather than ethical integrity.

Social Influence and Group Dynamics

Individuals are influenced by the behavior of those around them. In criminal networks, group dynamics encourage participation, normalize misconduct, and reduce psychological barriers. Offenders may derive motivation from a desire to belong, earn respect, or avoid conflict within the group. Organized crime groups use social reinforcement to maintain loyalty, often combining financial incentives with intimidation or ideological alignment.

In corporate environments, group dynamics can also influence misconduct. When employees observe colleagues committing fraud without consequences, they may view criminal activity as a standard practice. This diffusion of responsibility allows individuals to feel less accountable because actions are shared across a group rather than performed alone.

Skill, Confidence, and Perceived Control

Offenders often commit financial crime because they believe they possess the skills necessary to succeed. Technical proficiency, familiarity with financial systems, or experience with regulatory environments can increase confidence. Cybercriminals, for example, are motivated not only by profit but by a belief in their ability to penetrate systems, avoid detection, and control their environment.

Perceived control influences decisions significantly. Individuals who believe they can manage risk or manipulate evidence feel empowered to commit more sophisticated crimes. This sense of control may stem from past success, specialized knowledge, or access to insider information. Offenders may escalate their activity over time as confidence grows.

Desire for Power or Influence

Certain financial crimes are motivated by a desire for influence rather than direct financial gain. Corruption often reflects a consolidation of power within political, corporate, or administrative systems. Offenders may use bribery or manipulation to gain authority, secure favors, or expand their decision-making reach. The financial component becomes a tool rather than a goal.

Similarly, criminals who control money laundering networks, cybercriminal infrastructures, or illicit trade routes often pursue dominance within their ecosystems. Their motivation is to expand operational capacity, gain strategic advantage, or build a reputation that ensures compliance from subordinates and partners.

Psychological Traits and Personality Factors

Personality traits can shape motivation. Some offenders exhibit risk-taking behavior, impulsiveness, or a lack of empathy. Others show high levels of manipulation, strategic planning, or resilience under pressure. Psychological traits do not determine criminal behavior, but they influence how individuals respond to opportunity, stress, and rationalization.

In white-collar crime, offenders often demonstrate capability, confidence, and an understanding of organizational processes. These traits, when paired with weakened ethical standards, can produce sophisticated misconduct with far-reaching consequences.

Environmental and Societal Factors

Broader societal conditions influence motivation as well. Economic instability, political corruption, and weak regulatory environments encourage misconduct by reducing deterrence. When individuals observe widespread corruption or systemic unfairness, they may believe financial crime is a normalized method of advancement.

Technological and cultural shifts also play a role. The rise of remote work, online transactions, and digital communication provides both opportunity and anonymity. Offenders motivated by ease of access may exploit these environments because barriers to entry are lower than in traditional criminal activity.

SYSTEMIC WEAKNESSES AND EXPLOITABLE GAPS

Financial crime persists not only because of the motivations of offenders but because systems and institutions contain vulnerabilities that can be exploited. These weaknesses are not limited to operational gaps in individual organizations; they exist across financial markets, regulatory frameworks, technological infrastructure, and even cultural or economic environments. Understanding these systemic weaknesses is fundamental to effective investigation and prevention. It allows practitioners to identify where controls are most likely to fail, where oversight is limited, and where criminals can operate with relative ease.

Regulatory Inconsistencies across Jurisdictions

One of the most significant systemic weaknesses arises from the uneven regulatory landscape governing financial activity. Financial systems operate globally, yet regulatory frameworks are designed nationally. This mismatch creates gaps that criminals exploit by shifting activity across borders, selecting jurisdictions with minimal oversight, or routing transactions through complex pathways that hinder detection.

Some countries have robust anti-money laundering (AML) frameworks, strict corporate transparency rules, and strong enforcement capacity. Others lack resources, political will, or institutional stability to implement similar standards. Even well-regulated jurisdictions may differ in definitions, reporting thresholds, beneficial ownership requirements, or sanctions enforcement. These variations create opportunities for offenders to arbitrage between regimes, exploiting the weakest links.

The lack of uniformity also impedes collaboration between authorities. Mutual legal assistance processes can be slow, fragmented, or encumbered by bureaucratic hurdles. Criminals rely on these delays to move funds, destroy evidence, or restructure operations. The global nature of financial activity demands harmonized rules, yet in practice, coordination remains inconsistent, providing criminals with exploitable gaps.

Gaps in Beneficial Ownership Transparency

A central vulnerability in financial systems is the opacity surrounding beneficial ownership. While corporate structures are essential for legitimate commerce, they can be manipulated to conceal the identities of those who ultimately control or benefit from assets. Shell companies, trusts, layered corporate arrangements, and nominee directors allow offenders to disguise their involvement, distance themselves from illicit activity, and obscure financial flows.

In many jurisdictions, beneficial ownership registers are incomplete, unreliable, or inaccessible. Some require minimal verification, allowing individuals to list fictitious or proxy owners without consequence. Others provide exemptions that shield politically influential or high-risk individuals from scrutiny. These gaps make it difficult for investigators to establish connections between transactions, identify control relationships, or trace assets.

Criminals exploit these weaknesses by creating multi-jurisdictional structures that obscure accountability. A company may be incorporated in one country, controlled through a trust in another, and owned by entities located in a secrecy jurisdiction. This layering frustrates attempts to identify who ultimately benefits from a transaction or asset, allowing criminals to operate behind legal façades.

Ineffective Oversight in Certain Sectors

Financial institutions are subject to rigorous oversight, but other sectors with significant exposure to financial crime risks operate with limited regulatory attention. These include real estate, luxury goods, casinos, art markets, professional services, and certain fintech entities. Criminals gravitate toward these sectors because they allow high-value transactions, limited scrutiny, and opportunities to integrate illicit funds.

For example, real estate transactions often involve large sums of money without routine assessment of the source of funds. High-value goods can be purchased, stored, transported, or resold anonymously. Professional facilitators such as lawyers, notaries, and accountants often claim client confidentiality or rely on exemptions that limit their reporting obligations. These gaps create environments where illicit activity can be concealed within legitimate commerce.

Fintech platforms, crowdfunding services, and digital asset exchanges may also present vulnerabilities. Rapid innovation can outpace regulatory adaptation, allowing businesses to operate without adequate compliance systems. Some platforms prioritize growth over risk management, inadvertently offering criminals a channel for movement of value.

Fragmented Institutional Controls

Within organizations, systemic weaknesses frequently arise from fragmented or inconsistent controls. Even institutions with strong compliance cultures may suffer from gaps in procedures, unclear responsibilities, or failures in information sharing. These gaps can occur for several reasons:

- inadequate coordination between departments
- inconsistent documentation standards
- outdated risk assessments
- reliance on manual processes
- insufficient staffing or training

When controls operate in silos, suspicious activity may appear benign within one department but concerning when viewed holistically. Criminals exploit these gaps by structuring transactions across multiple channels, manipulating internal processes, or relying on insiders who understand where oversight is weakest.

Weak governance exacerbates these vulnerabilities. When leadership lacks commitment to compliance, or when oversight committees do not receive accurate information, critical warnings may be overlooked. Institutions with rapid growth or complex operations may struggle to maintain adequate risk management frameworks, creating openings for misconduct.

Weaknesses in Digital Infrastructure

The growth of digital financial systems introduces both opportunities and vulnerabilities. Weaknesses in cybersecurity, authentication processes, data management, and system integration create openings for criminals to commit fraud, steal information, or hijack accounts.

Cybercriminals exploit inadequate patching procedures, outdated software, poor network segmentation, and weak user access controls. Systems designed for convenience—such as mobile banking applications, digital wallets, and automated payment platforms—may lack robust detection mechanisms. Criminals can automate attacks, test weaknesses at scale, or purchase ready-made tools on illicit markets.

Digital identity systems also present vulnerabilities. Synthetic identities, forged documentation, and manipulated credentials can be used to open accounts, apply for loans, or conduct illicit transfers. When institutions rely heavily on automated verification without sufficient human review, criminals can bypass controls with minimal effort.

The decentralized nature of digital asset ecosystems further complicates oversight. Transactions occur outside traditional banking channels, anonymity is enhanced, and regulatory frameworks are still developing. Criminals exploit these conditions to move funds across borders quickly and discreetly.

Human Factors and Organizational Culture

Systemic weaknesses often stem from human behavior rather than technology or regulation. Employees may not understand compliance obligations, overlook red flags, or fail to escalate concerns. High workloads, inadequate training, or unclear policies increase the likelihood of errors. Even well-designed systems fail when staff do not apply them consistently.

Organizational culture shapes how seriously employees take compliance responsibilities. In environments where ethical conduct is emphasized, employees are more likely to question unusual transactions, report concerns, and follow procedures. In weaker cultures, employees may fear retaliation, believe misconduct is tolerated, or assume compliance is someone else's responsibility.

Insider threats are amplified in institutions with poor supervision, weak segregation of duties, or ineffective monitoring systems. Criminals may intentionally target employees in such environments, offering bribes or exploiting vulnerabilities. A single insider with privileged access can bypass controls designed to prevent external threats.

Insufficient Information Sharing

Systemic vulnerabilities are exacerbated when information does not flow effectively between institutions, regulators, and enforcement authorities. Limited data sharing allows criminals to exploit gaps in visibility, moving activity across institutions or sectors to avoid detection. Some jurisdictions restrict information sharing due to privacy laws, while others lack the infrastructure to facilitate secure exchange.

Criminals exploit this fragmentation by engaging in activity across multiple platforms, creating patterns that appear harmless in isolation but harmful in aggregate. Without the ability to detect cross-institutional patterns, investigators may miss key connections or fail to identify networks operating at scale.

Even within institutions, limited information sharing between compliance teams, operational departments, and senior management can create blind spots. When concerns are not escalated or systems do not integrate data effectively, critical warnings may go unnoticed.

Volume and Velocity of Global Transactions

The global financial system processes an enormous volume of transactions daily. Monitoring every transaction in real time is not feasible, even with advanced technology. Criminals exploit this reality by structuring activity to blend into legitimate traffic, conducting low-value transactions that avoid thresholds, or routing funds through high-volume channels where scrutiny is limited.

The velocity of digital transactions also creates challenges. Illicit funds can move across multiple jurisdictions within minutes, significantly reducing opportunities for intervention. Investigators often face a race against time, particularly in cases involving ransomware, online fraud, or cryptocurrency transfers.

Volume and velocity also burden monitoring systems. High false-positive rates can overwhelm compliance teams, allowing true suspicious activity to be overlooked. Criminals take advantage of this by designing activity that triggers minimal alerts or mimics legitimate patterns.

Limited Capacity and Resource Constraints

Regulators and enforcement agencies often face resource limitations that hinder their ability to detect, investigate, and prosecute financial crime. Financial investigations are complex, requiring specialized skills, international cooperation, and extensive data analysis. When agencies lack funding, personnel, or technological tools, they are unable to address the full scale of financial crime risks.

Criminals recognize these constraints and design operations to fall below enforcement thresholds. They may use multiple small transactions, target sectors with fewer compliance requirements, or operate in jurisdictions with limited regulatory presence. Resource constraints also delay investigations, giving offenders time to reorganize, relocate, or destroy evidence.

Institutions face similar challenges. Compliance functions must often manage increasing regulatory expectations without proportional increases in staff or budgets. This imbalance strains systems, increases risk of oversight failures, and creates openings for misconduct.

Lack of Transparency in High-Risk Sectors

Certain sectors inherently carry high financial crime risk due to limited transparency, complex operations, or high-value transactions. Examples include luxury goods, art markets, private investment funds, and cross-border procurement. These sectors often rely on opaque pricing, confidential transactions, or private negotiations that make oversight difficult.

Criminals exploit these environments because transactions can be justified through subjective valuation, confidentiality norms, or specialized industry practices. High-value assets can be purchased, transferred, or stored with little documentation, providing an effective means of laundering or concealing illicit funds.

Impact of Technology Gaps in Enforcement

While criminals benefit from emerging technologies, enforcement agencies may struggle to keep pace. Investigating cryptocurrency crime, darknet markets, or advanced cyberattacks requires technical expertise that may not be widely available. Agencies with outdated tools face disadvantages against criminals who adapt quickly.

Moreover, legal frameworks may not yet address modern technology adequately. Gaps in regulation for digital assets, decentralized platforms, or algorithmic trading create uncertainty that criminals exploit. Enforcement agencies may find themselves constrained by laws written for traditional financial systems.

Overreliance on Automated Monitoring

Automated detection systems are essential for monitoring large volumes of financial activity. However, overreliance on these systems can create vulnerabilities. Criminals study how automated monitoring works and design transactions that avoid triggering alerts. They may use structuring techniques, break patterns into smaller components, or operate just below risk thresholds.

Automated systems also struggle with complex, multi-stage schemes that require contextual understanding. Without human judgment, suspicious behavior may be misclassified as routine activity. When institutions prioritize automation at the expense of analytical expertise, systemic weaknesses appear.

INTERCONNECTIONS BETWEEN CRIME TYPES

Financial crime is not a collection of isolated offenses but a network of interdependent activities that support, conceal, or enhance one another. Criminals often combine multiple methods to achieve their objectives, shifting between offenses depending on opportunity, risk, or operational need. Understanding these interconnections is essential for investigators because focusing on a single crime type often reveals only a fraction of the underlying conduct. Many schemes require a blend of activities - fraud to generate proceeds, money laundering to conceal them, corruption to facilitate access, and cyber tools to execute or expand operations. These interwoven components create a dynamic landscape in which financial crime cannot be understood in isolation.

Money Laundering as a Universal Enabler

Money laundering sits at the center of most financial crime networks. No matter the origin of illicit proceed s- bribery, fraud, drug trafficking, asset misappropriation, cybercrime, or sanctions evasion - criminals must eventually convert those proceeds into usable assets without attracting attention. This necessity makes money laundering a common companion to almost every other crime type.

The laundering process is often tailored to the nature of the underlying offense. Proceeds from corruption may be hidden through false consulting contracts or inflated procurement arrangements. Cybercrime proceeds may be moved through cryptocurrency tumblers or peer-to-peer exchanges. Fraud proceeds may be routed through personal accounts, shell companies, or high-value purchases.

Because laundering is so central, investigators often identify broader criminal activity by tracing the financial methods used to conceal funds. A single suspicious transaction may point not only to laundering but to the underlying crimes that produced the proceeds. Understanding this interconnectedness allows investigators to establish the full scope of misconduct rather than focusing solely on the concealment phase.

Fraud as a Source Crime for Multiple Schemes

Fraud frequently serves as a foundational offense that supports other criminal activities. The proceeds from investment fraud, procurement fraud, or internal misappropriation can be used to fund corruption, finance extremist organizations, or support organized crime networks. Fraud schemes often generate substantial and continuous inflows of money, making them attractive to criminals seeking sustained revenue streams.

Certain types of fraud also create opportunities for additional offenses. Identity theft can facilitate account takeover, unauthorized transfers, or synthetic identity creation. Mortgage and real estate fraud may involve falsified appraisals, circular financing, and layering of ownership structures—techniques that overlap with money laundering. Business Email Compromise activity often relies on mule accounts, which are later repurposed for laundering unrelated criminal proceeds.

Fraud and cybercrime increasingly operate in tandem. Phishing campaigns, malware attacks, and credential harvesting are used to commit unauthorized transactions or to support more complex schemes such as payroll diversion, insurance fraud, or payment redirection. These interconnected behaviors reflect how criminals view fraud not as a standalone activity but as a component within a broader operational model.

Corruption as a Facilitator of Financial Crime

Corruption enables financial crime by weakening systems designed to prevent misconduct. Bribery and abuse of power can influence procurement decisions, regulatory approvals, enforcement actions, and access to sensitive information. When corrupt actors occupy positions of authority, they reduce the likelihood of detection and increase opportunities for criminals to operate without scrutiny.

Corruption often intersects with money laundering because corrupt officials must hide the proceeds of their misconduct. It also intersects with sanctions evasion when political connections or influence are used to bypass restrictions on trade or financial activity. In some jurisdictions, corruption becomes deeply embedded within administrative systems, creating structural vulnerabilities that criminals exploit repeatedly.

Organized crime groups frequently use corruption to protect their operations. They may bribe customs officials to facilitate smuggling, law enforcement officers to avoid investigation, or corporate employees to approve fraudulent documentation. This integration between corruption and other offenses demonstrates how financial crime ecosystems rely on influence and access as much as on technical methods.

Sanctions Evasion and Trade-Based Crime

Sanctions evasion and trade-based financial crime are closely related because both involve the movement of goods and funds across borders using deceptive documentation or misrepresented transactions. Sanctioned entities may use trade channels to disguise payments, reroute goods through third countries, or mislabel items to avoid detection. Offenders exploit weaknesses in trade documentation, valuation systems, and cross-border oversight to obscure the involvement of prohibited parties.

Trade-based money laundering often mirrors these techniques. Over-invoicing, under-invoicing, phantom shipments, and container manipulation can all be used to move value covertly. Criminals operating in sanctioned jurisdictions frequently rely on these methods because traditional financial channels are blocked or monitored closely.

These interconnections highlight the importance of trade analysis in investigations. Understanding trade patterns, pricing discrepancies, and shipping routes provides insights into both sanctions evasion and laundering techniques. Investigators must consider trade-based behavior as part of broader financial crime networks rather than treating trade anomalies as isolated issues.

Cybercrime as a Force Multiplier

Cyber-enabled crime interacts with almost every financial crime type. Digital tools increase efficiency, expand victim pools, and reduce the need for physical presence. Criminals use malware, phishing campaigns, credential theft, and remote access tools to commit fraud, manipulate accounts, steal information, or disrupt systems. Once proceeds are obtained, cybercriminals often employ digital laundering techniques, using online exchanges, privacy coins, or decentralized platforms.

Cybercrime also supports corruption and insider schemes. Compromised accounts may be used to intercept procurement information, manipulate financial records, or gain unauthorized access to sensitive data. Criminals may use communication platforms to coordinate bribery or influence operations, reducing the risk of interception.

Furthermore, cyber infrastructure allows professional facilitators to offer illicit services globally. Darknet markets provide fake documents, hacking tools, identity kits, and money laundering services, enabling offenders with limited expertise to participate in complex schemes. This accessibility strengthens the connections between cybercrime and traditional financial crimes.

Terrorist Financing and Criminal Revenue Streams

Terrorist financing intersects with other crimes in several ways. While ideological objectives drive the financing, the methods used to obtain and move funds often mirror those used in criminal enterprises. Terrorist groups may engage in fraud, extortion, smuggling, drug trafficking, or cybercrime to generate revenue. They may also benefit from corruption or rely on facilitators who provide logistical or financial services.

Funds used for terrorist activities often flow through informal money transfer systems, charities, or trade-based channels—pathways also used by criminals seeking to avoid detection. These shared channels create challenges for investigators because distinguishing between terrorist financing and other illicit activity requires contextual and behavioral analysis rather than reliance on financial indicators alone.

Understanding the interconnected nature of terrorist financing helps investigators recognize signs of ideological activity hidden within broader criminal networks. Even small financial flows, when analyzed alongside behavioral patterns, may indicate links to extremist organizations.

Organized Crime and Multi-Layered Schemes

Organized crime groups rarely rely on a single crime type. Instead, they operate diversified portfolios of illicit activity to stabilize revenue and reduce risk. A single network may engage in human trafficking, narcotics distribution, counterfeiting, cybercrime, corruption, and money laundering simultaneously. The income from these offenses is consolidated, layered, and reinvested in legitimate businesses or further criminal operations.

These groups use corporate structures, trade channels, and corrupt connections to support their activities. They may use illicit proceeds from one crime to fund another, creating self-sustaining cycles. For example, proceeds from drug trafficking may be laundered through real estate, with profits reinvested into cybercrime infrastructure that then supports fraud campaigns. These complex interactions make organized crime resilient and difficult to disrupt.

Investigators must therefore understand not only individual offenses but how they merge within broader organizational strategies. A disruption in one area may simply cause the network to shift activity to another crime type unless the interconnected structure is addressed holistically.

Professional Facilitation and Complex Structures

Facilitators such as lawyers, accountants, corporate service providers, and financial intermediaries contribute to the interconnections between crime types by designing structures that conceal misconduct. These structures include layered companies, trusts, cross-border entities, back-to-back loan arrangements, and artificial transactions designed to mimic legitimate commerce.

These structures can be used simultaneously for laundering, tax evasion, corruption, sanctions evasion, and fraud. A single corporate vehicle may serve multiple illegal purposes depending on how it is used. The presence of professional facilitation also allows criminals to move seamlessly between different crimes because the infrastructure needed to conceal one type of offense can conceal others.

Professional enablers sometimes operate knowingly, but in other cases, they fail to conduct adequate due diligence, allowing criminals to misrepresent their intentions. The involvement of professionals increases the complexity of investigations, as the appearance of legitimacy conceals underlying connections between offenses.

Victim Exploitation Across Multiple Crime Types

Victims are sometimes targeted across different crime types, especially where personal information, account access, or identity documents are obtained. Data breaches, phishing attacks, and credential theft often precede fraud schemes. Mule account recruitment frequently relies on victims who are deceived or coerced into facilitating money movement. Once victim information is compromised, it may be sold or repurposed across various criminal networks.

Victims of romance fraud, investment scams, or online impersonation may unknowingly become facilitators of laundering activity, particularly when asked to receive or forward funds. Organized networks exploit these overlaps to expand the scale and reach of their schemes.

Cross-Sector Implications

Financial crime spanning multiple types frequently crosses sectors as well. An investigation into a suspicious transaction in the banking sector may reveal connections to real estate purchases, trade anomalies, nonprofit organizations, or digital asset platforms. Criminals use different sectors strategically, selecting the channels with the least oversight or the greatest opportunity for concealment.

The movement of funds across sectors also complicates oversight. Each sector may monitor only part of a criminal scheme, and without cross-sector insights, the full picture remains hidden. Effective investigation therefore requires understanding how behavior in one sector connects to vulnerabilities in another.

Adaptive Behavior and Evolution of Crime Types

The interconnections between crime types are not static. Criminals adapt based on regulatory changes, technological developments, and enforcement actions. When one method becomes risky, they shift to another that offers similar benefits with lower exposure. This adaptability strengthens the interconnected nature of financial crime because offenders borrow techniques, tools, and structures from various crime types to create hybrid schemes.

For example, the rise of cryptocurrency has influenced laundering, sanctions evasion, fraud, and cybercrime simultaneously. The growth of online marketplaces has influenced identity theft, illicit trade, and corruption. As criminals innovate, the boundaries between offense categories blur further, increasing the need for investigative strategies that recognize the fluid nature of these connections.

Implications for Investigators

Interconnected crime types require analytical approaches that recognize patterns rather than isolated incidents. Investigators must consider the broader context of suspicious activity, identify the relationships between offenses, and understand how criminals leverage multiple channels. This requires knowledge of how financial crime operates across sectors, how professional facilitators contribute, and how digital tools expand opportunities.

Recognizing interconnections also supports more effective prevention. Strengthening controls in one area may disrupt multiple crime types if those crimes rely on the same vulnerability. Conversely, ignoring interconnected risks may allow criminals to bypass controls by shifting activity from one channel to another.

CHAPTER 3

GLOBAL LEGAL AND REGULATORY FRAMEWORKS

INTERNATIONAL CONVENTIONS AND STANDARDS

FINANCIAL CRIME is a global problem that transcends borders, legal systems, and enforcement capabilities. No single country can effectively address money laundering, corruption, sanctions evasion, terrorist financing, or complex fraud schemes without international collaboration. Criminal networks exploit inconsistencies between jurisdictions, while legitimate institutions operate across multiple countries with interconnected risks. For these reasons, international conventions and standards form the backbone of the global response to financial crime. They establish common expectations, harmonize legal frameworks, and create mechanisms for cooperation, monitoring, and accountability.

These frameworks do not replace national laws; rather, they shape them by articulating principles that countries adapt into their domestic systems. Understanding these conventions is essential for investigators and compliance professionals because they influence national obligations, regulatory expectations, and enforcement priorities worldwide.

The United Nations Conventions

The United Nations (UN) has developed several conventions that form the foundation of international efforts against financial crime. These conventions promote global cooperation, define criminal offenses, and require member states to adopt legal and institutional measures that align with agreed standards.

UN Convention against Transnational Organized Crime (UNTOC)

Adopted in 2000, UNTOC is one of the most significant instruments for combating organized criminal activity. It requires member states to criminalize participation in organized criminal groups, money laundering, corruption, and obstruction of justice. UNTOC also contains protocols addressing human trafficking, migrant smuggling, and firearms trafficking—crimes that often intersect with financial crime due to the need to launder proceeds or conceal illicit financing.

UNTOC emphasizes international cooperation, including extradition, mutual legal assistance, and joint investigations. These mechanisms are critical because organized criminal groups often operate across multiple countries, exploiting legal gaps and jurisdictional barriers. By establishing shared definitions and procedures, UNTOC enhances the ability of states to respond collectively.

UN Convention against Corruption (UNCAC)

UNCAC, adopted in 2003, is the first global instrument dedicated exclusively to combating corruption. It provides comprehensive standards on preventing corruption, criminalizing a broad range of corrupt conduct, recovering stolen assets, and fostering international cooperation. UNCAC requires countries to criminalize bribery of domestic and foreign public officials, embezzlement, trading in influence, illicit enrichment, and other corrupt acts.

One of UNCAC's most significant contributions is its emphasis on asset recovery. Corruption cases frequently involve complex financial structures, hidden assets, and cross-border transfers. UNCAC outlines procedures for identifying, freezing, confiscating, and returning illicit assets, making it an essential reference for investigators and enforcement agencies.

UNCAC also recognizes the importance of prevention. It requires member states to strengthen public sector transparency, ensure merit-based hiring, reinforce procurement controls, and establish independent anti-corruption bodies. These measures reduce vulnerabilities that criminals exploit and promote an environment of accountability.

UN Drug Control Conventions

Before modern AML frameworks were established, the UN drug conventions - particularly the 1988 Convention against Illicit Traffic in Narcotic Drugs and Psychotropic Substances - played a pivotal role in shaping the global response to money laundering. The 1988 Convention was the first instrument to require countries to criminalize the laundering of drug trafficking proceeds and to establish mechanisms for freezing and confiscation.

While originally focused on narcotics, the principles in the convention influenced the development of broader AML standards. It recognized that financial systems could be manipulated to support criminal enterprises and emphasized the need for international cooperation, extradition, and information sharing.

The Basel Committee Standards

The Basel Committee on Banking Supervision, composed of central banks and financial regulators, sets global standards for banking regulation, including key principles related to AML/CTF and financial integrity. Although its standards are not legally binding, they are widely adopted because they influence regulatory expectations and institutional practices.

The Basel Committee's guidance includes the "Core Principles for Effective Banking Supervision," which require banks to identify and manage financial crime risks. It also issues detailed guidance on customer due diligence, beneficial ownership transparency, correspondent banking, and the responsibilities of financial institutions in preventing misuse of the banking system.

These standards affect how banks structure compliance frameworks, assess risks, and conduct monitoring. They emphasize risk-based approaches, accountability of senior management, and the integration of AML/CTF considerations into broader prudential oversight.

The Financial Action Task Force Standards

While the Financial Action Task Force (FATF) will be addressed in greater detail in a later section, it is important to acknowledge here that FATF's 40 Recommendations serve as the global benchmark for AML/CTF frameworks. FATF sets minimum standards that countries must incorporate into their legal and regulatory systems and evaluates compliance through a rigorous peer-review process.

The FATF standards influence national legislation across the world, requiring countries to criminalize money laundering and terrorist financing, implement preventive measures for financial institutions, establish financial intelligence units (FIUs), and ensure effective supervision, enforcement, and cooperation.

FATF has expanded its focus to include proliferation financing, beneficial ownership transparency, virtual assets, and new technologies.

OECD Anti-Bribery Convention

The Organisation for Economic Co-operation and Development (OECD) adopted the Anti-Bribery Convention in 1997 to combat bribery of foreign public officials in international business transactions. Unlike many conventions, which address corruption broadly, the OECD Convention focuses specifically on corporate bribery across borders.

The convention requires signatory countries to criminalize the act of bribing foreign officials and to hold companies accountable for bribery-related offenses. It also requires states to implement measures ensuring accurate accounting, auditing, and internal controls. This focus on corporate responsibility has influenced global enforcement trends, including major prosecutions related to foreign bribery, accounting manipulation, and internal control failures.

The OECD Working Group on Bribery monitors implementation through peer reviews, ensuring countries maintain high standards. This monitoring has been influential in shaping corporate compliance programs, transactional due diligence, and ethical expectations across international business.

Wolfsberg Principles

The Wolfsberg Group - composed of major global banks - developed principles and guidance for managing financial crime risks within financial institutions. Although not a formal convention, the Wolfsberg Principles have significant influence in shaping AML/CTF practices worldwide.

The principles cover areas such as:

- customer identification and due diligence
- correspondent banking
- transaction monitoring
- sanctions compliance
- anti-bribery and corruption controls

They emphasize practical implementation of controls, promoting consistent standards across global institutions. The Wolfsberg Principles complement regulatory requirements by addressing operational realities and providing clarity to banks on managing complex financial crime risks.

Egmont Group of Financial Intelligence Units

The Egmont Group provides a global framework for cooperation among FIUs. FIUs receive, analyze, and disseminate financial intelligence related to money laundering, terrorist financing, and other financial crimes. The Egmont Group facilitates information sharing, strengthens analytic capabilities, and supports best practices.

Although not a regulatory body, the Egmont Group enhances international cooperation by providing secure communication channels and training opportunities. Its role is critical because financial intelligence is often the first indicator of criminal activity and forms the basis for many investigations.

IMF and World Bank Standards

The International Monetary Fund (IMF) and World Bank integrate AML/CTF considerations into their country assessments, particularly for states receiving financial assistance or undergoing economic evaluation. These organizations evaluate systemic vulnerabilities, regulatory frameworks, governance quality, and the effectiveness of financial oversight.

Their involvement has elevated the importance of financial integrity within global economic policy, encouraging countries to strengthen laws, improve transparency, and enhance supervisory capacity. By linking financial crime risk to economic stability, the IMF and World Bank underscore the broader implications of weak AML/CTF controls.

International Sanctions Frameworks

While sanctions regimes are implemented at the national or regional level, they are guided by international conventions and UN Security Council resolutions. These resolutions require member states to implement sanctions related to terrorism, proliferation, and threats to international peace.

Sanctions frameworks frequently intersect with AML/CTF standards, requiring institutions to identify and block transactions involving designated parties. The integration of sanctions into global standards ensures a unified response to high-risk actors and emphasizes the responsibility of financial institutions to conduct thorough screening, monitoring, and reporting.

Importance of Harmonization

International conventions and standards create the foundation for harmonized approaches to financial crime, but their effectiveness depends on consistent implementation. Differences in legal systems, enforcement capabilities, and political priorities can undermine alignment. Criminals exploit these disparities by operating in jurisdictions with weaker controls or limited cooperation.

Harmonization is essential for:

- facilitating cross-border investigations
- standardizing reporting practices

- ensuring equal regulatory expectations
- reducing opportunities for arbitrage

Global standards also provide clarity to financial institutions operating across multiple jurisdictions, reducing the uncertainty that arises from inconsistent requirements.

Challenges in Adoption and Implementation

Despite the strength of international frameworks, countries face challenges when incorporating them into domestic systems. These challenges include limited resources, political resistance, legislative delays, and lack of technical expertise. Developing countries may struggle to implement complex standards due to capacity constraints, while others may face corruption or institutional weaknesses that impede enforcement.

Even where laws are adopted, they may not be applied consistently. Supervisory agencies may lack authority or independence, investigative bodies may lack training, and judicial systems may face backlogs or inconsistent interpretations. These challenges highlight the difference between formal adoption of standards and their practical effectiveness.

Influence on Domestic Regulation and Institutional Practice

International standards shape national laws in areas such as money laundering, terrorist financing, corruption, sanctions enforcement, and asset recovery. They also influence institutional practices, requiring financial institutions to implement:

- customer due diligence
- suspicious activity reporting
- sanctions screening
- beneficial ownership verification
- risk-based monitoring

Organizations that operate internationally must align with both national laws and international expectations. Failure to do so exposes them to regulatory penalties, reputational damage, and operational risk.

AML/CTF LAWS AND SUPERVISORY BODIES

Efforts to prevent, detect, and deter money laundering and terrorist financing depend on legal frameworks that impose clear obligations on institutions and grant oversight powers to regulators. These laws and supervisory structures form a protective system designed to safeguard financial integrity, reduce vulnerabilities, and ensure that financial channels cannot be easily exploited by criminals or extremist groups. While AML/CTF regimes vary across jurisdictions, they share common foundations shaped by international standards and reinforced through national enforcement. A clear understanding of these systems is essential for investigators, compliance professionals, and decision-makers who must interpret regulatory expectations and recognize how failures in implementation expose institutions to significant risk.

Purpose and Structure of AML/CTF Laws

Modern AML/CTF laws aim to do more than penalize criminals. Their primary function is preventive. They require institutions to build environments that make it difficult for illicit funds to enter, move through, or exit the financial system unnoticed. To accomplish this, legislation typically establishes three core components:

1. Definition of offenses - criminalizing money laundering, terrorist financing, and related conduct.
2. Preventive measures for institutions - customer verification, monitoring, reporting, and internal controls.

3. Supervisory and enforcement mechanisms -oversight agencies with authority to inspect, sanction, and guide institutions.

This framework transforms financial institutions into crucial partners in national security and public protection. By obligating them to recognize and escalate suspicious behavior, AML/CTF laws expand the capacity of law enforcement and intelligence agencies far beyond what government alone could achieve.

Criminalization of Money Laundering and Terrorist Financing

AML/CTF laws begin by defining the conduct that constitutes an offense. Money laundering statutes criminalize the processing of assets derived from crime, including possessing, transferring, concealing, or legitimizing illicit proceeds. Importantly, many jurisdictions extend these laws to a wide range of predicate offenses, ensuring that laundering is not limited to drug trafficking or organized crime but encompasses fraud, corruption, environmental crimes, tax evasion, cybercrime, and other serious misconduct.

Terrorist financing laws operate differently. Instead of focusing on the origin of funds, they criminalize the intentional provision, collection, or movement of funds for terrorist purposes, regardless of whether the assets themselves are lawful. This distinction is critical: legitimate funds can become illegal when used to support extremist causes.

These offenses form the legal basis for investigations and prosecutions. They also justify the extensive compliance requirements imposed on institutions, which are expected to identify behavior that may indicate involvement in these crimes.

Obligations for Financial Institutions

AML/CTF laws require institutions to implement preventive measures tailored to their risk profile. While specific obligations vary, the pillars of compliance are broadly consistent across jurisdictions.

Customer Identification and Verification

Institutions must establish the identity of customers before forming a business relationship. This includes verifying personal details, obtaining documentation, assessing beneficial ownership for legal entities, and confirming the purpose of the relationship. Accuracy at this stage is crucial because weakened identification processes create opportunities for criminals to operate anonymously.

Understanding Customer Risk

Institutions must assess the risk posed by each customer and apply controls proportionate to that risk. The risk-based approach allows for flexibility but requires rigorous documentation and justification. For high-risk customers—such as politically exposed persons, those operating in high-risk industries, or individuals using complex structures—enhanced due diligence is required.

Monitoring Transactions and Activity

Effective monitoring involves reviewing transactions for anomalies, identifying patterns inconsistent with the customer's profile, and assessing whether activity aligns with expected behavior. Monitoring systems may include automated tools, manual reviews, or a combination of both. Institutions must adjust these systems regularly to respond to new threats and typologies.

Reporting Obligations

When institutions detect activity that raises suspicion, they must submit reports to their national Financial Intelligence Unit (FIU). These reports are confidential and designed to trigger further analysis, investigation, or enforcement action. Timely reporting is critical to preventing criminals from exploiting financial systems without detection. Institutions must also comply with mandatory reporting thresholds for cash transactions or cross-border transfers, depending on national laws.

Internal Controls and Governance

AML/CTF laws require institutions to establish governance structures that support compliance. These include:

- designated compliance officers
- independent audit functions
- policies and procedures aligned with legal requirements
- staff training to ensure awareness of financial crime risks

Institutions must demonstrate that compliance is integrated into daily operations, not treated as an isolated or symbolic function.

Role of Supervisory Bodies

Supervisory bodies enforce AML/CTF laws by monitoring institutions, guiding policy implementation, and imposing remedial actions when deficiencies arise. Their effectiveness depends on independence, expertise, and the authority granted by legislation.

Supervisors conduct on-site inspections, review documentation, assess governance structures, and evaluate the adequacy of monitoring systems. They also analyze institutions' risk assessments, scrutinize customer files, and test the quality of internal controls. Where gaps are found, supervisors can mandate corrective measures, restrict business activities, or issue penalties.

Supervisory bodies operate across multiple sectors. In many jurisdictions, banking regulators oversee banks and credit institutions; securities regulators supervise investment firms; insurance authorities monitor insurers; and separate bodies regulate DNFBPs. Coordination among these bodies is essential to ensure consistent application of standards.

Financial Intelligence Units (FIUs)

FIUs are central to AML/CTF enforcement. Their role is to receive, analyze, and disseminate financial intelligence derived from suspicious activity reports and other sources. FIUs review patterns, identify networks, and develop insights that support law enforcement, tax authorities, customs agencies, and national security bodies.

FIUs vary in structure. Some operate as independent administrative agencies; others function within law enforcement or judicial branches. Regardless of structure, their effectiveness depends on access to information, data analysis capabilities, and cooperation with international counterparts.

FIUs also provide feedback to reporting institutions, helping them refine detection mechanisms and better understand emerging risks. This feedback loop reinforces the connection between public authorities and the private sector.

Supervision of DNFBPs

DNFBPs - lawyers, accountants, real estate agents, corporate service providers, dealers in luxury goods, and casinos—are increasingly recognized as key actors in AML/CTF frameworks. Criminals often use these sectors to establish corporate structures, move high-value assets, or disguise ownership.

Supervision of DNFBPs presents unique challenges. Professional associations may resist certain obligations, confidentiality rules must be balanced with AML requirements, and some trades lack formal regulation. Nonetheless, many jurisdictions now require DNFBPs to conduct customer due diligence, maintain records, apply risk-based controls, and report suspicious activity.

Sanctions Compliance and Enforcement

Sanctions systems operate alongside AML/CTF laws. Institutions must ensure they do not engage in transactions involving prohibited individuals, entities, or jurisdictions. Supervisors assess the effectiveness of screening tools, the timeliness of list updates, and the quality of escalation processes.

Sanctions enforcement is often strict because violations carry geopolitical implications. Penalties can be substantial, and institutions must maintain controls that address both domestic and foreign sanctions regimes.

The Interaction Between Prudential and AML/CTF Oversight

Prudential regulators - responsible for financial stability - play an important role in AML/CTF oversight because poor financial crime controls can threaten institutional soundness. AML/CTF failures expose institutions to fines, litigation, reputational damage, and restrictions that impair operations.

Prudential regulators evaluate whether boards and senior management demonstrate accountability, allocate adequate resources, and promote a culture that prioritizes integrity. Weak governance is often a leading factor in compliance failures, making prudential oversight a necessary complement to AML/CTF supervision.

Cross-Sector Collaboration

AML/CTF laws depend on cooperation between multiple authorities: FIUs, supervisory bodies, law enforcement agencies, tax authorities, customs, and intelligence services. Effective collaboration requires formal agreements, clear communication channels, and consistent interpretation of legal obligations.

Increasingly, jurisdictions are developing public-private partnerships, where institutions share typologies, indicators, and risk information with authorities. These partnerships enhance detection capabilities by combining operational knowledge with regulatory insight.

Challenges in Implementation

Despite strong legislative frameworks, challenges remain. These include:

- limited resources for supervision
- inconsistent application of risk-based approaches
- difficulty assessing complex ownership structures
- reliance on outdated technology
- insufficient training for staff
- slow cross-border cooperation

These challenges can reduce the effectiveness of AML/CTF laws and allow criminals to exploit weaknesses.

THE ROLE OF FATF AND REGIONAL REGULATORS

The international system for preventing and combating financial crime relies heavily on organizations that set global standards, evaluate countries, and coordinate regulatory expectations. Among these bodies, the Financial Action Task Force (FATF) holds the most influential position. Its role extends beyond offering guidance; FATF shapes national legislation, influences supervisory practices, and drives reforms that affect every sector exposed to money laundering and terrorist financing risks. Alongside FATF, several regional regulators and assessment groups contribute to raising standards, strengthening coordination, and ensuring that countries maintain effective frameworks. Together, these bodies form the architecture of global financial integrity.

Understanding their role is essential because institutions and investigators must interpret national rules within this broader context. The standards issued by these bodies guide regulatory expectations, enforcement priorities, and compliance practices internationally.

Origins and Mandate of FATF

FATF was established in 1989 by the G7 countries to address growing concerns about financial systems being misused by criminals. Initially focused on money laundering, FATF's mandate expanded over time to include terrorist financing, proliferation financing, and emerging threats such as misuse of virtual assets. FATF is not a treaty-based organization but operates as an intergovernmental policy-making body. Its strength comes from the influence its standards exert on national regulations and supervisory frameworks.

FATF's mission has several components:

- developing global standards
- assessing member countries' implementation
- identifying jurisdictions with significant shortcomings
- promoting legislative and institutional reforms
- analyzing emerging risks and issuing typologies

These functions ensure that countries not only adopt laws but apply them effectively in practice.

The FATF Forty Recommendations

FATF's most important contribution is its Forty Recommendations, which form the global benchmark for AML/CTF frameworks. Although not legally binding, the Recommendations have become de facto international law because countries cannot participate effectively in the global financial system without adopting them.

The Recommendations cover a wide range of obligations, including:

- criminalization of money laundering and terrorist financing
- customer due diligence
- beneficial ownership transparency
- record-keeping
- suspicious transaction reporting
- supervision of financial institutions and DNFBPs
- sanctions implementation
- powers of law enforcement
- international cooperation

These standards provide a foundation for national legislation, shaping how institutions design compliance frameworks and how regulators conduct oversight.

Mutual Evaluation Process

One of FATF's most powerful tools is its mutual evaluation process. Through periodic assessments, FATF and its regional bodies evaluate each country's compliance with the Recommendations and measure the effectiveness of its AML/CTF system. Evaluations focus on both technical compliance—whether laws meet FATF standards—and operational effectiveness, meaning whether those laws function well in practice.

A typical assessment examines:

- risk understanding at national and institutional levels
- supervision quality
- effectiveness of FIUs
- investigative and prosecutorial capabilities
- transparency of legal entities and arrangements
- cross-border cooperation
- convictions and asset recovery outcomes

This process places considerable pressure on governments to maintain strong systems. Poor evaluations can result in financial reputational harm, increased scrutiny from foreign banks, and difficulties participating in the global financial system.

The FATF Grey List and Black List

FATF maintains two public lists identifying jurisdictions with AML/CTF deficiencies:

1. The "grey list"- countries with strategic weaknesses that are actively working on improvements.
2. The "black list"- jurisdictions with severe deficiencies and no credible commitment to reform.

Placement on either list carries significant consequences. Grey-listed countries face enhanced monitoring and reputational risk, which can reduce foreign investment, complicate banking relationships, and strain domestic institutions. Black-listed countries face even greater isolation, often experiencing restrictions from international lenders, reduced correspondent banking access, and heightened scrutiny in cross-border transactions.

As a result, countries have strong incentives to align their legal systems with FATF's standards and to demonstrate effective enforcement.

Guidance on Emerging Risks

FATF regularly issues guidance papers to help countries and institutions understand new threats. These include analyses of virtual assets, trade-based money laundering, proliferation financing, beneficial ownership, corruption, migrant smuggling, and financial flows linked to terrorism.

This guidance influences policymaking globally. Legislators often model national reforms on FATF publications, and supervisors adjust expectations in response to FATF's identified priorities. Institutions similarly study these documents to strengthen internal controls and remain aligned with evolving regulatory expectations.

Regional FATF-Style Bodies

In addition to FATF, several regional groups - known as FATF-style regional bodies (FSRBs) - play a significant role in maintaining international standards. These groups apply FATF's methodology, conduct mutual evaluations, and support member countries in implementing reforms. Their regional focus allows them to understand local challenges, offer targeted assistance, and improve coordination among neighboring countries.

The primary FSRBs include:

- APG – Asia/Pacific Group on Money Laundering
- MONEYVAL – Council of Europe's AML/CTF body
- MENAFATF – Middle East and North Africa
- ESAAMLG – Eastern and Southern Africa
- GAFISUD/GAFILAT – Latin America
- GIABA – West Africa
- CFATF – Caribbean

FSRBs expand FATF's reach, ensuring that standards are adopted globally, even in jurisdictions that are not FATF members.

They also provide technical assistance, training, and regional risk assessments, helping countries strengthen institutional capacity.

Regional Supervisory and Regulatory Bodies

While FATF and FSRBs focus on standard setting and evaluation, other regional regulators oversee specific sectors. These bodies harmonize regulations, share intelligence, and strengthen cross-border supervision.

Some of the most influential include:

European Banking Authority (EBA)

The EBA sets AML/CTF guidelines for EU financial institutions, harmonizing expectations across member states. It conducts risk assessments, oversees national regulators, and issues opinions on compliance failures.

European Securities and Markets Authority (ESMA)

ESMA ensures market integrity in the EU, incorporating AML/CTF considerations into oversight of investment firms, trading venues, and securities markets.

European Insurance and Occupational Pensions Authority (EIOPA)

EIOPA guides insurance sector regulators within the EU on risk assessments, governance standards, and supervisory practices related to financial crime.

Gulf Cooperation Council (GCC) regulators

These authorities coordinate financial sector supervision in the Gulf region, promoting AML/CTF legislative alignment and supporting cross-border collaboration.

Each regional regulator translates global standards into rules appropriate for local markets, ensuring consistency across national borders.

Impact of FATF on National Policymaking

Countries often revise legislation following FATF evaluations. When FATF highlights weaknesses - such as insufficient beneficial ownership transparency, poor supervision of DNFBPs, or weak sanctions implementation - governments frequently respond with new laws, enhanced enforcement powers, and increased regulatory scrutiny.

This influence can be seen in reforms across:

- corporate registries
- FIU authorities
- sanctions frameworks
- supervision of digital asset providers
- customer due diligence standards

Institutions must stay alert to FATF-driven changes because national reforms can alter reporting obligations, risk classifications, and compliance expectations.

Influence on Financial Institutions

FATF indirectly governs how financial institutions operate. Banks, insurers, and intermediaries understand that failure to meet FATF-aligned standards exposes them to regulatory penalties, reputational harm, and loss of correspondent banking relationships.

Institutions therefore design compliance frameworks that align with:

- FATF's risk-based approach
- expectations for beneficial ownership verification
- monitoring and reporting standards
- sanctions controls
- governance and accountability requirements

FATF's focus on effectiveness encourages institutions not only to implement controls but to ensure they function in practice. Supervisors increasingly evaluate whether institutions identify risks accurately and escalate concerns appropriately.

Coordination with Law Enforcement and FIUs

FATF and regional regulators help strengthen collaboration between supervisory bodies, FIUs, and law enforcement agencies. Their recommendations encourage:

- joint risk assessments
- information sharing
- coordinated investigations
- training programs
- cross-border cooperation

This coordination is essential because financial crime flows across jurisdictions quickly, often involving entities and individuals operating in multiple countries simultaneously.

Addressing Technological Developments

FATF and regional regulators play a central role in responding to technological change. They issue standards and guidance covering:

- virtual assets and service providers
- digital identity systems
- online payment platforms

- artificial intelligence and machine learning in compliance
- regulatory technology and supervisory technology

Their work ensures that national systems evolve alongside innovations and that emerging technologies do not create unchecked vulnerabilities.

Encouraging Transparency and Accountability

FATF's emphasis on transparency influences global reforms related to beneficial ownership. Many countries have introduced or strengthened registries, required firms to identify controlling individuals, and expanded powers for authorities to access ownership information. Regional regulators reinforce these measures by ensuring that supervisory bodies consistently evaluate compliance.

Transparency initiatives also extend to public procurement, nonprofit oversight, and cross-border trade - all areas where financial crime risk is significant.

Consequences of Non-Compliance

Failure to meet FATF standards carries serious implications for countries and financial institutions. These consequences include:

- loss of international banking relationships
- reduced foreign investment
- increased compliance costs for cross-border transactions
- enhanced monitoring from international bodies
- reputational damage
- limited access to global financial markets

For institutions, aligning with FATF expectations is not merely a regulatory obligation - it is essential for operational survival in a global marketplace.

CROSS-BORDER ENFORCEMENT AND COOPERATION CHALLENGES

Financial crime rarely respects national boundaries. Funds move rapidly from one jurisdiction to another, companies operate across continents, and criminal networks exploit inconsistencies in legal frameworks, cultural practices, technological infrastructure, and enforcement capacity. As a result, no country can effectively combat financial crime in isolation. Cross-border cooperation is essential, yet it is also where some of the most persistent obstacles arise. These challenges limit the ability of law enforcement, regulators, and intelligence bodies to act quickly, share information effectively, and hold offenders accountable.

Understanding these challenges is fundamental for investigators and compliance professionals who must anticipate where enforcement breakdowns are most likely to occur and factor those weaknesses into risk assessments and investigative strategies.

Complexity of Multijurisdictional Crime

Modern financial crimes often involve multiple jurisdictions simultaneously. A fraud scheme may originate in one country, be executed through digital platforms in another, routed through offshore companies incorporated in a third, and laundered through banks in several more. Each jurisdiction has its own legal system, procedural rules, and institutional priorities.

Because of this complexity:

- evidence is dispersed
- legal thresholds differ
- authorities must coordinate across time zones
- investigations require alignment of laws that may not be fully compatible

This creates delays that criminals exploit. Even rapid enforcement action in one country may be ineffective if another jurisdiction is slow to respond or unwilling to cooperate.

Criminal networks deliberately design schemes to take advantage of these complexities. By distributing elements of a crime across multiple legal environments, they reduce the likelihood that any single authority can obtain a complete picture of the activity.

Differences in Legal Frameworks

One of the most significant obstacles to cross-border enforcement lies in the differences between national legal systems. Every country defines money laundering, terrorist financing, corruption, tax crimes, and corporate liability differently. The standards for admissible evidence, investigative authority, asset seizure, and data privacy also vary considerably.

These variations create inconsistencies in:

- what constitutes sufficient evidence for arrest or prosecution
- the threshold for obtaining financial information
- how courts interpret intent
- requirements for freezing or confiscating assets

Even when international conventions promote harmonization, national laws often retain unique characteristics. As a result, assistance requests may be denied because an act considered criminal in one country may not meet the definition elsewhere. This creates gaps that criminals use strategically, choosing jurisdictions where their conduct is less likely to be prosecuted or where enforcement is weak.

Mutual Legal Assistance Challenges

Mutual Legal Assistance Treaties (MLATs) are the formal channels through which countries request evidence, testimony, financial records, or law enforcement cooperation from one another. MLAT processes are essential, yet they are frequently slow and administratively burdensome.

Common challenges include:

- long processing times for formal requests
- strict documentation requirements
- translation needs
- court authorizations that take months
- bureaucratic backlogs
- lack of prioritization

By the time information is received, assets may have been moved again, companies may have dissolved, and suspects may have relocated. Cybercrime and digital asset movement exacerbate this issue because the speed at which funds disappear does not align with the pace of legal cooperation.

Some countries also lack the institutional capacity to handle complex MLAT requests, leading to incomplete or low-quality responses. Others may delay cooperation due to political considerations or concerns about sovereignty. This fragmented MLAT environment remains one of the most significant structural barriers to effective cross-border enforcement.

Barriers to Information Sharing

Timely information sharing between jurisdictions is essential to identify financial flows, freeze assets, and disrupt criminal networks. However, there are several barriers that consistently slow or block the exchange of information.

These include:

- data protection laws that restrict sharing of financial or personal data
- concerns about misuse of shared information
- limitations on sharing intelligence versus evidentiary material
- incompatible technical systems between agencies
- lack of standardized formats for sharing financial intelligence

Even when information is shared, differences in terminology, data structure, and context may hinder interpretation. Valuable intelligence may be overlooked if the receiving authority lacks the expertise, resources, or legal authority to act upon it.

Some jurisdictions fear that sharing information may expose sensitive national security operations or compromise ongoing investigations. These concerns create caution that slows the flow of information and reduces the effectiveness of global cooperation.

Variations in Supervisory Capacity

Supervisory oversight differs widely across jurisdictions. Some countries have strong, well-funded regulators with advanced analytical tools and experienced personnel. Others have limited resources, outdated technology, or insufficient training. When weak supervision exists in one jurisdiction, criminals can exploit that gap to establish entities, open accounts, or conduct transactions that would trigger immediate scrutiny elsewhere.

This disparity also complicates cooperation. Countries with strong supervisory systems may be reluctant to rely on assessments or documentation from jurisdictions where compliance environments are underdeveloped. Likewise, requests for assistance may go unanswered if agencies lack the staffing or authorization to respond promptly.

Political and Diplomatic Considerations

Financial crime enforcement often intersects with political considerations. Countries may be reluctant to pursue cases involving politically exposed persons, foreign investors, or entities tied to strategic interests. Diplomatic tensions may delay cooperation or limit the willingness of one jurisdiction to support investigations led by another.

Additionally:

- some jurisdictions prioritize domestic interests over international obligations
- political instability may disrupt enforcement agencies
- corruption in certain states weakens cooperation and undermines trust

Authorities may hesitate to share information if they believe the receiving country lacks safeguards against political misuse. This mistrust significantly limits cooperation in regions with inconsistent governance or histories of politically influenced enforcement.

Challenges in Asset Recovery

Recovering assets located abroad is one of the most difficult aspects of cross-border enforcement. Even when authorities identify illicit funds, seizing and repatriating those assets requires legal cooperation from the jurisdiction where they are held. Asset recovery is complicated by:

- divergent rules on property rights
- strict judicial standards for evidence
- appeals that can delay proceedings for years
- lack of transparency in beneficial ownership
- bank secrecy laws
- complex layering of funds across multiple accounts

Offenders often place assets in jurisdictions known for strong privacy protections, minimal transparency, or slow legal processes. These countries may comply only partially or require extensive documentation before approving asset seizures.

In corruption and large-scale fraud cases, asset recovery becomes even more complex because offenders frequently disperse funds across several countries, reinvest proceeds into businesses, or disguise ownership through professional intermediaries.

Digital Assets and Technology-Driven Challenges

Technological innovation has added new layers of complexity to cross-border enforcement. Digital assets can move instantaneously across borders without traditional intermediaries. Cryptocurrencies, privacy-enhancing technologies, decentralized platforms, and peer-to-peer transfers reduce visibility and challenge traditional investigative methods.

Enforcement challenges include:

- tracing transactions on non-transparent blockchain networks
- identifying wallet owners without institutional intermediaries
- freezing assets held in decentralized environments
- obtaining data from virtual asset service providers located abroad
- rapid dissipation of funds

These technological challenges demand international coordination because no country can fully police a decentralized digital ecosystem alone. Without coordinated regulatory frameworks, criminals exploit differences in how countries supervise digital assets and service providers.

Non-Cooperative and High-Risk Jurisdictions

Some jurisdictions have limited political will or capacity to combat financial crime. These may be countries with:

- weak AML/CTF frameworks
- limited regulatory independence
- extensive corruption
- entrenched secrecy laws
- strategic interest in attracting opaque financial flows

These jurisdictions are often used as incorporation hubs, banking intermediaries, or asset holding centers. Their reluctance to cooperate hampers global enforcement efforts. Criminals deliberately use non-cooperative jurisdictions to block investigations, obscure financial trails, or protect beneficial owners.

International bodies like FATF attempt to pressure such jurisdictions through greylisting and blacklisting, but compliance varies, and improvements often take time.

Fragmentation of Responsibilities

Financial crime enforcement involves multiple agencies - regulators, FIUs, law enforcement, customs authorities, tax bodies, and intelligence agencies. In some jurisdictions, coordination is strong; in others, responsibilities are fragmented with overlapping mandates and inconsistent priorities.

Fragmentation complicates cross-border cooperation because foreign authorities may not know which domestic agency holds relevant information or has the authority to act. Even when domestic cooperation exists, different operational cultures, technology systems, and legal traditions complicate collaboration with foreign partners.

Differences in Enforcement Priorities

Countries differ in their enforcement priorities. Some emphasize tax evasion, others focus on corruption, terrorist financing, organized crime, or sanctions. These differences influence how quickly authorities respond to foreign requests, how aggressively they pursue international cases, and how they allocate resources.

As a result, a case viewed as critical in one jurisdiction may be considered low priority in another, leading to delays or limited cooperation. This misalignment weakens global efforts and creates openings that criminals exploit.

Resource Constraints

Many authorities lack the personnel, expertise, or funding to address complex cross-border cases. Financial crime investigations require specialized skills in forensic accounting, digital analysis, asset tracing, corporate law, and international procedure. Training these professionals and maintaining advanced technology requires significant investment.

Countries with limited resources often struggle to engage fully in international cooperation or to respond quickly to information requests. This creates bottlenecks that hinder global enforcement efforts, particularly in cases involving rapid fund movement or sophisticated laundering networks.

Improving Cross-Border Cooperation

While challenges persist, several initiatives aim to improve cooperation:

- enhanced information-sharing platforms
- regional intelligence task forces
- public-private partnerships
- standardized reporting formats

- bilateral and multilateral agreements
- global networks of FIUs and regulators

Such initiatives promote trust, reduce delays, and streamline communication channels. The effectiveness of these mechanisms depends on consistent political commitment, adequate resourcing, and active participation from all jurisdictions involved.

PART II

CORE FINANCIAL CRIME TYPES

CHAPTER 4

MONEY LAUNDERING

STAGES

MONEY LAUNDERING is a structured process through which criminals convert illicit proceeds into assets that appear legitimate. Although the specific methods vary widely, the process is typically described in three primary stages: placement, layering, and integration. These stages should not be viewed as rigid or sequential steps; in many schemes, they overlap or occur in modified forms. However, understanding each stage clearly provides investigators with a framework for identifying risk, recognizing suspicious activity, and understanding how criminals disguise the origins of unlawful funds.

The purpose of each stage is distinct. Placement introduces illicit proceeds into the financial system. Layering obscures the origin through complex movements, restructuring, or transformation of funds. Integration brings the funds back to the criminal in a form that appears to be legitimate income or assets. Together, these stages enable criminals to distance themselves from the unlawful origins of their revenue and blend their profits with legitimate economic activity.

Placement: Introducing Illicit Funds into the System

Placement is the initial stage, and for many criminals, it is the most vulnerable. At this point, cash or other illicit proceeds still bear clear connection to the crime. Introducing these funds into the financial system without detection requires careful planning, reliance on accomplices, and an understanding of institutional weaknesses.

Methods of Placement

Criminals use several techniques to place illicit funds:

- Depositing cash into bank accounts in small increments designed to avoid detection thresholds.
- Using cash-intensive businesses - such as restaurants, retail operations, or service-based enterprises - to mix illegal funds with legitimate revenue.
- Purchasing high-value goods or financial instruments with cash and then selling them to generate ostensibly legitimate proceeds.
- Using informal value transfer systems or unregulated intermediaries to move funds without passing through traditional banking channels.

These techniques allow criminals to convert physical cash into digital or financial form, reducing the immediate visibility of the illicit origin.

Placement is not limited to cash. Digital proceeds from cybercrime, fraudulent transfers, or misappropriation may also be placed through accounts controlled by intermediaries or through mixing services. Regardless of the form of proceeds, placement introduces funds into channels where subsequent stages can occur.

Challenges for Criminals in the Placement Stage

Criminals face risk because financial institutions are required to identify and report suspicious cash deposits, unusual business activity, and transactions inconsistent with a customer's profile. Large cash deposits, structuring behavior, or sudden changes in transactional patterns can draw the attention of compliance teams. For this reason, criminals often rely on individuals acting as "money mules" or use businesses with high cash turnover to disguise the origin of funds.

Placement may also occur across borders. Criminals may physically transport cash to jurisdictions with weaker controls or use intermediaries who specialize in moving funds across borders discreetly. Such transfers exploit differences in regulation and oversight, reducing the likelihood of early detection.

Layering: Obscuring the Origin through Complexity

Layering is the stage in which illicit funds are moved, transformed, or restructured to obscure their origin. It is the most complex phase of money laundering, involving a range of techniques designed to make tracing the funds extremely difficult. The objective is to create distance between the criminal and the money, reducing the likelihood that authorities can identify the connection between the illicit proceeds and the underlying crime.

Purposes of Layering

Layering aims to:

- break the audit trail
- confuse investigators
- exploit gaps between jurisdictions
- mix illicit funds with legitimate financial activity
- create multiple ownership or transactional layers

By dispersing funds across multiple channels, criminals increase the difficulty of tracing, especially when these channels span different countries with inconsistent supervisory capabilities.

Common Layering Techniques

Criminals employ many layering methods, including:

- transferring funds through multiple accounts, often in different jurisdictions
- purchasing and selling financial instruments that change form and ownership quickly
- using shell companies, trusts, and complex corporate structures to obscure beneficial ownership
- routing funds through professional intermediaries such as lawyers, accountants, or corporate service providers
- engaging in trade-based schemes involving mispriced invoices, fictitious shipments, or circular trade
- converting funds into digital assets or virtual currencies

The goal is not necessarily to hide funds completely but to create such complexity that authorities lack the time, resources, or legal reach to trace them effectively.

The use of digital assets has introduced new layering methods. Criminals may use mixing services, decentralized exchanges, or privacy-focused cryptocurrencies to obscure transaction histories. These tools reduce transparency and require specialized investigative expertise, making detection more challenging.

The Importance of Jurisdictional Arbitrage

Jurisdictional arbitrage plays a significant role in layering. Criminals deliberately route transactions through countries that have weak AML controls, limited transparency in beneficial ownership, or strong privacy protections. Offshore financial centers may be used to hold companies, trusts, or accounts that add additional layers between the funds and the criminal.

Even when a country has strong laws, complex corporate structures may exploit gaps in implementation. Some jurisdictions require minimal documentation to establish companies or trusts, allowing criminals to create entities that obscure ownership. Other jurisdictions lack resources to validate information provided, creating openings for manipulation.

Integration: Reintroducing Funds as Legitimate Wealth

Integration is the final stage of the laundering process, where illicit proceeds are converted into assets or income that appear legitimate. Once funds are successfully integrated, they can be used without raising suspicion. Integration is typically the most stable stage for criminals because the funds have been transformed sufficiently to avoid easy detection.

Methods of Integration

Integration techniques vary widely, including:

- investing in real estate, businesses, or other durable assets
- purchasing luxury items such as vehicles, jewelry, or artwork
- using holding companies to receive “returns” from investments that are in fact financed by illicit proceeds
- creating loans or contracts between controlled entities to justify the movement or possession of funds
- placing laundered proceeds into investment portfolios or bank accounts in the criminal’s name

In many cases, integrated funds appear indistinguishable from legitimate wealth. They may support lifestyles, fund new criminal activity, or finance legitimate business ventures.

The Role of Professionals in Integration

Professional intermediaries often play a critical role in integration. Lawyers, real estate agents, brokers, accountants, and corporate service providers may facilitate transactions without fully understanding—or in some cases, while knowingly ignoring—the source of funds. Their involvement gives illicit assets an appearance of legitimacy.

In some schemes, professionals design financial structures that produce artificial income streams. For example, a shell company owned by the criminal may "earn" payments from another company the criminal controls. These payments appear legitimate but are financed by laundered proceeds. This technique allows criminals to build wealth and maintain a façade of lawful activity.

Integration Through Legitimate Businesses

One of the most effective integration methods is the use of legitimate businesses. Criminals may acquire existing businesses or establish new ones that appear to generate genuine revenue. By commingling illicit funds with legitimate income, criminals create plausible explanations for their wealth.

Certain industries are particularly vulnerable to misuse due to their cash-intensive nature, rapid cash flow, or high-value transactions. Restaurants, retail operations, construction firms, import-export businesses, and consulting companies are common vehicles for integration.

Interdependence of the Three Stages

Although placement, layering, and integration are often described as separate stages, they are deeply interconnected. In many schemes, these stages occur simultaneously or in rapid succession. A single transaction may serve multiple purposes—for example, a wire transfer may introduce funds into the financial system (placement) while simultaneously obscuring their origin (layering).

Understanding the interdependence of stages is critical for effective investigation. Detecting unusual activity in one stage may reveal information about activity in other stages. For example:

- identifying unusual cash deposits may provide early indicators of placement
- discovering complex corporate structures may reveal layering
- observing luxury purchases inconsistent with income may point to integration

Each stage contains potential "choke points" where criminals face risk. Institutions and investigators must recognize these points to intervene effectively.

Impact of Technology on the Stages

Technology affects each stage of money laundering in different ways.

During placement, online payment platforms and fintech services allow criminals to introduce funds into digital channels rapidly. Some platforms have limited oversight or operate in jurisdictions with inconsistent regulation.

During layering, digital assets and online financial services enable rapid movement of funds across borders. Automated tools and decentralized platforms reduce reliance on traditional intermediaries, complicating detection.

During integration, technology allows criminals to invest in digital assets, online businesses, and remote services. Illicit funds can be converted into seemingly legitimate income streams via online marketplaces, digital investments, or virtual real estate.

Technology accelerates money laundering and reduces friction, but it also creates opportunities for detection through advanced analytics, machine learning, and real-time monitoring. Institutions capable of leveraging technology for detection can identify anomalies earlier in the process.

Challenges in Detecting Each Stage

Detection challenges vary by stage:

Placement challenges involve identifying unusual cash activity, recognizing patterns inconsistent with a customer's profile, and distinguishing legitimate high-cash businesses from those used to disguise illicit funds.

Layering challenges stem from complexity. Transactions may appear legitimate individually but, when viewed collectively, reveal patterns of concealment. Fragmented oversight across jurisdictions also hampers detection.

Integration challenges arise because funds appear legally justified. Once assets are integrated, they resemble legitimate wealth, making it difficult to identify the illicit origin without detailed investigation or intelligence.

For these reasons, institutions must adopt a holistic approach. Monitoring must examine both individual transactions and broader customer behavior. Investigators must analyze corporate structures, financial flows, and contextual information rather than focusing solely on isolated indicators.

TRADITIONAL TYPOLOGIES AND MODERN VARIANTS

Money laundering typologies have evolved significantly over time. Early schemes relied heavily on physical cash and straightforward concealment methods, while today's typologies reflect a far more complex ecosystem involving digital channels, globalized financial markets, decentralized technologies, and highly specialized intermediary networks. Understanding both traditional and modern typologies is essential for investigators and compliance professionals, as many contemporary schemes combine elements from multiple typologies or adapt older methods to new environments. Criminals continuously adjust their techniques in response to regulatory pressure, market innovation, and enforcement trends, creating a landscape in which traditional methods remain relevant but are often enhanced by sophisticated modern variants.

Traditional Typologies

Traditional money laundering typologies developed during periods when financial controls were less sophisticated, technology played a limited role, and cash-based economies were more prevalent. Despite advancements in regulation and oversight, these typologies continue to be used because they exploit fundamental weaknesses in human behavior, documentation processes, and operational oversight.

Cash-Based Laundering

Cash-based laundering is one of the oldest methods and continues to pose challenges in regions where cash remains widely used. The simplicity of physical currency enables criminals to move funds with anonymity, particularly in environments where high-value cash transactions are not subject to stringent reporting.

Common forms of cash-based laundering include:

- depositing cash into bank accounts through structuring or smurfing
- using cash-generating businesses to mix illicit funds with legitimate revenue

- purchasing high-value goods with cash and selling them to generate bankable proceeds

Although regulators have imposed tighter controls on cash transactions, criminals still exploit weak enforcement, limited oversight of cash-intensive sectors, and regional disparities in cash usage.

Use of Front and Shell Companies

Front companies and shell companies remain central to many laundering schemes. A front company combines legitimate business operations with illicit financial activity, enabling criminals to blend illegal funds with legal revenue. A shell company, by contrast, may have no real business activity and exists solely to obscure ownership and facilitate illicit transfers.

Traditional misuse of such companies includes:

- concealing beneficial ownership
- providing false invoices to justify transfers
- hiding the origin of proceeds by routing funds through controlled entities

These methods remain popular because they exploit weaknesses in corporate registry systems, especially in jurisdictions with limited transparency or minimal documentation requirements.

Trade-Based Money Laundering (TBML)

TBML involves disguising the movement of illicit value through legitimate trade transactions. This typology predates modern digital platforms and remains highly effective because global trade is inherently complex and subject to wide pricing variations.

Traditional TBML techniques include:

- over- or under-invoicing goods
- misrepresenting the quality or quantity of shipments

- phantom shipments - declaring goods that are never shipped
- using intermediaries to route goods through multiple countries

Trade provides natural cover for value movement, making TBML a persistent typology even in well-regulated jurisdictions.

Use of Financial Instruments

Before the proliferation of digital assets, criminals relied on conventional financial instruments to obscure funds. These included:

- cashier's checks
- money orders
- traveler's checks
- bearer bonds
- prepaid cards

These instruments were attractive because they could be purchased with cash and transferred easily. Although declining in use, these methods still appear in regions where such instruments remain accessible or where oversight is limited.

Smuggling and Bulk Cash Movement

Bulk cash smuggling is a traditional method used when formal financial systems impose strict controls. Criminals physically transport cash across borders to deposit it in jurisdictions with weaker supervision or to convert it into other assets.

Despite technological advancements, bulk cash smuggling continues due to:

- differences in AML controls across jurisdictions
- the anonymity afforded by physical transport
- the involvement of criminal networks that control transportation routes

Modern Variants

Modern money laundering variants reflect advancements in digital technology, globalization, and the increasing complexity of financial markets. These methods provide criminals with sophisticated tools for concealing ownership, obscuring transactions, and transferring value across borders quickly.

Laundering Through Digital Assets

Digital assets - including cryptocurrencies - have introduced new challenges. Their borderless nature, speed, and varying degrees of anonymity make them attractive for laundering activities.

Modern digital asset–related methods include:

- converting illicit proceeds into cryptocurrency through exchanges or mixers
- using privacy-enhancing coins that obscure wallet history
- transferring funds through decentralized exchanges without traditional intermediaries
- using cross-chain bridges to obscure transaction trails

These methods complicate monitoring because they fall outside traditional banking structures and may involve service providers operating in weakly regulated environments.

Use of Professional Enablers and Complex Structures

While the use of professionals is not new, modern laundering schemes rely far more heavily on specialized expertise. Lawyers, accountants, corporate service providers, trust administrators, and consultants may design intricate structures that combine international tax planning, financial engineering, and corporate layering.

These structures may involve:

- multiple offshore entities operating across different secrecy jurisdictions
- specialized trusts or foundations designed to obscure ownership
- contractual arrangements that create the appearance of legitimate financial flows

Criminals exploit the fact that professional services appear legitimate, making detection more difficult.

Online Payment Platforms and Fintech Services

Modern payment platforms allow criminals to move funds across borders quickly, often with minimal verification. These platforms are attractive because they offer:

- instant transfers
- global reach
- varying compliance standards
- access to large transaction volumes that obscure suspicious behavior

Criminals may misuse fintech services by creating multiple accounts, exploiting referral systems, or routing transactions through peer-to-peer platforms to obscure origins.

Trade-Based Laundering Enhanced by Logistics Technology

Although TBML is a traditional typology, modern versions are more sophisticated due to digital logistics platforms, container tracking systems, and global supply chains. Criminals may exploit weaknesses in digital documentation, fraudulent shipping records, or manipulation of automated tracking systems to disguise illicit movements.

Modern TBML variants may include:

- routing goods through free-trade zones with minimal oversight
- manipulating electronic bills of lading
- using e-commerce platforms to justify payments for goods that never move

These methods exploit the complexity of supply chain technology, creating new opportunities for concealment.

Use of Money Mules and Digital Smurfing

Digital banking has transformed smurfing into a more efficient and scalable method. Criminals recruit individuals online to open accounts, transfer funds, or withdraw money. These "money mules" may be unaware of the criminal origins of the funds.

Modern variants involve:

- online recruitment through social media
- automated coordination of multiple mule accounts
- rapid transfers across multiple platforms
- mixing illicit proceeds with gig-economy payments

The digital environment enables criminals to manage mule networks with minimal physical contact.

Laundering through Online Gambling and Virtual Gaming

Online gambling platforms and virtual gaming environments offer new avenues for laundering. Criminals may:

- deposit illicit funds into online gaming accounts
- purchase virtual items with real money
- transfer assets between players
- convert digital assets or gaming currencies back into cash

The global nature of these platforms and the limited regulatory oversight in some jurisdictions make them vulnerable to exploitation.

Sophisticated Use of Corporate Finance

Laundering increasingly involves sophisticated corporate finance strategies. Criminals may use mergers, acquisitions, venture capital investments, or complex debt arrangements to justify large transfers. By embedding illicit funds within corporate operations, criminals create plausible explanations for financial flows.

Modern techniques include:

- creating shell investment vehicles to finance controlled entities
- purchasing distressed businesses with illicit funds
- using high-value cross-border loans with artificially inflated terms

These methods require significant expertise but offer high levels of concealment.

Use of High-Frequency Financial Markets

The growth of global markets introduces typologies involving:

- rapid buying and selling of securities
- wash trading
- use of brokers in weak regulatory environments

Although these techniques are more common in fraud and market abuse cases, they also support money laundering by creating transaction histories that mask illicit origins.

Hybrid Typologies

Criminals rarely rely on a single typology. Instead, they combine traditional and modern methods to create multilayered schemes. For example:

- cash proceeds may be placed through a front company, layered through trade, and integrated via cryptocurrency investments
- digital fraud proceeds may be layered through mule accounts and then integrated through real estate purchases
- corruption proceeds may move through trusts, be converted to digital assets, and later reinvested in legitimate businesses

Hybrid typologies take advantage of both old and new vulnerabilities, making them especially challenging to detect.

Impact of Regulatory Evolution

As regulators strengthen controls in one area, criminals adjust by shifting to others. This "pressure-shift effect" has shaped the evolution of typologies:

- increased scrutiny of cash deposits pushed criminals toward trade and digital assets
- enhanced monitoring of traditional banks increased misuse of fintech platforms
- improved corporate transparency led criminals to exploit trusts, offshore jurisdictions, and complex intermediaries

Typologies evolve in response to enforcement actions, technological change, and market innovation. Understanding this evolution allows investigators to anticipate new risks.

CONCEALMENT METHODS AND LAYERING SCHEMES

The process of obscuring the origin, control, and movement of illicit funds is a core function of money laundering. While placement introduces the proceeds into the financial system, concealment and layering transform those funds through patterns designed to overwhelm investigators, bypass controls, and exploit structural and jurisdictional weaknesses. Concealment methods range from simple disguises to complex arrangements that involve multiple actors, technologies, and legal entities. Layering schemes take these methods further by dispersing and restructuring funds in a manner that severs any clear connection to the predicate crime.

Understanding how concealment and layering operate is essential because they represent the most sophisticated and least transparent phases of money laundering. These stages often define whether a laundering operation survives scrutiny or collapses under investigation.

Foundations of Concealment

Concealment techniques focus on hiding the connection between a criminal and the illicit proceeds. These techniques may be used before, during, or after the placement stage, and may intersect with layering and integration. At their core, concealment methods aim to manipulate information - faulty records, disguised ownership, false documentation, or misleading transaction patterns.

Criminals understand that documentation and transparency requirements form the backbone of modern financial oversight. They therefore create or exploit gaps where ownership, purpose, or value cannot be easily verified. These gaps may be legal, procedural, or technological.

Concealment methods commonly involve:

- obscuring identity
- disguising ownership
- masking the value or origin of assets
- blending illicit transactions with legitimate economic activity
- creating complexity that deters scrutiny

Although methods vary widely, all share the purpose of undermining visibility and reducing traceability.

Obscuring Customer Identity

One of the most direct forms of concealment involves falsely representing or disguising the identity of individuals involved in transactions. Criminals employ several approaches, depending on the jurisdiction and opportunity.

Some techniques include:

- using intermediaries to conduct transactions on behalf of criminals
- fabricating identities through fraudulent documentation
- using stolen or synthetic identities
- coercing vulnerable individuals into acting as account holders

Identity concealment is effective because it misleads financial institutions and investigators about who truly controls the funds. Once accounts are opened under false or manipulated identities, criminals can perform transactions that appear legitimate on the surface but conceal their true origins.

Digital identity systems create both challenges and opportunities. While biometric verification and robust identity controls improve detection, online platforms with limited verification standards allow criminals to open accounts quickly and with minimal traceability. Additionally, some criminals exploit identity verification gaps in emerging fintech ecosystems where enforcement may lag behind technological innovation.

Concealing Beneficial Ownership

Obscuring beneficial ownership is one of the most powerful concealment strategies. This typically involves the use of legal entities - companies, partnerships, trusts, or foundations - to hide who ultimately controls or benefits from the proceeds.

Concealment strategies related to beneficial ownership include:

- using nominee directors or shareholders
- employing corporate service providers to establish opaque structures
- creating multi-layered ownership chains across multiple jurisdictions
- exploiting jurisdictions with minimal disclosure requirements
- using bearer shares or corporate forms that allow ownership to change without registration

These structures may appear legitimate, but their purpose is to remove direct links between criminals and their assets. When authorities attempt to trace ownership, they encounter layers of intermediaries, often spanning several countries. This slows investigations and increases the likelihood that the trail becomes too complex or costly to pursue.

Trusts and foundations are particularly challenging because they provide genuine legal and economic functions that obscure control without requiring public disclosure. Integrated into multi-layered schemes, these structures create formidable barriers to identifying the real parties involved.

False Documentation and Misrepresentation

Documentation is central to financial and commercial transactions, and criminals exploit this reliance by manufacturing or altering records that support false narratives. Examples include:

- fabricated invoices
- altered contracts
- falsified shipping documents
- manipulated financial statements
- counterfeit bills of lading or customs records

These documents help justify the movement of funds or assets, allowing criminal proceeds to blend into ordinary business activity. False documentation is especially prevalent in trade-based schemes, where discrepancies in quality, quantity, and valuation can be hidden behind complex logistics chains.

Financial institutions may struggle to verify the authenticity of foreign documents, particularly when information systems, languages, or regulatory standards differ. Criminals use this lack of uniformity to their advantage.

Embedding Illicit Funds within Legitimate Business Activity

One of the most effective concealment strategies involves commingling illicit funds with legitimate earnings. This is especially common in cash-intensive businesses or industries with inconsistent revenue patterns.

Common concealment environments include:

- restaurants
- retail stores
- construction firms
- logistics companies
- consultancy firms with subjective pricing

Through the embedding of illicit funds within genuine economic activity, criminals create complexity that makes detection difficult. The combination of real transactions and falsified revenue obscures the true source of funds and creates plausible explanations for high cash turnover or abnormal profit margins.

Some businesses, particularly those operating in fragmented or informal sectors, may lack robust accounting practices, creating opportunities for manipulation. Criminals may also acquire legitimate businesses solely for the purpose of laundering funds.

Layering Schemes: Creating Distance Through Complexity

While concealment focuses on disguising the relationship between a criminal and the proceeds, layering breaks the financial trail itself. Layering schemes rely on complexity, speed, and cross-border movement to overwhelm investigators and exploit jurisdictional inconsistencies.

Layering commonly involves multiple transactions, accounts, and legal entities designed to create fragmentation. The overarching goal is to make it difficult, time-consuming, and resource-intensive for investigators to follow the trail.

Multi-Jurisdictional Transactions

The most sophisticated layering schemes move funds across several countries, often chosen for their regulatory weaknesses, low transparency, or reluctance to cooperate internationally. Criminals exploit differences in legal systems, reporting thresholds, and compliance expectations to create layers of barriers investigators must cross.

Techniques include:

- routing funds through accounts in different jurisdictions
- transferring money through intermediary institutions
- using payment services that operate in loosely regulated countries
- combining online transfers with physical cash movement

By the time investigators identify a suspicious transfer, the funds may have passed through several countries, each with its own procedural and legal hurdles. This fragmentation dramatically increases the difficulty of asset tracing.

Use of Complex Corporate Structures

Layering often involves intricate combinations of companies, trusts, and nominee arrangements. These structures may span multiple jurisdictions, each adding a layer of opacity. Criminals exploit differences in reporting requirements, making it challenging to identify the ultimate beneficial owner.

Layers within corporate structures serve several functions:

- they create plausible business justifications for fund transfers
- they hide criminal involvement behind professional intermediaries
- they disperse funds in a manner that appears operational rather than suspicious

Corporate layering is especially effective when combined with professional facilitators who provide legal or accounting services that give the appearance of legitimate financial operation.

Rapid Movement Through Financial Instruments

Another layering method involves converting funds into various financial instruments and moving them rapidly. These instruments may include:

- securities
- derivatives
- insurance products
- investment funds

By exchanging illicit funds for instruments that change value or ownership quickly, criminals create transaction histories that obscure the original source. These instruments may then be sold or redeemed in different jurisdictions, further distancing the funds from their origin.

These strategies exploit the complexity and volume of global financial markets, where high transaction volumes make it difficult for institutions to isolate irregularities without advanced monitoring tools.

Conversion Into Digital Assets

Digital assets and online platforms offer criminals new opportunities for layering. They can convert proceeds into cryptocurrency, transfer it through peer-to-peer networks, and convert it back to fiat currency in another location.

Common digital layering techniques include:

- using mixing services to obscure transaction history
- transferring funds through multiple wallets
- routing funds through decentralized platforms
- converting between multiple cryptocurrencies

These strategies increase anonymity and introduce technical challenges for investigators, particularly when transactions involve non-custodial wallets or platforms that do not maintain robust compliance programs.

Trade-Based Layering Schemes

Layering through trade remains one of the most challenging typologies to detect because trade flows naturally involve complex logistics, variable pricing, and diverse documentation. Criminals exploit these complexities by moving funds through trade transactions that appear legitimate but are structured to obscure the underlying value movement.

Trade-based layering may involve:

- overvalued or undervalued invoices
- fictitious shipments masked by legitimate trade flows
- use of wholesale intermediaries and free-trade zones
- circuitous routes designed to confuse shipping records

These schemes take advantage of global supply chains, where oversight is fragmented and documentation can be manipulated without immediate detection.

Integration of Layering with Professional Networks

Layering schemes increasingly rely on professional intermediaries—lawyers, accountants, brokers, corporate service providers—who facilitate movement of funds or assets. Some may be complicit; others may be unaware of criminal intent.

Professionals contribute by:

- drafting contracts that justify fund transfers
- creating legal structures that obscure ownership
- opening accounts in multiple jurisdictions
- providing advice on regulatory arbitrage

The involvement of professionals lends legitimacy to transactions, making investigative efforts more complicated.

RED FLAGS AND DETECTION CHALLENGES

Identifying money laundering requires more than monitoring individual transactions. Financial institutions must interpret patterns, behaviors, and contextual details that indicate potential misuse of the financial system. While many indicators—often referred to as "red flags"—signal unusual or suspicious activity, these flags rarely provide definitive proof of wrongdoing on their own. Instead, they provide early warning signs that require further investigation, escalation, or reporting. At the same time, institutions face significant challenges in detection due to evolving criminal methods, data limitations, operational constraints, and the inherent ambiguity of many financial behaviors.

Understanding red flags and the obstacles that complicate detection is essential for professionals responsible for maintaining the integrity of financial systems. This section explores key categories of red flags and the structural challenges that make detecting money laundering complex, resource-intensive, and sometimes uncertain.

Behavioral Indicators and Customer Activity

Money laundering is not defined solely by transactions; it is also reflected in customer behavior and overall account usage. Behavioral indicators often provide early signals that something is amiss. These behaviors may be subtle, inconsistent, or contradictory to the customer's stated profile.

Examples include sudden changes in account activity, unexplained increases in transaction volume, or reluctance to provide documentation that most customers offer without hesitation. Criminals may appear overly knowledgeable about AML requirements, avoid in-person meetings, or rely heavily on intermediaries when conducting basic account activities. In some cases, criminals attempt to manipulate or intimidate staff to discourage scrutiny.

Other behavioral red flags include the use of inconsistent contact information, multiple addresses in different jurisdictions, or a pattern of opening and closing accounts quickly. These behaviors may indicate attempts to avoid monitoring or create layers of distance between the criminal and their funds.

Financial institutions must recognize that behavioral indicators often signal deeper patterns. A single anomaly may not justify suspicion, but repeated unusual behavior across multiple accounts, entities, or channels suggests increased risk.

Transaction Patterns

Suspicious transaction patterns often provide the clearest early warnings of money laundering. These patterns may reflect the placement, layering, or integration stages and may arise from inconsistencies between expected and observed activity.

Unusual transaction patterns include repeated deposits of cash just below reporting thresholds, transfers to or from jurisdictions known for secrecy, or rapid movement of funds between accounts without a clear business purpose. Transactions that circulate among related entities for no legitimate financial reason may indicate layering. Similarly, payments for goods or services that do not match the customer's business profile may signal misuse of corporate accounts.

Another red flag involves the use of multiple accounts with similar names or ownership structures that engage in parallel transactions. This behavior may be an attempt to distribute funds across various channels to limit detection. Rapid movement of funds immediately after deposit is also a concern, especially when such movements occur in round numbers or at regular intervals without a clear commercial explanation.

Patterns involving digital assets also present challenges. Transfers between wallets without visible commercial purpose, repeated use of mixing services, or movement of funds through decentralized platforms are all indicators of potential misuse.

Geographic Indicators

Geographic risk plays a central role in money laundering detection. Jurisdictions differ widely in transparency, regulatory enforcement, and corruption levels. When funds move between low-risk and high-risk jurisdictions in ways that do not align with expected business activity, institutions must examine the nature of the relationship more closely.

Geographic red flags include transfers involving:

- countries with minimal AML regulations
- jurisdictions subject to sanctions or enhanced monitoring
- regions known for extensive corruption
- offshore financial centers used primarily for secrecy
- countries frequently linked to organized crime or terrorism

In many cases, the risk arises not from the jurisdiction itself but from the pattern of movement. For example, routing funds through multiple jurisdictions without clear commercial rationale, or conducting transactions that appear to circumvent geographic restrictions, may indicate layering.

Institutions must also consider domestic geographic risks. Some regions within a country may be known for illicit activity, such as drug trafficking corridors, areas with widespread illegal mining, or zones with high levels of unregistered businesses. Activity involving these areas may require heightened scrutiny.

Corporate and Structural Indicators

Complex or opaque corporate structures often conceal illicit activity. Red flags arise when companies operate with inconsistent, incomplete, or misleading information. This may include businesses with unclear ownership, entities that share contact information or directors, or companies with no physical presence despite claiming substantial activity.

Suspicious structural indicators also include:

- frequent changes in ownership or management
- mismatch between the business purpose and transactional behavior
- companies registered in jurisdictions with poor transparency
- unusually large cash flows for businesses that are not cash-intensive
- the use of multiple intermediary companies without a legitimate purpose

In some cases, criminals create chains of corporate entities to distribute funds and obscure their source. These chains may cross multiple borders and rely on corporate service providers that offer anonymity. When companies present inconsistent financial information, lack a verifiable business history, or engage in unusually complex transactions, institutions must consider the possibility that they are part of a layering scheme.

Integration Indicators

During the integration stage, criminals attempt to legitimize illicit funds by blending them into the formal economy. Identifying integration requires understanding the customer's business model, revenue streams, and financial capabilities. Red flags include substantial increases in the value of assets or investments without a clear explanation.

Integration red flags include:

- real estate purchases far beyond the customer's expected financial means
- investment activity that does not match the customer's stated risk profile
- personal or business loans that do not appear economically justified
- luxury purchases that are inconsistent with declared income
- unusually high profit margins for businesses with no market justification

These indicators do not prove wrongdoing, but they raise concern when they contradict verified information about the customer or lack a transparent business rationale.

Challenges in Detecting Money Laundering

Although red flags provide important clues, the detection of money laundering remains difficult. Criminals actively study AML controls and adapt their methods to exploit weaknesses. Several structural challenges complicate the work of financial institutions, investigators, and regulators.

Ambiguity in Financial Behavior

The greatest challenge is ambiguity. Many legitimate activities resemble suspicious ones, and many suspicious activities appear legitimate. High-value cash transactions may reflect genuine business operations. Transfers to offshore jurisdictions may involve tax planning. Rapid fund movement may reflect treasury practices.

The line between normal and suspicious behavior is often blurred. Institutions must rely on context, patterns, and risk assessments rather than isolated indicators. This ambiguity demands judgment, experience, and careful documentation.

Data Limitations and Fragmented Information

Financial institutions rely on the data available to them, which is often incomplete. They may not have visibility into external corporate registries, beneficial ownership databases, foreign account information, or cross-institutional transaction patterns. Criminals exploit this fragmentation by distributing activity across multiple institutions or jurisdictions.

Data quality is also inconsistent. In some jurisdictions, customer information may be incomplete, inaccurate, or outdated. Corporate ownership records may be difficult to obtain or fully opaque. Transactions involving digital assets may lack the documentation necessary to identify the individuals behind the activity.

These gaps make it difficult to form a clear picture of the customer's behavior and intent.

Resource Constraints

AML teams frequently face resource constraints. Complex cases require time, expertise, and technology. Large institutions may have thousands of alerts daily, many of which are false positives. Analysts must balance timely processing with thorough analysis, and limited staffing can lead to oversight.

Smaller institutions face additional challenges because they may lack advanced transaction monitoring systems, experienced analysts, or the ability to invest in specialized technology. Criminals take advantage of these limitations by targeting institutions with weaker defenses.

Evolving Criminal Techniques

Criminals adapt quickly. When controls tighten around one typology, they shift to another. When institutions strengthen monitoring in one channel, criminals migrate to channels with fewer controls. Digital assets, online payment platforms, and decentralized structures create new challenges because they evolve faster than regulations.

The speed of innovation means institutions must constantly adapt. Traditional monitoring systems, designed for linear and predictable patterns, often struggle with the dynamic behavior of modern laundering operations.

International Coordination Barriers

Because laundering often spans borders, detection requires cooperation between institutions, regulators, and jurisdictions. However, information sharing may be restricted by privacy laws, conflicting regulations, or lack of technical capability. Criminals exploit inconsistent national frameworks by structuring schemes across borders where detection is less likely.

These international challenges make it difficult for institutions to identify full patterns of activity, particularly when they operate only in one jurisdiction or lack visibility into foreign financial systems.

The Role of Technology in Enhancing Detection

Although technology aids criminals, it also provides powerful tools for detection. Institutions increasingly rely on:

- machine learning models
- risk-scoring systems
- behavioral analytics
- network analysis
- anomaly detection tools

These tools help identify complex patterns and correlations that human analysts cannot easily detect. They enhance efficiency by reducing false positives and enabling teams to focus on higher-risk cases.

However, technology is not a complete solution. Models must be regularly recalibrated, and systems must be integrated with high-quality data. Over-reliance on automated tools can cause institutions to overlook contextual factors that machines cannot interpret.

CHAPTER 5

FRAUD

INTERNAL VS. EXTERNAL FRAUD MECHANISMS

FRAUD TAKES many forms, but at its core it reflects an intentional misuse of systems, information, or authority to obtain an unfair benefit. Understanding how fraud occurs requires distinguishing between internal and external mechanisms, because each category interacts with an institution in different ways and exposes distinct vulnerabilities. Internal fraud arises from those who operate within an organization's structure, while external fraud is driven by actors outside the institution who exploit customers, processes, technologies, or public confidence. The distinction is not simply academic; the investigative approach, detection methods, and prevention frameworks differ substantially depending on where the threat originates. A clear assessment of these mechanisms is essential for designing effective controls and building a resilient fraud risk environment.

The Nature of Internal Fraud

Internal fraud refers to misconduct carried out by employees, contractors, executives, or any individual who has authorized access to an organization's systems, information, or operational processes. Because internal actors operate within established trust structures, they are positioned to bypass controls more easily than external criminals. Their knowledge of internal workflows, approval methods, system limitations, and oversight weaknesses gives them an advantage that external actors must compensate for through testing, probing, or social engineering. Internal fraud can therefore be subtle, difficult to detect, and prolonged if institutions do not maintain strong oversight.

Internal actors engage in misconduct for various reasons, but they often share an ability to recognize opportunities presented by inadequate segregation of duties, weak supervisory oversight, outdated systems, or cultural tolerance for unethical behavior. These opportunities allow them to manipulate transactions, divert funds, falsify records, or facilitate unauthorized payments without immediately drawing attention. Some insiders engage in small acts of misconduct initially, motivated by personal financial pressure or frustration, and expand their behavior when they perceive that controls are ineffective. Others plan sophisticated schemes that involve falsified documents, collusion with external parties, or strategic misuse of their authority.

The types of internal fraud are wide-ranging. Unauthorized transactions carried out through privileged user accounts, manipulation of account balances, theft of cash or assets, submission of inflated expense claims, and misuse of customer information are all common. Internal fraud may also involve intentional overrides of automated controls or exploitation of temporary workarounds put in place during operational disruptions. Some insiders use their authority to approve fraudulent payments or alter information in ways that conceal the misconduct. In severe cases, misconduct may involve collusion between multiple employees, creating layers of concealment that hinder detection.

One of the most challenging aspects of internal fraud is the breach of trust it represents. Organizations rely on employees to act with integrity, and controls are often designed with the assumption that staff apply procedures as intended. When this trust is violated, the resulting harm extends beyond financial loss. Internal fraud can damage organizational culture, weaken morale, and erode confidence in governance. It can also expose the institution to regulatory penalties if misconduct results in misreporting, inaccurate records, or failure to protect customer data.

The Dynamics of External Fraud

External fraud is initiated by individuals or networks operating outside the institution. These actors have no inherent access to internal systems and therefore must exploit weaknesses in customer behavior, system vulnerabilities, public information, or institutional processes. External fraudsters often rely on deception, impersonation, social engineering, or unauthorized access to misappropriate funds or obtain confidential data. Because external attempts may occur at scale and target multiple institutions simultaneously, they frequently evolve in response to countermeasures and technological changes.

External criminals vary widely in sophistication. Some operate alone, using straightforward tactics such as phishing emails or fraudulent account applications. Others belong to organized networks that employ specialized roles, advanced technologies, and coordinated strategies to test controls across institutions. These networks may purchase stolen data, create synthetic identities, compromise credentials, or use malware to bypass authentication systems. They often conduct large-scale attempts in which only a small percentage must succeed to generate substantial illicit proceeds.

Unlike internal actors, external fraudsters lack detailed knowledge of an institution's internal workflows. To compensate, they study publicly available information, analyze communication patterns, or test response behaviors through staged attempts. Some rely on information purchased from illicit online marketplaces, including identity documents, login credentials, or leaked customer records. Others exploit vulnerabilities in digital infrastructure, such as insufficient multi-factor authentication, weak password policies, or inadequate monitoring of account access anomalies.

External fraud commonly includes unauthorized electronic transfers, account takeovers, false applications for credit or services, and scams that involve impersonation of trusted organizations. Social engineering plays a central role, as offenders frequently manipulate victims into providing access or performing actions on their behalf. Because these schemes typically occur outside institutional boundaries, organizations must rely on behavioral indicators, transactional patterns, and customer education to detect and mitigate them.

The Role of Access and Opportunity

A crucial distinction between internal and external fraud lies in how the actor gains access to systems or information. Internal actors already possess privileged access by virtue of their role, meaning they do not need to breach the institution's perimeter. Their misconduct occurs inside the environment controls are meant to protect. This significantly influences detection challenges. Internal actors may know which transactions are reviewed manually, which alerts are typically ignored, or which supervisors are unlikely to question certain activities. They may also understand how to circumvent approval hierarchies or exploit relationships with colleagues who trust their judgment.

External actors have no such advantage. Their ability to commit fraud depends on finding an entry point through impersonation, technology, or exploitation of customer behavior. They must test accounts, exploit software vulnerabilities, or deceive victims into granting access. As a result, external fraud attempts often leave visible signs of probing, failed logins, unusual device activity, or inconsistent customer behavior. While sophisticated networks can conceal their attempts effectively, many external schemes produce indicators that can be identified through automated monitoring and behavioral analytics.

Opportunity also differs significantly between internal and external actors. Internal actors may see opportunities that are not visible to outsiders, such as gaps in documentation requirements, poorly monitored reconciliation processes, or approval functions that rely on trust rather than verification. External actors seek opportunities created by system weaknesses, human error, or customer vulnerabilities. They exploit institutions that lack strong authentication, have outdated fraud detection systems, or maintain slow response processes for suspicious activity reports.

Collusion Between Internal and External Actors

Although internal and external fraud can be analyzed separately, they often intersect in practice. Collusion between insiders and external criminals represents one of the most damaging forms of fraud because it combines the insider's knowledge and access with the external actor's operational resources. External networks may recruit employees to provide confidential information, approve fraudulent transactions, or overlook suspicious activity. In some cases, insiders proactively approach criminals, offering their assistance in exchange for compensation.

Collusion schemes can be especially harmful because they undermine the assumptions upon which controls are built. Automated monitoring systems may not detect unusual patterns if an insider approves transactions or enters information that appears legitimate. Documentation may seem complete and consistent because a knowledgeable insider has prepared it to avoid raising concerns. Investigating such schemes often requires forensic examination, cross-functional analysis, and a willingness to challenge long-standing internal assumptions.

Detectability and Control Challenges

The mechanisms that enable internal and external fraud also influence how easily each type is detected. Internal fraud may continue unnoticed for extended periods because the actor understands how to avoid alerts and may occupy a position of trust. Detection often relies on independent oversight, robust audit functions, behavioral monitoring, and strict segregation of duties. Institutions with weak governance, insufficient monitoring, or high employee turnover face heightened risk because insiders may operate without consistent scrutiny.

External fraud tends to generate a higher volume of detectable anomalies. Automated systems can identify unusual login attempts, unexpected transaction patterns, or inconsistencies in new account applications. Customers may also report suspicious activity if they notice unauthorized transactions or receive suspicious communications. The challenge with external fraud is not necessarily identifying single attempts but distinguishing genuine threats from large volumes of false positives. External offenders frequently test institutions repeatedly, requiring strong analytic capabilities and real-time monitoring.

Detection challenges also reflect differences in concealment strategies. Internal actors conceal misconduct through manipulation of records or misuse of authority. External actors rely on rapid movement of funds, stolen identities, or techniques that obscure digital footprints. Each category requires tailored controls that address the specific ways offenders hide their activity.

Institutional Implications

Internal and external fraud affect institutions differently. Internal fraud damages organizational culture, weakens trust between management and employees, and raises questions about oversight effectiveness. External fraud, while damaging in financial and operational terms, typically affects customer confidence and public perception of the institution's security. Both forms expose institutions to regulatory and legal consequences, but internal fraud often carries a deeper reputational impact because it suggests governance failures.

Understanding these distinctions allows institutions to design targeted prevention measures. Internal fraud requires strong access controls, rigorous oversight, clear accountability, robust ethics programs, and effective whistleblowing mechanisms. External fraud requires robust authentication methods, advanced monitoring technology, customer education, and coordinated intelligence to identify criminal networks. When institutions fail to differentiate these mechanisms, they risk applying controls that do not match the threat.

MAJOR FRAUD SCHEMES

Fraud manifests through numerous schemes that exploit trust, information gaps, and weaknesses in financial or administrative structures. Among the most persistent and damaging are investment fraud, mortgage fraud, pension fraud, and Business Email Compromise (BEC). Although each scheme operates differently, they share common elements: manipulation of perception, exploitation of vulnerabilities, and concealment of critical information. Understanding how these schemes function helps investigators identify the behavioral and transactional indicators that accompany them, and it enables institutions to establish strong preventive frameworks.

Investment Fraud

Investment fraud is characterized by deceptive practices that induce individuals or institutions to commit funds to a product, service, or opportunity that is misrepresented or entirely fictitious. These schemes manipulate expectations of financial gain, often taking advantage of individuals who lack expertise in evaluating complex investment pitches. The schemes vary widely in sophistication - from straightforward misrepresentations to structured programs supported by falsified documents, professional endorsements, or fabricated financial results.

A common feature of investment fraud is the illusion of legitimacy. Offenders construct an appearance of credibility through polished marketing materials, staged meetings, false compliance claims, or references to fictitious regulatory approvals. Some schemes use fabricated statements showing non-existent returns, while others rely on misinterpretation of genuine market data. Fraudsters often present themselves as experienced financial professionals, leveraging personal charm or perceived expertise to gain victims' confidence. They may also rely on social relationships to reduce skepticism, targeting communities, affinity groups, or professional networks where trust is assumed.

Ponzi-style schemes represent a well-known form of investment fraud. In such arrangements, returns to earlier investors are funded by contributions from new investors rather than genuine profit. These schemes require continuous recruitment to sustain payouts, and they collapse when inflows are insufficient to meet promised returns. Detecting these schemes requires attention to unexplained consistency in returns, vague descriptions of investment strategies, or resistance to independent verification.

Other investment fraud schemes involve misrepresentation of the underlying asset. Offenders may promote nonexistent real estate, exaggerated valuations of commodities, or fabricated technology ventures. Some schemes exploit emerging sectors, such as digital assets, by capitalizing on the lack of established regulatory frameworks. The complexity of these offerings can obscure the absence of real economic value, allowing offenders to operate for extended periods before detection.

Mortgage Fraud

Mortgage fraud occurs when individuals, intermediaries, or institutions intentionally misrepresent information in order to obtain a loan, secure a higher loan amount, or influence a lending decision. Because mortgage processes depend heavily on documentation related to income, assets, employment, property valuation, and identity, fraudulent actors manipulate these elements to bypass lending criteria. Mortgage fraud affects not only lenders but also financial markets, as widespread misrepresentation can distort loan portfolios and undermine property market stability.

One common form involves falsification of borrower information. Applicants may inflate income, misstate employment, fabricate bank statements, or conceal existing debt obligations. Sometimes the borrower is complicit; in other cases, an intermediary—such as a mortgage broker—prepares falsified documents to secure approval. Fraudulent applications distort lenders' assessment of creditworthiness and may lead to significant losses when borrowers default.

Property valuation manipulation is another frequent mechanism. Appraisers, property developers, or intermediaries may participate in schemes that inflate property values beyond their true market worth. Overvaluation enables larger loan amounts, allowing offenders to extract surplus funds through immediate resale, rental schemes, or diversion of loan proceeds. Some schemes rely on collusion between insiders and external actors to ensure that inflated valuations pass through approval channels without scrutiny.

Straw-buyer schemes add another dimension to mortgage fraud. In these cases, individuals with stronger credit profiles are recruited - often with promises of payment - to apply for mortgages on behalf of others who cannot qualify. Properties may be purchased for fraudulent purposes, used to launder money, or abandoned after funds are extracted. These schemes are particularly harmful because they create obscured ownership structures, complicating recovery efforts and distorting lending data.

Mortgage fraud is often concealed within genuine real estate activity, making detection challenging. Patterns such as repeated use of the same professionals, inconsistent borrower information, rapid property transfers, or dramatic valuation changes may indicate fraud. Because the real estate sector intersects with multiple financial and professional services, effective detection requires cooperation across institutions, regulatory bodies, and property market participants.

Pension Fraud

Pension fraud targets retirement savings and benefits, exploiting the complexity of pension systems, the vulnerability of retirees, and the long time horizons associated with pension management. These schemes may be committed by external criminals, insiders managing pension funds, or intermediaries offering fraudulent services. Pension fraud is particularly damaging because victims often have limited capacity to recover financially, and losses may not be detected until long after the fraudulent activity has occurred.

One major category involves misappropriation of pension funds by those entrusted with managing them. Fund managers, administrators, or trustees may siphon assets, divert contributions, or invest in illegitimate ventures for personal gain. These schemes may be disguised through falsified records, manipulated valuations, or fictitious investment vehicles. The long-term nature of pension investments allows misconduct to continue unnoticed, as beneficiaries typically do not monitor daily fund performance.

Another form of pension fraud occurs when criminals persuade individuals to transfer their savings to fraudulent schemes. These scams often involve false promises of higher returns, early access to retirement funds, or specialized investment opportunities. Offenders may create professional-looking materials, establish fake advisory firms, or impersonate legitimate pension administrators. Once funds are transferred, victims may be left with no legal recourse, as the perpetrators vanish or declare insolvency.

Identity-based pension fraud is also prevalent. Criminals may submit claims using stolen or fabricated identities to access pension benefits of deceased individuals or individuals who have not yet claimed their entitlements. Weak verification processes, outdated records, or inconsistent coordination across agencies can facilitate these schemes. The victims - often elderly or inactive pension holders - may never realize their benefits were misappropriated.

The detection of pension fraud requires careful scrutiny of fund management practices, transaction flows, and beneficiary information. Institutions responsible for pension oversight must maintain strong controls, including independent audits, transparent reporting, and robust authentication procedures. Because the consequences of pension fraud extend deeply into individuals' long-term financial wellbeing, the importance of prevention and early identification cannot be overstated.

Business Email Compromise

Business Email Compromise (BEC) has emerged as one of the most financially damaging fraud types worldwide. Unlike many cyber-related offenses, BEC relies primarily on social manipulation rather than technical intrusion. Offenders impersonate senior executives, suppliers, or trusted partners to persuade employees to authorize transfers, disclose confidential information, or modify payment instructions. These schemes exploit human judgment, organizational structure, and communication processes.

A BEC scheme typically begins with reconnaissance. Offenders gather information about the organization's reporting lines, communication styles, key personnel, and vendor relationships. They may acquire this information through public sources, social media profiling, phishing, or prior data breaches. Once equipped with sufficient knowledge, they craft emails or messages that appear legitimate, often mimicking internal language patterns or referencing ongoing business activities.

Offenders frequently impersonate senior executives who have the authority to request urgent payments. These messages emphasize confidentiality or time sensitivity, pressuring employees to bypass standard verification procedures. Another variant targets accounts payable teams by impersonating suppliers and requesting updated bank details. Because these requests align with normal business operations, they may not raise immediate suspicion unless institutions enforce strong authentication and verification controls.

BEC schemes often rely on subtle manipulation rather than overt deception. Attackers may send emails from domains that differ by a single character from legitimate ones, or they may compromise actual email accounts to send authentic-looking messages. Some schemes involve hybrid methods, combining phishing with direct impersonation to increase credibility. Offenders also take advantage of organizational changes, holidays, or high-pressure periods when employees may be less vigilant.

The impact of BEC extends beyond financial loss. Institutions may face operational disruption, regulatory scrutiny, and reputational harm. Because BEC exploits trust in internal communication channels, it can weaken employee confidence in routine processes. Detection requires attention to unusual communication patterns, deviations from standard payment practices, and inconsistencies in sender information. Prevention relies on employee training, strict verification protocols, secure email systems, and organizational awareness of how these schemes operate.

The Importance of Contextual Understanding

Although investment fraud, mortgage fraud, pension fraud, and BEC represent different mechanisms, they share structural characteristics that allow investigators to identify them early. Each involves manipulation of information, exploitation of trust, and the use of persuasive methods tailored to the victim or institution. Understanding their mechanics requires attention to behavioral cues as much as transactional data. Fraudsters construct narratives that appear legitimate, conceal critical details, and rely on victims or employees to act without full verification. Recognizing those patterns is central to effective detection.

Each scheme also illustrates how fraud adapts to economic trends, regulatory shifts, and technological developments. Investment schemes evolve alongside financial innovation; mortgage fraud responds to property market dynamics; pension fraud exploits demographic vulnerabilities; and BEC leverages communication technologies. Investigators must therefore maintain awareness of the broader environment in which fraud occurs, as changes in one sector often influence emerging risks in others.

SOCIAL ENGINEERING, PHISHING, AND BEHAVIORAL PATTERNS

Social engineering has become one of the most prevalent and effective methods used by fraudsters to compromise individuals and institutions. Unlike purely technical attacks, social engineering relies on manipulating human behavior. Criminals exploit trust, authority, fear, urgency, curiosity, or routine habits to persuade victims to act against their own interests. Phishing - one of the most common expressions of social engineering - extends this manipulation into digital environments, using fraudulent messages, websites, or communication channels to obtain confidential information or create unauthorized access. Understanding how these schemes operate requires examining the behavioral principles that guide victim decision-making and the tactics offenders employ to influence those decisions.

Foundations of Social Engineering

Social engineering targets human vulnerabilities rather than technological weaknesses. Offenders recognize that even the most secure systems depend on human interpretation and compliance at critical points. By influencing perception, manipulating communication cues, and creating psychological pressure, social engineers convince individuals to disclose information, transfer funds, or bypass established procedures.

These schemes often begin with information gathering. Criminals study their targets using public sources, leaked data, professional profiles, or previous breaches. They seek knowledge about organizational roles, reporting structures, personal relationships, and communication habits. This preparation gives them the context needed to craft persuasive interactions that appear legitimate. When an offender references a real project, known colleague, or familiar communication style, the victim is more likely to comply without further scrutiny.

The strength of social engineering lies in its alignment with natural cognitive tendencies. Humans are inclined to trust perceived authority, respond to urgency, avoid conflict, and cooperate with requests framed as routine. Offenders exploit these instincts by constructing scenarios that appear credible, compelling, or time-sensitive. Once a victim responds to the initial request, social engineers may escalate the interaction, gradually increasing the level of access or information acquired.

Forms and Techniques of Phishing

Phishing is a broad term covering fraudulent messages designed to prompt recipients to reveal information, click malicious links, or engage in actions that benefit the attacker. While early phishing attempts were often unsophisticated and easily identified, modern phishing schemes are highly tailored, using personalized details and realistic design elements to mimic genuine communication.

Email phishing remains the most common form. Attackers use messages that appear to come from trusted institutions, colleagues, or service providers. These emails may include urgent messages about account security, payment issues, or administrative requirements. They often contain links to fraudulent websites that mimic real login portals, prompting victims to enter credentials. Some include attachments loaded with malware that enables remote access or data extraction. The quality of these messages has improved significantly, with professional formatting and accurate branding that reduce suspicion.

Spear-phishing is a more targeted technique. Instead of sending bulk messages to random recipients, attackers focus on specific individuals or groups. They reference internal projects, personal information, or organizational context to increase credibility. Spear-phishing is commonly used in Business Email Compromise schemes and in attacks designed to gain entry to high-value systems.

Smishing and vishing represent similar techniques conducted through SMS and voice calls. Smishing messages often mimic delivery notifications, banking alerts, or two-factor authentication prompts. Vishing involves direct voice manipulation, where attackers impersonate customer service representatives, bank officers, government agencies, or internal staff. These calls frequently rely on urgency, emphasizing immediate action to prevent supposed account closure, fines, or service disruption.

Clone phishing is another advanced technique in which attackers replicate legitimate messages previously sent to the victim. By replacing attachments or links with malicious versions, offenders capitalize on established trust. This method is particularly effective when the original communication came from a credible source or contained information the victim expects to receive again.

Psychological Drivers Behind Victim Response

Victims of social engineering and phishing schemes are not necessarily careless or uninformed. These schemes succeed because they exploit universal behavioral patterns. Several psychological drivers are consistently observed in successful attacks.

Authority is one of the most influential factors. Individuals tend to comply with instructions from figures perceived to possess higher status or specialized knowledge. When an email appears to come from a senior executive or recognized institution, victims may act quickly to fulfill the request without verifying authenticity.

Urgency is another powerful driver. Social engineers often

frame their requests as time-sensitive, claiming that immediate action is required to avoid financial loss, service interruption, or disciplinary consequence. The pressure created by urgency disrupts rational evaluation and encourages rapid decision-making.

Familiarity reduces suspicion. When messages reference known colleagues, current projects, or recognizable patterns of communication, victims may not question their legitimacy. Attackers exploit this by studying organizational dynamics and mimicking natural communication styles.

Fear is frequently used to prompt compliance. Threats of account closure, legal action, or data exposure can cause victims to respond reflexively. Offenders take advantage of this fear by invoking authority figures or regulatory consequences.

Routine behavior also plays a role. Many fraudulent requests mimic everyday administrative actions such as invoice processing, password updates, or document downloads. Victims may process these requests without extensive thought because they appear consistent with normal workflows.

Curiosity can be exploited through unexpected attachments, intriguing subject lines, or messages implying personal relevance. Offenders rely on the natural human tendency to investigate information that seems important or interesting.

Social Engineering in Organizational Contexts

Within institutions, social engineering often succeeds because it targets operational processes that depend on human judgment rather than automated controls. Fraudsters may impersonate suppliers, request payment updates, or pose as IT personnel seeking access to systems. Employees who regularly manage high volumes of communication may overlook subtle signs of deception, particularly when a request appears routine or aligns with their responsibilities.

Organizational hierarchies contribute to the risk. Employees may hesitate to question instructions from individuals they believe to be senior executives. Attackers exploit this hesitation by impersonating leadership figures in emails or calls, requesting confidential data or urgent payments.

Remote work environments have increased vulnerability by reducing face-to-face interactions and introducing communication methods that are easier to spoof. Without direct access to colleagues for quick verification, employees may rely on electronic cues that are susceptible to manipulation.

Social engineering also intersects with insider risk. Attackers may attempt to exploit employees who appear disengaged, pressured, or unaware of security procedures. They may also use personal information gathered from social platforms to increase credibility or build rapport.

Behavioral Indicators of Deception

While social engineering and phishing schemes are designed to appear legitimate, they often produce subtle behavioral or contextual clues. Understanding these indicators supports early detection.

Inconsistencies in language or tone may signal impersonation. Attackers may imitate the general structure of institutional communication but fail to replicate specific habits, such as preferred greetings or signature formats. Timing may also be unusual, with requests sent outside regular business hours or at moments when verification is difficult.

Requests that bypass standard procedures or reduce oversight should raise concern. Attackers often discourage verification, claiming confidentiality or urgency. They may instruct victims to communicate through alternative channels, avoid copying colleagues, or limit discussion.

Unusual payment instructions, unexpected login prompts, or messages that encourage actions outside established workflows also present red flags. Social engineers often attempt to shift the victim away from familiar systems into environments where fraud is easier to execute.

Behavioral signs of pressure - such as repeated messages, attempts to create fear, or insistence on secrecy - may indicate manipulation. Legitimate institutions rarely use tactics that force immediate response without verification.

Broader Implications for Fraud Prevention

Understanding social engineering and phishing requires more than identifying specific schemes. It demands recognition of how human behavior interacts with institutional processes. Fraudsters design their techniques around predictable human responses, adapting their methods in response to increased awareness or organizational controls.

Institutions must acknowledge that even well-designed technical defenses can be compromised when employees are influenced to bypass them. Effective prevention therefore includes building a culture of awareness, reinforcing verification practices, and ensuring staff understand that questioning unusual requests is not only acceptable but expected.

Training must focus on practical decision-making rather than abstract concepts. Employees should learn to recognize psychological triggers, understand common techniques, and apply structured verification steps without hesitation. Clear escalation pathways, accessible support from security teams, and consistent reinforcement of expectations help reduce vulnerability.

Technology can support human judgment through email

filtering, warning banners, behavioral analytics, and multi-factor authentication. However, these tools must complement - not replace - the human ability to recognize manipulation. Social engineering succeeds when individuals believe they are acting in accordance with legitimate expectations; therefore, prevention relies on strengthening their ability to evaluate context and challenge assumptions.

Phishing and social engineering are persistent because they evolve in response to organizational defenses. As long as human decision-making remains central to institutional operations, these techniques will continue to pose significant risk. Investigators must therefore maintain a clear understanding of behavioral patterns and the psychological principles that offenders exploit. Recognizing these dynamics provides a foundation for developing detection strategies that address both human and technological vulnerabilities.

DETECTION APPROACHES AND PREVENTION CONTROLS

Detecting and preventing fraud requires a coordinated approach that combines technology, human judgment, organizational discipline, and a clear understanding of how criminals exploit weaknesses. Fraud detection is not a single function or system; it is an ongoing process shaped by analytical capability, operational awareness, and institutional responsiveness. Effective prevention depends not only on identifying suspicious activity but also on reducing opportunities, strengthening oversight, and ensuring that employees and customers understand their role in protecting financial integrity. As fraud evolves, institutions must maintain controls that are flexible, intelligence-driven, and grounded in a realistic assessment of current risks.

Foundations of Fraud Detection

Fraud detection begins with the ability to recognize patterns of behavior that deviate from normal activity. This requires establishing clear baselines against which anomalies can be measured. Baselines take many forms depending on the environment: typical transaction sizes, customer spending habits, expected account behaviors, normal communication practices, or standard procedural steps. When activity falls outside these expected boundaries, investigators and monitoring systems can examine it more closely.

Modern detection systems rely heavily on analytics, yet analytics alone are insufficient. Systems must capture high-quality data, integrate information across multiple platforms, and interpret results in context. Without strong data governance and clear classification of behaviors, detection systems may produce excessive false positives or fail to identify subtle but meaningful irregularities. Institutions must therefore invest in structures that ensure data accuracy, completeness, and consistency.

A layered detection model is most effective. Automated tools screen for unusual patterns, while analysts examine outliers for intent, context, and explanation. Experienced investigators understand how fraudsters manipulate systems to disguise malicious activity. Their judgment complements automation by identifying signals that algorithms may overlook, such as inconsistencies in narrative explanations, discrepancies in documentation, or behavioral cues that do not align with legitimate operations.

Transaction Monitoring and Analytical Capabilities

Transaction monitoring is a core component of fraud detection. Systems review financial activity in real time or near real time, using rules, statistical models, and machine learning to identify transactions that warrant review. These tools screen for behaviors such as rapid movement of funds, unusual account activity, payment requests outside standard channels, or transaction flows inconsistent with a customer's historical profile.

Rule-based systems remain useful for detecting known patterns, such as structured transactions or prohibited account combinations. However, as fraudsters adapt to predictable controls, institutions increasingly rely on behavioral analytics and anomaly-detection models. These systems evaluate activity holistically, comparing it to peer groups or population norms. They also adapt over time, refining thresholds and expectations based on observed behavior.

Machine learning enhances detection by identifying relationships that may not be apparent through static rules. For example, complex interactions between account activity, device usage, and communication patterns may reveal coordinated schemes. Predictive models can identify subtle signals that precede fraud, enabling interventions before losses occur. However, machine learning models must be carefully managed to prevent bias, maintain transparency, and ensure regulatory compliance.

Despite advances in technology, transaction monitoring is only as effective as its interpretation. Analysts must understand how fraudsters manipulate timing, channels, and amounts to avoid detection. They must also differentiate between legitimate anomalies and suspicious irregularities. Contextual understanding, supported by strong escalation procedures, ensures that alerts receive the appropriate level of scrutiny.

Identity Verification and Authentication

Fraud detection increasingly relies on robust identity verification and authentication methods. Fraudsters often rely on false identities, synthetic profiles, or compromised credentials to initiate activity. Institutions must verify not only who customers claim to be but also whether the behavior and device patterns associated with an identity are consistent with legitimate use.

Strong authentication measures, such as multi-factor authentication, device fingerprinting, and behavioral biometrics, reduce the likelihood that fraudsters can impersonate legitimate users. Behavioral biometrics examine how individuals interact with systems - typing patterns, navigation habits, or device handling characteristics - to identify anomalies that may indicate misuse. These tools complement traditional authentication by providing continuous verification rather than relying solely on login credentials.

Identity verification must also address onboarding risks. Fraudsters may attempt to create accounts using fabricated documents or stolen information. Digital identity verification tools analyze document authenticity, cross-check data with external records, and use facial recognition technologies to confirm that the individual presenting the document matches the identity on record. Effective onboarding reduces upstream fraud by preventing criminals from entering the system through misrepresentation.

Strengthening Organizational Controls

Prevention controls are most effective when embedded throughout an organization's operations. Institutions must implement clear governance structures, strong oversight, and consistent enforcement of policies. Fraud thrives where processes are opaque, responsibilities are unclear, or controls are inconsistently applied.

Segregation of duties is a foundational principle. No single individual should have unilateral control over critical processes such as payments, reconciliations, or account adjustments. Segregation reduces opportunities for internal fraud by requiring multiple approvals, independent verification, and oversight. Even small lapses - such as temporary overrides during staff shortages - create opportunities criminals may exploit.

Access controls are equally important. Employees should have access only to the systems and information necessary for their role. Regular review of access rights helps prevent accumulation of unnecessary privileges, which increases risk. Access should be revoked promptly when employees change roles or leave the institution.

Exception handling processes must be tightly managed. Fraudsters often exploit exceptions, workarounds, or manual interventions that bypass automated controls. Institutions should document exceptions, require justification, and subject them to independent review. Inconsistent or poorly documented exceptions frequently indicate underlying issues that warrant investigation.

Document Verification and Information Integrity

Fraud detection depends on the ability to verify that documentation, records, and information presented during transactions are authentic and accurate. Fraudsters use falsified invoices, manipulated statements, counterfeit identification, or fabricated contracts to support their schemes. Institutions must implement controls that scrutinize both the content and source of documents.

Document analysis tools can detect alterations, inconsistencies, or irregular formatting. Cross-verification with external data sources - such as public records, regulatory registers, or credit bureaus - helps confirm accuracy. Institutions must also examine the narrative coherence of documentation: whether the information aligns with the customer's profile, financial history, and expected behavior.

Information integrity extends to internal records. Inaccurate or incomplete data can obscure patterns, weaken monitoring systems, and create gaps that fraudsters exploit. Regular audits and data-quality assessments ensure that internal information supports effective detection.

Employee Awareness and Human Judgement

Human judgment is central to fraud detection. Employees who understand fraud risks, recognize suspicious behavior, and know how to escalate concerns play a critical role in prevention. Awareness programs must focus on practical scenarios, teaching staff how fraudsters manipulate communication, exploit procedural gaps, or impersonate trusted partners.

Training should emphasize critical thinking. Employees must feel confident questioning unusual requests, even when they appear to come from senior colleagues or long-standing business partners. Institutions should create a culture where verification is encouraged, not viewed as obstructive. Clear escalation channels, accessible support from risk or compliance teams, and consistent reinforcement of expectations strengthen organizational resilience.

Frontline employees, such as customer service agents and payment processors, are particularly important. Their proximity to operational processes allows them to identify irregularities that automated systems may overlook. Encouraging staff to report concerns, supported by whistleblowing mechanisms, enhances detection and promotes accountability.

Fraud Intelligence and External Collaboration

Fraud detection improves when institutions share intelligence, observe external trends, and maintain awareness of emerging techniques. Criminals often repeat successful methods across institutions, sectors, or regions. Participation in industry forums, information-sharing partnerships, and regulatory working groups helps institutions anticipate new fraud patterns.

Fraud intelligence includes analysis of compromised credentials, emerging phishing techniques, new social engineering strategies, and changes in criminal infrastructure. Combining internal data with external insights allows institutions to strengthen controls proactively rather than responding only after incidents occur.

Cross-sector collaboration is especially valuable in combating organized fraud networks. These networks often operate across telecommunications, financial services, digital platforms, and international jurisdictions. Coordinated intelligence efforts support faster identification of connected events, reducing losses and disrupting criminal operations.

Incident Response and Remediation

Detection is only the first step in managing fraud. Effective response ensures that incidents are contained, investigated, and remediated. Institutions must establish procedures for isolating compromised accounts, halting suspicious transactions, and securing affected systems. Rapid response reduces financial loss and protects evidence needed for further investigation.

Investigations should examine not only the fraudulent activity but also the underlying control failures that allowed it to occur. Root cause analysis identifies weaknesses in processes, systems, or oversight. Remediation must address these weaknesses through improved controls, policy updates, training enhancements, or technology upgrades.

Communication is crucial. Customers and partners affected by fraud require timely information, clear guidance, and assurance that corrective measures are in place. Transparent communication supports trust and demonstrates institutional accountability.

Building a Resilient Framework

Fraud detection and prevention are not static exercises. They require continuous refinement, informed by changing criminal behavior, technological evolution, and regulatory expectations. Institutions that adopt a proactive and integrated approach - combining analytics, governance, human awareness, and external collaboration - are better positioned to protect themselves and their customers.

The goal is not to eliminate all risk, which is impossible, but to create systems capable of identifying suspicious activity, reducing opportunities for misconduct, and responding effectively when incidents occur. A resilient framework recognizes that fraud is dynamic, adaptive, and persistent. It integrates controls that address both technical vulnerabilities and human factors, acknowledging that prevention depends equally on systems and behavior.

CHAPTER 6

BRIBERY AND CORRUPTION

MECHANICS OF BRIBERY, KICKBACKS, AND INFLUENCE ABUSE

BRIBERY and CORRUPTION undermine the integrity of financial systems, commercial environments, and public institutions by distorting decision-making processes for private benefit. These offenses operate through mechanisms designed to exchange value -whether monetary or non-monetary - in return for favorable outcomes. Understanding these mechanics is essential because thc methods used to disguise improper influence often mimic legitimate business conduct. Investigators must therefore distinguish between acceptable commercial practices and actions intended to manipulate authority. The mechanics of bribery, kickbacks, and influence abuse illustrate how individuals and organizations exploit positions of power, conceal illicit value transfers, and subvert fair processes.

Foundations of Bribery

Bribery involves offering, giving, receiving, or soliciting something of value to influence the actions of an individual entrusted with decision-making authority. The value exchanged may take many forms: cash payments, gifts, travel, entertainment, employment opportunities, political contributions, or personal favors. The essence of bribery lies in the intention to secure advantage by undermining impartial judgment.

The act of bribery usually develops through a sequence of interactions. It begins when an individual identifies a decision that can be influenced- an award of a contract, approval of a permit, regulatory clearance, procurement selection, or confidential information that provides commercial benefit. The bribe payer evaluates the decision-maker's vulnerabilities, motivations, or pressures. The bribe may then be structured to appear as a legitimate transaction, such as a consulting fee, marketing expense, sponsorship, or service agreement.

The bribe recipient accepts the benefit in exchange for altering their decision or providing access. Their actions may include recommending a specific supplier, accelerating an approval, withholding adverse findings, or granting exemptions. The benefit may be delivered directly or indirectly through intermediaries who create distance between the payer and recipient. The arrangement succeeds when the exchange of value remains hidden beneath the appearance of ordinary business activity.

Sophisticated schemes often involve multiple layers of justification. Offenders may create fictitious service invoices, inflate legitimate expenses, or channel funds through controlled companies to disguise the benefit. These methods allow participants to conceal the bribe in accounting records, making detection more difficult unless the underlying purpose is scrutinized.

Nature and Purpose of Kickbacks

Kickbacks are a type of bribery that typically occur within procurement, contracting, and supply-chain activities. In a kickback scheme, a supplier or contractor secretly pays a portion of the contract value to an insider in return for favorable treatment. This insider may have authority to select vendors, approve payments, or influence evaluations.

Kickbacks distort commercial outcomes by prioritizing the financial interest of the insider rather than the organization they serve. They often result in inflated prices, substandard goods, or acceptance of unnecessary services. In some cases, the supplier's pricing explicitly incorporates the amount required to fund the kickback, shifting the cost to the victim organization or, in public-sector environments, the taxpayer.

The mechanics of kickbacks require concealment of both the payment and the relationship. Offenders may arrange for the insider to receive funds through personal accounts, unrelated businesses, or offshore entities. They may disguise payments as consulting fees, commissions, or subcontracting arrangements. When intermediaries are involved, they often serve as conduits who funnel funds while presenting themselves as service providers.

The insider's involvement may also include adjusting procurement specifications to favor a particular supplier, bypassing competitive tender processes, manipulating scoring criteria, or approving invoices without verification. Because kickbacks typically involve collusion, they can persist for extended periods, especially when organizational oversight is weak.

Influence Abuse Beyond Direct Payments

Corruption is not limited to explicit transfers of money. Influence abuse includes any action through which authority is misused to benefit a private interest. This may occur through nepotism, favoritism, conflicts of interest, or granting advantages to individuals or entities with personal connections to decision-makers.

Influence abuse often operates without a direct financial transfer. Decision-makers may award contracts to relatives, appoint unqualified individuals to positions, or direct resources to organizations aligned with their personal interests. These actions still constitute corruption because they undermine fairness and transparency. In many cases, influence abuse functions as a precursor to more explicit bribery or as a mechanism for sustaining corrupt networks.

Another form of influence abuse occurs when individuals leverage their position to secure future benefits rather than immediate payment. This includes promises of employment, business partnerships, or political support. The expectation of future reward shapes current decisions and compromises impartiality.

The mechanics of influence abuse rely heavily on discretion, authority, and lack of oversight. When processes lack transparency, decision-makers may exercise authority in ways that are difficult to challenge or review. Without clear accountability, actions motivated by improper interests may appear routine or justified, even when they harm the organization or the public.

Use of Intermediaries and Third Parties

Intermediaries play a central role in many bribery and corruption schemes. They provide a buffer between payer and recipient, allowing the illicit nature of the transaction to be concealed. Intermediaries may include agents, consultants, distributors, lawyers, lobbyists, or local partners. Their involvement adds credibility to transactions and obscures the true purpose of payments.

Third-party intermediaries often have legitimate roles within business environments. This makes their misuse particularly challenging to detect. A consultant may receive a fee that appears consistent with industry standards, yet the service may be fabricated or unnecessary. A distributor may be granted unusually high margins that are then used to fund bribes. A local representative may arrange introductions or expedite approvals but use corrupt payments to influence decisions without the principal's direct knowledge.

Intermediaries may also be used to disguise kickbacks. Funds can be routed through shell companies or entities controlled by insiders, allowing participants to mask the flow of money under the guise of subcontracting or referral arrangements. Some intermediaries specialize in facilitating corruption, using networks of contacts, offshore accounts, or opaque corporate structures to hide illicit activity.

The use of intermediaries complicates investigations because the connection between the bribe and the benefit is intentionally fragmented. Effective examination requires scrutiny of contractual terms, analysis of value provided, assessment of compensation structures, and identification of personal or commercial links between parties.

Structuring and Concealment Techniques

Bribery and corruption depend on concealment. Offenders must disguise both the transfer of value and the improper influence exerted. This often involves complex structuring techniques designed to integrate illicit payments into legitimate financial flows.

One method involves falsified or inflated invoices. A supplier may issue an invoice for services not rendered or exaggerate the cost of genuine services. The excess funds are then used to pay the bribe. Because the transaction appears legitimate, it may pass through routine verification without question.

Another technique involves misallocation of corporate funds through expense claims, cash advances, or petty cash withdrawals. These small transactions may accumulate into substantial illicit payments, especially when records are manipulated to obscure their purpose.

Charitable donations, sponsorships, and community projects can also be misused to disguise bribes. A company may contribute funds to an organization connected to a government official, or sponsor an event that indirectly benefits the decision-maker. The payment appears altruistic but is intended to secure favorable treatment.

Offenders also use sophisticated financial structures, such as offshore entities, trusts, or layered transactions, to obscure beneficial ownership and payment trails. These structures make it difficult for investigators to trace funds or identify connections between parties.

Conditions That Enable Corruption

Bribery and corruption thrive in environments where oversight is weak, processes lack transparency, or discretion is concentrated in the hands of a few individuals. When decision-making criteria are not clearly documented, it becomes easier for corrupt actors to justify decisions that deviate from objective standards. Inadequate record-keeping further obscures improper actions.

High-risk environments also include sectors where the stakes are significant - public procurement, natural resource management, construction, healthcare, infrastructure, and licensing. These areas often involve large budgets, complex projects, or discretionary approvals, making them attractive targets for corrupt actors.

Cultural factors can also influence susceptibility to bribery. In some environments, gift-giving or facilitation payments may be normalized, blurring the line between acceptable conduct and illicit influence. Where organizational culture tolerates informal practices, employees may struggle to identify when behavior becomes improper.

Corruption is self-reinforcing. Once established, it can grow into networks that protect participants, suppress reporting, and deter transparency. These networks may include insiders, intermediaries, and external actors who share benefits and risks. Breaking such systems requires strong leadership, accountability mechanisms, and consistent enforcement.

Consequences for Institutions and Society

The mechanics of bribery and corruption impose significant harm. For institutions, corruption leads to financial loss, reputational damage, operational inefficiency, and regulatory exposure. Decisions influenced by private interests undermine strategic objectives and weaken trust within the organization.

For governments, corruption erodes public confidence, distorts policy decisions, and diverts resources away from essential services. It undermines economic development by discouraging investment, inflating costs, and reducing competitiveness. In environments where corruption becomes systemic, it can destabilize political structures and diminish institutional legitimacy.

For individuals, corruption restricts opportunities, reinforces inequality, and undermines confidence in both public and private institutions. It diminishes the fairness of commercial markets and limits accountability for those in positions of power.

COMMON TYPOLOGIES AND HIGH-RISK SCENARIOS

Bribery and corruption manifest through varied patterns that reflect both the intent of offenders and the systems they exploit. While methods change over time, certain typologies recur across jurisdictions, sectors, and organizational structures because they reliably create opportunities for improper influence. Understanding these typologies is essential for investigators and compliance practitioners, as it allows them to recognize consistent markers of misconduct even when schemes are adapted to local contexts or disguised through legitimate channels. High-risk scenarios typically arise where discretion is concentrated, oversight is weak, or significant financial or political interests are involved.

Procurement and Contracting Manipulation

Procurement is one of the most common environments for bribery and corruption because it frequently involves large sums of money, complex decision-making processes, and reliance on technical evaluations. Bribery in procurement can occur at any stage - from drafting specifications to contract award, performance monitoring, or payment approval.

One recurring typology involves tailoring procurement specifications to favor a specific bidder. Offenders may write requirements that only one supplier can meet or introduce technical criteria that eliminate competitors. This manipulation reduces competition, inflates prices, and restricts access to qualified vendors.

Another typology is bid rotation or coordinated bidding. In these schemes, suppliers collude to alternate winning contracts while submitting artificially high bids to create the appearance of competition. Officials involved may receive bribes or kickbacks for facilitating this arrangement, approving manipulated processes, or overlooking irregularities.

Contract inflation and change-order abuse also represent significant risks. A contract may be awarded at a reasonable price to avoid scrutiny, but subsequently inflated through amendments, supplemental agreements, or change orders that were planned from the outset. Insiders and suppliers may share the inflated proceeds.

In environments where procurement oversight is weak, payments may be approved without verification of delivery, quality, or necessity. Fake invoices, fictitious suppliers, or improper use of single-source procurement mechanisms often accompany these schemes. Because procurement spans multiple departments—such as technical teams, finance, and operations—it provides ample opportunity for corrupt actors to exploit gaps in coordination.

Licensing, Permits, and Regulatory Approvals

Interactions with regulatory authorities present frequent opportunities for bribery because approvals often involve discretion, specialized knowledge, and considerable impact on commercial activities. This includes permits for construction, environmental compliance, land use, import/export operations, and business licensing.

A typical typology involves paying officials to accelerate approval processes. Offenders exploit delays or bureaucratic complexity by offering payments or benefits in exchange for prioritization. While the facilitation of speed may appear harmless, it creates unfair advantage and normalizes corrupt relationships between applicants and officials.

Another scenario involves influencing regulatory inspections. Inspectors may accept bribes to overlook violations, reduce penalties, or issue favorable reports. These schemes can endanger public safety when applied to construction, food safety, healthcare, or environmental compliance.

In sectors subject to health and safety regulations, bribes may be used to secure certification for products or facilities that do not meet required standards. Such practices pose material risk to consumers and undermine confidence in regulatory systems.

Foreign businesses operating in countries with high corruption risk may also encounter demands for unofficial payments during licensing or inspection processes. Even when such payments are framed as customary or administrative, they constitute corrupt practices and expose organizations to legal consequences under international anti-bribery laws.

Public Sector Influence and Political Corruption

Political environments present significant bribery risks because officials have authority over public funds, policy decisions, licensing, and access to state resources. Political corruption can take many forms, including campaign finance abuses, manipulation of public contracts, or diversion of state assets.

One common typology involves awarding public contracts in exchange for political contributions or personal favors. Officials may ensure that contracts are directed toward businesses owned by relatives, associates, or supporters. In return, these businesses may channel funds back to political campaigns, personal accounts, or controlled entities.

Another mechanism is the misuse of discretionary budgets or development funds. Officials may allocate public resources to projects where they or their associates benefit financially. Funds may be diverted through inflated contracts, fictitious vendors, or shell companies.

Political interference in appointments is also a form of corruption. Officials may place unqualified individuals in key roles within public agencies or state-owned enterprises to facilitate access to resources or weaken oversight. These networks may perpetuate corrupt practices over long periods, protected by political patronage.

In some jurisdictions, corruption may become systemic, involving multiple levels of government and private partners who maintain influence through payments, threats, or reciprocal benefits. These environments pose substantial challenges for investigators because corruption is embedded in routine operations rather than isolated acts.

Third-Party Agents and Intermediaries

The involvement of intermediaries is a defining feature of many bribery schemes. Agents, consultants, distributors, and local partners are often used to facilitate payments, exert influence, or secure approvals while shielding the principal from direct involvement.

One typology involves paying excessive commissions or fees to agents who then use a portion of the funds to bribe officials. Because the payment to the agent appears legitimate, institutions may not immediately question the arrangement unless they analyze the value provided.

Distributors in certain markets may receive unusually high margins intended to fund illicit payments. These arrangements are particularly difficult to detect because the distributor's compensation may appear to be a commercial decision rather than a mechanism for corruption.

Local partners may also be used to access government contracts or approvals. In some countries, joint ventures or partnerships with politically connected individuals serve as a conduit for influence. The partner may not perform meaningful services but is included to facilitate access or secure favorable treatment.

Because intermediaries often operate outside the institution's direct oversight, they present significant risks. Weak due diligence, inadequate monitoring, or reliance on opaque commercial practices can allow bribery to occur without the principal's explicit knowledge.

Procurement in High-Risk Sectors

Certain sectors are inherently susceptible to bribery because they involve large financial flows, technical complexity, and discretionary decision-making. Construction, infrastructure, pharmaceuticals, defense, extractive industries, and telecommunications frequently appear in corruption investigations.

In construction and infrastructure, contracts are large, timelines are long, and specifications are complex. These conditions create opportunities for inflated pricing, kickbacks, and manipulation of certification processes. Contractors may submit claims for work not performed or engage in collusion to control bidding outcomes.

Pharmaceutical and healthcare sectors face high bribery risk due to the influence officials have over drug approvals, procurement of medical supplies, and allocation of healthcare budgets. Bribery may occur through sponsorships, travel, consulting arrangements, or incentives paid to healthcare professionals to promote specific products.

Extractive industries carry heightened risk because licensing of natural resources often rests with a small number of officials. Bribes may be paid to secure exploration rights, influence taxation terms, or obtain access to land. Weak governance in resource-rich countries amplifies these risks.

Defense and security procurement is another high-risk environment due to confidentiality, complexity, and political sensitivity. Bribes may be paid to secure arms deals, equipment purchases, or technology transfers.

High-Risk Corporate Structures and Payment Channels

Corporate structures can be manipulated to facilitate bribery. Shell companies, trusts, and opaque ownership arrangements allow individuals to disguise their involvement in transactions. Fraudulent consulting contracts or service agreements may be used to justify payments that fund illicit activity. These mechanisms create layers of separation between payers and recipients, complicating detection.

Payments routed through offshore accounts or jurisdictions with weak transparency laws also pose elevated risk. Offenders may use complex financial pathways to obscure the flow of funds, making it difficult to trace the ultimate beneficiary. Even small payments can be concealed within large volumes of international transactions when institutions do not conduct adequate scrutiny.

Cash-intensive sectors present additional risks, as cash transactions reduce traceability and provide opportunities for unrecorded payments. In environments with weak financial controls, cash may be used to pay bribes directly or fund informal networks.

Situations Involving Conflicts of Interest

Conflicts of interest are a frequent precursor to bribery. When individuals have personal or financial interests that intersect with their professional responsibilities, they may be influenced to act improperly. Conflicts become high risk when they are undisclosed, unmanaged, or systemic.

A typical scenario involves an employee or official with ownership interests in a supplier. Even without direct payments, the decision-maker may favor the supplier due to personal benefit. This advantage may escalate into overt corruption if not identified and addressed.

Conflicts also arise when employees seek future employment with companies they supervise or regulate. They may make favorable decisions to position themselves for recruitment, creating improper incentives that undermine integrity.

Emerging Risks and Evolving Typologies

As business practices evolve, so do bribery typologies. Digital platforms, government digitalization, and new financial technologies introduce novel risks. Online procurement portals can be manipulated through insider access. Digital payment systems can facilitate rapid, concealed transfers. Cryptocurrencies and decentralized platforms may be used to route bribes in ways that obscure origin and ownership.

Foreign investment initiatives also create high-risk scenarios. When projects involve multiple jurisdictions, intermediaries, and regulatory regimes, the potential for corruption increases. Companies may face demands for unofficial payments to secure land, permits, or infrastructure access.

RED FLAGS AND CONTROL FAILURES

Bribery and corruption often operate beneath the surface of organizational activity, concealed within seemingly legitimate transactions and interactions. Yet even the most carefully hidden schemes leave behind indicators - behaviors, inconsistencies, and anomalies that signal potential misconduct. These indicators, often referred to as red flags, do not prove wrongdoing on their own; instead, they highlight areas where further scrutiny is necessary. Understanding red flags is only one part of the equation. Bribery and corruption also thrive where institutional controls are weak, inconsistently applied, or poorly designed. Examining how control failures arise provides insight into why certain environments are more vulnerable and how institutions can strengthen their defenses.

Behavioral and Transactional Red Flags

Individuals involved in bribery or corruption often exhibit behavioral patterns that contradict normal professional conduct. These behaviors may be subtle or easily rationalized as personal style, but collectively they can indicate risk. Unusual secrecy around decisions, reluctance to involve colleagues, or insistence on operating outside formal channels often suggests an attempt to limit visibility. When employees guard information excessively or resist routine oversight, it may reflect a desire to avoid detection.

Another common red flag is a sudden improvement in an individual's lifestyle that cannot be explained by known income or personal circumstances. While such changes do not necessarily indicate corruption, they warrant heightened attention when paired with control gaps or unexplained decision-making patterns. Individuals engaged in corruption may also demonstrate defensive attitudes when questioned or display an unusual willingness to approve high-value transactions without proper documentation.

Transactional red flags frequently appear when payments or contracts do not align with business needs. These may include repeated use of the same supplier without competitive tendering, sudden changes in supplier selection without clear justification, or contracts awarded under conditions that appear inconsistent with standard procedures. Transactions involving vague service descriptions, inflated fees, or deliverables that cannot be substantiated should be scrutinized.

Irregularities in financial records are also notable indicators. Payments routed through unfamiliar accounts, outbound transfers to jurisdictions known for secrecy, or invoices lacking detail may signal improper activity. Even small inconsistencies - such as mismatches between purchase orders, invoices, and received goods - can reveal larger schemes when examined collectively.

Third-Party Red Flags

Third parties play a central role in many corruption schemes, making monitoring of their behavior essential. A third party's unwillingness to disclose ownership information, provide references, or clarify the nature of its role is a significant concern. Entities that appear recently formed, have no clear business history, or operate through opaque structures present elevated risk.

A red flag arises when a third party requests compensation that is significantly higher than market rates or insists on unusual payment terms, such as payments to offshore accounts, cash transactions, or split transfers across multiple jurisdictions. These requests may indicate an intention to conceal the destination of funds or finance illicit activity.

A third party's political connections also require careful assessment. While connections alone do not imply wrongdoing, failure to disclose such relationships - especially when the third party interacts with public officials on behalf of the organization - raises concerns about potential influence abuse.

Additionally, when a third party consistently achieves outcomes that appear unusually favorable, such as rapid approvals in heavily regulated sectors, it may suggest reliance on improper methods. Excessive success without a clear, legitimate explanation is a key indicator that warrants further inquiry.

Environmental and Structural Red Flags

Some red flags emerge from the broader environment rather than from specific individuals or transactions. High-risk environments include jurisdictions with weak governance, limited transparency, or histories of systemic corruption. In these contexts, bribery may be embedded within institutional processes, making it difficult to distinguish between legitimate and illicit interactions.

Other environmental indicators include sudden changes in regulatory requirements, unexplained delays in approvals, or inconsistent application of rules by authorities. These situations create opportunities for corrupt actors to exploit uncertainty or pressure organizations into providing improper payments.

Within an organization, excessive reliance on informal processes, lack of documentation, or inconsistent enforcement of policies creates fertile ground for corruption. When employees or departments operate without clear oversight, individual discretion can exceed appropriate boundaries, enabling misconduct to flourish with limited risk of detection.

Control Failures That Enable Corruption

Bribery and corruption do not emerge solely because individuals choose to engage in wrongdoing; they flourish when institutional controls fail. Control failures may stem from poor design, inadequate implementation, or organizational culture that tolerates or ignores improper conduct.

One common failure is insufficient segregation of duties. When a single individual has authority to approve contracts, select suppliers, and verify payments, opportunities for manipulation expand significantly. Without checks and balances, even well-designed processes become vulnerable. Segregation of duties is essential not only in procurement but also in financial reporting, vendor management, and regulatory interactions.

Another frequent failure is weak due diligence on third parties. Organizations often conduct surface-level assessments that focus on commercial capability but overlook ownership structures, reputation, and potential conflicts of interest. Inadequate due diligence allows corrupt actors to infiltrate supply chains and service networks, using their position to facilitate illicit payments or influence authorities.

Documentary controls also commonly fail. Corrupt actors rely on vague contracts, incomplete records, or unverified invoices to conceal illicit activity. When organizations do not enforce strict standards for documentation, individuals can justify questionable transactions without fear of challenge. Poor record-keeping not only hinders detection but also compromises an institution's ability to investigate allegations effectively.

Oversight mechanisms may also be underdeveloped. Audit functions that lack independence, resources, or technical expertise may miss clear indicators of corruption. When internal audit focuses on procedural compliance rather than substantive review of transactions, it overlooks opportunities to identify concealed bribery schemes.

Cultural and Leadership Failures

Controls can only function effectively when supported by a strong organizational culture. Corruption often emerges in environments where leadership tolerates unethical behavior, prioritizes results over integrity, or disregards compliance obligations. When employees observe that improper conduct is ignored or rewarded, they may believe that bribery is an acceptable means of achieving business objectives.

A culture of fear or retaliation also represents a significant control failure. Employees who fear repercussions are unlikely to report concerns, even when they observe clear signs of misconduct. Without safe reporting channels and visible support from leadership, red flags remain unaddressed.

Another cultural issue arises when organizations normalize informal practices. When employees rely on personal networks, verbal agreements, or undocumented decisions, transparency is reduced. These practices may evolve into environments where bribery is considered routine.

Leadership failures also include assigning compliance responsibilities without adequate authority or resources. Compliance functions must have independence and the ability to challenge decisions at all levels. When compliance is seen as an administrative formality, rather than a core safeguard, corruption risk increases substantially.

Control Gaps in Complex or Decentralized Operations

Large or decentralized organizations face unique risks because responsibilities are dispersed across multiple locations, teams, or business units. In such environments, inconsistent application of policies creates opportunities for corrupt actors to exploit weaknesses.

Subsidiaries operating in high-risk jurisdictions may adopt practices inconsistent with headquarters' expectations. Local teams may face pressure from authorities or competitors who rely on corrupt methods, and without strong oversight, they may rationalize similar behavior.

Another challenge arises from rapid expansion, particularly in emerging markets. Organizations that scale quickly may outpace their control frameworks, creating gaps in due diligence, monitoring, and policy enforcement. These gaps can persist for years if not identified early.

Joint ventures also pose significant risk, especially when partners have different standards of governance or operate under informal norms. Without clear contractual rights to monitor operations, the organization may lack visibility into bribery risks within the joint venture.

Failures in Monitoring and Response

Even when red flags are visible, corruption continues when institutions fail to respond appropriately. Monitoring systems may generate alerts, but if investigators lack expertise or resources, underlying issues may remain undetected. A failure to investigate anomalies—such as repeated use of specific suppliers, unusual payment patterns, or unexplained delays in project timelines—allows corrupt practices to continue unchecked.

Another failure occurs when organizations identify misconduct but take limited action due to fear of reputational damage, political pressure, or financial impact. When consequences are inconsistent, employees may perceive that corruption is tolerated or selectively enforced. This perception undermines the credibility of control frameworks.

REGULATORY EXPECTATIONS AND ENFORCEMENT TRENDS

The global landscape for anti-bribery and anti-corruption enforcement has evolved significantly over the past two decades. Regulators across jurisdictions have intensified scrutiny, expanded legal frameworks, and increased expectations for how organizations should prevent, detect, and respond to corruption risks. These developments reflect growing recognition that bribery undermines economic stability, distorts competition, weakens public trust, and fuels broader criminal activity. Understanding regulatory expectations and enforcement trends is essential for institutions seeking to maintain compliance and protect themselves from legal, financial, and reputational consequences.

Expanding Legal Frameworks and Global Reach

Anti-corruption laws have broadened in scope and extraterritorial reach. The U.S. Foreign Corrupt Practices Act (FCPA), the U.K. Bribery Act, and similar legislation in France, Brazil, Canada, and other jurisdictions have established comprehensive standards for corporate behavior. Many of these laws apply not only to domestic conduct but also to actions involving foreign officials or international business activities. As a result, organizations operating across borders face overlapping legal requirements and increased exposure.

A significant shift in recent years has been the focus on corporate responsibility for the actions of third parties. Regulations increasingly recognize that intermediaries play a central role in corruption schemes. Consequently, companies can be held liable for bribes paid by agents, distributors, or consultants acting on their behalf, even when senior management is not directly involved. This shift has elevated the importance of robust due diligence, monitoring, and oversight of third-party relationships.

Another development is the expansion of laws targeting private-sector bribery. While early anti-corruption efforts concentrated on public officials, modern regulations address corruption within commercial relationships. This includes bribery between private companies, kickbacks in procurement, and improper influence in supply chains. Organizations must therefore implement controls that address both public-sector and private-sector risks.

Increasing Regulatory Expectations for Compliance Programs

Regulators now expect organizations to maintain comprehensive and effective anti-corruption compliance programs. These programs are evaluated based on their design, implementation, and effectiveness, not merely their existence. A well-structured compliance program should reflect the organization's risk profile, industry, geographic footprint, and operational complexity.

Tone from the top is a central expectation. Regulators look for evidence that senior leadership actively supports anti-corruption measures, communicates expectations clearly, and demonstrates commitment through actions rather than statements alone. Leadership engagement influences organizational culture and provides the foundation upon which compliance controls operate.

Risk assessments are another core expectation. Organizations must conduct regular, thorough assessments to identify areas of heightened corruption risk, such as high-value procurement, interactions with officials, or operations in high-risk jurisdictions. These assessments guide decisions about resource allocation, controls, and monitoring.

Training and communication are also key requirements. Employees and third parties must understand corruption risks, reporting procedures, and the consequences of misconduct. Training should be tailored to job functions, rather than delivered as generic content, and should be updated as risks evolve.

Regulators also expect organizations to maintain effective reporting and investigation procedures. Whistleblower channels must be accessible, confidential, and free from retaliation. Investigations must be timely, independent, and well-documented, demonstrating the organization's willingness to respond to concerns seriously.

Greater Use of Data Analytics in Regulatory Oversight

Regulatory bodies increasingly rely on data analytics to identify patterns indicative of corruption. This includes analysis of procurement activity, transactional flows, third-party payments, and market anomalies. Regulators compare data across industries and regions to identify outliers that may indicate systemic issues.

This trend has raised expectations for organizations to use similar analytical tools within their compliance programs. Companies that fail to use available technology may be perceived as lacking adequate detection capabilities. Regulators have expressed that organizations should use tools proportionate to their size and risk, meaning that larger institutions with complex operations are expected to adopt more sophisticated monitoring methods.

Analytics also contributes to enforcement strategy. Authorities can identify clusters of suspicious activity, link multiple cases to broader corruption networks, and build a more comprehensive understanding of how bribery is facilitated. This enhances the likelihood of detection and reduces the ability of offenders to hide within fragmented systems.

Focus on Corporate Accountability and Individual Liability

Enforcement trends reflect a growing emphasis on holding both corporations and individuals accountable. While corporate penalties remain significant, regulators increasingly pursue individual executives, managers, and employees who authorize or turn a blind eye to corruption. This approach is intended to deter misconduct by demonstrating that personal consequences accompany institutional failures.

Penalties for corporations continue to rise, and settlements often include requirements for enhanced compliance controls, external monitoring, or detailed reporting obligations. Deferred prosecution agreements and non-prosecution agreements are common mechanisms used to enforce accountability while allowing organizations to continue operations under supervision.

For individuals, consequences may include fines, imprisonment, and disqualification from professional roles. Authorities often focus on individuals who had decision-making authority or who deliberately circumvented controls. This focus reinforces the expectation that corporate leaders must actively oversee compliance efforts and ensure that risk areas are appropriately managed.

Cross-Border Collaboration and Joint Investigations

Modern bribery investigations frequently involve multiple jurisdictions, reflecting the global nature of commerce. Regulatory bodies increasingly collaborate across borders, sharing information, coordinating investigative efforts, and aligning enforcement strategies. This trend has led to coordinated settlements involving multiple agencies, with penalties allocated among jurisdictions.

Collaboration is facilitated by international bodies such as the OECD Working Group on Bribery, the International Anti-Corruption Coordination Centre, and regional anti-corruption taskforces. These groups promote best practices, harmonize standards, and enable rapid information exchange.

Cross-border cooperation increases enforcement risk for global organizations. Misconduct that might previously have remained hidden within local operations can now trigger investigations in multiple jurisdictions simultaneously. Companies must ensure consistent compliance standards across all subsidiaries and maintain documentation demonstrating adherence to global expectations.

Emphasis on Beneficial Ownership Transparency

Regulators have increasingly focused on beneficial ownership transparency as a tool to combat corruption. Shell companies, opaque structures, and layered transactions often conceal the true recipients of bribe payments. Many jurisdictions have introduced beneficial ownership registries or strengthened requirements for corporate transparency.

Organizations are expected to understand the ownership structures of their business partners, suppliers, and third parties. Failure to identify beneficial owners is viewed as a significant control weakness. Transparency measures also assist regulators in tracing the flow of illicit funds, identifying undisclosed conflicts of interest, and uncovering networks that facilitate corruption.

Heightened Scrutiny of High-Risk Sectors

Enforcement continues to concentrate on sectors where corruption risk is greatest—public procurement, extractive industries, healthcare, construction, telecommunications, and defense. These sectors involve large contracts, significant regulatory involvement, and complex supply chains, all of which increase the likelihood of improper influence.

Regulators also monitor emerging industries where governance frameworks are still developing, such as renewable energy, digital infrastructure, and certain technology markets. In these sectors, the absence of mature controls can enable corruption to occur more easily.

Organizations operating in high-risk sectors must demonstrate that they apply enhanced due diligence, monitoring, and oversight. Generic compliance programs are insufficient; controls must be tailored to sector-specific risks.

Expectations for Remediation and Continuous Improvement

Regulators expect organizations to respond to identified corruption issues with comprehensive remediation efforts. This includes addressing control weaknesses, disciplining involved individuals, enhancing policies, and strengthening monitoring systems. Remediation must be well-documented and proportional to the severity of the misconduct.

Continuous improvement is a core expectation. Compliance programs should evolve in response to new risks, regulatory guidance, and lessons learned from internal and external incidents. Static programs are viewed as inadequate, especially in rapidly changing environments.

Regulators also emphasize the importance of sustainable compliance. Programs must be integrated into business operations rather than treated as separate or symbolic. This requires clear accountability, appropriate resourcing, and regular evaluation of program effectiveness.

Future Enforcement Trends

Enforcement trends indicate increasing use of technology, greater demand for organizational transparency, and more coordinated global action. Regulators are expanding investigative capabilities, improving access to cross-border financial data, and focusing on complex networks rather than isolated actors.

Future enforcement is likely to emphasize the role of intermediaries, the misuse of digital payment channels, and corruption linked to supply chain vulnerabilities. Organizations will be expected to demonstrate not only compliance with legal requirements but also proactive management of emerging risks.

CHAPTER 7

TERRORIST FINANCING

IDEOLOGICAL VS. PROFIT-DRIVEN CRIME

TERRORIST FINANCING differs fundamentally from most other forms of financial crime because its primary purpose is not personal enrichment but the advancement of political, religious, or ideological objectives. While many financial crimes seek private gain, terrorism relies on financing to support activities intended to intimidate, coerce, or destabilize society. Understanding the distinction between ideological motives and profit-driven motives is central to effective investigation. It shapes how networks operate, how funds are generated and moved, and how financial institutions identify risks within transactional flows.

The Nature of Ideological Motivation

Ideological crime is driven by commitment to a cause rather than personal benefit. Terrorist organizations seek resources to sustain their operations, recruit members, disseminate propaganda, establish logistical networks, and execute violent acts. Because their motivation is ideological, not financial, they may use diverse funding methods, including legitimate activities, informal transfers, and illicit fundraising. Profit is merely a means to support operations; the ultimate goal is the advancement of an ideological vision.

This distinction has important implications for investigators. Individuals involved in ideological crime may not display the typical behavioral indicators associated with financial crimes. They may live modestly, avoid conspicuous consumption, and reinvest funds into the organization's mission rather than personal gain. Ideologically motivated individuals often demonstrate a level of discipline that enables them to operate under financial constraints, relying on small donations, community support, or volunteer contributions.

Ideological networks often emphasize trust, shared beliefs, and loyalty. These relationships reduce the need for formal contracts or financial incentives. Funds may move through family networks, long-standing social ties, or informal community channels, making detection more difficult. In some contexts, ideology provides a higher level of internal cohesion than monetary compensation could achieve, enabling operations to continue even under significant financial pressure.

Profit as a Tool for Ideological Crime

Although ideological crime is not motivated by profit, terrorist groups frequently engage in profit-generating activities to fund their operations. This blend of ideology and profit complicates traditional financial crime analysis. Terrorist organizations may rely on smuggling, extortion, trafficking, counterfeiting, or other forms of organized crime to generate income. These activities have profit motives, but the proceeds do not enrich the perpetrators personally; instead, they sustain the organization's ideological mission.

The overlap between terrorism and organized crime creates complex investigative challenges. Criminal networks may collaborate with terrorist entities when profit interests align, despite differing motivations. For example, organized crime groups may smuggle goods or provide logistical support in exchange for payment, even if they do not share the terrorist group's ideology. Conversely, terrorist organizations may adopt criminal methods because they offer reliable revenue streams.

In some regions, ideological groups evolve into hybrid organizations that combine political objectives with economic activities. They may control territory, extract taxes, or operate black-market enterprises. While the ideological motivation remains present, the group's financial operations increasingly resemble those of organized crime. Investigators must therefore avoid oversimplifying motives and instead examine how ideology and profit converge to sustain illicit networks.

Recruitment and Financial Commitment

Ideological groups rely on a mix of committed members and peripheral supporters. Core members may provide voluntary contributions, pool resources, or sacrifice personal income for the cause. These contributions are often modest but consistent, enabling long-term operational sustainability. Unlike profit-driven criminals, ideological supporters may have no expectation of material return. Their involvement may stem from belief in the cause, social pressure, or sense of duty.

Peripheral supporters may provide financial assistance without direct operational involvement. They may donate under the impression that they are supporting charitable or humanitarian objectives, unaware that their funds are diverted to extremist activities. Ideological groups frequently exploit emotional appeals, religious narratives, or political grievances to generate support. This makes fundraising difficult to monitor, as it may blend seamlessly with legitimate charitable giving.

Recruitment also influences the financial profile of ideological crime. Individuals motivated by belief may be willing to accept lower compensation for high-risk tasks, reducing the organization's need for large financial resources. This contrasts with profit-driven criminals, who typically demand payment commensurate with risk. Ideological commitment therefore allows terrorist groups to operate with fewer financial incentives and lower operational costs.

Financial Behavior of Ideologically Motivated Actors

The financial behavior of ideologically driven actors differs from that of profit-focused criminals in several key ways. First, ideological actors often prioritize operational secrecy over financial efficiency. They may use methods that are slower or more cumbersome, such as informal value transfer systems, hand-to-hand cash exchanges, or use of intermediaries within trusted communities. These methods reduce exposure to formal monitoring systems, even if they are less efficient than electronic transfers.

Second, ideological groups may maintain decentralized financial structures. Funds may be held by multiple individuals rather than centralized in a single account. Decentralization reduces vulnerability to asset freezes or law enforcement seizures. It also reflects the operational structure of many terrorist organizations, which rely on small, independent cells capable of functioning even when other cells are disrupted.

Third, ideological networks often accept small contributions rather than relying exclusively on large transactions. This creates a fragmented financial footprint that can be difficult to detect using traditional monitoring systems designed to identify large or unusual transactions. The accumulation of low-value contributions may generate enough resources to support operations while avoiding regulatory thresholds that trigger scrutiny.

Fourth, ideological actors may engage in fundraising activities that appear legitimate. They may operate businesses, collect donations, or participate in community events. Without clear evidence of wrongdoing, these activities may blend with legitimate economic activity. Investigators must therefore assess context, relationships, and underlying intent rather than relying solely on transactional anomalies.

Distinguishing Ideological Ops from Profit-Driven Crime

Distinguishing ideological crime from profit-driven crime requires understanding the underlying purpose of financial flows. While both may involve illicit methods, the intent shapes how funds are used, the behavior of participants, and the structure of the network.

Profit-driven criminals prioritize personal or organizational financial gain. Transactions often exhibit patterns associated with enrichment - luxury purchases, asset accumulation, or reinvestment into criminal enterprises. Offenders may use sophisticated laundering techniques to conceal proceeds while enjoying financial benefit.

In contrast, ideological groups direct resources toward operational objectives. Funds support recruitment, training, travel, logistics, weapons procurement, or propaganda. Personal gain is minimized unless it serves organizational needs. Ideologically motivated individuals may even avoid spending patterns that would attract attention, choosing modest lifestyles that reduce exposure and demonstrate commitment to the cause.

The structure of networks also differs. Profit-driven groups may operate with hierarchical or market-based structures, emphasizing efficiency and division of labor. Ideological organizations often combine hierarchy with decentralized cells, enabling resilience and operational secrecy. This affects financial flows, which may move through informal channels aligned with trust networks rather than through coordinated financial systems.

Overlap and Convergence

Despite clear distinctions, ideological and profit-driven crime often overlap. Terrorist groups may adopt criminal activities to raise funds, while organized crime groups may collaborate with ideological entities when mutually beneficial. In some cases, ideological groups evolve into profit-seeking enterprises, losing ideological focus over time as economic activities dominate.

Conversely, profit-driven criminals may adopt ideological narratives to justify activities, attract support, or exploit community grievances. This creates a hybrid environment where motivations are intertwined and where simplistic categorization fails to capture operational reality.

Investigators must therefore evaluate each case based on evidence rather than assumptions. Motivation should be inferred from behavior, structure, financial patterns, and operational objectives. Misinterpreting motivation can lead to ineffective response strategies, inappropriate risk assessments, or missed opportunities to identify broader networks.

Implications for Detection and Prevention

Recognizing the distinction between ideological and profit-driven crime enhances detection efforts. Ideological activity may be signaled by frequent low-value transactions, community-based fundraising, use of informal transfer systems, or engagement with high-risk jurisdictions. Profit-driven crime may exhibit patterns associated with laundering, asset accumulation, or reinvestment.

Institutions must design monitoring frameworks that account for both categories. Traditional anti-money laundering systems often focus on detecting large, unusual, or unexplained financial flows. These models may overlook distributed, low-value networks typical of ideological financing. Enhanced behavioral analysis, contextual reviews, and integration of external intelligence can improve detection.

LOW-VALUE FUNDING AND DISTRIBUTED NETWORKS

Terrorist organizations increasingly rely on low-value funding and distributed financial networks to sustain their operations. These methods are designed to minimize detection, reduce dependence on large transactions, and ensure operational resilience even when significant financial channels are disrupted. Unlike traditional money laundering schemes that often involve substantial sums, terrorist financing frequently operates through small, fragmented contributions that accumulate over time. This approach reflects the adaptability of terrorist groups and poses distinct challenges for financial institutions and investigators. Understanding the mechanics, motivations, and operational implications of low-value and distributed funding provides critical insight into how these networks evade detection.

The Strategic Logic Behind Low-Value Funding

Many terrorist organizations intentionally rely on low-value contributions because small transactions are unlikely to trigger alerts within formal monitoring systems. Most financial institutions design detection models to identify unusual or high-value activity, leaving routine, low-level transactions largely unexamined unless they exhibit other suspicious characteristics. Terrorist groups exploit this by operating beneath thresholds that would otherwise prompt closer scrutiny.

Low-value funding serves an additional strategic purpose. It reduces reliance on wealthy backers or centralized revenue streams, making the organization less vulnerable to targeted financial disruption. If authorities shut down one supporter or channel, the group can still sustain operations through other small contributors. This resilience is crucial for groups operating under intense counterterrorism pressure.

Using small contributions also aligns with ideological narratives. Many groups emphasize collective involvement, encouraging supporters to contribute modest amounts rather than relying on a few donors. This approach diffuses responsibility, strengthens communal identity, and broadens the network of individuals connected - willingly or unknowingly - to the organization's activities.

Fragmented and Decentralized Funding Streams

Distributed networks rely on multiple independent nodes that contribute funds, move resources, or facilitate transactions. These nodes may have no direct connection to one another and may not understand their role within a broader structure. Decentralization increases resilience by ensuring that disruption of one element does not destabilize the entire network.

In many cases, supporters contribute through informal community channels such as religious groups, social clubs, or cultural associations. These channels provide opportunities for fundraising without attracting suspicion, particularly when contributions are framed as charity or humanitarian assistance. Funds collected in this way may be pooled gradually and transferred through methods designed to obscure their ultimate destination.

Decentralized networks also use family and social ties to move funds. Relatives living abroad may send remittances that appear legitimate but are intended to support extremist activities. These funds often move through informal value transfer systems, such as hawala or similar mechanisms, which operate outside traditional banking frameworks. The absence of formal documentation or standardized oversight makes these channels difficult for investigators to trace.

Another characteristic of distributed networks is the use of multiple, low-level facilitators who execute isolated tasks - such as purchasing equipment, renting property, transporting cash, or collecting donations. These individuals may be peripheral supporters whose involvement is limited to a single action. Their small, compartmentalized roles reduce the likelihood of detection and complicate efforts to identify a central organizer.

Role of Informal Value Transfer Systems

Informal value transfer systems (IVTS) are frequently used to support low-value, distributed financing. These systems rely on trusted brokers who transfer value through personal networks rather than through formal bank accounts. They are particularly prevalent in regions where banking infrastructure is limited or where cultural practices emphasize informal financial arrangements.

Terrorist groups use IVTS because transactions leave minimal digital footprints. Funds may be transferred across borders without passing through formal financial channels, and settlement may occur through trade, cash exchanges, or balancing transactions within the IVTS network. The decentralized nature of these systems aligns naturally with low-value contributions and distributed networks.

While IVTS mechanisms are widely used for legitimate purposes, including remittances and community support, their anonymity and informality can be exploited. Investigators face difficulty distinguishing between lawful use and illicit activity, especially when transaction amounts fall within normal ranges.

The challenge increases when transfers occur across jurisdictions with limited regulatory oversight.

Use of Legitimate Business Activity

Low-value and distributed funding often intersect with legitimate businesses. Small retail shops, informal traders, transportation services, and community organizations may be used to collect or move funds. These businesses can integrate small contributions into daily cash flows, making the proceeds difficult to isolate.

Some businesses are established with the explicit intent of facilitating terrorist financing. Others may be legitimate enterprises unknowingly exploited by individuals sympathetic to extremist causes. Because the businesses appear to operate normally and handle a large volume of small transactions, detecting illicit financial flows requires careful analysis of patterns, relationships, and context rather than reliance on transaction size alone.

In some cases, businesses are used as fronts to launder funds generated through criminal activities such as smuggling, theft, or fraud. The proceeds are integrated gradually into legitimate revenues through small, routine deposits. When funds are transferred out of the business, the amounts may be small enough to avoid triggering alerts.

Online Platforms and Micro-Financing Models

Digital platforms have expanded opportunities for low-value terrorist financing. Social media, crowdfunding sites, online payment services, and digital wallets enable individuals to contribute small amounts quickly and anonymously. Terrorist organizations may solicit support using coded messages, disguised appeals, or fraudulent charitable campaigns.

The digital environment supports distributed networks by connecting supporters across geographic boundaries. Individuals who would otherwise lack direct access to extremist groups can contribute small sums online, often without recognizing the full implications of their actions. This creates a diffuse financial footprint that spans multiple jurisdictions and payment platforms.

Cryptocurrencies also play a role in low-value financing. While not necessarily used for large-scale transactions, cryptocurrencies offer opportunities for small, anonymous transfers that bypass traditional banking systems. Terrorist groups may post digital wallet addresses through encrypted channels or public platforms, encouraging supporters to send micro-donations.

Digital wallets, prepaid cards, and mobile payment systems further complicate detection. They allow rapid movement of small amounts, sometimes across borders, with minimal verification. When funds are withdrawn or spent, they may be used to purchase goods or services that support operational needs, such as communication tools, travel tickets, or supplies.

Operational Efficiency of Small Contributions

Despite the small size of individual transactions, low-value funding can effectively support terrorist activity. Many operations require limited financial resources, particularly those involving lone actors or small cells. For example, travel expenses, basic equipment, communication tools, and small-scale weapons can be acquired with modest funds. Even attacks with significant impact may cost relatively little compared to the effort required to detect and prevent them.

Low-value funding also supports operational security. Small transactions are less likely to attract attention, and purchasing everyday items rarely raises suspicion. Terrorist groups intentionally design operations around accessible resources, reducing reliance on large financial inflows that might expose them to monitoring.

Distributed networks enhance efficiency by spreading tasks across many individuals. Each participant handles a small component of the process, such as collecting donations, moving funds, or purchasing items. This division of labor minimizes risk to the organization and complicates investigative efforts, as no single participant has a complete understanding of the operation.

Challenges for Detection and Disruption

Low-value and distributed funding networks pose significant challenges for traditional detection systems. Monitoring frameworks designed to identify large or unusual transactions may overlook routine, small-value movements. Analysts must therefore rely on behavioral indicators, contextual analysis, and intelligence from non-financial sources.

Detection becomes even more difficult when transactions occur outside formal banking systems. Cash-based activity, informal transfers, and peer-to-peer exchanges leave limited records. Even when suspicious patterns are identified, connecting individual transactions to broader networks requires substantial investigative effort and collaboration across jurisdictions.

Disrupting distributed networks also requires a different approach than dismantling hierarchical criminal organizations. Instead of targeting central leaders or large financial channels, authorities must identify multiple nodes and understand how they interact. This requires intelligence sharing, analysis of social networks, and long-term monitoring of community dynamics.

Another challenge lies in balancing security measures with protection of legitimate activity. Many low-value transfers involve migrants, small businesses, or community groups with no link to terrorism. Overly aggressive enforcement could hinder legitimate financial inclusion and erode trust between communities and authorities.

Implications for Financial Institutions and Policy Makers

Financial institutions must adapt their monitoring frameworks to identify risks associated with low-value and distributed financing. This involves shifting from a primarily quantitative approach to one that incorporates behavioral, geographic, and relational indicators. Institutions should consider patterns such as frequent small transfers to high-risk jurisdictions, use of multiple senders or recipients within short periods, or unusual activity involving accounts linked to informal businesses.

Policymakers must also recognize the importance of regulating informal value transfer systems while preserving their legitimate functions. Effective regulation requires outreach, community cooperation, and capacity-building rather than heavy-handed enforcement alone.

MISUSE OF CHARITIES AND NON-PROFITS

Charities and non-profit organizations occupy a unique position in society. They provide essential humanitarian services, deliver community support, respond to crises, and operate in regions where government capacity is limited. Their work often involves moving funds rapidly across borders, providing assistance to vulnerable populations, and managing resources in challenging environments. These characteristics make them indispensable - but they also create opportunities for exploitation by terrorist organizations seeking to raise, move, or disguise financing.

Understanding how charities and non-profits can be misused, the vulnerabilities inherent in their operations, and the consequences of such misuse is crucial for effective prevention and oversight.

Why Charities Attract Misuse

Charities and non-profits operate with high levels of public trust. Donors often assume that contributions are being used for legitimate purposes, and regulatory authorities may provide these organizations with simplified reporting requirements or exemptions from certain financial controls. Terrorist groups exploit these advantages because they allow funds to move with less scrutiny than in commercial settings.

In many countries, charities enjoy tax-exempt status, which reduces the visibility of financial flows and may limit the depth of financial review. Donations, grants, and relief funds can be collected from broad sources, including individuals, corporations, and international partners. Because these contributions often come in small amounts from diverse donors, they can resemble ordinary, legitimate activity even when some of the funds are diverted for illicit purposes.

Another reason charities are vulnerable is their presence in high-risk regions. Humanitarian organizations frequently operate in areas affected by conflict, instability, or poverty - precisely the environments where terrorist groups are active. Providing aid in these regions often requires negotiating access with local power brokers, navigating unpredictable security conditions, and working with informal logistics networks. Terrorist groups may exploit these conditions by imposing taxation, demanding "fees" for access, infiltrating local staff, or diverting supplies.

Methods of Misuse

Terrorist groups misuse charities and non-profits in several distinct ways, each reflecting the flexibility of these organizations and the environments in which they operate.

One common method is the creation of sham charities. These entities may appear legitimate on paper, complete with mission statements, registration documents, and bank accounts, yet exist solely to raise funds for extremist activities. They may conduct minimal genuine charitable work to maintain an appearance of legitimacy while funneling the majority of donations to affiliated groups. In some cases, sham charities are established abroad to take advantage of weaker regulatory oversight.

In other cases, legitimate charities are infiltrated by individuals sympathetic to extremist causes. These insiders may redirect funds, manipulate procurement processes, or provide material assistance under the guise of humanitarian support. Because they operate within legitimate structures, their actions can be difficult to identify without thorough monitoring.

Diversion of aid is another method. Terrorist groups may intercept supplies intended for civilian beneficiaries, then redistribute them in ways that strengthen their influence. Food, medicine, building materials, and other resources can be seized, taxed, or used to support fighters. When aid is diverted, the organization may unknowingly contribute to the group's operational capacity or legitimacy within the local population.

Charities may also be used to move funds across borders. They often have permission to operate in multiple jurisdictions, maintain relationships with international partners, and use fund transfer channels designed to support rapid response. Terrorist financiers exploit these channels to transfer money under the cover of humanitarian activity. Transfers may be described as project funding or emergency relief, masking their true purpose.

Another misuse involves the employment of charity networks for recruitment and propaganda. Organizations providing genuine services may inadvertently create opportunities for extremist groups to target vulnerable populations. While this does not necessarily involve financial misuse, it strengthens the organization's broader support network and creates an environment conducive to future fundraising.

Operational Vulnerabilities in Non-Profit Structures

Non-profit organizations often operate with lean administrative budgets, prioritizing program delivery over internal controls. While this is understandable from a mission perspective, it can create significant vulnerabilities. Weak financial oversight, limited segregation of duties, and reliance on volunteers may allow individuals with bad intentions to manipulate processes.

Many non-profits face resource constraints that limit their ability to conduct due diligence on partners, vendors, or staff. In high-risk areas, they may depend on local intermediaries to distribute aid, hire personnel, or coordinate logistics. These intermediaries may have undisclosed ties to extremist groups, making it difficult to ensure that funds and supplies reach intended beneficiaries.

Cash-based operations also present risks. In areas where banking infrastructure is limited, charities may rely on cash payments for salaries, supplies, and transport. Cash transactions reduce traceability and are susceptible to theft, diversion, and extortion. Terrorist groups may demand cash payments in exchange for allowing aid convoys to operate, creating a direct financial pathway between the charity and the extremist organization.

Another vulnerability arises from limited visibility into sub-grantee activity. Many international non-profits work through local partner organizations to implement programs. When oversight is inadequate, sub-grantees may divert funds or collaborate with extremist actors without the knowledge of the parent organization.

Regulatory Challenges

Regulating charities is inherently challenging. Authorities must balance the need for oversight with the importance of supporting legitimate humanitarian work. Excessive regulation can hinder the ability of charities to deliver aid quickly and effectively, while insufficient regulation leaves gaps that terrorists can exploit.

Regulators often face difficulty distinguishing between legitimate humanitarian operations and intentional misuse. Many non-profits operate in volatile environments where documentation is minimal, communication is unreliable, and rapid adaptation is necessary. This complexity makes traditional compliance models difficult to apply.

International coordination is another challenge. Charities may operate across multiple jurisdictions with varying regulatory standards. A non-profit registered in one country may send funds to partners in another country with weaker controls. Without consistent global standards, it is difficult to ensure that funds are properly monitored throughout their movement.

In some regions, governments may lack the capacity or political will to regulate charities effectively. Weak oversight, corruption, or conflict may allow extremist groups to operate openly within the charitable sector. This creates opportunities for both deliberate misuse and unintentional diversion.

Consequences of Misuse

The misuse of charities and non-profits has serious implications for humanitarian organizations, donors, governments, and the populations they serve. Financial diversion undermines the mission of legitimate charities by reducing resources available for intended beneficiaries. In severe cases, it can lead to loss of life when critical supplies do not reach those in need.

When charities are implicated in terrorist financing - whether intentionally or inadvertently - their reputations suffer. Donors may withdraw support, regulatory scrutiny may increase, and operational permissions may be revoked. Reputational damage can be long-lasting and may affect the broader non-profit sector by eroding public trust.

Misuse also has strategic consequences. When resources intended for humanitarian purposes are co-opted by terrorist groups, these groups strengthen their capacity to conduct operations, build legitimacy, or expand influence. This undermines stability, prolongs conflict, and complicates peacebuilding efforts.

Strengthening Integrity in the Charitable Sector

Preventing misuse requires strong governance, rigorous oversight, and collaboration across the non-profit, regulatory, and financial sectors. Charities must implement controls proportionate to their risk exposure. This includes due diligence on partners, segregation of financial duties, clear audit trails, and transparent reporting. Organizations operating in high-risk environments should adopt enhanced measures such as independent monitoring, secure fund transfer mechanisms, and background checks on staff and intermediaries.

Financial institutions play a critical role by identifying suspicious transactions involving non-profit accounts. Banks must understand the operating profiles of their non-profit clients, recognize legitimate patterns of activity, and identify anomalies that may indicate misuse.

DETECTION COMPLEXITIES AND EMERGING RISKS

Detecting terrorist financing is significantly more challenging than identifying many other forms of financial crime. Unlike money laundering or fraud, which often display patterns associated with personal gain or large-scale transactions, terrorist financing may involve modest sums, fragmented networks, informal channels, and shifting operational methods. These characteristics reduce the visibility of financial flows and force investigators to rely on contextual interpretation rather than clear transactional indicators. At the same time, new technologies, evolving organizational structures, and geopolitical changes continue to introduce emerging risks. Understanding the complexities and anticipating future challenges is essential for effective detection and prevention.

The Challenge of Identifying Purpose

One of the core complexities in detecting terrorist financing is that the financial activity itself often appears ordinary. Many transactions linked to terrorist financing are indistinguishable from legitimate behavior when viewed in isolation. A low-value transfer between family members, a donation to a charitable organization, or a cash withdrawal for local expenses may serve benign purposes or may support a terrorist operation. Financial institutions cannot rely solely on transaction size, frequency, or direction to identify risk. Context is essential, yet obtaining context requires information beyond what is typically available in transactional data.

Compounding this difficulty is the fact that many terrorist operations require minimal funding. A disrupted plot may reveal that the entire effort cost only a few hundred dollars. This means that large wire transfers, complex layering strategies, and expensive purchases - common indicators in money laundering - are not always present. Detecting terrorist financing requires attention to subtle behavioral patterns, regional risk factors, and intelligence-driven insights rather than reliance on traditional financial monitoring techniques.

Informal Transfer Mechanisms and Limited Transparency

Informal value transfer systems, cash couriers, and unregulated service providers greatly complicate detection. These channels operate outside formal banking frameworks, leaving little documentation for investigators. Transfers may be recorded in handwritten ledgers, communicated verbally, or settled through trade rather than monetary exchange. Such systems often rely on trusted brokers who maintain anonymity and limit access to internal records.

Cash couriers present another challenge. Carrying physical cash across borders or within conflict zones is difficult to detect unless authorities intercept the courier at the right moment. Cash is portable, untraceable, and widely accepted. Terrorist groups rely on cash for operational security, especially when working in remote areas or regions with unstable financial infrastructure.

Where banking access exists, terrorist financiers may use multiple accounts with low balances, frequent small deposits, or transfers through intermediaries. These patterns may not appear suspicious unless institutions have strong behavioral monitoring systems capable of identifying anomalies in customer activity.

Overlap with Legitimate Activity

Terrorist financing frequently intersects with legitimate economic and humanitarian activity. Community fundraising, charitable giving, remittances, and small business operations can all be used as cover. This overlap makes it difficult to determine whether a transaction supports legitimate needs or illicit activity.

For example, charitable organizations may move funds to conflict zones for genuine humanitarian purposes. These same regions may also host extremist groups. Distinguishing between legitimate aid and diversion is difficult even for authorities operating on the ground. Financial institutions must therefore make assessments based on limited information, relying on indirect indicators rather than definitive proof.

Similarly, remittances to family members in high-risk regions may reflect genuine support, but they may also provide a channel for transferring funds to extremists. Because remittances often follow predictable patterns related to migration, employment, and family support, anomalous activity may be subtle or absent altogether.

Decentralized Operational Structures

Modern terrorist organizations increasingly adopt decentralized structures that rely on small, autonomous cells or lone actors. These structures reduce the need for centralized financing and limit the number of financial transactions associated with operational planning. Lone actors may fund their activities using personal savings, salary income, or small contributions from peers. They may not require direct financial support from a larger organization, making detection nearly impossible without behavioral intelligence or reporting from community members.

Decentralization also leads to fragmented financial footprints. Instead of a single funding stream supporting multiple operations, each cell or individual may manage its own financial activities. This fragmentation further diminishes the possibility of identifying suspicious patterns within banking systems.

Technological Advancements and Digital Platforms

Technological innovation has introduced new risks that complicate detection. Digital payments, mobile money services, online fundraising platforms, and cryptocurrencies allow rapid, low-cost transfers across jurisdictions. These services often provide convenience and financial inclusion for legitimate users, but they also introduce vulnerabilities when exploited for illicit purposes.

Cryptocurrencies, for example, offer varying degrees of anonymity and can be transferred globally without reliance on traditional banking systems. Terrorist groups may publish wallet addresses online, solicit micro-donations, or use privacy-enhancing technologies to obscure transaction trails. While blockchain analysis tools exist, they require significant expertise and do not fully eliminate anonymity when users employ sophisticated methods.

Online crowdfunding platforms also present risks. Terrorist supporters may disguise fundraising campaigns as charitable initiatives, political activism, or community support efforts. Because contributions are often small and dispersed, platforms may overlook the true purpose. Identifying such misuse requires coordination among financial institutions, platform providers, and law enforcement agencies.

Mobile payment systems introduce additional complexity. In many regions, individuals rely on mobile wallets rather than bank accounts. These systems allow peer-to-peer transfers without the oversight typical of traditional banks. While they play an important role in economic development, their accessibility and informality provide opportunities for misuse.

Exploitation of Humanitarian Crises and Conflict Zones

Terrorist groups often operate within regions experiencing humanitarian crises, political instability, or natural disasters. These environments create opportunities to move funds under the guise of humanitarian assistance, because large volumes of aid and remittances naturally flow into these areas.

Humanitarian organizations may struggle to maintain rigorous oversight when operating in insecure environments. Terrorist groups may impose taxes, demand payments for safe passage, or infiltrate local distribution networks. These conditions make it difficult to distinguish between legitimate aid delivery and financial diversion.

Conflict zones also lack stable regulatory environments. Financial institutions may have limited presence, and oversight bodies may be ineffective or absent. This creates opportunities for terrorists to receive funds, procure supplies, or facilitate operations without interference from authorities.

Limited Information Sharing and Institutional Silos

Financial institutions often operate with incomplete information. Privacy laws, differing regulatory standards, and siloed data systems limit the sharing of intelligence across institutions and jurisdictions. Even when authorities possess relevant intelligence, dissemination may be restricted due to sensitivity or classification.

This fragmentation undermines detection efforts. A transaction that appears benign to one institution may form part of a broader pattern recognizable only when combined with data from multiple sources. Terrorist networks exploit these gaps by distributing transactions across institutions, jurisdictions, and channels.

Efforts to improve information sharing - such as public-private partnerships, financial intelligence units, and multiagency taskforces - have strengthened detection capabilities, but challenges remain. Global cooperation is essential, yet varies significantly across regions.

Emerging Risks in the Evolving Landscape

New and emerging risks continue to shape the future of terrorist financing detection. One growing concern is the use of online sales platforms. Terrorist supporters may sell merchandise, digital content, or services to generate small, distributed revenue streams. These activities blend into the global digital economy and may go unnoticed without detailed analysis.

Another emerging risk involves synthetic identities created using digital tools. Fraudulently obtained or fabricated identities can be used to open accounts, access digital wallets, or conduct transactions without revealing the true user. This complicates due diligence and undermines traditional customer verification processes.

Additionally, emerging technologies such as decentralized finance (DeFi) platforms, privacy-enhancing cryptocurrencies, and peer-to-peer networks introduce new opportunities for anonymous transfers. These tools enable transactions outside centralized exchanges, making oversight more difficult.

Artificial intelligence can also be misused. Extremist groups may use AI-generated content to enhance propaganda, recruit supporters, or solicit funds. While AI also offers opportunities for enhanced detection, the technology's misuse creates new vulnerabilities.

Finally, geopolitical shifts influence terrorist financing risks. Changes in control over territory, movement of displaced populations, and disruptions to international markets can alter patterns of financial activity. Terrorist groups adapt quickly to these shifts, seeking new funding sources and exploiting emerging vulnerabilities.

CHAPTER 8

SANCTIONS EVASION AND TRADE-BASED CRIME

SANCTIONS FRAMEWORKS AND EXPOSURE POINTS

SANCTIONS are among the most powerful tools available to governments seeking to influence the behavior of foreign states, organizations, and individuals without resorting to military action. They serve as instruments of national security, foreign policy, and international stability, designed to constrain access to financial systems, commercial markets, and global trade. Understanding how sanctions frameworks operate -and where exposure points arise - is essential for institutions responsible for compliance, risk management, and financial crime investigation. These frameworks are complex, dynamic, and far-reaching, creating both obligations and vulnerabilities for organizations across the world.

The Purpose and Structure of Sanctions

Sanctions aim to restrict the ability of specific entities or regimes to finance prohibited activities, procure sensitive goods, or participate in global commerce. Their targets may include countries, government agencies, political elites, terrorist organizations, criminal groups, corporations, and individuals involved in corruption, proliferation, or destabilizing conduct. Sanctions seek to change behavior by imposing economic and political pressure, limiting access to resources, and isolating targets from international systems.

Most sanctions frameworks include several categories of measures. These may include asset freezes, which prohibit dealing with funds or economic resources belonging to designated parties; trade restrictions, which limit the export or import of certain goods; activity prohibitions, which restrict financial services, investment, or specific types of transactions; and sectoral restrictions, which target key economic areas such as energy, defense, shipping, or finance. Each measure carries distinct compliance requirements and exposure points.

Sanctions frameworks vary by jurisdiction, but many share common principles. For example, the United States implements sanctions primarily through the Office of Foreign Assets Control (OFAC), while the European Union applies sanctions through regulations binding on member states. The United Kingdom, Canada, Australia, and other jurisdictions operate independent regimes, sometimes aligned and sometimes diverging from global partners. Multilateral organizations such as the United Nations also impose sanctions through Security Council resolutions, though the strength and enforcement of these measures vary depending on member-state participation.

Extraterritorial Reach and Global Impact

One of the defining characteristics of modern sanctions is their extraterritorial effect. Even organizations operating outside the jurisdiction of the sanctioning authority may face consequences for dealings that support sanctioned parties. U.S. sanctions are particularly influential in this regard because the U.S. dollar dominates global trade and financial flows. Any transaction cleared through the U.S. financial system may fall under OFAC oversight, exposing foreign institutions to penalties and restrictions.

This global reach means that organizations must consider not only local laws but also the implications of foreign sanctions when conducting international business. A company may face enforcement action even without direct dealings with sanctioned entities if it facilitates transactions that indirectly benefit them. The risk extends to subsidiaries, branches, intermediaries, and partners across supply chains.

The extraterritorial nature of sanctions creates significant exposure points for financial institutions, shipping companies, manufacturers, and commodity traders. Organizations must understand how their operations intersect with sanctioned jurisdictions, how their goods may be reexported or diverted, and how their financial channels may be exploited by actors seeking to evade restrictions.

Exposure Points in Financial Systems

Financial institutions are central to sanctions enforcement because they facilitate payment flows, letters of credit, trade finance, and international transfers. As a result, they face numerous exposure points.

One major exposure point involves customer onboarding and due diligence. Institutions must verify the identities of customers, beneficial owners, and controlling parties to ensure no sanctioned parties are involved. Shell companies, opaque ownership structures, and nominees create challenges, as sanctioned actors may hide behind intermediaries to access financial systems.

Another exposure arises through payment screening. Institutions must screen incoming and outgoing payments against sanctions lists, but evasion methods often include minor alterations to names, use of aliases, or use of intermediary banks in jurisdictions with weaker oversight. Screening systems may fail to detect misspellings, partial matches, or subtle variations intentionally designed to bypass controls.

Trade finance presents additional vulnerabilities. Letters of credit, bills of lading, invoices, and shipping documents may appear legitimate while concealing the involvement of sanctioned entities. Financial institutions may unknowingly finance shipments of prohibited goods, fund front companies controlled by sanctioned actors, or process payments for transactions routed through high-risk jurisdictions.

Correspondent banking relationships introduce further risks. When a bank provides services to a foreign institution, it may indirectly process transactions involving sanctioned parties. Weak oversight by the respondent bank can expose the correspondent bank to liability, even if it has no direct contact with the sanctioned entity.

Exposure Points in Trade and Supply Chains

Trade networks are a major avenue for sanctions evasion because they involve multiple parties, jurisdictions, and documentation layers. Companies engaged in manufacturing, shipping, logistics, and distribution face significant risks.

One exposure point is reexportation. Goods that are legally exported from one jurisdiction may be redirected to a sanctioned country through third-party intermediaries. Dual-use goods - items with both civilian and military applications - are particularly vulnerable because they may be disguised as routine commercial products. Companies must understand where their goods ultimately end up, even when dealing with distributors or resellers.

Another exposure point is the use of transshipment hubs. Goods may be shipped to intermediaries in regions with limited enforcement capacity, then repackaged and forwarded to sanctioned destinations. Changes in packaging, labeling, or documentation may obscure the original origin of the goods.

Supply chains often involve complex ownership structures. Sanctioned parties may control companies indirectly through minority ownership stakes, board influence, or informal arrangements. Without effective due diligence, organizations may unknowingly supply goods or services to entities linked to sanctioned actors.

Additionally, sanctioned jurisdictions may attempt to access technology, raw materials, or specialized equipment by using intermediaries that appear legitimate. Companies may receive inquiries from unfamiliar firms, often offering premium prices for goods that are difficult to obtain due to sanctions. Without thorough scrutiny, these transactions pose significant risk.

Exposure Points in Shipping and Transportation

The global shipping industry contains numerous mechanisms that can facilitate sanctions evasion. Ships can change ownership, registry, name, or flag with relative ease, complicating efforts to track sanctioned vessels or operators. Some shipping companies may intentionally obscure ownership through layered corporate structures.

Automatic Identification System (AIS) manipulation is a common exposure point. Ships may turn off AIS transponders to conceal movements, particularly when approaching sanctioned ports. Others may engage in "dark activity," during which no location data is transmitted, making it difficult for authorities to track routes.

Ship-to-ship transfers present another challenge. Vessels may transfer cargo at sea to disguise origin or destination. These transfers often occur in remote locations where monitoring is limited, allowing sanctioned oil, coal, or other commodities to enter global markets.

Shipping documentation also presents vulnerabilities. Bills of lading, certificates of origin, and cargo manifests may be falsified to hide connections to sanctioned jurisdictions. Unscrupulous freight forwarders or port agents may assist in altering documents to bypass controls.

Impact of Rapidly Changing Sanctions Lists

Sanctions regimes evolve quickly, often in response to geopolitical developments, military actions, or international negotiations. The rapid introduction or expansion of sanctions presents challenges for organizations that must adjust compliance systems quickly to avoid violations.

Frequent updates mean that organizations must maintain real-time screening tools, continuously monitor regulatory announcements, and ensure staff understand new restrictions. Failure to implement updates promptly can lead to inadvertent dealings with newly sanctioned parties.

Rapid changes also create operational strain. Contracts already in progress may suddenly become prohibited. Goods en route may need to be rerouted or returned. Financial institutions may freeze assets unexpectedly or halt transactions mid-process. These decisions carry legal and commercial consequences.

The Regulatory Expectation for Risk-Based Programs

Regulators increasingly expect organizations to adopt risk-based sanctions compliance programs. These programs must account for the organization's sector, geographic footprint, customer base, trade relationships, and exposure to high-risk jurisdictions.

A risk-based program relies on governance, due diligence, screening, escalation procedures, and continuous training. Organizations are expected to understand their exposure points and deploy controls accordingly. A one-size-fits-all approach is no longer acceptable; compliance must reflect actual operational risks.

This expectation extends beyond financial institutions. Manufacturers, insurers, shipping companies, logistics providers, and technology firms all face sanctions-related obligations. Their risk-based programs must incorporate supply chain monitoring, vendor assessments, and controls tailored to their activities.

Broader Implications for Global Commerce

Sanctions affect not only the targeted parties but also the global commercial landscape. Companies must weigh commercial opportunities against legal risks, reputational consequences, and the potential for unintentional violations. High-risk jurisdictions may become difficult to serve, and business relationships may require enhanced scrutiny.

For governments, sanctions offer a way to exert influence without direct conflict. But they also introduce diplomatic tensions, compliance burdens, and risk of retaliation by targeted states. As sanctions become more complex and interconnected, the potential for unintended consequences increases, affecting global markets, trade routes, and supply chains.

EVASION METHODS AND DUAL-USE GOODS

Sanctions evasion is an adaptive and highly sophisticated practice that exploits weaknesses in global trade, finance, and regulatory oversight. Actors seeking to bypass restrictions - including sanctioned states, criminal groups, and commercial intermediaries - use complex methods to disguise their identities, obscure trade flows, and obtain restricted goods. Their techniques evolve rapidly, often mirroring legitimate commercial practices to avoid attracting attention. Understanding evasion methods and the risks associated with dual-use goods is essential for identifying exposure points and implementing effective controls. These methods demonstrate how sanctions can be undermined through subtle manipulation of trade and financial systems, making vigilance essential for institutions involved in cross-border commerce.

The Use of Front Companies and Layered Ownership

One of the most common evasion methods involves the use of front companies, shell entities, and complex ownership structures. Sanctioned actors may create companies in jurisdictions with limited transparency, weak reporting requirements, or permissive incorporation laws. These companies appear legitimate on paper, maintaining registration documents, bank accounts, and commercial relationships. In reality, they exist primarily to conceal the involvement of sanctioned individuals or entities.

Layered ownership is a key tactic. Instead of directly controlling a company, sanctioned actors may hold minority stakes, influence decision-making through proxies, or exert informal control through family members or associates. The goal is to distance themselves from the entity and obscure beneficial ownership. Investigators may struggle to trace ownership through multiple jurisdictions, especially when corporate registries are incomplete or inaccessible.

Front companies are often used to procure restricted goods, secure financing, or facilitate trade transactions. They may purchase items for civilian use on the surface while transferring them to sanctioned destinations. The ability to operate through intermediaries allows sanctioned actors to maintain access to global markets even when direct transactions are prohibited.

Manipulation of Documentation and Payment Flows

Documentation abuse is a widespread evasion method. Shipping documents, invoices, certificates of origin, and customs declarations may be falsified or altered to conceal links to sanctioned jurisdictions. Common manipulations include mislabeling goods, underreporting value, altering destination information, or presenting intermediaries as end-users to mask the true recipient.

Payment flows may also be structured to avoid detection. Instead of directly sending funds from a sanctioned jurisdiction, actors may route payments through multiple banks in different countries. Intermediary banks may not recognize the connection to sanctions if the information provided is incomplete or intentionally misleading. In some cases, payment chains involve several account holders and correspondent banks, creating layers that obscure the source of funds.

Evasion networks may also use barter arrangements or trade credits to avoid formal financial channels altogether. When goods are exchanged directly, without monetary transfers, financial institutions receive no visibility into the transaction. These alternative arrangements make detection extremely difficult unless customs or trade authorities identify discrepancies.

Circumvention Through Transshipment and Reexportation

Transshipment and reexportation schemes exploit the complexity of global supply chains. Goods originating from one jurisdiction may be routed through multiple intermediaries before reaching their final destination. Sanctioned actors use this method to disguise the origin or end-user of goods, taking advantage of free-trade zones, strategic geographic hubs, and jurisdictions with weak enforcement.

In a typical scheme, goods may be legally exported to a country not subject to sanctions. Once there, they are repackaged, relabeled, or consolidated with other shipments, then reexported to a sanctioned destination. Documentation accompanying the shipment may present the intermediary country as the origin, obscuring the true supply chain.

Free-trade zones present particular risks because they often allow goods to move with reduced customs oversight. Repackaging and relabeling are common practices, and the volume of trade may overwhelm local authorities. Sanctioned actors understand these gaps and use them to disguise illicit shipments.

Reexportation fraud also occurs through diversion. Goods intended for one legitimate end-user may be diverted to a sanctioned party after leaving the exporter's control. This occurs when exporters fail to verify the final recipient or when intermediaries exploit weak due diligence.

Dual-Use Goods and Their Risks

Dual-use goods are items that have civilian applications but can also be used for military, surveillance, or weapons-related purposes. These goods include electronics, advanced machinery, chemical precursors, navigation systems, industrial equipment, and software with potential military use. Because these items serve legitimate commercial purposes, restricting them requires careful classification and oversight.

Sanctioned actors prioritize dual-use goods because they enable development of weapons programs, military capabilities, and surveillance technologies. Obtaining these items is essential for regimes seeking to advance ballistic missile programs, nuclear development, or military modernization. The subtlety of dual-use goods makes them difficult to control, as exporters may not always understand the potential risks associated with the products they sell.

Evasion schemes involving dual-use goods often use front companies to present civilian end-use certificates. These certificates claim that the goods will be used for benign purposes, such as scientific research or industrial production. Once exported, the goods may be diverted to military applications. Exporters who fail to verify the legitimacy of end-users may inadvertently support prohibited activities.

Another risk arises when goods are broken down into components and shipped separately through different channels. This fragmentation prevents authorities from recognizing the full purpose of the shipment. Components sent to one location may be assembled elsewhere to form restricted equipment.

Misuse of Technology and Digital Platforms

Digital platforms and technologies have expanded the methods available for evading sanctions. Online marketplaces may be used to procure restricted goods using aliases, forged identities, or proxy buyers. Payments may be made through digital wallets or cryptocurrencies, which provide anonymity and bypass traditional banking systems.

Cryptocurrency mixing services, decentralized finance platforms, and peer-to-peer exchanges allow sanctioned actors to convert digital assets, obscure transaction trails, and transfer value across borders with limited oversight. Although blockchain provides transparency in theory, sophisticated users employ privacy-enhancing tools to avoid detection.

Digital communication platforms also facilitate coordination among evasion networks. Encrypted messaging, secure file-sharing services, and anonymous forums allow sanctioned actors to share instructions, documentation templates, and procurement strategies.

Exploiting Gaps in International Coordination

Sanctions are only as strong as the enforcement mechanisms supporting them. Gaps in international coordination provide opportunities for evasion. Some jurisdictions may lack political will to enforce sanctions, especially if they benefit economically from continued trade. Others may lack regulatory capacity, facing resource constraints that limit inspection, monitoring, or investigation.

Differences in sanctions regimes further complicate enforcement. A country may impose restrictions on certain goods or entities while another country does not. Sanctioned actors exploit these discrepancies by routing trade through jurisdictions with weaker or less aligned controls.

Additionally, global supply chains often involve many intermediaries. Exporters, freight forwarders, customs brokers, financial institutions, insurers, and end-users all play roles in trade. When even one link in this chain fails to conduct adequate due diligence, sanctioned actors gain an opportunity to evade restrictions.

Why Evasion Methods Remain Effective

Sanctions evasion persists because it thrives in complexity. The global economy operates with high volumes of trade, intricate supply chains, and diverse regulatory environments. Many businesses lack visibility into the full life cycle of their goods once they are exported. Financial institutions often receive incomplete transaction information. Shipping companies may not know the true beneficial owner of a vessel.

Sanctioned actors exploit these blind spots with precision. They adapt quickly to enforcement actions, shifting methods, restructuring networks, and leveraging new technologies. Their agility contrasts with the slower pace of regulatory reform and compliance adaptation.

TRADE-BASED MONEY LAUNDERING (TBML) TECHNIQUES

Trade-based money laundering is one of the most sophisticated and resilient methods used by criminal networks, terrorist financiers, and sanctions evaders to disguise the origins of illicit funds. Unlike traditional laundering, which relies primarily on financial channels, TBML exploits the complexity of international trade. It manipulates legitimate commercial transactions - often across multiple jurisdictions, modes of transport, and documentation systems - to obscure illicit value transfers. Because global trade operates at enormous scale, identifying anomalies requires deep understanding of trade patterns, pricing norms, and supply chain behavior. TBML thrives when oversight is fragmented and when compliance frameworks focus narrowly on financial indicators rather than the broader commercial context.

The Foundations of TBML

TBML operates by embedding illicit value within trade transactions. Instead of moving funds directly, criminals manipulate the price, quantity, quality, or terms of goods and services. These manipulations create imbalances that allow value to be transferred between parties while appearing legitimate to outside observers.

The method is attractive because international trade involves countless transactions daily, much of which is not closely inspected. Customs authorities may inspect only a small percentage of cargo, and financial institutions often see only a portion of trade documentation. Criminal networks exploit these gaps by using shipping routes, free-trade zones, and intermediaries to mask illicit flows.

Because TBML involves real goods, or at least the appearance of them, it benefits from a veneer of legitimacy that can withstand scrutiny unless investigators examine price discrepancies, trade routes, and supply chain behavior.

Over- and Under-Invoicing of Goods

One of the most common TBML techniques is the manipulation of invoice values. Over-invoicing occurs when the exporter inflates the price of goods beyond their market value. The importer pays the inflated invoice, thereby transferring extra funds to the exporter under the guise of a legitimate purchase. This method is often used to move proceeds of crime or circumvent capital controls.

Under-invoicing accomplishes the opposite. The exporter lists a lower price on the invoice, enabling the importer to receive goods of higher value while paying significantly less. The difference in value is transferred outside formal channels, often through cash transactions, informal value transfer systems, or offshore accounts. Under-invoicing also allows sanctioned actors to acquire goods they otherwise could not afford or legally procure.

These schemes rely on the difficulty of determining accurate market value, especially for specialized goods, commodities with volatile prices, or items for which international pricing data is not readily available. Unless investigators compare invoice prices to reliable benchmarks, discrepancies may go unnoticed.

Misrepresentation of Quantity or Quality

TBML schemes frequently involve misrepresenting the quantity or quality of goods shipped. A shipment may be documented as containing more units than it actually does, allowing criminals to justify large payments to exporters. Alternatively, the shipment may include goods of higher value than those described in documentation, enabling the importer to receive greater value than reflected in the invoice.

Quality manipulation is particularly difficult to detect because evaluating quality requires technical expertise and physical inspection. Goods may be labeled as premium when they are low-grade or may be declared defective when they are not. These discrepancies serve as mechanisms for transferring value across borders under the cover of legitimate commerce.

Criminal networks may also ship empty containers or goods with no value. These fictitious shipments create documentation that supports payments for nonexistent trade. Because vast quantities of containers move globally each day, detecting such schemes is challenging unless authorities inspect specific shipments based on intelligence or anomalies.

Phantom Trade and Fictitious Documentation

Another prevalent TBML method involves phantom trade - transactions in which no goods move at all. Instead, criminals create a set of fabricated documents, including invoices, bills of lading, packing lists, letters of credit, and customs declarations. These documents support payments that appear legitimate but correspond to nonexistent shipments.

Fictitious documentation is difficult to detect when it mirrors authentic forms and follows expected trade patterns. Criminal networks may use advanced printing technology, fraudulent corporate seals, or compromised intermediaries to create documents indistinguishable from genuine versions. They may also exploit weaknesses in digital systems that allow alterations without detection.

Phantom trade can occur in both import and export scenarios. For example, an exporter may claim to have shipped goods to a foreign buyer and receive payment from a third party that seeks to launder funds. Alternatively, an importer may declare the arrival of goods that were never shipped, allowing funds to be transferred overseas with no physical transaction.

Use of Third Parties and Intermediaries

Criminal networks often rely on third-party intermediaries to facilitate TBML. These may include freight forwarders, customs brokers, distributors, or trading companies that act as conduits for illicit value transfers. Some intermediaries knowingly participate in TBML schemes, while others are used without their knowledge.

A common tactic is to route goods through multiple intermediaries and jurisdictions, creating complexity that discourages investigation. Each intermediary adds a layer of separation between the criminal actors and the final transaction.

The involvement of multiple parties also complicates efforts to trace goods or payments, as investigators must coordinate across legal and regulatory frameworks that differ significantly.

Intermediaries located in free-trade zones or jurisdictions with weak oversight play a particularly important role. These areas often allow repackaging, relabeling, or consolidation of goods without full customs scrutiny. Criminals exploit these environments to alter the appearance of shipments, disguise origin, or change documentation.

False Descriptions and Misclassification of Goods

Misclassification of goods is another TBML technique that exploits tariff systems, regulatory differences, and customs procedures. Criminals may classify goods under incorrect tariff codes to reduce duties, evade controls, or conceal the nature of the items being shipped.

For example, restricted items may be declared as agricultural products, textiles, or consumer goods. This allows them to pass through customs with minimal inspection. Alternatively, high-value goods may be classified as low-value items to justify lower invoice values.

In some cases, criminals intentionally use vague descriptions such as "parts," "electronics," or "machinery," which make it difficult for authorities to verify whether the goods match documentation. Such ambiguity enables manipulation of both pricing and commodity identification.

Dual-Purpose Trade Finance Instruments

Trade finance instruments, including letters of credit, guarantees, and bills of exchange, can be manipulated to support TBML schemes. These instruments rely on documentation rather than physical verification of goods, creating opportunities for criminals to exploit gaps.

A letter of credit may be issued based on fraudulent documents, enabling funds to be transferred even when the underlying trade is fictitious. Similarly, banks may process payments for shipments that exist only on paper if documents appear authentic. Because financial institutions often do not inspect goods directly, they must rely on the accuracy of trade documentation - a vulnerability exploited by TBML networks.

Criminals may also use back-to-back letters of credit or circular payments involving multiple banks to create complex financial pathways that obscure the movement of funds. These pathways make it challenging to trace value and identify the true beneficiaries.

Integration of Illicit Funds into the Formal Economy

One of the strengths of TBML is its ability to integrate illicit funds into the legitimate economy. Once value is transferred through trade manipulation, it appears as revenue, cost of goods sold, or trade expenses. This integration provides a plausible explanation for the movement of funds, reducing the likelihood of scrutiny.

Criminal networks may establish trading companies that engage in both legitimate and illicit transactions. Blending lawful trade with manipulated transactions allows them to obscure the true purpose of their activities and complicates enforcement efforts.

TBML also supports the movement of funds across borders without reliance on traditional financial channels. By shifting value through trade, criminals bypass monitoring systems that focus on financial transactions. This method is particularly attractive in regions with strict capital controls, unstable financial systems, or heavy surveillance of banking activity.

Why TBML Remains Difficult to Detect

Traditional anti-money laundering controls are designed for financial transactions, not trade. Banks may see only partial information, such as invoice values or payment instructions, without visibility into shipping routes, cargo contents, or customs declarations. Customs authorities may see the goods but lack insight into financial flows. This fragmentation of oversight creates significant detection challenges.

TBML also benefits from the complexity of global pricing. Many goods have variable market values depending on region, season, and product specifications. Determining whether an invoice is reasonably priced requires specialized knowledge and access to reliable data. Without these resources, authorities may overlook manipulations.

PHANTOM SHIPPING, DOCUMENTATION ABUSE, AND CASE EXAMPLES

Phantom shipping and documentation abuse are central components of sanctions evasion and trade-based crime. These schemes exploit the complexity of global shipping systems, the vast volume of maritime traffic, and the reliance on documentation rather than physical inspection. By manipulating records, obscuring vessel identity, or inventing trade activity entirely, illicit actors create an appearance of legitimacy that conceals unlawful transactions. Understanding how these schemes function - and examining real-world examples - provides insight into the scale, sophistication, and persistence of maritime and trade-based financial crime.

The Concept of Phantom Shipping

Phantom shipping refers to trade activity that exists on paper but does not occur in reality. It often supports money laundering, sanctions evasion, tax fraud, and illicit commodity trading. In a phantom shipping scheme, parties create documentation implying that goods were shipped, transported, or delivered, even though no cargo was actually moved. These schemes may involve fictitious bills of lading, fabricated shipping routes, or vessels that never made the voyage described.

Because global shipping relies heavily on documentation to confirm transactions, phantom shipping can go undetected without physical verification. Shipping records, customs declarations, and bank documents may align perfectly despite the absence of real movement. Financial institutions funding such transactions may never suspect wrongdoing, as invoices and transport records appear authentic.

Phantom shipping can also be used to justify payments between companies in different jurisdictions. Criminal groups may claim that goods were exported or imported and move funds accordingly, masking illicit financial flows under the guise of trade settlement. This makes phantom shipping particularly attractive for both money laundering and sanctions evasion.

AIS Manipulation and Concealment Tactics

A key method used in maritime evasion schemes involves manipulation of the Automatic Identification System (AIS), a tracking mechanism intended to enhance safety and transparency in shipping. AIS broadcasts a vessel's identity, location, heading, and speed. Although intended for safety, it is also a critical tool for regulators and compliance teams monitoring maritime activity.

Criminal actors may disable AIS transponders entirely, allowing vessels to "go dark" for hours or days at a time. These dark activities often occur near sanctioned ports, in areas known for ship-to-ship transfers, or along routes commonly used to smuggle commodities. When AIS signals resume, vessels often appear to continue their journey without any indication of what occurred during the blackout.

More advanced schemes involve AIS spoofing, where vessels broadcast false coordinates or identity information. In some cases, a vessel at sea may transmit location data suggesting it is moored safely at a foreign port, misleading authorities and insurers. Spoofing complicates efforts to track movements and detect illicit transfers, particularly when combined with false documentation.

Fabrication and Alteration of Shipping Documentation

Documentation abuse lies at the heart of many trade-based crimes. Bills of lading, certificates of origin, cargo manifests, insurance certificates, and customs declarations represent the official record of a shipment. Criminal schemes manipulate these documents to conceal origin, mask destination, misstate cargo details, or fabricate entire shipments.

One method involves creating duplicate sets of documents with conflicting information. One set may show a legitimate cargo destined for a permitted jurisdiction, while another, used internally, reflects the true nature of the shipment. Dual documentation enables sanctioned entities to receive prohibited goods while maintaining plausible deniability in case of inspection.

Another method involves altering genuine documents. Forgers may change the stated port of loading, adjust tonnage, substitute commodity descriptions, or falsify container numbers. Because many customs and financial systems rely on scanned or digital copies rather than original documents, alterations can be difficult to detect unless discrepancies appear elsewhere.

Certificates of origin are frequently abused. These documents indicate where goods were produced, which is critical for sanctions enforcement. By presenting forged certificates from non-sanctioned countries, actors can disguise goods originating from restricted jurisdictions, such as oil or metals exported illicitly.

Ship-to-Ship Transfers and Obscured Commodity Flows

Ship-to-ship (STS) transfers allow vessels to exchange cargo at sea, often far from regulated ports or surveillance. These transfers may involve oil, coal, grain, or metals. STS operations are not illegal in themselves, but they are frequently exploited in sanctions evasion schemes.

A sanctioned tanker may approach a non-sanctioned vessel, transfer cargo, and then retreat to international waters. The receiving vessel, now with mixed or fully substituted cargo, can enter foreign ports with documentation that obscures the origin of the goods. When combined with AIS manipulation, STS transfers can effectively erase the connection between a commodity and its sanctioned source.

Illicit networks may also use floating storage units or idle vessels to hold cargo offshore until documentation is arranged or markets align. This practice complicates efforts to determine the origin, ownership, or intended destination of goods.

Fraudulent Commodities and Empty Containers

In some cases, shipments contain no goods at all. Containers may be loaded with filler material, counterfeit products, or nothing whatsoever. These empty-container schemes support money laundering by generating documentation that justifies payments between exporters and importers. Because customs agencies inspect only a small fraction of containers, many fraudulent shipments pass undetected.

Other schemes involve counterfeit commodities - products that do not match their stated quality or specifications. For example, a shipment declared as high-grade metal may contain scrap material or unrelated products. These discrepancies serve as vehicles for transferring value across borders, with the difference in quality representing the illicit transfer.

Fraudulent commodity schemes often intertwine with phantom shipping. The purpose is not to move valuable goods but to create a transactional footprint that supports the movement of illicit funds.

High-Profile Case Examples

Real-world cases illustrate how phantom shipping and documentation abuse operate on a global scale.

One notable example involves sanctions evasion networks transporting oil from embargoed jurisdictions. Tankers would disable AIS, conduct STS transfers at sea, obtain forged certificates of origin, and deliver oil to refineries claiming it originated elsewhere. Investigators later uncovered chains of falsified documents, including shipping manifests and customs filings, that masked the involvement of sanctioned actors. These schemes allowed millions of barrels of oil to enter global markets undetected for prolonged periods.

Another case involved a large commodity trading firm implicated in TBML schemes through inflated invoices and phantom shipments. The company declared shipments of agricultural goods that never existed, allowing criminal groups to launder funds through fabricated trade flows. Banks processed associated letters of credit, unaware that the shipments were fictional. The exposure was discovered only after authorities noticed discrepancies between port records and declared cargo volumes.

A separate investigation revealed criminal networks smuggling gold by misdeclaring tonnage and purity. Shipments were routed through multiple countries with falsified documentation to disguise the origin of the gold and avoid sanctions or export restrictions. The illicit gold was then sold in major markets with official certification, generating clean revenue for criminal organizations.

In another example, a freight forwarding company assisted sanctioned entities by providing forged shipping documentation. The firm created multiple versions of bills of lading to conceal the final destination of goods, enabling sanctioned parties to acquire prohibited technology. The involvement of legitimate intermediaries made detection difficult, as financial institutions accepted the fraudulent documents as genuine.

Systemic Weaknesses Exposed by These Schemes

These case studies highlight systemic weaknesses in global trade oversight. Authorities often lack full visibility into maritime movements, especially when vessels manipulate AIS or operate in remote areas. Customs agencies may not have resources to inspect cargo thoroughly. Financial institutions frequently rely on documentation provided by clients, which may be inaccurate or intentionally deceptive.

The decentralized nature of global trade further complicates enforcement. Multiple jurisdictions, intermediaries, and logistical partners create layers of separation between illicit actors and the final transaction. Criminal networks exploit these gaps through coordination, deception, and rapid adaptation to enforcement measures.

Improving Detection and Mitigation

Addressing phantom shipping and documentation abuse requires closer collaboration among regulators, financial institutions, shipping companies, and international agencies. Technology plays a growing role. Satellite imagery, machine learning tools, and vessel behavior analytics can help identify suspicious maritime patterns. Enhanced verification of documentation through blockchain-based systems may improve authenticity and traceability.

CHAPTER 9

CYBER-ENABLED FINANCIAL CRIME

RANSOMWARE, CRYPTO SCAMS, AND ONLINE FRAUD

CYBER-ENABLED FINANCIAL CRIME continues to expand in scale and sophistication, reshaping the threat landscape for institutions, governments, and individuals. Unlike traditional financial crime, which often relies on physical access, personal interaction, or human intermediaries, cybercrime exploits digital systems, global connectivity, and automation. This allows offenders to operate across jurisdictions, target victims worldwide, and scale their operations rapidly. Among the most pervasive forms of cyber-enabled financial crime are ransomware, cryptocurrency-based scams, and online fraud. Each presents distinct risks, yet they share common characteristics: remote execution, anonymity, global reach, and the ability to generate significant illicit revenue with limited upfront cost.

The Mechanics and Impact of Ransomware

Ransomware is a form of malicious software that encrypts a victim's data, systems, or networks, rendering them unusable until a ransom is paid. Attackers typically demand payment in cryptocurrency to obscure their identity and avoid the scrutiny associated with traditional banking channels. Ransomware has evolved from opportunistic attacks to highly coordinated operations involving specialized roles, support networks, and profit-sharing structures.

Modern ransomware attacks often begin with phishing emails, credential theft, or exploitation of software vulnerabilities. Once attackers gain entry, they move laterally across systems, identify critical data, disable backups, and prepare the environment for maximum impact. Some groups spend weeks inside a network before launching the attack. When encryption is initiated, victims may receive instructions directing them to a portal on the dark web, where they are told how to pay the ransom and negotiate with the attackers.

The impact of ransomware extends beyond financial loss. Organizations may face operational disruption, reputational damage, legal exposure, and regulatory consequences. Critical infrastructure, hospitals, and public-sector agencies have been targeted, demonstrating that ransomware can have life-threatening consequences when essential services are interrupted.

Ransomware groups frequently adopt a "double extortion" model. In addition to encrypting data, they exfiltrate sensitive information and threaten to publish it if the ransom is not paid. This increases pressure on victims and expands the potential harm beyond immediate system paralysis. Some groups have introduced "triple extortion," where they pressure clients, partners, or patients of the affected organization to demand payment.

Ransomware as an Organized Criminal Enterprise

Ransomware is no longer limited to technically skilled hackers; it has become a commercial ecosystem. Many groups operate under the "ransomware-as-a-service" (RaaS) model, providing malware, infrastructure, and negotiation tools to affiliates in exchange for a share of the proceeds. This model lowers the barrier to entry and accelerates the spread of ransomware.

The ecosystem includes developers who write the malware, operators who distribute it, negotiators who interact with victims, and money launderers who move the proceeds. Some groups even maintain customer service portals where victims can ask questions or request proof that decryption is possible. This level of organization mirrors legitimate business operations but serves criminal objectives.

International law enforcement efforts have disrupted some major ransomware groups, but new variants continually emerge. Many groups operate in regions with limited extradition cooperation, further complicating countermeasures.

Cryptocurrency's Role in Cybercrime

Cryptocurrency plays a central role in ransomware and many online scams because it enables cross-border transfers with limited oversight. While blockchain technology provides transparency in principle, attackers rely on anonymity-enhancing tools, mixers, privacy coins, and complex layering to obscure transaction trails.

Criminals may move funds through multiple wallets, use automated bots to fragment transactions into hundreds of small transfers, or exploit decentralized finance platforms to convert one asset into another. These techniques complicate efforts to trace illicit funds, although blockchain analytics has improved significantly in recent years.

Some ransomware groups specify the exact cryptocurrency to be used, the wallet address, and the process for confirming payment. They may demand additional fees if payment is delayed, mimicking the structure of commercial invoicing systems. The professionalization of this ecosystem underscores the financial sophistication underlying many ransomware operations.

Crypto Scams

Crypto scams span a wide spectrum, from simple confidence tricks to highly structured investment fraud. Their common feature is the exploitation of cryptocurrency's novelty, volatility, and perceived anonymity.

One common scam is the fraudulent investment platform. Criminals create websites that claim to offer high returns, automated trading, or insider strategies. Victims are encouraged to deposit cryptocurrency, which may initially appear to grow in value through fabricated dashboards. When victims attempt to withdraw funds, they encounter hidden fees, delays, or total loss of access. The platform disappears once enough deposits have been collected.

Another major category is impersonation scams. Fraudsters pose as legitimate exchanges, financial advisors, government officials, or well-known public figures. They may contact victims through social media, messaging apps, or email, offering "guaranteed returns" or urgent instructions to transfer funds for safekeeping. These scams rely heavily on psychological manipulation and social engineering.

"Romance scams" involving cryptocurrency have become increasingly common. Victims form online relationships with individuals who gradually introduce the idea of cryptocurrency investment. Trust is established over weeks or months, making the victim more vulnerable. Once funds are transferred, the scammer disappears. These cases often involve sophisticated networks that automate communications, share victim profiles, and reuse scripts across multiple targets.

A growing threat is "rug pull" schemes. Developers create new tokens or decentralized finance projects, promote them aggressively, and attract substantial investment. Once the price rises, developers drain liquidity pools or abandon the project, causing the token's value to collapse. Because these schemes operate in decentralized and lightly regulated environments, perpetrators often evade accountability.

Online Fraud and Digital Deception

Online fraud encompasses a wide range of schemes that exploit trust, convenience, and the impersonality of digital communication. Criminals use phishing attacks, fake marketplaces, malware, and credential theft to obtain financial information or induce payments.

Phishing remains one of the most effective methods. Attackers craft messages that mimic trusted institutions, directing victims to fraudulent websites where they enter credentials or personal information. These details are then used to access bank accounts, drain funds, or commit identity theft. Criminals leverage current events, regulatory announcements, or company branding to make their messages convincing.

Online marketplace fraud is another common problem. Fraudsters list products that do not exist, accept payment, and vanish. Some operate at scale, using automated tools to create multiple listings, manage fake reviews, and coordinate logistics. Others intercept legitimate transactions by compromising seller accounts or manipulating payment flows.

Business email compromise (BEC) schemes, while not purely online fraud, share many characteristics with cyber-enabled deception. Attackers impersonate executives, suppliers, or partners and instruct employees to make urgent payments. Although these frauds do not always involve hacking into systems, they rely on digital communication channels and social engineering.

Credential compromise underpins many online fraud schemes. Criminals collect usernames, passwords, or authentication tokens through phishing, malware, or exploitation of data breaches. These stolen credentials may be used to access bank accounts, payment apps, or cryptocurrency exchanges. Because many users reuse passwords across platforms, a single compromised credential may expose multiple accounts.

The Scale and Flexibility of Cyber-Enabled Fraud

Cyber-enabled financial crime benefits from scalability. Once a scam is developed, it can be executed repeatedly at minimal cost. A phishing template can target thousands of victims in minutes. A fraudulent website can process deposits from victims in numerous jurisdictions. Cryptocurrency fraud can attract global investment without physical infrastructure.

Criminals also adapt rapidly. When law enforcement disrupts one channel, they shift to new platforms, develop new narratives, or change technical methods. This adaptability challenges traditional enforcement models that rely on reaction rather than proactive intelligence.

Cyber-enabled crime is also facilitated by the accessibility of illicit tools. Ransomware kits, phishing templates, malware-as-a-service, and compromised credentials are sold on darknet markets. Individuals with limited technical expertise can launch cyber fraud campaigns by purchasing these tools and following step-by-step instructions.

Institutional Exposure and Risk Implications

Financial institutions face significant risk from ransomware, crypto scams, and online fraud. Banks may process transactions linked to ransomware payments, host accounts used in fraudulent schemes, or become targets of credential theft. Cryptocurrency exchanges face exposure when criminals use their platforms to launder funds or pay ransoms. Payment processors may unknowingly facilitate transactions associated with scams.

Institutions must maintain strong cybersecurity, transaction monitoring, and fraud detection capabilities. They must understand the behavior of cybercriminals, not just their financial patterns. Emerging technology such as behavioral analytics, threat intelligence, and network monitoring plays a critical role.

IDENTITY THEFT AND CREDENTIAL COMPROMISE

Identity theft and credential compromise represent some of the most pervasive and damaging forms of cyber-enabled financial crime. These offenses undermine the integrity of digital systems, exploit gaps in authentication processes, and enable criminals to assume control of personal or corporate identities. Unlike crimes that rely on overt deception, identity theft involves silent infiltration. Criminals operate in the background, collecting fragments of data, combining them into exploitable profiles, and using stolen credentials to impersonate victims, steal funds, or facilitate broader schemes. As financial services, government systems, and commercial platforms increasingly depend on digital authentication, identity-related crime has become central to the cybercrime ecosystem.

The Value of Identity in the Digital Economy

In modern financial systems, identity functions as a gateway to access resources, services, and authority. When criminals obtain personal identifiers - such as names, dates of birth, national identification numbers, or account credentials - they acquire the ability to impersonate victims across multiple platforms. Even seemingly insignificant data points can be valuable when aggregated. A single stolen password, security question, or email address may open pathways to broader compromise.

The value of identity data lies not only in its immediate use but also in its resale potential. Criminal marketplaces trade vast quantities of compromised credentials, selling them individually or in bulk. Buyers may use these credentials for fraud, extortion, or broader cyber operations. High-value targets, such as executives or government employees, command greater prices due to their elevated access and potential for exploitation.

Identity data also enables social engineering attacks. Criminals can impersonate legitimate individuals to build trust, manipulate decisions, or direct financial transfers. In many cases, identity theft is the precursor to more complex crimes rather than the final objective.

Methods of Data Acquisition

Criminals employ numerous methods to obtain identity data. Phishing remains one of the most common. By sending emails or text messages that mimic legitimate organizations, attackers trick victims into entering passwords, card numbers, or personal information into fraudulent websites. These attacks are increasingly tailored to specific individuals or organizations, making them more convincing.

Malware is another key method. Keyloggers, form-grabbers, and remote access tools capture data directly from victims' devices. More advanced malware infiltrates operating systems and extracts stored credentials, browser cookies, or authentication tokens. These tools allow criminals to bypass passwords entirely by hijacking authenticated sessions.

Data breaches provide attackers with large volumes of identity data in a single incident. When companies are compromised, attackers may obtain customer records, login details, or financial information. These breaches fuel the cybercrime ecosystem, providing material for credential stuffing attacks, account takeovers, or secondary fraud.

Public information also plays a role. Social media profiles, company websites, and online directories often contain details that can support identity theft. Criminals combine publicly available data with stolen information to build full identity profiles. Even security questions—such as mother's maiden name or first school—are often answerable through public research.

Credential Compromise and Account Takeover

Credential compromise enables criminals to access victim accounts directly. This account takeover (ATO) risk affects financial services, e-commerce, insurance platforms, and online tools that store payment or personal information. Once criminals obtain valid credentials, they attempt to log into accounts manually or through automated scripts. If successful, they may reroute funds, change contact details, or lock out legitimate users.

Credential stuffing is a common technique, leveraging the fact that many individuals reuse passwords across platforms. Criminals test stolen credentials against multiple websites simultaneously, using automated tools that simulate human behavior to avoid detection. Even if only a small percentage of attempts succeed, the scale of the operation makes it highly profitable.

Once inside an account, criminals may immediately withdraw funds or conduct high-value transactions. Others maintain long-term access, monitoring account activity, collecting additional data, and preparing for more complex fraud. In corporate environments, compromised credentials may allow attackers to access sensitive systems, internal communications, or payment processes.

Synthetic Identity Creation

One of the more complex forms of identity fraud involves synthetic identities. Rather than stealing a complete identity, criminals combine real and fabricated data to create a new digital persona. For example, they may use a legitimate identification number combined with a fictitious name and date of birth. Over time, they build credit profiles for these synthetic identities by applying for loans, opening accounts, or conducting small transactions.

Synthetic identities are challenging to detect because they do not correspond to a single real individual. They blend into financial systems by appearing to be legitimate new customers. Once synthetic profiles develop creditworthiness, criminals exploit them by obtaining large loans or credit lines, then disappearing without repayment. This form of identity crime often targets financial institutions rather than individuals.

Children's identities are particularly vulnerable to synthetic misuse. Because minors rarely use financial services, fraudulent activity may go undetected for years. By the time the identity is compromised, the damage to credit records may be extensive.

Corporate Identity Theft

Identity theft does not affect individuals alone; businesses are also targets. Criminals impersonate companies to obtain credit, defraud suppliers, or conduct invoice manipulation schemes. They may register domains similar to legitimate companies, forge documents, or compromise email systems to impersonate senior executives.

Attackers may also steal credentials belonging to employees with privileged access. Such compromises allow entry into financial systems, payroll accounts, or vendor management tools. Corporate identity theft can lead to unauthorized payments, data breaches, regulatory violations, and reputational harm.

Another form involves creating fictitious companies that mimic real firms, using similar names, logos, or industry affiliations. These entities may approach banks for credit, solicit investors, or transact with suppliers. Because they often provide fabricated documents, detection requires careful verification and external due diligence.

The Role of Social Engineering

Social engineering is often intertwined with credential compromise. Attackers exploit trust and human error to bypass security measures. Even sophisticated technical controls may be defeated when victims are manipulated into sharing information or approving transactions.

Techniques include impersonating customer service representatives, contacting employees through messaging apps, or calling victims directly while spoofing legitimate phone numbers. Criminals leverage urgency, authority, or fear to pressure victims into taking action. Identity data gathered through breaches or public sources enhances their credibility.

Business email compromise schemes frequently rely on social engineering combined with credential compromise. Attackers may intercept communications, alter payment details, or issue fraudulent instructions. Because messages appear to come from legitimate accounts, recipients may not question their authenticity.

Consequences of Identity Crime

Identity theft has far-reaching consequences for both individuals and institutions. Victims may face financial loss, damaged credit, emotional stress, and difficulty restoring their reputations. In some cases, fraudulent activity may continue for years, especially when synthetic identities are involved.

For institutions, identity-related crime undermines trust and exposes them to financial loss, regulatory scrutiny, and operational disruption. Fraudulent accounts drain resources through loans, credit card charges, or unauthorized transactions. Moreover, institutions must invest heavily in identity verification tools, fraud detection systems, and remediation processes.

The broader economic impact is substantial. Identity theft fuels other crimes - ransomware, online fraud, tax fraud, and money laundering. Criminals depend on credential compromise to operate anonymously, access systems, and launder proceeds. The interconnected nature of these crimes means that identity theft serves as a foundational component of the cybercrime ecosystem.

Evolving Threats and Detection Challenges

Identity theft continues to evolve as attackers adopt more sophisticated techniques. Deepfake technology, voice synthesis, and AI-generated content introduce new vectors for impersonation. Criminals may use synthetic voices to bypass phone-based verification or AI-generated documents to support fraudulent applications. As digital identity systems expand, the methods for compromising them grow increasingly advanced.

Traditional authentication - passwords, security questions, SMS verification - has proven insufficient against modern threats. Even multi-factor authentication can be circumvented through SIM swapping, phishing kits, or man-in-the-middle attacks. Institutions must adopt layered security strategies that incorporate behavioral analytics, device profiling, and biometric verification.

DARKNET MARKETS AND CRIMINAL INFRASTRUCTURE

Darknet markets and the broader criminal infrastructure supporting them form the backbone of many cyber-enabled financial crimes. These environments operate outside conventional internet channels, using hidden networks, encrypted communications, and anonymity-enhancing tools to shield participants from detection. While popular narratives often portray the darknet as a chaotic marketplace saturated with illicit activity, its structure is highly organized and supported by specialized service providers who enable commerce, communication, and financial exchange. Understanding how these markets function is essential to identifying how criminals acquire tools, launder proceeds, and coordinate global operations.

The Structure and Purpose of Darknet Markets

Darknet markets operate on hidden layers of the internet that require specialized software - most commonly Tor - to access. These networks obscure user identity by routing traffic through multiple encrypted nodes, making it difficult for investigators to trace participants. Within these environments, marketplaces resemble legitimate e-commerce platforms, with product listings, vendor profiles, customer reviews, and payment portals. But instead of lawful products, these platforms predominantly offer illegal goods and services.

Common offerings include malware kits, stolen identity data, forged documents, narcotics, weapons, and fraudulent financial tools. Vendors operate from jurisdictions around the world, taking advantage of the anonymity provided by the platform. Buyers similarly benefit from anonymity, enabling them to acquire illicit products with minimal risk of exposure.

The success of darknet markets relies on maintaining trust among participants, despite the inherently criminal nature of activity. Market administrators implement rating systems, escrow services, dispute resolution mechanisms, and vendor verification processes to provide consistency and reduce the likelihood of fraud. This infrastructure creates a commercial ecosystem that mirrors legitimate commerce but serves illegal purposes.

Criminal Infrastructure Supporting Darknet Activity

Beyond the marketplaces themselves, a sophisticated infrastructure supports the operation of darknet crime. This includes hosting providers specializing in bulletproof servers - systems designed to ignore takedown requests or law enforcement subpoenas. These services often operate in jurisdictions with weak regulatory frameworks or political resistance to international cooperation.

Another key component is encrypted communication. Many darknet vendors require buyers to use encrypted messaging platforms or PGP encryption when exchanging sensitive information. This ensures that even if communications are intercepted, the contents remain unreadable. Criminal groups also use private forums, chat channels, or invitation-only platforms to coordinate operations, share intelligence, or vet new members.

Fraud services form another layer of infrastructure. These include escrow providers for illicit transactions, reputation management services, and money laundering facilitators. Some actors specialize in cashing out stolen funds, converting cryptocurrency into fiat currency, or transferring proceeds across borders using complex layering techniques. Others offer tutorials, customer support, and tools that enable even inexperienced individuals to engage in cybercrime.

The Role of Cryptocurrencies in Darknet Commerce

Cryptocurrencies are integral to darknet transactions. Bitcoin remains widely used, though privacy-focused coins such as Monero are increasingly preferred due to their enhanced anonymity. Payments typically flow through mixing services, tumblers, or decentralized protocols that fragment transactions, making them difficult to trace.

Marketplaces themselves may provide built-in wallets or escrow systems. These features allow buyers to deposit funds into platform-controlled accounts before completing a purchase. Vendors receive payment only when the buyer confirms receipt of goods. While this system supports trust, it also exposes the marketplace to risk; law enforcement operations sometimes target escrow wallets to seize funds.

Criminal infrastructures have also adopted decentralized finance tools. Peer-to-peer exchanges, privacy layers, and liquidity pools allow criminals to move value rapidly, converting between cryptocurrencies or cashing out without relying on centralized exchanges. These tools reduce the effectiveness of traditional anti-money laundering measures, which depend heavily on regulated intermediaries reporting suspicious activity.

Darknet Markets as Procurement Hubs for Cybercrime Tools

Darknet markets are essential sources of cybercrime tools. Vendors sell malware, ransomware variants, phishing kits, credential harvesters, and exploit packs. Some offer ready-made attack tools that require minimal technical expertise. Others provide highly specialized kits that enable sophisticated operations.

Stolen data is another major commodity. Criminals buy and sell email accounts, social media profiles, bank credentials, and credit card information. They may purchase data in bulk or acquire targeted information for specific operations. Identity packages, sometimes referred to as "fullz," include multiple data points - addresses, identification numbers, account credentials - which enable synthetic identity creation or account takeover.

Darknet markets also offer infrastructure services such as botnets, proxy networks, and distributed denial-of-service (DDoS) tools. These services allow criminals to deploy attacks without exposing their own systems. Some vendors provide subscription models for continuous access to compromised machines or malicious software.

Resilience and Evolution of Darknet Markets

Darknet markets demonstrate remarkable resilience despite persistent law enforcement pressure. When authorities shut down major platforms, new ones often appear within months. In some cases, successor markets launch with enhanced security features designed to address vulnerabilities exploited during prior takedowns.

Decentralized marketplaces represent a newer advancement. Instead of operating on centralized servers, these markets use distributed ledger technology or peer-to-peer networks, minimizing single points of failure. They may store listings on decentralized file systems and accept payments through smart contracts. While still emerging, these models erode traditional enforcement strategies that depend on seizing centralized infrastructure.

Another trend is fragmentation. Instead of relying on large, centralized markets, criminals increasingly use smaller, invitation-only platforms or private channels. This reduces exposure to law enforcement infiltration and creates tighter-knit communities where trust is essential. Many cybercrime groups now operate primarily through encrypted messaging channels rather than public marketplaces.

Cross-Jurisdictional Challenges

Darknet crime presents significant jurisdictional challenges. Participants often operate across several countries, making it difficult to identify which authority has responsibility for enforcement. Legal frameworks vary, and cooperation between jurisdictions may be slow or politically constrained. Even when law enforcement identifies suspects, extradition may not be possible.

Hosting infrastructure may be located in countries with limited enforcement capability, and cryptocurrency transactions may cross multiple jurisdictions. This fragmentation complicates investigations and slows response efforts. Criminals exploit these weaknesses, structuring operations to minimize exposure to aggressive law enforcement environments.

Case Examples Demonstrating Darknet Activity

Over the past decade, several major cases have highlighted the scale and complexity of darknet markets. One notorious platform facilitated the sale of narcotics, forged documents, and cybercrime tools. It relied on sophisticated encryption, vendor ranking systems, and a large community of buyers. After authorities infiltrated the platform and arrested its operator, investigators discovered extensive financial infrastructure supporting the site, including cryptocurrency wallets, mixing services, and offshore servers.

In another case, a darknet forum specializing in stolen financial data was dismantled after a multinational investigation. The forum hosted millions of compromised credit card numbers and account credentials. Members included data brokers, fraud specialists, and money laundering facilitators. Law enforcement recovered detailed logs showing how criminals used compromised data to commit fraud across multiple countries.

A further example involved a ransomware group that operated through darknet channels, selling ransomware kits and providing customer support to affiliates. The group coordinated operations through encrypted forums and used darknet marketplaces to recruit new participants. When authorities disrupted the group, they found extensive documentation demonstrating the structured nature of the operation, including training materials and profit-sharing agreements.

These cases illustrate how darknet platforms serve as operational hubs for multiple forms of cybercrime. They also highlight the challenges authorities face in dismantling networks that operate across borders and rely heavily on anonymizing technologies.

TECH-STACK OF CYBERCRIMINALS AND DIGITAL LAUNDERING

Cybercriminals operate with a level of technological sophistication that rivals, and in some cases exceeds, that of legitimate organizations. Their tools, infrastructure, and laundering techniques evolve rapidly in response to law enforcement pressure, improved cybersecurity standards, and changes in the digital economy. The "tech-stack" used by cybercriminals includes a wide array of software, hardware, platforms, and services that support activities ranging from system intrusion and data theft to illicit fund movement and concealment. Understanding how these components interact provides critical insight into the operational capability of cybercriminals and the challenges facing investigators.

Core Infrastructure and Anonymity Tools

Anonymity is fundamental to cybercrime operations. Criminals rely on technologies designed to conceal identity, location, and communications. The Tor network remains central to this infrastructure, enabling access to hidden services and suppressing the ability of investigators to trace IP addresses. Virtual private networks (VPNs) are widely used as an additional layer of masking, often purchased from providers that advertise "no logs" policies or operate in jurisdictions with limited regulatory oversight.

Proxies and botnets expand anonymity even further. Botnets - large networks of compromised devices -serve as distributed infrastructures for launching attacks, sending spam, or masking the origin of malicious traffic. These systems often consist of thousands of infected machines, and their decentralized nature makes them difficult to dismantle. Criminals may rent access to botnets for specific operations, lowering the technical barriers for newcomers.

Dedicated hosting also supports anonymity. "Bulletproof hosting" services allow criminals to deploy websites, malware distribution sites, or command-and-control servers with minimal fear of shutdown. These providers often operate in regions with weak enforcement, and they deliberately ignore complaints or takedown requests. Their infrastructure can host phishing pages, malware kits, darknet storefronts, or fraudulent investment platforms.

Malware Development and Exploit Kits

A critical component of the cybercriminal tech-stack involves the creation, distribution, and operation of malware. Malware families include ransomware, keyloggers, remote access tools, credential harvesters, and banking trojans. Many are modular, allowing attackers to add plug-ins to enhance capabilities such as data exfiltration, privilege escalation, or lateral movement.

Exploit kits automate the process of identifying vulnerabilities in target systems. These kits scan victims' devices for weaknesses in browsers, plugins, or operating systems. Once a vulnerability is found, the kit deploys a tailored exploit that installs malware without requiring the victim to click anything. Exploit-kits-as-a-service are sold on darknet markets, enabling individuals with limited technical expertise to execute sophisticated attacks.

Zero-day exploits - vulnerabilities unknown to software vendors - are among the most valuable tools. Criminal groups with financial resources can purchase zero-day exploits from brokers or underground markets. Once deployed, these exploits allow silent infiltration of high-value targets such as financial institutions, government agencies, or corporate networks.

Data Harvesting, Credential Theft, and Automated Tools

Cybercriminals rely on massive volumes of data to execute fraud and laundering schemes. Automated scraping tools collect email addresses, password hashes, personal identifiers, and financial information from compromised websites or unsecured databases. Malware on infected devices can capture keystrokes, screenshots, and stored credentials, giving attackers access to sensitive accounts.

Credential stuffing tools test stolen usernames and passwords across numerous platforms. These tools integrate proxy lists to avoid detection and incorporate automation to handle thousands of login attempts within minutes. Once an account is compromised, attackers may use it directly or sell access on darknet forums.

Session hijacking tools intercept authentication tokens or cookies, allowing attackers to bypass passwords entirely. This technique is particularly dangerous because it can circumvent multi-factor authentication when improperly implemented.

Encryption, Obfuscation, and Anti-Forensics

To evade detection, cybercriminals use sophisticated encryption and obfuscation techniques. Malware samples may be packed or encrypted to evade anti-virus detection. Attackers regularly rotate encryption keys, modify file signatures, or deploy polymorphic malware that changes its code structure with each infection.

Secure communication is another priority. Criminal groups use end-to-end encrypted messaging platforms, such as Signal or private Telegram channels, to coordinate operations. Many employ PGP encryption for email communications, ensuring that even intercepted messages remain unreadable.

Anti-forensics tools allow attackers to wipe logs, erase metadata, or alter system artifacts that investigators rely on. These tools limit the ability of forensic teams to reconstruct attack timelines, identify compromised systems, or attribute operations to specific actors.

Cryptocurrency Wallets, Mixers, and Privacy Tools

Digital laundering is integral to cybercrime. Fraud, ransomware, darknet commerce, and data sales often produce cryptocurrency proceeds that must be moved, converted, or concealed. This process relies on specialized wallets, obfuscation layers, mixing services, and decentralized exchange platforms.

Criminals begin by collecting payments in cryptocurrencies such as Bitcoin, Ethereum, or Monero. Bitcoin, while traceable, remains widely accepted due to liquidity. Monero and other privacy coins offer stronger anonymity, attracting groups that prioritize concealment.

Mixing services fragment cryptocurrency transactions by blending illicit funds with large pools of unrelated transactions. Tumblers may operate on centralized servers or through decentralized protocols. The goal is to sever the link between the sender and the final recipient. Some criminals run their own mixers to avoid reliance on third-party services.

Chain-hopping is another laundering method, involving quick conversion between different cryptocurrencies to obscure the transaction trail. These conversions may occur through decentralized exchanges (DEXs) that require no identity verification. Automated bots may handle these transfers to reduce human error and accelerate movement.

Criminals also use "peel chains," where funds are divided into smaller increments and distributed across numerous wallets.

This technique creates long transaction chains that are time-consuming for investigators to trace.

Cash-Out Infrastructure and Global Facilitators

Once digital funds are sufficiently obfuscated, criminals use cash-out methods to convert cryptocurrency into fiat currency or usable value. Cash-out services may involve over-the-counter (OTC) brokers, unregulated exchanges, or peer-to-peer marketplaces. Some OTC brokers knowingly assist criminal groups, offering discreet conversion services for high fees.

Gift card conversion schemes represent another method. Criminals purchase digital gift cards using illicit cryptocurrency and resell them at a discount. While inefficient in value retention, this method provides anonymity and access to physical goods.

In some cases, criminals rely on money mules -individuals who receive funds and transfer them on behalf of the main actors. Mules may be recruited unknowingly through job advertisements or knowingly as members of organized networks. Their involvement creates an additional layer between criminals and the proceeds of crime.

Automation, AI, and Offensive Capabilities

Automation plays a central role in cybercrime. Attackers use bots to launch large-scale campaigns, manage phishing distribution, run credential attacks, and monitor compromised accounts. This allows them to operate with minimal human oversight.

Artificial intelligence enhances these capabilities. AI tools can analyze massive datasets of stolen credentials, identify valuable targets, and optimize attack strategies. Machine learning models can generate phishing messages that mimic writing styles, making them more convincing. Deepfake technology allows creation of synthetic voices and videos used in fraud schemes, such as impersonating executives to authorize transfers.

AI-supported malware can modify its behavior in real time, avoiding detection by adapting to the system it infects. These tools significantly increase the complexity of analysis and require equally advanced defensive measures.

The Integration of Technology into Organized Cybercrime

Cybercrime groups often operate like structured organizations with defined roles and clear division of labor. Developers create tools, operators deploy them, brokers launder proceeds, and administrators manage infrastructure. This industrialization mirrors legitimate technology sectors, with rapid product cycles, customer support, and revenue-sharing agreements.

Darknet markets facilitate the procurement of components within this tech-stack. Virtually every tool required - malware, stolen credentials, hosting, encryption, laundering services - is available for purchase or rental. This reduces entry barriers and allows individuals with limited technical skills to execute complex crimes.

Because each component of the tech-stack can be swapped or upgraded independently, cybercriminals maintain resilience. When law enforcement disrupts one service, alternative providers emerge quickly.

Challenges for Detection and Enforcement

The sophistication of cybercriminal technology poses significant challenges for investigators. Traditional financial crime detection relies on transactional data, but digital laundering exploits systems that lack robust regulation or transparency. Blockchain analytics has improved, but privacy coins and decentralized exchanges continue to hinder traceability.

Attribution remains one of the greatest challenges. Anonymity tools, compromised devices, and proxy networks obscure the identity of attackers. Even when one infrastructure component is removed, the distributed nature of the tech-stack enables rapid recovery.

PART III

INVESTIGATION METHODOLOGIES

CHAPTER 10

PLANNING A FINANCIAL CRIME INVESTIGATION

DEFINING SCOPE, OBJECTIVES, AND STRATEGY

A FINANCIAL CRIME INVESTIGATION is most effective when it is guided by a clearly defined scope, precise objectives, and a structured strategy. Without these elements, investigations can become fragmented, reactive, or unfocused, increasing the risk of missed evidence, misdirected resources, or flawed conclusions. Establishing clarity at the outset ensures that investigators understand what they are examining, why they are examining it, and how the investigation will proceed. This structured approach also provides accountability, enhances decision-making, and supports the defensibility of investigative outcomes in legal, regulatory, and internal contexts.

Establishing a Clear Scope

The first step in designing an investigation is defining the scope. Scope determines the boundaries of the investigation - what will be examined, what falls outside the mandate, and how far investigators are authorized to go. Scoping begins with understanding the triggering event, which may be an internal red flag, an external complaint, a regulatory inquiry, an audit finding, or intelligence suggesting misconduct. From there, investigators must articulate the specific subject matter under review.

Scope definition typically includes identifying the relevant time period, individuals or entities involved, business lines affected, systems implicated, and the types of transactions or behaviors under scrutiny. A narrow scope may focus on a specific transaction or a single employee's conduct, whereas a broader scope may examine systemic vulnerabilities, operational failures, or an entire product line. The challenge lies in ensuring that the scope is neither overly expansive nor too restrictive. An investigation that is too broad risks inefficiency and unnecessary diversion of resources. One that is too narrow risks overlooking material facts.

Effective scoping balances precision with flexibility. Investigators must be prepared to refine the scope as new evidence emerges, expanding or contracting their focus to reflect the reality of the misconduct. Early documentation of the scope is essential, providing a reference point for decision-making and helping stakeholders understand the rationale behind investigative boundaries.

Defining Core Objectives

Objectives articulate what the investigation aims to achieve. While scope identifies what is being examined, objectives define the purpose of the examination. Clear objectives reduce ambiguity and prevent investigative drift. They also communicate to senior management, regulators, and legal counsel what the investigation is designed to accomplish.

Common objectives include establishing whether misconduct occurred, identifying the individuals or entities responsible, determining the financial impact, assessing control failures, evaluating regulatory exposure, and recommending corrective actions. Some investigations may focus on fact-finding alone; others may be designed to support remediation, self-disclosure, or disciplinary action.

Objectives must align with legal and regulatory obligations. If the investigation arises from a regulatory inquiry, objectives may include responding thoroughly to regulators' questions, providing evidence to address compliance concerns, and demonstrating that internal controls are functioning effectively. When misconduct potentially involves criminal exposure, objectives may include preserving evidence for potential law enforcement action.

Well-defined objectives support strategic planning and help ensure that investigative work remains purposeful and targeted.

Developing an Investigative Strategy

A strategy outlines how the investigation will be executed. It sets the methodology, sequencing, timeline, and approach to evidence collection. An effective strategy ensures that investigators proceed systematically, anticipate potential obstacles, and manage risk proactively.

Strategy development typically begins with identifying the information sources. These may include transaction records, email communications, messaging logs, financial statements, customer files, surveillance footage, third-party data, whistleblower reports, or system access logs. The strategy must identify which sources are most relevant, how they will be obtained, and in what order they will be reviewed.

Interviews form another core component of the strategy. Investigators must determine who should be interviewed, the sequence of interviews, and which topics to address. Witness interviews require careful preparation, as errors in questioning can compromise evidence or influence testimony. Interview strategy must consider legal privilege, employee rights, and the potential need to conduct interviews in coordination with legal counsel.

A well-designed strategy also addresses analytical methods. For example, data analytics may be used to identify anomalies in transaction patterns, trace fund flows, or identify relationships between individuals. Forensic accounting may be required to quantify financial impact. Technical expertise may be needed to review digital evidence, such as log files or metadata.

The strategy must also account for the need to preserve evidence. This may require issuing litigation holds, securing electronic devices, restricting system access, or duplicating data sources to prevent tampering. Preservation failures can undermine the credibility of the investigation and expose the organization to legal risk.

Aligning Strategy with Risk and Complexity

Not all investigations require the same level of intensity or technical complexity. A strategic approach considers the severity of allegations, the potential financial and regulatory impact, and the likelihood of escalation. Investigations involving senior executives, high-value transactions, sanctions exposure, or suspected criminal conduct require heightened rigor and may involve external counsel or forensic specialists.

Risk assessment informs strategic decisions such as whether to notify regulators, when to brief senior leadership, and how to structure communications. It also informs whether the investigation should proceed discreetly or transparently. Discretion may be necessary to prevent evidence destruction, preserve the integrity of interviews, or avoid market impact.

Complex cases may require phased strategies. Early phases may involve preliminary assessments, triage, or rapid fact-finding to determine whether a full investigation is warranted. Subsequent phases may involve deeper analysis, broader document collection, or targeted inquiries.

Coordinating Stakeholders and Advisers

An investigation requires coordination among internal and external stakeholders. Legal counsel plays a central role in ensuring compliance with legal obligations, preserving privilege, and advising on risk. Compliance teams provide expertise on regulatory frameworks and control environments. Human resources may be involved when allegations concern employee conduct. Senior management may require regular updates to make informed decisions.

External advisers may include forensic investigators, auditors, industry specialists, or cybersecurity experts. Their involvement depends on the nature of the allegations and the skills required. External involvement also enhances independence, which may be important when investigating sensitive issues or senior personnel.

The strategy must define communication protocols. This includes identifying who receives updates, how often updates are provided, and which decisions require escalation. Clear communication channels prevent misunderstandings and ensure that the investigation progresses efficiently.

Avoiding Investigative Drift and Ensuring Discipline

Investigative drift occurs when teams pursue tangential issues or expand the investigation without clear justification. This leads to inefficiency, increased cost, and potential confusion. Well-defined scope and objectives help prevent drift, but investigators must remain disciplined in adhering to them.

Any change to scope or objectives must be deliberate and documented. Adjustments may be necessary when new evidence emerges or when initial assumptions prove incorrect. However, such decisions must be justified and approved by the appropriate stakeholders. Uncontrolled expansion undermines the structure and credibility of the investigation.

Maintaining discipline also requires careful documentation of decisions, evidence collection, and analytical processes. This documentation ensures transparency, supports defensibility, and enables the investigation to withstand external scrutiny from regulators, courts, or auditors.

LEGAL AND REGULATORY CONSTRAINTS

Financial crime investigations operate within a complex framework of laws, regulations, and obligations that shape every aspect of the investigative process. These constraints define not only what investigators are permitted to do, but also how evidence must be collected, preserved, and used. Failure to adhere to these requirements can compromise findings, expose organizations to liability, and undermine relationships with regulators and law enforcement. Understanding legal and regulatory constraints is therefore essential to planning a defensible, efficient, and compliant investigation.

The Role of Legal Authority and Mandate

Every investigation must begin with a clear understanding of the legal authority under which it is conducted. Internal investigations draw their mandate from corporate policies, employment contracts, and governance frameworks. External investigations triggered by regulators, law enforcement, or litigation require adherence to specific statutory obligations. Clarity on the mandate ensures that investigators operate within their authorized boundaries and avoid actions that infringe on rights or exceed their legal powers.

Different jurisdictions impose varying requirements on evidence collection, employee interviews, data protection, and disclosure. Organizations operating across multiple jurisdictions must consider the most restrictive legal environment that may apply. An investigative action permissible in one country may be prohibited in another, particularly when data privacy or labor laws affect the process.

Data Protection and Privacy Obligations

Data protection is one of the most significant constraints in contemporary financial crime investigations. Regulations such as the EU's General Data Protection Regulation (GDPR), the UK Data Protection Act, and similar laws across Asia, Latin America, and other regions restrict how organizations may collect, process, and transfer personal data.

Investigators must determine whether accessing an employee's email, reviewing customer records, or extracting system logs constitutes the processing of personal data. If so, they must ensure that their actions comply with requirements such as purpose limitation, minimization, secure storage, and restricted access. In many cases, organizations must rely on legitimate interest, contractual necessity, or regulatory obligation to justify processing.

Cross-border data transfer introduces additional complexity. Moving data from one jurisdiction to another may require specific safeguards such as contractual clauses, encryption, or adherence to approved frameworks. In some countries, exporting certain categories of data is prohibited or subject to regulatory approval. These restrictions influence decisions about where data is reviewed, who has access, and which tools may be used.

Privacy obligations also extend to surveillance. Monitoring employee communications, reviewing messaging logs, or accessing personal devices may be subject to consent requirements or statutory limitations. Investigators must balance the need for evidence with the legal rights of individuals.

Legal Privilege and Confidentiality

Legal privilege protects certain communications between legal counsel and clients from disclosure. In the context of investigations, privilege plays a critical role in ensuring that sensitive communications remain confidential and shielded from regulators, counterparties, or litigation. Understanding how privilege applies - and how it can be preserved - is essential.

Privilege typically applies when legal advice is sought or provided, or when communications are prepared for litigation. To maintain privilege, investigators must ensure that legal counsel is meaningfully involved and that communications are properly marked and restricted to those who need to know. Failure to preserve privilege may result in compelled disclosure of sensitive materials, undermining the organization's position.

Privilege considerations can influence how interviews are conducted, how findings are documented, and how stakeholders are briefed. External counsel may be engaged to enhance privilege protections, especially in cases involving potential criminal exposure or regulatory breaches.

Confidentiality obligations also apply to whistleblower reports, internal audit findings, and communications with regulators. Investigators must ensure that sensitive information is not disclosed improperly, particularly when it concerns personal data, trade secrets, or regulatory matters.

Employment Law and Individual Rights

Investigations that involve employees must comply with employment laws that govern interviews, disciplinary actions, and workplace rights. These requirements vary across jurisdictions and may impose obligations such as informing employees of their rights, allowing representation during interviews, or providing notice of investigatory actions.

In some jurisdictions, employees have the right to refuse to answer certain questions, particularly when criminal exposure exists. Others may require that interviews be conducted in a specific manner or that employees receive written notice of allegations. Employment contracts and internal policies may impose additional requirements.

Investigators must also consider the risk of retaliation. Whistleblower protection laws often require the organization to safeguard individuals who report misconduct. Actions perceived as retaliatory - such as demotion, termination, or informal pressure - may result in legal liability.

Regulatory Expectations and Cooperation Requirements

Regulators expect organizations to conduct thorough, timely, and independent investigations into financial crime matters. This expectation applies across banking, insurance, securities, and payments sectors. Failure to investigate adequately may result in enforcement actions, fines, or restrictions on business activities.

In many jurisdictions, organizations are required to report specific findings to regulators. Suspicious activity reports, fraud notifications, sanctions breaches, and cybersecurity incidents may carry mandatory reporting timelines. Investigators must therefore understand what triggers reporting obligations and ensure that disclosures are made accurately and promptly.

Regulators may also require access to investigative findings, supporting evidence, or interview transcripts. In some cases, they may direct the scope or methodology of the investigation. Cooperation obligations vary, but generally require openness, transparency, and responsiveness. However, organizations must balance cooperation with legal privilege, confidentiality, and data protection obligations.

Regulators increasingly scrutinize the quality of investigations. They expect clear documentation, well-supported findings, and evidence of senior oversight. Investigations viewed as superficial or incomplete may prompt deeper regulatory scrutiny or independent reviews.

Law Enforcement Interaction and Criminal Exposure

When investigations uncover potential criminal conduct, organizations may need to engage with law enforcement. This introduces additional legal considerations. Cooperation with law enforcement must be structured to avoid compromising privilege, violating data protection laws, or exposing individuals to undue risk.

Organizations must assess whether to make voluntary disclosures, which may mitigate penalties but also expose the organization to increased scrutiny. In some jurisdictions, failure to disclose certain categories of misconduct is itself an offense.

Law enforcement may issue subpoenas, search warrants, or production orders. Responding to these requests requires careful coordination with legal counsel to ensure compliance while protecting rights. Investigators must understand the limits of law enforcement authority, particularly regarding extraterritorial claims or access to privileged information.

Criminal exposure creates risks for employees as well. Individuals may require separate legal representation, and interviews may need to be structured to avoid self-incrimination concerns.

Litigation Risks and Evidence Handling

Investigations often create litigation risk. Employees may challenge disciplinary actions, customers may dispute findings, or regulators may initiate enforcement proceedings. Evidence collected during the investigation must therefore be handled in a manner consistent with legal standards for admissibility, chain of custody, and accuracy.

Digital evidence requires particular care. Logs, emails, and system data must be collected using forensically sound methods to ensure they are not altered. Metadata must be preserved. Physical devices must be imaged. Failure to follow proper procedures may render evidence inadmissible or reduce its weight.

Documentation must be clear, factual, and free of speculation. Investigative reports should distinguish between findings, assumptions, and unresolved issues. Ambiguous or poorly documented evidence invites legal challenges.

Cross-Border Complexity and Conflicting Obligations

Multinational organizations face additional challenges when investigations span multiple jurisdictions. Conflicting legal obligations may arise. A jurisdiction may require disclosure of findings, while another may prohibit sharing certain information. Data protection laws may restrict access to documents needed to comply with regulatory inquiries. Employment laws may impose constraints on interviewing personnel based in different locations.

Investigators must work with legal counsel familiar with each jurisdiction's requirements. In some cases, investigations may need to be segmented by region or structured to comply with the strictest applicable laws.

Ethical Responsibilities and Fairness

Beyond legal requirements, investigators must uphold ethical standards. Investigations must be impartial, evidence-driven, and respectful of individual rights. Biased assumptions, leading questions, or selective evidence review undermine credibility. Organizations that fail to conduct fair investigations may face reputational harm and lose trust among employees, customers, and regulators.

Fairness includes ensuring that allegations are assessed objectively, that individuals are given an opportunity to respond, and that findings reflect the evidence rather than assumptions. Ethical discipline reinforces the legitimacy of the investigation and supports its long-term value.

RESOURCE ALLOCATION AND STAKEHOLDER COORDINATION

Conducting a financial crime investigation requires a structured framework for managing resources and coordinating the many stakeholders involved. Investigations are often complex, time-sensitive, and multidisciplinary, requiring contributions from legal counsel, compliance officers, forensic analysts, human resources, technology teams, auditors, and external advisers. Without careful planning and coordinated execution, even well-designed investigations risk delays, duplication of effort, or gaps in critical evidence. Allocating the appropriate resources and ensuring that stakeholders work cohesively are central to achieving reliable outcomes and maintaining institutional credibility.

Determining the Resources Required

Resource planning begins with understanding the scope and complexity of the investigation. Allegations involving simple misconduct may require only a limited team, while those involving sanctions breaches, fraud networks, cyber intrusions, or cross-border activities demand a broader range of expertise. Decision-makers must assess which skills, tools, and personnel are necessary to conduct an effective investigation. This assessment must be made early, since delays in deploying key resources can compromise evidence, hinder progress, and create regulatory challenges.

Human resources are the foundation of the investigative effort. Analysts, investigators, and subject-matter experts must have the appropriate training and experience to interpret complex financial data, assess control environments, review legal issues, or analyze digital evidence. In some cases, internal teams possess sufficient expertise; in others, organizations may need to supplement internal capability with external forensic specialists, cybersecurity experts, or legal advisers. Choosing the right team is not simply a matter of availability - it requires judgment about the unique demands of the investigation.

Technology resources are equally important. Investigations commonly require secure data extraction tools, forensic imaging software, encrypted storage environments, communication monitoring systems, and analytical platforms capable of handling large quantities of structured and unstructured data. When these tools are not readily accessible, the investigation may be delayed while systems are procured or configured. Adequate planning ensures that investigators have timely access to the infrastructure necessary to preserve and analyze evidence.

Budgeting and Cost Management

Investigations can be resource-intensive, especially when they involve specialized expertise, external advisers, or cross-border coordination. Budgeting must therefore be undertaken thoughtfully, balancing the need for thoroughness with realistic cost constraints. A poorly budgeted investigation risks both inefficiency and insufficient depth.

The budgeting process should account for personnel hours, consultant fees, technology costs, data processing charges, travel (when required), and potential legal expenses. While costs may be difficult to estimate precisely, establishing an initial budget helps set expectations and provides a framework for monitoring spending throughout the investigation. As the investigation progresses and new information emerges, budget adjustments may be necessary. Transparent reporting ensures that leadership remains informed and that financial decisions support investigative needs rather than restrict them arbitrarily.

Budget considerations also influence decisions about external assistance. Outsourcing can provide specialized expertise but comes at a premium. Internal teams may handle certain tasks more efficiently, while outsourcing others improves objectivity and independence. An effective resource strategy weighs these trade-offs and aligns them with investigative priorities.

Coordinating Key Internal Stakeholders

Financial crime investigations often span multiple departments, each with distinct responsibilities, perspectives, and priorities. Effective coordination ensures that all stakeholders understand their roles, cooperate constructively, and avoid working at cross-purposes.

Legal counsel typically guides overall strategy, ensuring compliance with regulatory and legal requirements. Their involvement is particularly important when investigations involve potential criminal exposure, regulatory breaches, or sensitive employment matters. Compliance teams provide insight into the regulatory framework, existing controls, and risk assessment processes. They help interpret how alleged misconduct fits within the broader compliance environment.

Technology teams facilitate access to systems, logs, and digital evidence. Their cooperation is essential in preserving devices, retrieving communications, or analyzing security incidents. Human resources may be involved when conducting employee interviews, managing disciplinary processes, or ensuring that employment laws are respected.

Internal audit teams may contribute by identifying control weaknesses or reviewing historical assessments related to the subject matter. Senior management serves as the decision-making authority, approving budgets, endorsing strategy, and determining escalation pathways.

To ensure alignment, the investigation should establish a stakeholder communication structure. This may include regular updates, defined points of escalation, and clear lines of responsibility. Documentation should be shared through secure channels, and sensitive information disclosed only on a need-to-know basis.

Engaging and Managing External Stakeholders

Certain investigations require external expertise due to their scale, complexity, or potential regulatory impact. Engaging external forensic firms, law firms, cybersecurity specialists, or data analytics providers can enhance credibility and provide skills not available internally.

External stakeholders must be selected carefully. Their qualifications, objectivity, and experience are critical to ensuring that investigative work is conducted thoroughly and defensibly. Retainers or engagement letters should clarify scope, deliverables, confidentiality, and reporting lines. Effective coordination requires integrating external teams into the investigative process without compromising internal controls or privileged communications.

Regulators are another category of external stakeholder. Depending on the nature of the misconduct, organizations may need to inform regulators early in the process or provide periodic updates. Transparency with regulators can build trust, but premature disclosure may create unnecessary risk. Decisions regarding regulatory engagement must be coordinated with legal counsel and senior management.

Law enforcement may also become involved, especially when investigations uncover criminal behavior. Cooperation with law enforcement must be managed carefully to preserve privilege, comply with legal obligations, and avoid disrupting the internal investigation. Timing, content, and method of communication with authorities must be strategically considered.

Other external stakeholders may include auditors, insurers, business partners, or external whistleblower channels. Coordination with these groups must be tailored to legal requirements, contractual obligations, and investigative needs.

Sequencing Tasks and Managing Dependencies

Investigations often involve complex dependencies. Document collection may require system access, which depends on technology teams. Interviews may require prior document review. Analytical work may depend on receiving structured data from external systems. Understanding these dependencies allows investigators to sequence tasks in a way that maximizes efficiency and reduces downtime.

A well-structured investigation plan outlines the order in which tasks should occur, identifies potential bottlenecks, and highlights areas where delays are likely. For example, if data extraction requires approval from multiple departments, those approvals should be sought early to avoid hindering later stages of analysis. Interviews with key personnel may need to be scheduled before memories fade or before individuals alter their behavior in response to the investigation.

Managing dependencies requires continuous oversight. Investigative leads must monitor progress, identify obstacles, and adjust the sequence of activities when unexpected developments arise. Clear communication among stakeholders helps ensure that tasks proceed as planned.

Ensuring Independence and Avoiding Conflicts of Interest

Investigations must be conducted objectively. Independence is crucial when allegations involve senior personnel, sensitive business units, or potential regulatory violations. Conflicts of interest - whether actual or perceived - can undermine the credibility of findings. To maintain independence, investigators must avoid involvement in prior decisions related to the subject matter or relationships that could impair objectivity.

In some cases, independence concerns require external investigators or counsel. This is especially true when investigating senior leadership or issues that may result in regulatory enforcement. External involvement also provides assurance to stakeholders that the findings are unbiased and defensible.

Internal governance structures may require oversight by committees, such as audit or risk committees, which help ensure independence and monitor progress. These bodies provide an additional layer of scrutiny and reinforce accountability.

Communication Protocols and Information Management

Clear communication protocols are essential to managing a complex investigation. Protocols must define who receives updates, how frequently updates are provided, and which decisions require escalation. Poor communication can lead to misunderstandings, delays, or inadvertent disclosure of sensitive information.

Information management requires secure systems for storing evidence, draft reports, interview notes, and correspondence. Access must be restricted to authorized individuals, with audit trails documenting who viewed or modified materials. Secure communication channels must be used for sharing documents, especially when external stakeholders are involved.

Communication with employees must be handled carefully. Rumors or misinformation can undermine morale and affect cooperation. Transparent but controlled messaging helps maintain confidence while protecting the confidentiality of the investigation.

Aligning Resources with Strategic Objectives

Ultimately, resource allocation and coordination must reinforce the strategic goals of the investigation. Resources should not be applied indiscriminately; they must be directed where they add value. Skilled personnel should focus on complex analytical tasks, while routine work can be delegated. Technology should support efficient evidence collection and analysis, not complicate it.

Stakeholder coordination must support timely decision-making and ensure that findings are communicated to the appropriate authorities. Effective resource management enhances the quality of the investigation, reduces the risk of oversight, and supports a defensible final report.

INTERNAL GOVERNANCE AND DOCUMENTATION STANDARDS

Internal governance and documentation standards form the structural foundation of any financial crime investigation. They ensure that investigative work is accountable, defensible, and aligned with organizational expectations as well as regulatory requirements. Strong governance provides oversight and clarity, while meticulous documentation demonstrates that the investigation was conducted thoroughly, professionally, and without bias. Together, these elements sustain the credibility of the investigative process and support appropriate decision-making by leadership, regulators, and other stakeholders.

Governance as the Framework for Oversight

Effective governance begins with a clear structure that defines who is responsible for directing, supervising, and approving investigative activity. This structure may include oversight committees, investigation leads, legal counsel, compliance officers, and senior management. Although each investigation varies in complexity, every case should have an established chain of accountability. This ensures that decisions are made consistently, risks are managed proactively, and the investigation remains aligned with organizational objectives.

Committees play an important role, particularly audit, risk, and ethics committees. These bodies provide high-level oversight and help ensure that investigations involving significant financial, reputational, or regulatory exposure receive appropriate scrutiny. They also provide an independent perspective when allegations involve senior employees or conflicts of interest. Their involvement reinforces impartiality and establishes a direct link between investigative findings and organizational governance.

Governance also requires documented protocols that define how investigations should be initiated, approved, and conducted. These protocols help ensure consistency across cases and prevent ad-hoc approaches that may lead to gaps or weaknesses. They may define the threshold for launching an investigation, the process for appointing investigators, and the expectations for communication, reporting, and escalation.

Clear governance structures support timely decision-making. Investigations often confront situations requiring swift action, such as evidence preservation, employee suspension, or reporting to regulators. A well-defined governance model enables investigators to act quickly without uncertainty about their authority or responsibilities.

Maintaining Independence and Objectivity

Governance mechanisms must also promote independence. Investigations lose credibility when stakeholders perceive bias, undue influence, or inappropriate intervention. Independence is especially critical when allegations implicate senior leadership, involve substantial financial exposure, or touch on compliance failures.

To preserve independence, organizations may implement strict conflict-of-interest controls. Individuals with involvement in the underlying business area should not lead or influence an investigation concerning that area. When internal independence is insufficient, external investigators or counsel should be engaged.

Objectivity must be embedded at every stage. Investigators must follow evidence wherever it leads, without pre-judging outcomes or dismissing leads that do not fit initial assumptions. Governance structures provide safeguards by requiring periodic review, supervision, and peer challenge of investigative work. This ensures that conclusions are grounded in evidence rather than interpretation or convenience.

Standards for Documentation and Recordkeeping

Documentation is central to investigative integrity. It creates a permanent record of decisions, reasoning, evidence, and findings. It allows future reviewers - such as regulators, courts, auditors, or internal committees - to understand how and why an investigation reached its conclusions. Without robust documentation, even a well-executed investigation can appear incomplete or unreliable.

Documentation standards apply to every component of the investigation: evidence collection, interview notes, analytical work, decision logs, and reporting. These records must be accurate, complete, and contemporaneous. Reconstructing decisions after the fact introduces risk, as memory may be incomplete or influenced by subsequent developments.

Investigators should maintain a documented rationale for key judgments - such as why certain witnesses were selected, why certain documents were prioritized, or why the scope was modified. This transparency supports defensibility and reduces the risk of allegations that investigators acted arbitrarily or ignored relevant evidence.

Records must be stored securely and preserved in accordance with legal requirements. This may include encryption, restricted access, and retention policies that meet regulatory expectations. Improper handling can compromise confidentiality, undermine privilege, or expose the organization to litigation risk.

Evidence Management and Chain of Custody

Evidence management is a critical component of documentation standards. The integrity of evidence is essential for establishing facts and supporting conclusions. Poor evidence handling can undermine the investigation and weaken its credibility in regulatory or legal contexts.

Chain of custody procedures must be established for all forms of evidence - digital, physical, and documentary. These procedures track who collected the evidence, when it was collected, where it was stored, and how it was preserved. Even minor lapses can create questions about authenticity or potential tampering.

Digital evidence presents particular challenges. Logs, emails, databases, and devices must be collected using structured forensic methods. Metadata must remain intact. Access must be limited to authorized individuals, and any analysis should be performed on verified copies rather than original files. Documentation of each step ensures transparency and preserves evidentiary value.

Physical evidence - such as paper documents, financial records, or handwritten notes - must also be handled consistently. Secure storage, labeling, and controlled access help prevent loss or unauthorized use.

Interview Documentation and Witness Records

Interviewing witnesses is a core investigative activity, and documentation of these interviews must meet high standards. Interview notes should capture both the substance and context of statements. This includes relevant questions, witness responses, clarifications, and any observable behaviors that may influence interpretation. Audio or video recordings may be used when appropriate and legally permissible.

Summaries should be prepared promptly after each interview to avoid memory distortion. These summaries must remain factual and avoid speculation. Where possible, witnesses may be asked to confirm that summaries accurately reflect their statements. This practice enhances the reliability of the record and reduces disputes later in the process.

Interview documentation must remain organized and accessible. Investigators should be able to trace how witness statements informed conclusions and how inconsistencies were resolved or evaluated.

Reporting Standards and Content Expectations

The investigative report is the final expression of the investigation's findings. It must be clear, objective, and supported by evidence. The report should present facts accurately, distinguish between conclusions and assumptions, and avoid ambiguous or subjective language.

Many investigations require reports suitable for multiple audiences: senior management, regulators, auditors, or legal counsel. While the core findings remain consistent, the level of detail or emphasis may differ. Governance structures often include formal review processes to ensure accuracy, consistency, and compliance with reporting protocols.

A well-structured report typically includes an overview of the scope and objectives, a summary of investigative steps, a factual narrative, analysis of evidence, findings, and recommended actions. The report should avoid unnecessary technical jargon without sacrificing precision. Appendices may contain supporting documents, data tables, or reference materials.

Documentation of dissenting views, unresolved questions, or limitations encountered during the investigation is also important. Transparency about limitations enhances credibility and allows decision-makers to understand the boundaries of the findings.

Governance Linkages to Training and Continuous Improvement

Governance and documentation standards must be integrated into organizational training and oversight. Investigators, managers, and relevant staff should receive regular training on investigative protocols, evidence handling, and documentation best practices. This ensures that standards are applied consistently across cases.

Periodic reviews of prior investigations can identify weaknesses, gaps, or opportunities for improvement. Organizations should maintain a governance framework that incorporates lessons learned into policies, procedures, and training programs. Continuous improvement enhances investigative capability and reinforces trust among internal and external stakeholders.

CHAPTER 11

GATHERING AND ANALYZING EVIDENCE

COLLECTING FINANCIAL, DOCUMENTARY, AND TRANSACTIONAL RECORDS

COLLECTING FINANCIAL, documentary, and transactional records is a central component of any financial crime investigation. These records provide the factual foundation upon which all subsequent analysis rests. Without complete, accurate, and well-organized evidence, investigators cannot determine what occurred, quantify the impact, or identify those responsible. The process requires precision, legal awareness, and methodical execution. It also demands an understanding of how different categories of records interact and how they collectively contribute to a reliable reconstruction of events.

Establishing a Collection Framework

Before gathering records, investigators must establish a structured framework that outlines what is needed, why it is needed, and how it will be obtained. This framework helps prevent oversights, ensures compliance with legal obligations, and guides the sequencing of evidence collection. It also helps distinguish between essential data and supplemental materials. The goal is to gather all relevant information in a manner that is organized, complete, and defensible.

At the outset, investigators must identify the range of systems, repositories, and sources likely to contain relevant records. This can include internal financial systems, customer management platforms, communication archives, archived reports, third-party provider systems, and physical documentation held in secure storage. Establishing access pathways early in the process prevents delays and protects against inadvertent data loss.

Financial Records as Primary Evidence

Financial records often serve as the most critical category of evidence, especially in investigations involving fraud, bribery, money laundering, misappropriation, or sanctions breaches. These records reveal patterns of activity that may support or contradict allegations. They also provide objective data that can be compared against internal controls, regulatory requirements, and established procedures.

The types of financial records investigators may need include account statements, general ledger entries, journal postings, payment records, loan documentation, expense reports, remittance instructions, wire transfers, procurement files, and audit trails. Each category offers unique insight. For example, bank statements may identify suspicious withdrawals or transfers; journal entries may show attempts to conceal losses; procurement files may reveal inflated invoices or duplicate billing.

A thorough review requires not only collecting these documents but assessing their completeness. Investigators must confirm that records cover the relevant time period, reflect all transactions, and are free from alteration. Where discrepancies appear, investigators must determine whether they indicate error, incomplete data capture, or intentional manipulation.

Documentary Records and Their Contextual Value

Documentary records—emails, memos, contracts, meeting notes, policies, and correspondence—provide context that financial records alone cannot supply. While financial records show what happened, documentary records often explain how and why it happened.

Contracts and agreements may reveal undisclosed obligations, unauthorized changes, or exploitable weaknesses. Internal communications may identify individuals involved in decision-making, discussions about irregularities, or attempts to conceal misconduct. Policy documents help investigators assess whether employees followed required procedures and whether controls were adequate.

Investigators must systematically collect documents from all relevant custodians. This includes primary actors, support staff, managers, and anyone involved in approving or reviewing questionable transactions. Requests should be specific, time-bounded, and consistent with data protection rules. Oversight from legal counsel ensures compliance with privacy, labor, or regulatory obligations.

Documentary records must also be evaluated for authenticity. For example, investigators may compare email metadata against server logs or verify that document versions match timestamps. This prevents reliance on manipulated or incomplete information.

Transactional Records and Behavioral Patterns

Transactional records reflect discrete events: payments, deposits, withdrawals, trades, shipments, or system access logs. These records create a chronological trail that investigators can use to reconstruct sequences of activity. Transactional evidence is often highly detailed, making it invaluable for identifying anomalies or patterns indicative of misconduct.

In complex investigations - such as those involving trade-based money laundering, sanctions evasion, or cyber-enabled fraud - transactional records may span multiple systems and jurisdictions. This requires coordination with internal technology teams and, in some cases, external institutions. Investigators must be precise in defining search parameters, such as account numbers, time periods, counterparty identifiers, or transaction types.

Patterns often emerge only after consolidating data across multiple sources. For example, investigators may identify a recurring structure in payments, a consistent relationship between certain accounts, or irregular timing of transactions. These insights can support deeper analysis or guide interview strategies.

Ensuring Completeness and Accuracy

Thorough evidence collection depends on confirming that the records obtained are complete. Missing data can distort analysis or create gaps in the narrative. Investigators must therefore validate the completeness of extracted records by cross-checking system logs, reviewing access histories, or confirming retrieval with system administrators.

Accuracy is equally important. Records must reflect genuine activity. Investigators must be alert to signs of tampering, such as altered entries, overwritten logs, missing invoices, or inconsistent timestamps. Where anomalies arise, they must determine whether the root cause is technical, procedural, or intentional.

In some cases, investigators may need to recreate missing data using alternative sources. For example, if internal records are incomplete, investigators may obtain bank statements from external institutions, retrieve archived documents, or use backup systems. The goal is to create the most complete evidence set possible.

Coordinating with Technology and Data Teams

Modern financial investigations rely heavily on digital information. Collaboration with IT teams is therefore essential. Technology staff help investigators identify locations of data, extract it securely, and preserve system integrity during the process. They also help verify metadata, trace user activity, and confirm whether records have been altered or deleted.

Investigators must communicate clearly about the scope and urgency of requests. Poor coordination can cause delays, inadvertently overwrite key data, or expose sensitive information. Clear protocols for data extraction, storage, and review ensure that investigators receive usable evidence without compromising privacy or security.

In large organizations, data may be dispersed across multiple platforms or cloud environments. Robust inventory procedures and system mapping allow investigators to identify all relevant repositories. Without this knowledge, critical evidence could remain undiscovered.

Legal and Regulatory Considerations in Evidence Collection

Evidence collection must always comply with legal requirements. Data protection rules may restrict access to certain records or require specific safeguards. Employment laws may limit how employee emails or devices can be reviewed. Financial regulations may impose retention obligations that determine what records are available.

Investigators must understand these constraints to avoid procedural violations that could invalidate evidence or expose the organization to liability. Legal counsel plays a key role in determining what may be collected, how it should be handled, and which safeguards must be implemented.

Regulatory expectations also influence evidence collection. Many regulators emphasize thoroughness, independence, and accuracy. Failure to obtain and analyze relevant records can be interpreted as inadequate oversight, leading to penalties or remediation requirements.

Organizing and Cataloging Evidence

Once records are collected, they must be organized systematically. Poor organization can undermine even the most thorough collection effort. Investigators must create a structured catalog that identifies the source, type, date, custodian, and relevance of each item.

A searchable database or evidence management system is essential for large investigations. It allows investigators to locate documents quickly, cross-reference information, and track review progress. Proper cataloging also supports chain-of-custody requirements and strengthens evidentiary reliability.

Organized evidence allows investigators to build timelines, compare statements against records, and identify contradictions or confirmations within the data. It forms the basis for analytical work that will follow in later stages.

Building a Cohesive Evidentiary Record

The ultimate objective of evidence collection is to build a cohesive record that supports accurate conclusions. Each document, transaction, or communication contributes to a broader understanding of events. Investigators must therefore evaluate not only individual pieces of evidence but how they interact.

A cohesive record allows investigators to identify causes, quantify losses, determine responsibility, and evaluate control failures. It also provides the foundation for reporting, remediation recommendations, regulatory submissions, or legal proceedings.

A strong evidentiary record reflects thorough, consistent, and lawful collection practices. It demonstrates that investigators acted objectively, gathered all relevant information, and preserved it in a manner suitable for scrutiny by internal and external stakeholders.

DIGITAL EVIDENCE AND CHAIN OF CUSTODY

Digital evidence plays a decisive role in modern financial crime investigations. As organizations rely heavily on electronic systems, communication platforms, and online transaction channels, misconduct often leaves a digital footprint that can reveal activities, timelines, user interactions, and attempts to conceal wrongdoing. However, digital evidence is also fragile. It can be overwritten, altered, or corrupted if not handled properly. Chain of custody procedures therefore become indispensable for maintaining the integrity, admissibility, and reliability of digital information. Together, digital evidence preservation and chain of custody form the technical backbone of a defensible investigation.

The Nature of Digital Evidence

Digital evidence includes any data stored or transmitted using electronic devices or systems. This category is broad and may range from emails and instant messages to system logs, metadata, mobile device extractions, cloud storage content, financial database entries, and network activity trails. What sets digital evidence apart from physical documents is its dynamic nature. Electronic data can change automatically through routine system activity, software processes, or user actions. Even opening a file may alter metadata.

Because of this volatility, investigators must act promptly and methodically. They cannot rely on traditional approaches used for paper documents or physical records. Digital evidence requires specialized tools, skilled personnel, and strict handling protocols. Failing to approach it with precision can lead to unintentional alteration or data loss, which weakens the investigation and may compromise the credibility of findings.

Identifying Sources of Digital Evidence

Before collecting digital evidence, investigators must identify all potential sources, which may be more extensive than initially expected. Modern organizations rely on complex technology ecosystems involving local servers, cloud platforms, mobile devices, outsourced systems, and communication tools. Misconduct may touch multiple components of this environment.

Potential sources include corporate email servers, collaboration platforms, financial systems, application logs, shared drives, virtual desktops, virtual meeting transcripts, customer support systems, content management repositories, mobile devices, laptops, and removable storage. In some cases, evidence may reside with third-party vendors or external partners.

A structured inventory of systems and applications helps investigators understand where relevant data may be stored. Collaboration with technology teams is essential at this stage, as investigators may not fully understand internal system architecture without their support. Identifying sources early prevents oversight, ensures comprehensive evidence collection, and reduces the risk of losing time-sensitive information.

Preserving Digital Evidence

Preservation is the most critical step in the digital evidence lifecycle. Once misconduct is suspected, investigators must act quickly to prevent automatic system processes from overwriting logs, to secure devices used by potential subjects, and to restrict access to relevant systems. Preservation measures may include disabling auto-deletion settings, implementing data holds, restricting user access, creating forensic images of devices, and preserving backup environments.

Forensic imaging - an exact, bit-by-bit copy of a device - is the preferred method for capturing digital evidence. It ensures that investigators work with a duplicate rather than the original, maintaining evidentiary integrity while allowing for analysis without risk of modifying the source data. Forensic imaging also captures deleted files, slack space, registry entries, and other system artifacts invisible to standard users.

Preservation must extend to cloud-based data, which often operates under shared responsibility models. Investigators may need to coordinate with cloud providers to secure logs, audit trails, or user activity records before those records expire according to retention settings.

All preservation steps must be documented carefully, noting what was preserved, when, by whom, and using which method. These details contribute directly to the chain of custody and help demonstrate that evidence has remained intact throughout the investigation.

Collection Techniques and Forensic Precision

Digital evidence collection requires tools and techniques that avoid altering the data. Investigators typically use forensic software capable of extracting data in a manner that maintains authenticity while capturing metadata and system artifacts. The process must be conducted by trained personnel who understand the risks of improper extraction.

Forensic collection should also account for encryption, password protection, access controls, and system-level restrictions. Devices may require legal authorizations or internal permissions before they can be accessed. Investigators must respect privacy laws, employee rights, and regulatory constraints throughout the process.

In many investigations, advanced techniques are required. These may include recovering deleted files, decrypting protected data, reconstructing fragmented information, or analyzing volatile memory captured before a device is powered down. Each technique must be justified, appropriate, and well-documented to ensure the evidentiary reliability of the results.

Verifying Authenticity and Integrity

Digital evidence must be demonstrably authentic. Investigators use methods such as hashing - applying mathematical algorithms that generate unique identifiers for data sets - to prove that files remain unchanged during collection and analysis. If a data set's hash value is consistent throughout the investigation, integrity is confirmed.

In many cases, digital evidence includes metadata that helps establish authenticity. Metadata may include timestamps, user identifiers, file origin, device information, and modification history. These attributes can confirm the circumstances of creation or reveal attempts to conceal or alter information.

Authenticity also requires demonstrating that evidence was obtained through proper technical procedures. When investigators use recognized forensic tools, follow established protocols, and maintain a complete chain of custody, they strengthen the credibility of their findings. Regulators and courts place significant weight on adherence to forensic standards because digital evidence is so susceptible to accidental alteration.

Analyzing Digital Evidence

After preservation and collection, investigators analyze digital evidence to uncover patterns, reconstruct events, and identify inconsistencies. Digital evidence analysis involves reviewing logs, email content, communication threads, device activity, file histories, and user access records. Investigators may need to correlate data across platforms - for example, comparing emails against login logs or aligning financial transactions with device activity.

Digital timelines are particularly valuable. By arranging activities chronologically, investigators can identify actions taken to commit or conceal misconduct. Timelines reveal how quickly events occurred, who participated, and which systems were used.

Investigators must also account for technical artifacts. System logs, cache files, browser histories, and registry entries may reveal behaviors not captured by primary data sources. These artifacts often play a critical role in exposing attempts at deletion, manipulation, or evasion.

Challenges Unique to Digital Evidence

Digital evidence presents challenges not found in traditional investigations. Devices may contain massive volumes of data, requiring advanced tools to filter relevant information. Cloud environments may involve shared infrastructure, making it difficult to isolate data belonging to specific users. Encryption and privacy settings may require special methods or legal authorizations.

Another challenge is the rapid pace of technological change. New communication platforms, remote work tools, and cybersecurity enhancements continuously reshape how data is created and stored. Investigators must keep current with emerging technologies to ensure evidence is collected effectively.

Cybercriminals also intentionally obscure their digital footprints. Techniques such as masking IP addresses, encrypting communications, using disposable accounts, or wiping devices require investigators to employ advanced forensic methods to reconstruct events.

The Role of Documentation in Digital Evidence Handling

Every step of the digital evidence process must be documented thoroughly. Documentation supports transparency, allows for peer review, and enables external stakeholders to assess the investigation's rigor. It is also essential for ensuring that findings are defensible in legal or regulatory settings.

Documentation should describe the tools used, the rationale for each method, the sequence of events, and the results of hash verifications. It must also record any anomalies or complications encountered during the process.

FORENSIC EXAMINATION AND ANALYTICAL TECHNIQUES

Forensic examination and analytical techniques are crucial in transforming raw evidence into meaningful, defensible conclusions. Financial crime investigations rely not only on collecting records but also on interpreting them through structured, disciplined methods that uncover hidden relationships, identify anomalies, and reveal patterns of behavior. Forensic work bridges the gap between data and insight, ensuring that findings are supported by objective analysis rather than assumptions or intuition. The quality of this work often determines whether an investigation withstands external scrutiny, influences remediation decisions, or supports regulatory reporting.

The Role of Forensic Methodology

Forensic methodology provides a systematic framework for examining evidence. It ensures that investigators apply consistent procedures and analytical logic across every case, regardless of the specific misconduct under review. This approach reduces bias, enhances accuracy, and creates a disciplined environment in which evidence is assessed objectively.

Forensic methodology typically includes defining analytical objectives, establishing hypotheses, identifying relevant data sets, applying appropriate analytical techniques, and testing findings against multiple sources. These steps help ensure that conclusions are grounded, replicable, and resistant to challenge.

Following a structured methodology, investigators avoid relying solely on surface-level observations. Instead, they explore underlying causes, compare multiple lines of evidence, and examine whether results align with both the documentary and transactional record.

Financial Forensic Analysis

A major component of forensic examination is financial analysis, which seeks to reconstruct account activity, quantify losses, identify irregularities, and assess compliance with policies or regulations. Investigators may conduct reconciliations, review journal entries, compare internal records against external statements, and trace the movement of funds across accounts or entities.

Tracing is one of the most common techniques in financial crime work. It involves following money flows from origin to destination, identifying how funds moved, which accounts were involved, and whether transactions served legitimate or improper purposes. Tracing often reveals attempts to hide the origin of funds, structure transactions to avoid detection, or route money through intermediaries to obscure links between parties.

Variance analysis is another important tool. Investigators compare actual results against expected or historical patterns to identify anomalies. For example, an unexplained spike in vendor payments, unusual fluctuations in cash balances, or irregular timing of transactions may signal misconduct.

In more complex cases, investigators may conduct ratio analysis, examining financial indicators such as turnover rates, expenditure ratios, or liquidity measures. Significant deviations from norms may indicate fraud, manipulation, or concealed liabilities.

Digital Forensic Techniques

Digital forensic techniques support the analysis of electronic evidence collected from devices, systems, and network environments. These techniques help investigators uncover activities that may not be visible in traditional financial records.

Digital forensic work may involve reviewing file system metadata, analyzing system logs, examining deleted files, reconstructing internet browsing histories, or reviewing email and messaging content. These techniques allow investigators to determine what users accessed, when actions occurred, and whether attempts were made to alter or erase evidence.

In some investigations, registry analysis, artifact recovery, or memory analysis may be necessary. These techniques reveal details such as program executions, USB device connections, or remnants of encrypted communications. They are particularly useful in cyber-enabled financial crime where individuals rely on sophisticated methods to conceal digital footprints.

Network forensics may be required when misconduct involves unauthorized access or external communication channels. Investigators may analyze network traffic, firewall logs, or intrusion detection alerts to determine whether systems were breached or whether sensitive data was transmitted outside authorized channels.

Behavioral and Pattern Analysis

Forensic examination is not limited to numerical or digital data. Behavioral and pattern analysis plays a significant role in understanding how individuals acted and whether those actions align with misconduct indicators.

Behavioral analysis may involve reviewing sequences of actions taken by employees or external actors, assessing whether those actions were consistent with legitimate job duties, or determining whether activity appeared calculated, concealed, or opportunistic. For example, repeated after-hours system access by an employee with no operational need may warrant further scrutiny.

Pattern analysis helps identify trends that may not be visible within individual data points. Investigators may examine clusters of transactions, recurring activity near reporting thresholds, correlations between different accounts, or repeated behaviors across time. Patterns often reveal deliberate strategies, such as structuring payments to avoid detection or repeatedly manipulating invoices.

In some investigations, linguistic or communication analysis may be used. This involves reviewing emails, messages, or reports to identify coded language, inconsistent explanations, or coordinated activity among individuals. This technique helps investigators evaluate intent, which often cannot be captured through transactional evidence alone.

Analytical Tools and Technology

Modern forensic examination relies heavily on analytical tools capable of processing large volumes of data. Advanced software allows investigators to analyze transactions, visualize relationships, search unstructured documents, and identify anomalies quickly and accurately.

Data analytics platforms help investigators sort and filter millions of records, apply algorithms that flag suspicious activity, and build models that estimate expected behavior. Visualization tools transform raw data into maps, timelines, or flowcharts that make complex information easier to interpret. These tools are particularly helpful in cross-border investigations or cases involving numerous entities.

Text analytics and machine learning tools assist in reviewing unstructured data such as emails or reports. These tools can identify key terms, emotional tone, communication patterns, or document clusters. While human judgment remains essential, technology accelerates the review process and highlights areas that warrant deeper analysis.

However, the use of technology requires discipline. Tools must be configured properly, results validated, and interpretations supported by evidence. Analytical tools do not replace forensic judgment; they enhance it.

Testing and Validating Findings

A central part of forensic examination is testing and validating findings to ensure accuracy and reliability. Investigators must challenge their own conclusions, seek alternative explanations, and verify results with independent data sources.

For example, if tracing suggests that certain payments were diverted for illicit purposes, investigators must confirm the legitimacy of each intermediary account, verify transaction dates, and consider whether the behavior could have a benign explanation. Validation helps prevent false conclusions and strengthens the defensibility of findings.

Cross-referencing is essential. Evidence from emails should match financial data; system logs should align with user activity; physical records should correspond to digital entries. When discrepancies appear, investigators must understand whether they reflect error, manipulation, or limitations in the available data.

Review by senior investigators or technical experts further enhances quality. Peer review helps identify analytical gaps, confirm assumptions, and ensure that conclusions are well-supported and consistent with industry standards.

Quantifying Financial Impact

Forensic examination often involves calculating the financial consequences of misconduct. This may include determining losses, identifying unjust enrichment, calculating improper payments, or estimating liabilities arising from regulatory breaches.

Quantification requires a detailed understanding of the underlying transactions. Investigators must consider the time frame of misconduct, the direct and indirect effects, and the financial implications for the organization. They may need to reconstruct financial statements, adjust for market conditions, or interpret contractual provisions.

Precise quantification is important not only for internal decision-making but also for reporting to regulators, supporting recovery efforts, or pursuing legal action. Numerical accuracy and clear documentation are essential.

Integrating Findings into a Coherent Narrative

Ultimately, forensic examination must produce a coherent narrative that explains what occurred, how it occurred, and what evidence supports those conclusions. Analytical techniques are tools; their purpose is to contribute to a factual storyline grounded in documented activity.

A coherent narrative integrates financial, digital, documentary, and behavioral evidence. It explains links between individuals, systems, and transactions. It outlines timelines, identifies critical junctures, and highlights the mechanisms used to commit or conceal misconduct.

This narrative becomes the basis for the final investigative report. It provides clarity to decision-makers, regulators, or law enforcement and ensures that the investigation's findings are understood within the broader context of organizational controls and risk exposure.

ASSESSING EVIDENCE RELIABILITY AND INTEGRITY

Assessing the reliability and integrity of evidence is essential for ensuring that investigative findings rest on a stable foundation. Even the most comprehensive evidence collection and forensic analysis become meaningless if the underlying material cannot be trusted. Reliability determines whether evidence accurately reflects the events it purports to describe. Integrity determines whether the evidence has remained whole, authentic, and untampered. Together, these concepts serve as the qualifying test for whether evidence can support conclusions that must withstand regulatory, legal, and organizational scrutiny.

The Principles of Reliability and Integrity

Reliability concerns the accuracy and consistency of evidence. Investigators must determine whether documents, digital files, statements, or transactional data match objective reality and align with other evidence. Reliability asks the question: *Can this evidence be depended upon as a truthful representation of events?*

Integrity concerns the condition of the evidence - whether it has been altered, manipulated, or degraded. Even reliable evidence can lose its value if integrity is compromised through improper handling, system errors, or intentional interference.

These principles are interconnected. Integrity issues often undermine reliability, and unreliable evidence often raises integrity concerns. An investigation must examine both dimensions with equal rigor.

Authenticity as the Foundation of Integrity

Authenticity is the starting point for assessing integrity. Investigators must confirm that each piece of evidence is genuinely what it claims to be. For physical documents, authenticity might involve reviewing signatures, letterheads, or consistency with established templates. For digital evidence, authenticity often depends on metadata, audit logs, and technical artifacts that verify origin, creation date, user activity, and modification history.

Digital authenticity also relies on hashing - generating cryptographic values that uniquely represent a file. Matching hash values confirm that the evidence has not changed from its original form. When evidence lacks metadata or displays unusual attributes, investigators must explore whether this resulted from system limitations, human error, or deliberate manipulation.

Authenticity assessments extend to statements and verbal accounts. Investigators must evaluate whether witness explanations align with objective evidence, whether memories appear consistent over time, and whether statements change as new information emerges. Authenticity does not guarantee truthfulness but serves as a starting point for reliability analysis.

Evaluating Completeness and Accuracy

Reliability requires evidence to be both complete and accurate. Completeness refers to whether the evidence set covers the full scope of events under review. Incomplete evidence creates gaps that may distort interpretation or conceal critical elements of misconduct. Accuracy refers to whether the contents of the evidence reflect factual events without error or distortion.

For documentary evidence, investigators must confirm that versions are final, not drafts, and reflect all relevant information. For digital records, completeness may depend on whether system logs span the entire review period, whether emails were archived properly, or whether backup files provide continuity where primary data is missing.

Financial evidence must be checked for omissions or inconsistencies. A series of transactions may appear complete on the surface but may exclude off-ledger activity, manual adjustments, or external accounts. Comparing internal records with external statements helps verify accuracy.

Ensuring completeness often requires triangulation - cross-referencing multiple sources to confirm that all relevant data has been captured. When gaps appear, investigators must determine whether they result from retention policies, technical failures, human oversight, or intentional concealment.

Identifying Signs of Manipulation

Evidence manipulation can take many forms, some subtle and others overt. Detecting manipulation requires an understanding of normal patterns, system behaviors, and typical documentation practices.

For digital evidence, investigators must examine metadata anomalies, irregular file timestamps, sudden absence of logs, or inconsistencies between audit trails and user activity. Unusual deletion patterns, overwritten files, or attempts to disable logging mechanisms are common indicators of tampering.

For financial records, manipulation may appear as duplicate entries, unexplained adjustments, forced journal postings, sudden reversals, or transactions that bypass established controls. Investigators must determine whether discrepancies are the result of legitimate corrections or signals of concealment.

Document manipulation may involve altered signatures, mismatched formatting, inconsistent terminology, or content that conflicts with contemporary communications. In some cases, investigators may encounter fabricated documents created to justify unauthorized actions or hide discrepancies.

When manipulation is suspected, investigators must document the basis for concern, collect supporting data, and evaluate whether the conduct was intentional or negligent. Intent matters, particularly when determining misconduct severity or regulatory exposure.

Assessing Witness Credibility

Witness statements form an important component of many investigations, but witness reliability cannot be assumed. People may provide inaccurate information due to faulty memory, misunderstanding, fear of consequences, or deliberate misrepresentation.

To assess credibility, investigators must compare statements with objective evidence, examine consistency across different interviews, evaluate whether the individual has a personal interest in the outcome, and consider the witness's proximity to relevant events. Investigators should also observe whether statements evolve unnecessarily over time or whether key details shift depending on the questions asked.

Credibility assessment does not mean dismissing imperfect statements. Instead, it involves contextualizing witness testimony and determining how it fits into the broader evidence. Witness evidence often helps explain motivations, provide context, or clarify why certain decisions were made. Even when credibility concerns arise, witness accounts may still contain useful insights, but they must be interpreted cautiously.

Evaluating System Reliability

When evidence originates from electronic systems, investigators must assess whether those systems operate reliably. System reliability refers to whether the underlying platform consistently records data in a complete, accurate, and tamper-resistant manner.

Systems vary greatly in terms of logging capabilities, retention settings, data accuracy, and security controls. Investigators must understand whether logs overwrite automatically, whether audit trails capture all user actions, and whether system administrators have privileges that could affect integrity. Evaluating system reliability may require discussions with IT staff or reviewing technical documentation.

When systems have known weaknesses - such as outdated software, limited logging, or weak access controls - investigators must account for these limitations when assessing evidence.

System deficiencies do not invalidate the evidence but influence how much weight it can carry.

Corroboration across Evidence Types

One of the most effective methods for assessing reliability is corroboration. Because individual pieces of evidence may be incomplete or ambiguous, investigators must evaluate whether different sources align. This cross-verification helps strengthen conclusions and reduces reliance on any single record or statement.

For example, if a financial record indicates a suspicious payment, investigators may corroborate it through bank statements, emails discussing the transaction, system logs showing who initiated it, or interviews confirming its purpose. Consistency across sources enhances reliability; inconsistency signals the need for deeper examination.

Corroboration also helps identify misinterpretations. Evidence that appears suspicious in isolation may seem benign when contextualized through other sources. Conversely, evidence that appears normal may reveal misconduct when paired with another data set.

Understanding Context and Organizational Environment

Evidence cannot be assessed reliably without understanding the context in which it was created. Investigators must consider policies, procedures, business practices, industry norms, and operational constraints. This contextual awareness helps differentiate between errors caused by weak controls and actions that suggest misconduct.

For example, if a system allows manual overrides, an override may not be suspicious unless it occurs unusually often, is used in high-risk transactions, or is tied to individuals with a motive to conceal activity. Similarly, variations in documentation quality may reflect inconsistent administrative practices rather than deliberate manipulation.

Understanding context also helps investigators assess whether evidence aligns with typical behavior. Reliable assessments require distinguishing between normal deviations and meaningful anomalies.

Documenting Reliability Assessments

Every judgment about evidence reliability and integrity must be documented. Investigators should record how evidence was evaluated, what anomalies were found, how they were interpreted, and what corroboration was identified. Documentation ensures that others reviewing the investigation - whether regulators, courts, or internal supervisors - can understand the basis for conclusions.

Proper documentation includes noting limitations or uncertainties. Transparency about constraints strengthens investigative credibility by acknowledging areas where evidence was lacking or inconclusive.

CHAPTER 12

INTERVIEWING AND HUMAN INTELLIGENCE

INTERVIEW STRATEGIES AND PREPARATION

EFFECTIVE INTERVIEWING is one of the most critical components of financial crime investigation. Documents, data, and digital evidence establish facts, but interviews provide insight into intent, decision-making, and relationships that cannot be captured through records alone. For this reason, interviews must be approached with methodical planning rather than improvisation. Thorough preparation not only increases the likelihood of uncovering accurate information but also prevents misinterpretation, reduces risks, and strengthens the credibility of investigative outcomes.

Establishing the Objective

Every interview must begin with a clear understanding of its purpose. Investigators should identify the specific information that the interview is intended to confirm, clarify, or challenge. Without a defined objective, interviews often become unfocused conversations that consume time without producing meaningful insight. Objectives should be based on gaps in existing evidence, inconsistencies in documentation, unexplained behavior, or areas where intent is not yet established.

Defining the objective also determines the structure of the interview. A discussion aimed at understanding a transaction's rationale will differ from one examining internal control failures or assessing an individual's knowledge of irregular activity. Preparing with precision allows the investigator to choose the right approach, determine the appropriate sequence of questions, and anticipate potential areas of resistance.

Understanding the Interviewee's Role and Perspective

An interview is more effective when the investigator understands the interviewee's responsibilities, access, and potential incentives. Individuals behave differently depending on their role within an organization, their involvement in the matter under investigation, and their perception of personal or professional risk. Reviewing job descriptions, reporting lines, performance history, and prior involvement in relevant processes helps contextualize statements made during the interview.

Investigators must also consider how the interviewee is likely to perceive the interview. A witness may be cooperative but anxious. An employee implicated in misconduct may arrive defensive or evasive. A subject with technical expertise may attempt to challenge the investigator's understanding. Anticipating these perspectives helps the investigator maintain control of the interview and prevent the interviewee from influencing its direction.

Reviewing available Evidence

Preparation requires a comprehensive review of available information before any interview takes place. This includes transactional data, internal emails, system logs, contracts, policy documents, and any previous statements provided by the interviewee. Investigators should identify inconsistencies, unanswered questions, and areas where the evidence is incomplete or ambiguous.

The review must be analytical rather than superficial. It is important to understand not just what occurred but how events align with normal patterns and institutional procedures. An interviewee is less likely to provide misleading explanations when the investigator demonstrates familiarity with operational details and can challenge vague answers with specific references.

A detailed review also helps the investigator determine whether potentially sensitive issues should be introduced at the outset or held until later in the interview. Strategically timing certain questions can elicit more candid responses or expose contradictions that reveal insight into motive and intent.

Selecting the Interview Format and Setting

The environment in which an interview takes place influences the quality of information obtained. A neutral and private setting reduces distractions, encourages focus, and minimizes the pressure that the interviewee may feel from colleagues or external observers. The space should be arranged to promote open communication while ensuring the investigator retains control of the interaction.

In-person interviews remain the preferred format for most financial crime investigations because they allow assessment of non-verbal cues, rapport, and behavioral indicators. However, remote interviews may be necessary in cross-border cases or when logistical constraints arise. When remotely conducted, investigators must ensure that the interviewee is alone, not being coached, and not accessing external information. Confirmation of the interviewee's environment should be an explicit part of the opening procedure.

Regardless of format, investigators should confirm that all necessary technology - recorders, secure connections, or note-taking tools - is functioning properly. Technical issues can compromise credibility, delay proceedings, or create grounds for disputing the accuracy of the interview record.

Structuring the Interview

Although interviews should appear conversational, they must be structured with clear intention. A well-designed structure creates a balance between allowing the interviewee to express themselves freely and ensuring that critical topics are thoroughly explored.

A common structure begins with establishing rapport and clarifying the purpose of the interview. Investigators should explain the scope of the discussion, expectations regarding truthfulness, and any confidentiality limitations. This sets boundaries and reinforces the seriousness of the process.

The next stage typically focuses on general questions that encourage the interviewee to describe their role, responsibilities, and routine activities. This baseline provides context and allows the investigator to identify inconsistencies later in the interview.

Once foundation information is established, the investigator transitions into targeted questions related to the core subject matter. These questions should be precise, structured, and based on evidence already reviewed. Open-ended questions help uncover detail, while specific questions test accuracy and consistency. The investigator must maintain control of the sequence to prevent the interviewee from diverting the discussion into irrelevant or distracting areas.

The interview should conclude with an opportunity for the interviewee to clarify or add information, followed by a summary of key points to ensure mutual understanding. Closing the interview with clarity reduces the risk of misinterpretation and reinforces the accuracy of the record.

Developing Questioning Strategies

Effective questioning strategies require a balance between open-ended and closed questions. Open questions encourage the interviewee to provide narrative responses that offer insight into thinking, behavior, and motivation. Closed questions help verify facts, test consistency, and narrow down ambiguous statements.

The investigator should avoid leading questions that suggest a preferred answer, as these undermine credibility and may distort the interviewee's responses. Instead, neutral phrasing allows the interviewee to articulate their perspective without feeling directed or influenced.

Questions must be sequenced logically. Starting with foundational facts builds momentum and reduces defensiveness. As the interview progresses, questions can gradually become more probing. This strategic escalation encourages candor and builds pressure on deceptive interviewees without appearing confrontational.

It is also important to anticipate where the interviewee may offer incomplete, vague, or evasive answers. Preparing follow-up questions allows the investigator to explore these areas immediately, preventing the interviewee from controlling the narrative or avoiding uncomfortable subjects.

Managing Documentation and Records

Accurate documentation is essential for maintaining the integrity of the interview. Investigators should take detailed notes, even when the interview is recorded. Notes help capture tone, emphasis, pauses, and other nuances that may not be evident from the recording alone.

Documentation should focus on facts rather than interpretation. It must be clear, objective, and organized. The investigator should note key statements, contradictions, and any behavioral cues that may be relevant in later analysis. Documentation must also comply with legal and regulatory requirements, including retention periods and confidentiality protocols.

Immediately after the interview, investigators should review their notes to ensure completeness. Delays in documentation can lead to errors or gaps that undermine the reliability of the interview record.

Anticipating Risk and Resistance

Financial crime interviews frequently involve individuals who may experience personal or professional risk. Some may fear disciplinary action; others may worry about potential legal consequences. These fears shape behavior and can lead to resistance, defensiveness, or attempts to control the interview.

Preparation must therefore include assessing where resistance is likely to occur. Investigators should identify potential points of tension - such as gaps in documentation, conflicting evidence, or sensitive topics - and plan strategies for addressing them. This may involve preparing alternative question paths, determining when to introduce certain evidence, or deciding whether confrontation is necessary.

Risk assessment also includes evaluating the interviewee's potential access to counsel, external influence, or internal support structures. These factors determine the level of preparedness required and influence the investigator's strategy.

Final Preparation and Mental Readiness

Technical preparation is not sufficient on its own. The investigator must also be psychologically ready for the interview. Interviews require concentration, patience, and control. The investigator must manage their own demeanor, maintain neutrality, and remain alert to subtle shifts in tone or behavior. Any sign of bias, frustration, or assumption can compromise the interview.

MANAGING SUSPECTS, WITNESSES, AND INFORMANTS

Financial crime investigations rely heavily on human intelligence. Documents, data, and digital evidence establish patterns and timelines, but people provide information that reveals motive, intent, and the reasoning behind actions that may appear ambiguous on paper. The approach to managing individuals during interviews varies significantly depending on whether the person is a suspect, a witness, or an informant. Each category requires different strategies, expectations, and safeguards. An investigator must be able to distinguish these roles clearly while adjusting communication, structure, and control to obtain reliable and legally defensible information.

Understanding Role Distinctions

Suspects, witnesses, and informants occupy different positions within the investigative landscape. Their incentives, risks, and expected behaviors differ, which in turn shapes how they should be approached.

A suspect is an individual who may have participated in misconduct or benefited from it. Their statements carry legal implications, and they often enter interviews with defensive postures, concerns about exposure, or intentions to conceal or minimize wrongdoing. The investigator must balance respect for legal rights with rigorous questioning.

Witnesses, by contrast, are individuals who observed, interacted with, or indirectly contributed information relevant to the matter under review. They are not themselves implicated, but their reliability varies based on memory, involvement, and personal interests. Witnesses require reassurance, clarity, and structured questioning to ensure accuracy.

Informants occupy a unique category. They provide information voluntarily, often in confidence, and may seek protection, incentives, or anonymity. Their motivations are mixed - ranging from ethical concerns to personal disputes, professional grievances, or attempts to negotiate favorable treatment. Managing informants requires strict control, careful evaluation of credibility, and awareness of risks.

Understanding these distinctions helps the investigator adapt both strategy and tone to extract the most reliable and useful information from each category.

Managing Suspects

Managing suspects requires a disciplined approach. The investigator must maintain control of the interview while adhering to procedural fairness. Suspects should understand the purpose of the interview, the seriousness of the matter, and their obligation to provide truthful information. However, the investigator should avoid appearing confrontational or accusatory, as this may cause the suspect to withdraw or adopt rigid, defensive behavior.

The key to managing suspects is preparation. The investigator must enter the interview with a detailed understanding of the evidence, including discrepancies, unexplained patterns, and conflicting accounts. Suspects often test the investigator's knowledge by offering partial truths, vague explanations, or attempts to shift blame. A well-prepared investigator is able to challenge such statements calmly and methodically, using evidence to prompt clarification or highlight inconsistencies.

Tone is critical. The investigator should remain professional, patient, and neutral. Displays of frustration, disbelief, or bias can undermine the credibility of the interview and give the suspect grounds to dispute the fairness of the process. Suspects frequently monitor the investigator's reactions, and any emotional response may influence their behavior.

Another important strategy is pacing. Suspects may try to control the interview by speaking rapidly, providing excessive detail, or introducing irrelevant information. The investigator must regulate the pace, pause where necessary, and redirect attention to essential points. Structured questioning - beginning with foundational facts and gradually progressing to more sensitive or contradictory topics - enables the investigator to maintain control while reducing opportunities for manipulation.

Finally, managing a suspect requires recognizing when pressure should escalate and when it should be reduced. Some individuals respond to firm, direct questioning; others may become more cooperative when allowed to speak at length before being challenged. The investigator must read behavioral signals and adjust accordingly, ensuring the interview remains both productive and fair.

Managing Witnesses

Witnesses often play an essential role in constructing timelines, understanding internal processes, and providing context that evidence alone cannot fully reveal. However, their reliability depends on memory, perspective, and willingness to speak candidly. Managing witnesses requires a combination of reassurance, clarity, and structured questioning.

Witnesses should feel safe to provide information without fear of retaliation or misinterpretation. The investigator must explain the interview's purpose, how their information will be used, and any confidentiality limitations. This clarity reduces anxiety and encourages open communication.

Because witnesses may not fully understand the broader context of events, they often provide information based on their perception rather than factual knowledge. The investigator must distinguish between direct observation, assumptions, and interpretations. This requires careful questioning, with the investigator prompting witnesses to describe what they saw, heard, or did, rather than asking them to draw conclusions.

Witnesses may also have biases - some subtle, others pronounced. A witness who is close to a suspect may unintentionally minimize suspicious behavior. Another who resented a colleague may exaggerate concerns. The investigator must remain alert to emotional cues, inconsistencies, or signs that the witness is influenced by personal motives. Comparing witness accounts with documentary evidence helps verify accuracy.

Memory lapses are common, especially when events occurred months or years earlier. The investigator should approach gaps calmly and avoid suggesting answers. Leading questions can distort memory and undermine the integrity of the interview. Instead, the investigator should give the witness time to recall information and provide prompts grounded in known facts without implying desired responses.

Managing witnesses effectively means maintaining a supportive but structured environment—one that encourages candor while ensuring the information collected is precise, accurate, and grounded in reality.

Managing Informants

Informants are both valuable and potentially risky sources of information. They provide insight that may be inaccessible through ordinary investigative methods, but they also present complex challenges relating to credibility, motivation, and safety.

Motivation must be assessed carefully. Some informants come forward because they are genuinely concerned about misconduct. Others may have personal grievances, conflicts of interest, or expectations of reward. The investigator must evaluate whether the informant's motives affect the reliability of their statements. This does not mean discarding information based on motive alone, but it requires careful corroboration.

Confidentiality is essential. Informants often fear retaliation or professional consequences. The investigator must explain what can and cannot be kept confidential and must adhere strictly to any protections promised. Even minor breaches of confidentiality can expose informants to harm and damage the credibility of the entire investigation.

Control is equally important. Informants sometimes attempt to shape the investigation's direction, exaggerate claims, or withhold information to maintain influence. The investigator must remain objective, avoiding undue reliance on any single informant and maintaining full independence in decisions.

Documentation of informant interactions is critical. Each discussion should be recorded in detail, noting the information provided, the informant's attitude, and any relevant background. This documentation helps later assess reliability and prevents disputes regarding what was said or promised.

Managing informants also requires an awareness of legal boundaries. Some jurisdictions impose strict rules about how informants may be used, especially if they themselves are implicated in wrongdoing. The investigator must ensure that interactions comply with legal requirements to prevent the investigation from being compromised.

Building and Maintaining Rapport

Although the strategies for managing suspects, witnesses, and informants differ, rapport is important in all interviews. Rapport does not mean friendship; it means creating an environment in which the interviewee feels willing to communicate. This involves demonstrating respect, active listening, and professionalism.

Neutrality helps maintain rapport. Interviewees should not feel judged or dismissed, even when their statements conflict with evidence. If the investigator remains calm and objective, interviewees are more likely to remain engaged and less likely to shut down.

Rapport also allows the investigator to observe shifts in tone, hesitation, or discomfort that may indicate areas requiring deeper exploration. These behavioral shifts often provide insight into underlying concerns or concealed information.

Evaluating Credibility across Interviewee Types

Credibility assessment is central to managing suspects, witnesses, and informants. It requires the investigator to examine not just what is said but how it is said, and how statements align with other evidence. Factors such as consistency, detail, plausibility, and demeanor all contribute to credibility evaluation.

The investigator must avoid assumptions based on personality, confidence, or communication style. Some individuals appear outwardly composed while providing false information, whereas others may appear nervous even when truthful. Credibility must therefore be assessed through structured analysis, not intuition.

Cross-referencing statements with documentation, digital records, and other interviews is essential. No interview should be treated as an isolated source of truth. The strength of an investigation comes from aligning human intelligence with objective evidence to create a coherent account.

Maintaining Professional Boundaries

Regardless of the interviewee type, maintaining boundaries is critical. Investigators must avoid personal involvement, emotional reactions, or leniency influenced by sympathy or hostility. Clear boundaries preserve objectivity and protect the integrity of the investigation.

HANDLING EVASION, DENIALS, AND MANIPULATION

Financial crime interviews often involve individuals who attempt to protect themselves, others, or an underlying scheme through evasive behavior, strategic denials, or deliberate manipulation. Such tactics are not always overt. They may appear in subtle shifts in tone, selective memory, excessive detail, or carefully crafted statements aimed at influencing the investigator's assumptions. Effective handling of these behaviors requires a combination of preparation, observational skill, psychological awareness, and methodical questioning. The goal is never to force confessions; rather, it is to obtain accurate information, expose inconsistencies, and assess credibility reliably.

Understanding the Nature of Evasive Behavior

Evasion manifests in many forms. Some interviewees avoid direct answers by shifting to unrelated topics, repeating general statements, or claiming they cannot recall events that appear central to their role. Others provide minimal responses designed to obscure details. Evasion may also take the form of excessive politeness or exaggerated cooperation, creating an appearance of openness while withholding substantive information.

Understanding why an individual engages in evasive behavior is important. Some do so because they fear personal consequences. Others attempt to protect colleagues or the organization. In certain cases, the interviewee may feel overwhelmed or unprepared. The investigator should not assume malicious intent immediately. Instead, they should analyze whether the evasive behavior is consistent with the interviewee's responsibilities, access, and documented interactions.

The most effective way to counter evasion is to maintain control of the interview's structure. By asking clear, precise questions and enforcing boundaries, the investigator reduces opportunities for diversion. If an interviewee avoids answering, the investigator should calmly return to the original question and repeat it in a slightly different form. Repetition of key points - without showing frustration or coercion - signals that evasion will not succeed.

Addressing Denials with Methodical Inquiry

Denials are common in interviews involving suspected misconduct. A denial may be factual, strategic, reflexive, or defensive. Some individuals deny involvement immediately as a protective mechanism, even before processing the question. Others present rehearsed or carefully framed denials crafted to minimize risk.

The investigator must treat denials neutrally. Accepting them at face value or confronting them aggressively both create vulnerabilities. A neutral approach allows the investigator to examine the denial objectively while reducing emotional escalation.

When a denial is issued, the investigator should explore it through structured inquiry. This involves examining surrounding behavior, verifying timelines, and testing the consistency of the denial with existing evidence. Rather than asking the interviewee to repeat or justify the denial, the investigator should seek factual detail. People who deny truthfully can usually provide coherent context and supporting information. Those who deny falsely often struggle with detail, shift stories, or rely on general statements.

Investigators must not attempt to "break" denials through pressure. The aim is to establish clarity, not to obtain admissions. Excessive pressure invites retraction, claims of coercion, or unreliable statements. Instead, the investigator should ask open but focused questions that gradually narrow the scope of acceptable answers. This creates a structured environment in which inconsistencies naturally emerge.

The investigator should also be alert to qualified denials. Statements such as "I don't recall doing that," "Not to my knowledge," or "That doesn't sound like something I would do" are forms of denial that offer flexibility to adjust later. These require careful follow-up. The investigator should seek clarification of what the interviewee does recall, what they would normally do in such a situation, and whether any documentation exists that might help confirm events.

Recognizing Manipulation Tactics

Manipulation presents a more deliberate form of obstruction. Manipulative interviewees seek to influence the investigator's perceptions, redirect responsibility, or control the narrative. Manipulation may appear subtle - such as excessive flattery, emotional appeals, or attempts to create rapport for strategic purposes. It may also be more direct, including accusations against colleagues, exaggerated claims of cooperation, or strategic withholding of information.

One common tactic is selective disclosure. An interviewee may voluntarily present information that appears helpful while avoiding key details that would expose misconduct. By appearing cooperative, they attempt to reduce the investigator's scrutiny. Another tactic is overloading the investigator with irrelevant detail, hoping to create confusion or reduce focus. Manipulative individuals may also adopt dramatic emotional displays - frustration, indignation, or distress - to disrupt the interview's structure or shift the investigator's attention.

The investigator must remain objective and unmoved by these tactics. Professional detachment is essential. Manipulation often becomes ineffective when the investigator maintains consistent tone, adheres to the interview structure, and refrains from reacting emotionally. By refusing to reward manipulative behavior with changes in questioning or tone, the investigator reinforces control.

Maintaining Control without Confrontation

Handling evasion, denials, and manipulation requires control, not confrontation. The investigator must create an environment in which the interviewee understands that evasive or manipulative behavior will not influence the outcome. Control is established through clarity, composure, and strategic questioning.

One effective technique is signposting. This involves telling the interviewee what topic will be addressed next. Signposting reduces opportunities for diversion because the interviewee understands that specific subjects will be explored. It also signals that the investigator is well-prepared and expects direct answers.

Another technique is summarizing. After the interviewee speaks, the investigator restates the key points neutrally. This ensures accuracy while preventing the interviewee from shifting the narrative without detection. Summarizing also helps the interviewer highlight contradictions that may not be obvious to the interviewee. When inconsistencies emerge, the investigator can revisit them calmly, presenting the discrepancy as something requiring clarification rather than confrontation.

A controlled interview is predictable in structure but flexible in approach. The investigator should not hesitate to pause, redirect, or revisit earlier points. Pauses can be particularly effective. When the investigator remains silent after an evasive or incomplete answer, the interviewee often fills the silence with additional information. Pausing also signals that the investigator is considering the response carefully, which may prompt the interviewee to elaborate or correct their statement.

Using Evidence Strategically

Evidence is a powerful tool when used strategically. The investigator should avoid presenting evidence prematurely, as doing so may allow an uncooperative interviewee to adjust their story. Instead, evidence should be introduced at moments where inconsistencies have already emerged. Presenting evidence in this way highlights contradictions and encourages the interviewee to address them directly.

The investigator should introduce evidence factually, without accusation. For example, referencing a document or transaction record should be done in a neutral tone. The goal is to reduce defensiveness and encourage explanation. When confronted with evidence that contradicts earlier statements, individuals often shift from denial to partial acknowledgment. These shifts provide insight into intent and may reveal areas requiring deeper exploration.

Technical evidence, such as system logs or audit trails, can be particularly useful. Interviewees rarely expect investigators to possess detailed digital records. When such evidence is presented later in the interview, it can disrupt rehearsed narratives and prompt more candid responses.

Managing Emotional Reactions

Handling emotional responses is part of managing evasion, denial, and manipulation. Some interviewees become frustrated when challenged. Others may express fear, indignation, or anxiety. Emotional reactions do not automatically indicate deception; they may reflect stress, misunderstanding, or concern about consequences. The investigator must acknowledge the emotion without allowing it to derail the interview.

Maintaining a calm, steady tone encourages the interviewee to regain composure. If emotions escalate to the point of disrupting the interview, the investigator may offer a short break. Breaks allow emotions to settle and reduce impulsive statements that may later be disputed.

The investigator should avoid responding emotionally. Showing irritation, sympathy, or disbelief gives manipulative interviewees opportunities to influence the interview. Emotional neutrality preserves control and protects the integrity of the process.

Assessing Patterns and Consistency

An individual response may not reveal deception, but patterns of behavior often do. Patterns such as repeated claims of memory loss, constant deflection to unrelated topics, inconsistent timelines, or shifting explanations indicate areas requiring deeper inquiry. The investigator should note these patterns and revisit them systematically.

Consistency is another key factor. Honest individuals typically maintain consistent accounts even when questioned in different ways. Deceptive individuals often struggle to maintain stability across multiple question sets. By varying the order of questions and revisiting previous topics later in the interview, the investigator can test the durability of the interviewee's statements.

Ensuring Integrity and Reliability

Handling evasion, denials, and manipulation requires adherence to investigative integrity. The investigator must ensure that questioning remains fair, objective, and legally compliant. Interviews must be properly documented, with clear records of statements and observable behaviors. This documentation provides critical support if an interviewee later challenges the interview's fairness or accuracy.

BODY LANGUAGE, BEHAVIORAL CUES, AND CULTURAL SENSITIVITY

Interviews require more than the ability to ask strategic questions and interpret verbal responses. Much of the insight an investigator gains comes from observing how individuals behave as they speak. Body language, tone, and non-verbal cues provide valuable context that complements the factual content of the interview. However, non-verbal cues must be treated as indicators, not evidence. Misinterpretation can lead to false assumptions, particularly when cultural differences, personal traits, or situational stress influence behavior. Effective use of behavioral cues requires careful observation, balanced judgment, and an understanding of the broader context in which the interview takes place.

The Role of Body Language in Financial Crime Interviews

Body language reflects psychological states, emotional reactions, and cognitive processes. During an interview, individuals often display non-verbal signals that reveal hesitation, discomfort, confidence, or uncertainty. These signals may support verbal statements or contradict them, offering clues about areas requiring deeper exploration.

However, body language must never be used as a standalone measure of credibility. Human behavior is complex, and individuals may display anxiety, restlessness, or discomfort for reasons unrelated to deception. Professional pressure, fear of misinterpretation, or unfamiliarity with investigative settings can influence posture and facial expressions. Therefore, the investigator must interpret body language cautiously and in combination with evidence, verbal responses, and the individual's baseline behavior.

Body language becomes most useful when it reflects change. A shift in posture, sudden tension, or altered eye contact may indicate that a particular topic has emotional or cognitive significance for the interviewee. Recognizing these shifts allows the investigator to adjust questioning strategically and explore the underlying reason for the reaction.

Observing Baseline Behavior

An essential step in interpreting body language is establishing a behavioral baseline. A baseline represents how the interviewee typically behaves when discussing neutral topics. It includes posture, eye contact, tone, speech rate, and gestures. Without this baseline, deviations could be misinterpreted.

The early moments of the interview provide the best opportunity to observe baseline behavior. When discussing routine responsibilities, background information, or general procedures, the interviewee is less likely to feel threatened. Their natural disposition emerges, allowing the investigator to note how they respond when comfortable.

Once a baseline is established, deviations may indicate increased cognitive load, emotional stress, or discomfort. For example, an individual who maintains steady eye contact during neutral discussion but consistently avoids it when addressing specific events may be signaling reluctance, uncertainty, or selective recall. The significance lies not in the behavior itself but in the change relative to the baseline.

Recognizing Indicators of Stress or Cognitive Load

In financial crime interviews, stress does not automatically equal deception, but it often signals areas where the interviewee feels vulnerable, uncertain, or pressured. Cognitive load increases when a person must fabricate, conceal, or alter information. It also increases when someone feels scrutinized or fears that their statements may be misinterpreted.

Common signs of increased cognitive load include longer pauses, slower speech, inconsistent gestures, or fragmented explanations. Some individuals may speak more rapidly as they attempt to offer extensive detail that fills gaps they cannot logically support. Others may attempt to control their movements, leading to unnaturally rigid posture.

Stress-related behaviors include fidgeting, throat clearing, touching the face, shifting in the chair, or repeatedly adjusting clothing. These behaviors, on their own, are not reliable indicators of dishonesty. Their value lies in recognizing when they appear consistently in response to certain questions or topics. Stress patterns help the investigator identify points in the narrative that warrant further examination.

Understanding Cultural Influences on Behavior

Cultural context significantly shapes how individuals communicate, express emotion, and respond to authority. Without awareness of cultural differences, an investigator may misinterpret behavior and draw incorrect conclusions about credibility or intent.

In some cultures, direct eye contact with authority figures is viewed as disrespectful or confrontational. In others, indirect communication is preferred, and individuals may avoid direct answers as a sign of politeness rather than evasion. Gesture frequency, personal space, tone modulation, and emotional expressiveness vary widely across cultures. Silence may indicate respect or thoughtfulness in some cultural environments, whereas in others, it may indicate uncertainty or reluctance.

Cultural sensitivity requires the investigator to recognize that behaviors cannot be universally interpreted. Before conducting interviews involving individuals from unfamiliar cultural backgrounds, the investigator should develop a basic understanding of regional norms. This preparation reduces risk of misinterpretation and promotes a respectful, effective interview environment.

Interpreting Tone and Speech Patterns

Verbal behavior extends beyond the words themselves. Tone, pacing, emphasis, and sequence provide insight into how confident or comfortable an interviewee feels. Sudden changes in tone when discussing certain subjects may indicate emotional significance. Hesitation may reflect uncertainty or an attempt to control the narrative.

Speech patterns also reveal cognitive processing. Individuals who speak smoothly when describing their responsibilities but hesitate when recounting specific events may be relying on memory for one topic and reconstruction for another. Similarly, excessive detail may indicate an attempt to distract from missing information, while overly concise answers may signal attempts to limit exposure.

The investigator must balance interpretation with caution. Some individuals naturally speak quickly or slowly. Others may struggle with language proficiency or feel intimidated by the interview setting. Observing patterns and context prevents misinterpretation.

Reading Micro-Expressions and Subtle Signals

Micro-expressions are brief, involuntary facial movements that can reflect underlying emotion. They may appear when an interviewee attempts to mask feelings such as frustration, fear, or irritation. Although micro-expressions can be informative, they are difficult to read reliably without specific training, and overreliance can lead to false assumptions.

Subtle signals - including quick glances toward the exit, tightening of the jaw, or slight shifts in posture - may indicate discomfort or a desire to avoid a topic. These cues are valuable when they align with verbal inconsistencies or changes in behavior. They do not confirm deception, but they help guide the investigator toward areas needing deeper inquiry.

Ensuring Non-Verbal Neutrality as an Interviewer

Interviewers must also be aware of their own non-verbal behavior. Body language influences the tone of the interview and affects how comfortable or defensive the interviewee becomes. An investigator who appears impatient, skeptical, or confrontational may unintentionally escalate tension or encourage evasive behavior.

Maintaining non-verbal neutrality involves stable posture, controlled gestures, and consistent eye contact. A calm presence promotes an environment where the interviewee feels able to speak without feeling judged. Even when the interviewee displays frustrating or manipulative behaviors, the investigator must avoid visible reactions that signal irritation or disbelief. Professional composure enhances credibility and supports the overall integrity of the interview.

Using Behavioral Cues to Shape Questioning

Behavioral cues are most valuable when they inform the investigator's strategy. If an interviewee displays sudden discomfort when asked about a specific transaction, the investigator may choose to explore that transaction further. If body language contradicts verbal confidence, the investigator may revisit the topic later in the interview to test consistency.

Strategic use of behavioral cues does not mean pressing aggressively. Instead, it guides the investigator to areas where additional clarification is needed. Subtle cues often reveal gaps in knowledge, emotional investment in certain outcomes, or attempts to protect others.

Behavioral observation also supports the timing of evidence presentation. Introducing documentation at a moment when an interviewee shows uncertainty or hesitation may prompt more candid explanations. Conversely, presenting evidence too early may shut down communication. The investigator must balance sensitivity and strategy.

Avoiding Overinterpretation

One of the greatest risks in behavioral assessment is overinterpretation. Non-verbal signals are influenced by personality, cultural norms, and situational stress. Even experienced investigators must resist drawing conclusions without supporting evidence. Behavioral cues are indicators, not conclusions.

To avoid overinterpretation, investigators should rely on patterns rather than isolated behaviors. A consistent mismatch between verbal statements and non-verbal cues may indicate that further exploration is needed. However, a single instance of discomfort or hesitation should not be treated as evidence of misconduct.

The investigator's task is to gather accurate information, not to diagnose psychology. Behavioral cues should inform the investigative strategy while maintaining a disciplined focus on evidence.

Integrating Behavioral Observation into Investigative Analysis

Following the interview, behavioral observations should be documented carefully and objectively. Notes should describe the behavior witnessed rather than interpret its meaning. For example, "The interviewee paused for several seconds before answering questions about approval processes" is factual. "The interviewee appeared deceptive" is an interpretation that offers little value without supporting evidence.

Integrating behavioral insight with documentary and digital evidence strengthens the investigative analysis. Patterns of hesitation may point to areas needing reconciliation with transactional data. Emotional reactions may highlight relationships or conflicts relevant to the case. Behavioral consistency across interviews may reinforce credibility.

CHAPTER 13

DIGITAL AND OPEN-SOURCE INTELLIGENCE (OSINT)

SOCIAL MEDIA AND PUBLIC INFORMATION MINING

DIGITAL and OPEN-SOURCE INTELLIGENCE has become an essential component of financial crime investigations. While traditional investigative methods remain vital, vast amounts of relevant information now exist in the public domain, particularly on social media platforms and publicly accessible online sources. These environments contain details that individuals voluntarily share, often without considering how such information may contradict official statements, reveal hidden associations, or expose indicators of misconduct. When approached with discipline and methodological rigor, public information mining provides investigators with valuable insight into personal networks, behavioral patterns, lifestyle indicators, business activities, and inconsistencies that would otherwise remain obscured.

The Value of Social Media in Financial Crime Investigations

Social media platforms - ranging from major global networks, such as Instagram, Facebook, and X (formerly known as Twitter), to specialized forums - capture real-time snapshots of individuals' lives. People share opinions, travel activities, employment updates, photographs, affiliations, and interactions that collectively form a digital footprint. This footprint often supplements structured evidence, providing context that helps investigators assess credibility, identify undisclosed relationships, or detect unexplained lifestyle indicators.

In cases of bribery, corruption, internal fraud, and money laundering, social media can expose inconsistencies between declared income and lifestyle. It may reveal undisclosed assets, travel patterns, or associations with individuals linked to suspicious activity. In complex fraud schemes, perpetrators sometimes use social media to promote false investment opportunities or display fabricated identities. Cybercriminals frequently operate in online communities where they share methods, tools, or illicit services.

However, public information must be interpreted carefully. Not all content is accurate. Some individuals exaggerate success, downplay professional roles, or post curated images that do not reflect reality. For this reason, social media intelligence must be corroborated with other sources. The investigator's task is to analyze the information with critical judgment, identifying patterns and contradictions rather than treating content as definitive proof.

Mapping Relationships and Networks

One of the most valuable uses of social media is mapping relationships. Individuals often identify friends, colleagues, family members, and professional contacts openly. Public interactions such as comments, "likes," group memberships, and shared content reveal social dynamics and networks that may not appear in formal records.

Relationship mapping can identify conflicts of interest, undisclosed business partners, or links to high-risk individuals. In corruption cases, social media may reveal personal connections between officials and contractors. In internal fraud, employees sometimes expose close relationships with vendors or customers that they failed to disclose. Organized crime groups frequently maintain visible online associations, even when attempting to conceal their activities offline.

Mapping networks also assists in identifying key influencers, intermediaries, or individuals who may act as facilitators. Public posts may show who travels together, attends events together, or interacts frequently. These patterns help investigators understand group dynamics, potential collusion, or shared interests relevant to the matter under review.

Lifestyle Indicators and Behavioral Insight

Social media allows investigators to assess lifestyle indicators. Posts showing expensive purchases, luxury travel, or high-value assets may suggest income inconsistent with declared earnings, particularly in cases of embezzlement, corruption, or money laundering. While lifestyle displays do not automatically indicate wrongdoing, they may help prioritize lines of inquiry or identify sources that require further verification.

Behavioral patterns also emerge. Some individuals reveal ideological stances, political affiliations, or personal grievances that provide context for decisions and actions relevant to financial crime. For instance, posts indicating resentment toward employers may support analysis in internal fraud cases. Comments expressing financial distress may provide context for unusual actions. Photographs showing frequent association with known high-risk individuals can help assess whether relationships presented during interviews are minimized or concealed.

Investigators must maintain objectivity when reviewing lifestyle indicators. The purpose is to identify discrepancies, not to judge personal preferences. A structured approach ensures that observations remain focused on relevance to the investigation.

Verifying Identities and Detecting Fabrication

Public information mining also assists in identity verification. Social media accounts often contain names, aliases, photographs, employment details, and educational history. By comparing this information to official records, investigators can identify inconsistencies, falsified credentials, or fabricated identities.

In fraud and cybercrime cases, individuals sometimes create multiple online identities to misrepresent qualifications or mislead victims. Public profiles may expose these inconsistencies when biography details conflict across platforms. Reverse image searches can identify whether profile photos appear elsewhere online, suggesting stolen or manipulated identities.

Identity verification is critical when assessing risk. Public information may reveal prior misconduct, involvement in questionable business ventures, or claims that contradict statements made during interviews. When inconsistencies appear, the investigator should cross-reference with documentation and additional sources before drawing conclusions.

Public Databases, Media Sources, and Community Platforms

Beyond social media, a wide range of public information sources support financial crime investigations. News articles, corporate websites, online marketplaces, government announcements, and community forums all offer insights that may support case analysis.

Media reporting is particularly valuable in corruption, sanctions, and organized crime cases. Local news sources sometimes publish details that would otherwise be unavailable through official channels. Public announcements may reveal business interests, political connections, or legal proceedings relevant to the investigation.

Online marketplaces and classified listings can reveal assets held by individuals, such as vehicles, artwork, or real estate. These platforms are especially helpful when evaluating whether individuals possess assets disproportionate to their known income.

Community platforms - ranging from professional forums to personal blogs - may contain statements or discussions that expose professional activities, business plans, or participation in unauthorized ventures. These platforms can also reveal attitudes toward compliance, ethical standards, or regulatory obligations.

Ensuring Ethical and Legal Compliance in OSINT Collection

Public information mining must comply with legal and ethical boundaries. Although information is publicly available, investigators must respect privacy laws, platform terms of service, and institutional policies. Unauthorized access, creation of deceptive accounts to obtain information, or attempts to circumvent privacy settings can compromise the integrity of the investigation and expose the organization to legal risk.

The investigator must ensure that only information intentionally made public is collected. When privacy settings restrict content, attempting to bypass them is prohibited. Information from public sources should be captured and stored in accordance with evidence preservation standards, ensuring that screenshots, metadata, and timestamps are documented accurately. This prevents challenges to authenticity and supports defensibility if findings are presented in legal or regulatory proceedings.

Ethical considerations extend to interpretation. Investigators must avoid drawing conclusions based solely on impression or assumption. Public information should guide inquiry, not determine guilt. The purpose of OSINT is to enhance understanding, not to intrude on personal privacy unnecessarily.

Assessing Reliability and Corroborating Information

The reliability of public information varies. Some posts are made impulsively, others deliberately manipulated. Photos may be edited or taken out of context. Comments may reflect exaggeration or humor. For these reasons, investigators must corroborate information with additional evidence.

Corroboration may involve comparing social media statements with employment records, transactional data, travel logs, or interview responses. A single post should not be treated as fact without supporting information. Instead, investigators should look for patterns that align with documented evidence.

Evaluating reliability also requires considering the source. Posts from the interviewee may carry different weight than posts from acquaintances. Content shared widely may reflect external commentary rather than personal truth. Investigators should document the origin of all information and consider whether it represents direct evidence, hearsay, or speculation.

Applying OSINT to Financial Crime Typologies

Public information mining directly supports multiple financial crime typologies. In corruption cases, it may reveal political affiliations, social connections, or unexplained wealth. In fraud investigations, it can uncover promotional materials, investor communications, or misrepresented credentials. In money laundering cases, it may help identify luxury holdings, international travel patterns, or links to high-risk jurisdictions. In insider trading investigations, public posts may reveal premature hints, coded references, or discussions with associates.

Cybercrime investigations particularly benefit from OSINT. Online communities used by cybercriminals often operate partly in public forums, even if tools and methods are traded privately. Open-source information can reveal handles, aliases, or communication patterns that help identify individuals behind fraudulent or malicious activity.

Structuring OSINT Findings

Public information must be organized clearly and systematically. Investigators should maintain records of the platform, URL, date of access, and any relevant metadata. Notes should describe why the information is relevant, how it supports or contradicts other evidence, and any limitations in interpretation.

Structured OSINT findings enable investigators to integrate insight into the broader case narrative. When used appropriately, public information strengthens fact patterns, clarifies relationships, and helps identify inconsistencies that warrant deeper analysis.

CORPORATE REGISTRIES AND BENEFICIAL OWNERSHIP DATA

Corporate registries and beneficial ownership records form a crucial foundation for understanding how individuals and entities operate within commercial environments. In financial crime investigations, these sources provide essential insight into legal structures, control relationships, operational legitimacy, and the movement of value through corporate networks. Although corporate registries differ significantly by jurisdiction, their central purpose remains consistent: they create transparency around the formal existence of companies and the individuals who ultimately control, direct, or benefit from them. When examined carefully, registry data helps investigators uncover hidden relationships, detect concealed interests, and identify entities that exist solely to obscure illicit activity.

Understanding the Role of Corporate Registries

Corporate registries serve as official repositories of information relating to legal entities. They typically include company names, incorporation dates, directors, registered addresses, and in some jurisdictions, shareholding information. Registries exist to provide public accountability and a reliable baseline from which stakeholders - regulators, auditors, investors, investigators, and the public - can assess the legitimacy of a business.

For investigators, corporate registry data helps establish whether an entity is genuinely operational or merely a construct used to facilitate misconduct. It allows identification of directors who appear repeatedly across multiple companies, registered addresses used by numerous entities without clear operational justification, and businesses that change ownership or management in ways that appear inconsistent with legitimate commercial behavior.

Because registry information is generally self-reported by companies, the accuracy of the data depends on jurisdictional requirements and enforcement. In jurisdictions with strong regulatory systems, the information is often reliable and regularly updated. In those with weak oversight, information may be outdated, incomplete, or intentionally misleading. Understanding these limitations is essential when evaluating corporate structures.

Beneficial Ownership as a Key Transparency Mechanism

Beneficial ownership refers to the natural persons who ultimately own, control, or profit from a legal entity, regardless of the names listed on official documents. The purpose of beneficial ownership transparency is to prevent individuals from hiding behind layers of corporate structures, shell companies, or nominees.

Financial crime typologies frequently rely on obscuring ownership. Money launderers, corrupt officials, tax evaders, and sanctions evaders commonly use complex structures - often spanning multiple jurisdictions - to conceal their identity. Beneficial ownership registers allow investigators to pierce these structures and identify the individuals behind an entity's formation and activity.

Some registers are public, while others are accessible only to regulated institutions or enforcement authorities. Even where information is restricted, investigators may obtain access through formal channels or through lawful OSINT methods if some portions of the data are published publicly.

Beneficial ownership transparency significantly enhances an investigator's ability to link individuals to entities used in suspicious transactions. When combined with registry data and financial records, it becomes possible to trace ownership chains, identify controlling interests, and detect discrepancies between declared roles and actual influence.

Identifying Suspicious Ownership Structures

Criminal networks often construct ownership structures designed to obscure true control. These structures may appear complex but typically share identifiable characteristics. Investigators should examine ownership layers carefully, assessing whether each component serves an operational purpose or exists primarily to create distance between the true owner and the entity's activity.

Multi-jurisdictional structures, for example, may involve companies incorporated in several countries, each with differing transparency requirements. A company registered in a low-transparency jurisdiction may hold shares in an entity incorporated in a jurisdiction with more robust oversight, thereby shielding the true owner's identity.

Nominee directors and shareholders are another common feature of suspicious structures. A nominee director may appear on dozens of companies without clear involvement in their operations. Their role is often administrative, allowing the true controller to remain hidden. While nominees may operate legally in some jurisdictions, their presence in high-risk investigations warrants further scrutiny.

Rapid, frequent changes in ownership or directorship may also indicate attempts to avoid detection. Transfers may occur just before or after suspicious transactions, suggesting that the entity serves as a temporary conduit. Similarly, companies with minimal operational history but substantial financial activity may indicate misuse as shell or front entities.

Using Registry Data to Trace Control and Relationships

Corporate registry searches provide a foundation for tracing control. By analyzing director names, shareholder information, and registered addresses, investigators can map connections between individuals and entities. When a single address houses dozens of companies with no apparent business alignment, it may indicate the presence of a corporate service provider used to facilitate anonymity.

Tracing relationships through registry data often reveals networks of associated individuals. A director appearing repeatedly across unrelated companies may signal the presence of a professional facilitator or nominee. When these names cross-reference with OSINT findings or internal records, investigators can construct detailed profiles of individuals involved in wider schemes.

Registry data can also reveal family relationships or close personal associations. In some cases, individuals attempt to conceal ownership by placing shares in the names of relatives or associates while retaining actual control. When registry information is analyzed alongside social media data, public records, and transactional evidence, these hidden ties become more apparent.

Integrating Beneficial Ownership Data with Financial Evidence

Beneficial ownership information achieves maximum value when combined with financial records. Ownership transparency helps investigators determine whether transaction flows align with declared business activity. If funds move between companies controlled by the same beneficial owner, despite claims of independence, the behavior may indicate self-dealing, layering, or other illicit purposes.

In corruption cases, beneficial ownership data helps identify whether entities receiving contracts or payments are connected to public officials or their associates. In fraud investigations, it may reveal that entities claiming independence are part of a coordinated network. In money laundering cases, ownership data often exposes the ultimate destination of funds, especially when layered through multiple corporate entities.

Cross-referencing ownership information with bank account data, trade documents, and internal emails strengthens the investigative narrative. It helps establish intent by demonstrating that individuals exercised control even when their names did not appear on surface-level documentation.

Challenges in Accessing and Interpreting Ownership Information

Although beneficial ownership transparency has improved globally, significant challenges remain. Jurisdictions vary widely in their requirements. Some require frequent updates and verification, while others rely on voluntary disclosures with minimal enforcement. Certain jurisdictions do not maintain beneficial ownership registers at all.

Even where registers exist, information may be inaccurate or incomplete. Individuals determined to conceal their involvement often exploit legal loopholes, register companies in opaque jurisdictions, or rely on trusts and private agreements that fall outside reporting requirements. Interpreting ownership structures therefore requires skepticism, cross-verification, and careful evaluation of context.

Investigators must also understand the legal limitations of registry data. Some records may be outdated due to delays in reporting. Others may omit important information such as bearer shares, which complicate ownership tracing. When interpreting registry data, investigators must consider whether gaps reflect administrative shortcomings, deliberate concealment, or both.

Using OSINT Tools to Enhance Corporate Research

Modern investigations benefit from a variety of tools designed to analyze corporate structures and beneficial ownership data. Some tools aggregate registry information across multiple jurisdictions, allowing investigators to visualize ownership chains and identify links that might otherwise go unnoticed. Others provide access to leaked datasets, regulatory filings, or historical company records that reveal changes over time.

These tools enhance efficiency but must be used carefully. Not all sources are equally reliable, and some datasets originate from leaks or unauthorized disclosures that may require legal evaluation before use. Investigators must ensure that any data accessed complies with legal and ethical requirements and that findings are validated through authoritative sources.

Evaluating the Purpose and Risk Profile of Entities

Not every complex corporate structure signals misconduct. Many legitimate businesses operate through holding companies, subsidiaries, or multi-jurisdictional arrangements for tax, regulatory, or operational reasons. The investigator must distinguish between commercial logic and suspicious complexity.

Evaluating an entity's purpose involves assessing whether its structure aligns with its stated business activity. For example, a small consulting firm incorporated through multiple offshore jurisdictions without employees or physical presence may raise questions. Likewise, an entity that conducts high-value transactions but reports minimal income or assets warrants closer examination.

Risk-based analysis combines ownership transparency, transactional patterns, and contextual evidence. When these elements suggest misalignment between declared and actual behavior, investigators should explore the structure in greater depth.

Documenting Findings and Ensuring Analytical Integrity

Corporate registry and beneficial ownership findings must be documented thoroughly and objectively. Records should include source registry information, dates of access, official filings, and any relevant observations about discrepancies, inconsistencies, or red flags. Documentation should distinguish between verified facts, reasonable inferences, and unconfirmed information requiring further investigation.

CRYPTO TRACING

Cryptocurrencies have become a central component in modern financial crime investigations. While digital assets provide legitimate benefits - speed, accessibility, and decentralized control - they also create opportunities for misuse. Criminal actors exploit cryptocurrencies to obscure transactions, transfer assets across borders, and operate outside traditional financial systems. Yet, contrary to popular belief, most cryptocurrency activity is traceable. Blockchains preserve permanent, chronological records of all transactions, and with the right tools and knowledge, investigators can reconstruct flows of value, identify involved addresses, and connect seemingly anonymous wallets to real-world actors. Effective crypto tracing requires a clear understanding of blockchain fundamentals, wallet structures, transaction patterns, and analytical tools that convert cryptographic records into actionable intelligence.

Understanding Blockchain Fundamentals

A blockchain is a distributed ledger maintained by a network of participants rather than a central authority. Each transaction is recorded in a block, and each block is linked cryptographically to the previous one, creating a permanent and tamper-resistant chain. This structure ensures transparency: every transaction ever executed on a public blockchain, such as Bitcoin or Ethereum, can be viewed publicly.

For investigators, this transparency is a powerful advantage. While users may not be identified directly by name, their wallets - represented by alphanumeric addresses - have complete transaction histories that cannot be deleted or altered. If investigators can associate even one address with an individual, they can often map an entire financial footprint.

Blockchains differ significantly depending on design. Bitcoin's blockchain records simple transactions, while Ethereum supports smart contracts, decentralized applications, and tokens. Stablecoins operate on multiple chains, and privacy-focused cryptocurrencies such as Monero use advanced cryptographic techniques to obscure transactions. Understanding these differences helps investigators determine which analytical techniques and tools are appropriate for a particular case.

Tracing Cryptocurrency Wallets

Wallets serve as the primary interface through which users interact with blockchains. They do not store cryptocurrency in the traditional sense; instead, they hold the cryptographic keys needed to authorize transactions. Wallets come in multiple types: custodial, non-custodial, hardware, software, and multi-signature.

Custodial wallets are managed by exchanges or service providers. Users rely on the platform to hold keys, making custodial accounts more similar to traditional financial accounts. These are the most straightforward for investigators because exchanges - if compliant - maintain customer information, including identity verification data. When investigators identify a wallet associated with a regulated exchange, subpoenas or legal requests can uncover the account holder.

Non-custodial wallets give users full control over their keys. They provide greater privacy but also generate investigative challenges. Even so, the transactions linked to these wallets remain visible on the blockchain. Patterns of deposits, withdrawals, and transfers allow investigators to map relationships between addresses and identify which services the wallet interacts with.

Hardware wallets store keys offline, reducing the risk of theft but leaving a digital footprint similar to other non-custodial wallets once transactions occur. Multi-signature wallets require multiple approvals for a transaction, often used by businesses or criminal groups seeking both security and anonymity. Understanding wallet types helps investigators interpret transaction behaviors and assess the level of traceability.

Following Transaction Flows

Crypto tracing involves reconstructing the flow of assets from one address to another. Most cryptocurrencies move through a predictable pattern: funding, transfers, exchange activity, and withdrawal. Investigators track these flows by examining transaction histories on the blockchain.

Transaction patterns often reveal intent. Straightforward transfers with clear endpoints may suggest legitimate activity. However, complicated patterns - rapid sequences of transfers, splitting funds across numerous addresses, or sending funds through multiple chains - may signal attempts to hide origin or ownership.

Mixing or tumbling services intentionally obscure transactions by pooling funds from numerous users and redistributing them. Although mixing complicates tracing, it does not eliminate it entirely. Investigators can sometimes trace funds entering and leaving mixers by analyzing timing, transaction size, and patterns. Some mixers have been taken down or compromised, allowing historical data to support investigations.

Cross-chain bridges transfer assets between blockchains. Criminals use bridges to obscure trails or convert assets into tokens with lower regulatory oversight. These transfers create additional complexity, but they also generate new data points that tools can analyze, especially when transfers involve centralized services or known wallet clusters.

In fraud or ransomware cases, the movement of currency quickly leads to exchanges, where actors attempt to convert funds into cash or other assets. These interactions provide key opportunities for intervention. Once funds reach a regulated exchange, investigators can request account information, freeze assets, or trace withdrawals.

Identifying Wallet Clusters and Behavioral Patterns

Tracing does not rely solely on following individual transactions. Investigators often examine clusters of addresses believed to belong to the same individual or organization. Clustering relies on behavioral analysis and technical heuristics, such as identifying addresses that share transaction inputs, timing patterns, or wallet management practices.

Many blockchain analytics platforms maintain extensive databases of known wallet clusters—including exchanges, darknet markets, fraud schemes, theft rings, and legitimate businesses. These clusters allow investigators to determine whether suspicious addresses belong to known entities, reducing investigative time and supporting risk assessments.

Behavioral patterns also help identify criminal activity. For example, ransomware actors often follow predictable patterns: receive payment, move funds immediately through several intermediate addresses, and send them to an exchange or mixing service. Investment fraud operators typically funnel funds from victims into central wallets before splitting assets across other chains or platforms.

Patterns that deviate from typical user behavior - such as simultaneous large transfers from unrelated sources or synchronized activity across multiple wallets - can indicate coordinated networks or automated systems.

Using Blockchain Analytics Tools

Several tools support crypto tracing by converting blockchain data into visual and analytical insights. These tools aggregate transactions, label known wallet clusters, and highlight patterns that would be difficult to detect manually.

Blockchain explorers, such as Etherscan and Blockchain.com, allow investigators to view individual transactions and wallet histories. These tools provide transparency but require manual analysis, which is feasible for simple cases but inefficient for complex schemes.

Advanced analytics platforms - offered commercially - provide automated clustering, risk scoring, entity labeling, and visualization of transaction flows. These platforms compile data from law enforcement cases, compliance filings, exchange disclosures, and OSINT sources, allowing investigators to identify connections that may not be evident from the blockchain alone.

Some tools specialize in tracing DeFi (decentralized finance) activity, analyzing smart contract interactions, liquidity pools, token swaps, and decentralized exchange transactions. Others focus on cross-chain movements, NFT transactions, or privacy-enhancing technologies. Selecting the right tool depends on the cryptocurrency involved, the nature of the suspicious activity, and available technical expertise.

Overcoming Privacy Enhancements and Evasion Techniques

Certain cryptocurrencies and technologies are specifically designed to increase privacy. Monero uses ring signatures and stealth addresses to obscure both sender and recipient. Zcash allows shielded transactions that hide amounts and addresses. Even on transparent blockchains like Bitcoin, criminals may use CoinJoin transactions, mixers, and chain-hopping to complicate tracing.

While these techniques introduce challenges, options remain. Investigators may analyze behavioral patterns, timing correlations, and off-chain intelligence to identify participants. Exchanges often block or monitor deposits linked to privacy-enhancing methods, especially when risk indicators are present. Law enforcement sometimes uncovers operational mistakes that expose addresses even when actors attempt to conceal identity.

Despite advanced obfuscation techniques, criminals often make errors. They reuse addresses, interact with services that require identity verification, or consolidate funds prematurely. These mistakes provide openings for investigators.

Linking On-Chain and Off-Chain Evidence

Crypto tracing depends on connecting blockchain activity with real-world identity. While the blockchain provides transparent records, off-chain evidence provides context. Linking the two requires careful analysis.

Off-chain evidence includes email correspondence, chat logs, IP addresses, account registration information, device data, and exchange records. When investigators identify a wallet associated with a particular individual - through exchange KYC (Know Your Customer) data, document analysis, or communication records - they can map all associated transactions.

This linkage is central to proving intent. On-chain analysis shows the flow of funds. Off-chain analysis shows who controlled the wallet and why the transactions occurred. When combined, they create a complete narrative of misconduct.

Preserving Evidence and Ensuring Analytical Integrity

Investigators must preserve blockchain evidence carefully. Blockchains evolve continuously as new blocks are added, so timestamps and block heights must be recorded to ensure accuracy. Screenshots, hash values, and exportable transaction histories should be documented systematically. Analytical tools often provide standardized reports that meet evidentiary standards, but investigators must still verify data and maintain a clear chain of custody.

OPERATIONALIZING OSINT IN INVESTIGATIONS

Open-source intelligence (OSINT) becomes meaningful only when it is integrated methodically into investigative processes. Collecting public information alone does not produce insight; investigators must transform data into structured intelligence that supports hypotheses, identifies risks, clarifies relationships, and guides decision-making. Operationalizing OSINT requires clear objectives, disciplined collection methods, systematic verification, and analytical rigor. When applied effectively,

OSINT strengthens every stage of financial crime investigation, from preliminary assessments to complex case development and enforcement actions.

Establishing Purpose and Scope

Before collecting OSINT, investigators must determine why it is needed and what questions it must answer. OSINT is most effective when used to fill gaps in existing information, validate or challenge internal records, or identify external factors that influence the case. Clear objectives prevent the investigation from becoming overwhelmed by irrelevant data.

Scope determination includes identifying which platforms, databases, and public sources are likely to contain relevant information. For example, social media may help clarify behavioral patterns, while corporate registries may reveal ownership structures. Public forums might provide insight into fraudulent schemes, while news archives may uncover historical disputes or allegations involving individuals or entities.

Purpose and scope act as the foundation for collection. They ensure that the investigative effort remains focused and that findings directly support case development.

Designing Structured Collection Strategies

OSINT collection must follow structured processes. Investigators should work systematically, beginning with broad searches and gradually refining queries as patterns emerge. Structured collection reduces biases that arise when investigators interpret information prematurely or rely too heavily on initial impressions.

Documentation is critical. Each search query, platform visited, and data point collected should be recorded meticulously. This ensures that OSINT findings can be verified, reproduced, and defended in regulatory or legal settings. It also prevents investigators from overlooking important sources or duplicating effort.

A structured approach includes methodical examination of primary sources - original posts, corporate filings, publicly accessible documents, or direct statements - before turning to secondary commentary or analysis. Primary sources provide more reliable evidence and allow investigators to interpret information without external influence.

Integrating OSINT with Internal and Third-Party Data

OSINT achieves maximum value when integrated with internal records, regulatory filings, transaction data, and information obtained through interviews. This integration creates a multi-dimensional view of individuals and entities under review.

For example, if internal transaction records show repeated transfers to an unfamiliar company, OSINT can help identify whether the company is legitimate, dormant, or linked to the subject. Similarly, if a witness claims limited interaction with a business partner, social media may reveal a pattern of communication or shared activities that contradicts that claim.

OSINT also supports risk assessment. Public information can show whether a company is associated with negative media coverage, legal disputes, or regulatory actions. It can identify whether individuals involved in a case have a history of misconduct or maintain ties to high-risk jurisdictions.

By combining OSINT with other data, investigators strengthen their understanding of the case and refine investigative hypotheses.

Verifying Accuracy and Ensuring Information Integrity

Public information varies widely in reliability. Investigators must verify OSINT findings through cross-referencing with credible sources. Verification prevents incorrect conclusions and protects the integrity of the investigation.

Verification may involve checking whether a corporate address listed online matches official registry filings, confirming whether a photograph corresponds to a known location, or assessing whether a social media post is authentic and unaltered. Multiple independent sources should support any claim before being incorporated into findings.

Investigators must distinguish between factual evidence, speculation, personal opinion, and manipulated content. Some public information is inaccurate due to user error, outdated postings, or deliberate misrepresentation. Critical evaluation includes assessing the source's credibility, context, and motivations.

Maintaining information integrity also requires careful preservation. Screenshots, URLs, timestamps, and metadata should be documented accurately. This ensures that findings can be reproduced and withstand scrutiny, especially when used in formal or adversarial settings.

Building OSINT Profiles and Intelligence Packages

One of the most effective ways to operationalize OSINT is by building structured profiles. A profile organizes information about an individual, company, or network into coherent categories - identity, affiliations, business activities, online behavior, and risk indicators. Profiles ensure that investigators have a comprehensive and logically organized understanding of the subject.

An OSINT intelligence package goes further, integrating findings into a narrative that explains relevance, connections, and implications. These packages support decision-making by summarizing what is known, identifying gaps, and recommending further investigative steps.

Profiles and intelligence packages must be factual, objective, and concise. They should highlight verified information, clearly identify assumptions, and avoid speculation. Well-constructed packages enable investigators to brief colleagues, support legal teams, and present findings to regulators or leadership with clarity and confidence.

Timing and Sequencing in OSINT Collection

Timing matters in OSINT investigations. Public information changes continuously. Social media posts may be deleted. Company records may be updated. Users may restrict access after becoming aware of scrutiny. For this reason, early OSINT collection is often critical. As soon as an investigation begins, investigators should capture publicly available information before subjects modify their online presence.

Sequencing is equally important. Conducting OSINT prematurely may lead investigators to form early assumptions that could bias interviews or documentary analysis. Conversely, conducting OSINT too late may lead to missed opportunities.

A balanced approach involves conducting initial OSINT early in the investigation, followed by targeted collection after interviews or document reviews raise new questions. This ensures that OSINT remains relevant, accurate, and responsive to emerging information.

Leveraging Technology to Enhance OSINT

Modern OSINT relies heavily on technology. Analytical tools automate data extraction, cluster related information, and visualize relationships. These tools improve efficiency and help investigators identify connections that are not immediately apparent through manual research.

Tools can aggregate corporate registry data across jurisdictions, identify social media accounts linked by email or phone numbers, and track digital footprints across platforms. Others monitor news sources, regulatory announcements, and online forums for mentions of individuals or entities.

Despite the value of these tools, investigators must interpret findings using professional judgment. Automated systems may misidentify connections or overlook nuances. Technology supports OSINT but does not replace analytical expertise.

Ethical and Legal Considerations in OSINT Operations

OSINT must be conducted ethically and in compliance with applicable laws. Investigators cannot attempt to bypass privacy settings, create deceptive accounts to access restricted content, or violate platform terms of service. Unlawful collection compromises investigations and exposes organizations to legal liability.

Ethical considerations also relate to proportionality. Investigators must ensure that OSINT collection is relevant to the case and not excessive. Publicly available information may be extensive, but only a portion may be necessary for the investigation's purpose.

All findings should be handled responsibly, stored securely, and disclosed only to individuals with a legitimate need to know. Ethical OSINT practices protect both the integrity of the investigation and the rights of individuals involved.

Translating OSINT Into Investigative Action

The true value of OSINT lies in its application. Findings must inform investigative strategy, influence interview planning, shape document requests, and support hypotheses. OSINT may reveal that certain individuals are more influential than initially assumed, that a company's ownership structure is more complex than expected, or that a subject's public statements contradict internal information.

OSINT may also guide decisions about escalation. For example, if public information links a subject to sanctioned individuals or high-risk jurisdictions, the investigation may require deeper review or referral to specialized teams.

Investigators must translate OSINT revelations into concrete actions. This may include conducting targeted interviews, requesting additional financial records, issuing subpoenas, or involving compliance or legal specialists. OSINT should guide next steps, not sit unused as a separate layer of information.

CHAPTER 14

FORENSIC TECHNOLOGY AND DATA ANALYTICS

TRANSACTION MONITORING AND AUTOMATED DETECTION

TRANSACTION MONITORING is a cornerstone of modern financial crime control. As financial systems expand and transaction volumes increase, manual review becomes impractical. Automated detection systems allow organizations to examine millions of transactions in real time, identifying unusual behavior, suspicious patterns, and potential risks that would otherwise remain unnoticed. Effective transaction monitoring is not simply a matter of deploying technology; it requires a clear understanding of risk typologies, data quality, operational needs, and the investigative processes that follow alerts. When implemented correctly, transaction monitoring provides early warning of misconduct, supports regulatory compliance, and strengthens an organization's overall control environment.

The Purpose and Scope of Transaction Monitoring

Transaction monitoring systems analyze financial activity to identify transactions or behaviors that fall outside expected norms. The objective is to detect potential indicators of money laundering, fraud, sanctions violations, terrorist financing, bribery, insider misuse, and other forms of financial crime. These systems are designed to distinguish legitimate customer activity from abnormal or high-risk behavior, allowing investigators to focus resources where they are most needed.

The scope of monitoring depends on the institution's risk profile. Banks, payment processors, cryptocurrency exchanges, insurance providers, and money service businesses face different risks and therefore require monitoring strategies tailored to their operations. Financial institutions must understand the customers, products, geographies, and channels that present elevated risk, ensuring that detection rules align with the organization's inherent exposure.

Core Components of Automated Monitoring Systems

Automated detection relies on multiple components working together to assess whether transactions warrant further review. The foundation is data. Systems must have access to accurate, complete, and timely information, including customer profiles, account history, transactional records, and relevant third-party data. Poor data quality undermines system performance, producing unreliable alerts and increasing operational strain.

Rules and scenarios form the backbone of traditional transaction monitoring. These rules define the conditions under which an alert is triggered. Examples include transactions exceeding certain thresholds, rapid movement of funds through multiple accounts, activity inconsistent with customer profile, or transfers involving high-risk jurisdictions. While rules-based detection is not sophisticated by modern standards, it remains essential because it is transparent, easy to audit, and adaptable to regulatory expectations.

More advanced systems incorporate behavioral analytics, statistical models, and machine learning. These methods identify subtle anomalies that rules cannot capture, such as changes in spending patterns, unusual transaction sequences, or deviations from peer groups. As financial crime techniques evolve, behavior-based models play an increasingly important role in recognizing suspicious activity that does not fit static rules.

Balancing Sensitivity and Precision

A persistent challenge in transaction monitoring is managing the balance between sensitivity and precision. If detection rules are too broad or thresholds too low, the system generates excessive alerts, overwhelming investigators and increasing false positives. If rules are too narrow or thresholds too high, genuine risks may go undetected.

Effective tuning requires iterative analysis. Institutions must review alert outcomes, identify patterns of false positives, and adjust rules accordingly. Tuning is not a one-time exercise; it must be revisited regularly to account for changes in financial behavior, evolving criminal methodologies, and new regulatory requirements. Institutions that neglect tuning often face inefficient investigations, increased operational cost, and potential regulatory scrutiny.

Precision can be improved by incorporating contextual data. For example, a transaction that appears suspicious when viewed in isolation may be reasonable when considered alongside the customer's known business activity. Systems that incorporate customer risk ratings, historical patterns, and peer comparisons generate more accurate alerts and improve investigative efficiency.

Real-Time Monitoring Versus Batch Processing

Transaction monitoring can occur in real time or through batch processing. Real-time monitoring evaluates transactions as they occur, allowing institutions to block or flag high-risk activity immediately. This is critical for environments involving rapid movement of funds, such as payments, remittances, and crypto asset transfers. Real-time monitoring is especially important when dealing with sanctions, where an institution must prevent prohibited transactions from completing.

Batch processing evaluates transactions after they occur, typically at scheduled intervals. While not as immediate, batch processing can be effective for large datasets, retrospective reviews, and complex behavioral analysis. It allows systems to examine long-term patterns, identify cumulative risk factors, and detect anomalies that emerge only when viewed over time.

Most institutions use a combination of both methods. Real-time monitoring protects against immediate risk, while batch processing supports in-depth analysis and trend identification.

Alert Generation and Triage

Transaction monitoring systems produce alerts when activity meets defined criteria. However, the presence of an alert does not automatically indicate wrongdoing. Alerts represent hypotheses - signals that require human analysis to determine whether further investigation is warranted.

Triage is the first step in the investigative process. Analysts review alerts for completeness, relevance, and clarity. They may request additional data, conduct initial research, or close the alert if it clearly reflects legitimate behavior. Effective triage requires trained analysts, strong processes, and access to contextual information.

Without proper triage, institutions face large backlogs and reduced investigative quality. Triage allows analysts to prioritize cases based on risk, ensuring that critical alerts receive immediate attention.

Investigative Follow-Up and Case Development

Once an alert is escalated, investigators examine the transaction in detail. This may involve reviewing account statements, customer documentation, historical activity, and public information. Investigators may identify links to known high-risk individuals or entities, connections to previous alerts, or inconsistencies in customer explanations.

Automated detection provides the starting point; investigative judgment completes the analysis. Investigators must assess whether activity matches known typologies, identify whether the transaction aligns with the customer's expected behavior, and determine whether escalation to compliance, legal, or external authorities is necessary.

Well-designed transaction monitoring systems support investigators by providing clear alert histories, data visualization, and access to relevant records. This reduces manual work and allows investigators to focus on substantive analysis.

Monitoring Across Products and Channels

Modern financial institutions operate across multiple channels - online banking, mobile apps, branch networks, payment processors, trading platforms, and digital wallets. Criminals exploit gaps between these channels, moving funds through less monitored pathways to avoid detection.

Effective transaction monitoring requires enterprise-wide coverage. Systems must aggregate activity across products and platforms, enabling investigators to identify patterns that span multiple environments. An isolated transaction may appear benign, but when viewed across channels, it may reveal a broader scheme or sequence of suspicious events.

Cross-channel monitoring is particularly important for institutions offering both fiat and digital asset services. Criminals often move between traditional and digital environments, exploiting differences in controls. Unified monitoring provides a comprehensive view of customer behavior.

Typologies and Red Flags in Automated Detection

Transaction monitoring systems are most effective when aligned with known financial crime typologies. These typologies reflect how criminals operate - whether layering funds, structuring cash deposits, misusing corporate accounts, operating mule networks, or exploiting trade finance systems.

Red flags must be incorporated into detection rules. Examples include transactions inconsistent with business purpose, rapid movement of funds through multiple accounts, transfers involving high-risk jurisdictions, unusual cash-intensive activity, or behavior indicative of third-party control.

Typologies evolve as criminals adapt. Institutions must continually update detection rules to reflect emerging risks such as crypto-fiat conversion schemes, synthetic identity fraud, and complex trade-based laundering. Ongoing review ensures that monitoring remains relevant.

Role of Data Quality and System Integrity

Transaction monitoring systems depend on high-quality data. Incomplete, inaccurate, or outdated data leads to both missed risks and excessive false positives. Common issues include incorrect customer risk ratings, outdated identification information, inconsistent data formatting, and missing transaction attributes.

Institutions must invest in data governance. Standardized inputs, automated data validation, and continuous monitoring of data integrity enhance system reliability. When data is wrong, monitoring fails.

System integrity is equally important. Access controls, audit logs, and change management procedures protect monitoring systems from manipulation or error. Regulators frequently assess these controls because improper system configuration can compromise the entire detection process.

PATTERN RECOGNITION AND BEHAVIORAL ANALYTICS

Pattern recognition and behavioral analytics play a central role in modern financial crime detection. While transaction monitoring identifies individual anomalies, behavioral analytics examines how events fit together, how individuals or entities behave over time, and how those behaviors compare to expected norms. Criminal activity rarely consists of isolated actions. It is the accumulation of small irregularities - changes in transaction timing, deviations from historical patterns, unusual connections, or unexplained shifts in behavior - that forms the foundation of suspicious activity. Behavioral analytics allows institutions to detect these subtleties and interpret them in context.

Understanding Behavioral Baselines

The starting point for behavioral analytics is establishing a baseline. A baseline represents what is normal for a customer, employee, account, or business line. It includes transaction size, frequency, geography, counterparties, and product usage. Without a baseline, analysts cannot determine whether behavior is unusual or concerning.

Baselines are dynamic rather than static. Customer situations change, businesses evolve, and economic conditions shift. Effective systems update baselines regularly to reflect current behavior without losing awareness of long-term patterns. This flexibility is essential. A rigid baseline might treat legitimate growth or seasonal variation as suspicious, while an overly permissive one may overlook subtle signs of criminal activity.

Establishing accurate baselines requires high-quality data and thoughtful segmentation. Customers should be grouped by realistic characteristics - industry, size, geography, account purpose - not arbitrary factors. When segmentation aligns with true behavior, deviations become easier to detect and interpret.

Identifying Behavioral Red Flags

Behavioral analytics is particularly effective in identifying patterns that appear benign when viewed individually but reveal risk when examined collectively. For example, a customer who makes several small transactions in a short period may not trigger an alert. But if those transactions represent a clear deviation from their usual behavior or closely resemble known typologies, they warrant closer scrutiny.

Common behavioral red flags include sudden increases in transaction velocity, changes in counterparties, inconsistent routing patterns, or unusual use of new products. Criminals frequently adjust their behavior to test system thresholds or identify weak points in monitoring processes. Behavioral analytics helps detect these adjustments by focusing not just on specific actions but on how those actions compare to established patterns.

Employee behavior is also subject to analysis. Insider threats, collusion, and unauthorized system access often involve subtle deviations in user behavior - accessing systems at unusual times, extracting large volumes of data, or interacting with accounts outside their normal scope. Behavioral monitoring tools track these deviations and alert investigators before harm occurs.

Temporal and Sequential Analysis

Time is a critical factor in behavioral analytics. Many financial crimes unfold gradually, with perpetrators attempting to mask activity through incremental changes. Temporal analysis examines the timing of events, identifying whether behaviors follow consistent patterns or exhibit sudden shifts.

Sequential analysis goes a step further by analyzing the order of events. Criminal activity often follows recognizable sequences - structuring deposits, moving funds through layers, converting assets, or rapidly shifting between accounts. By examining these sequences, investigators can detect typologies even when individual transactions do not appear suspicious.

For instance, fraudsters may initiate small test transactions before conducting large fraudulent transfers. Money launderers may deposit funds into one account, rapidly transfer them to multiple others, and then consolidate them again. These patterns are recognizable when viewed as sequences, even if the individual transactions do not breach thresholds.

Sequential analysis supports proactive detection. Instead of waiting for a single large or unusual transaction, systems identify the early stages of a pattern, allowing investigators to intervene sooner.

Comparing Behavior across Peer Groups

Peer comparison helps identify unusual behavior by placing an individual's actions within the context of their broader population. A customer operating a small retail business should not resemble a multinational trading company in terms of transaction volume, cross-border activity, or counterparties. When an entity behaves differently from peers with similar risk profiles, the deviation may signal misconduct or require explanation.

Peer grouping allows analytical models to understand expected ranges for transaction frequency, value, and velocity. When a customer significantly exceeds these ranges, investigators are alerted to potential risk. Peer comparisons are also useful for identifying outliers, which may represent emerging criminal typologies or new fraud schemes.

For employees, peer comparison highlights unusual system access patterns or deviations from standard workflows. If one employee consistently accesses high-risk accounts outside normal working hours while their peers do not, such behavior may warrant review.

Machine Learning and Adaptive Behavioral Models

Machine learning significantly enhances behavioral analytics by allowing systems to learn from data and adjust automatically. Unlike rule-based systems, which require manual updates, machine learning models adapt to new information, recognize emerging patterns, and detect anomalies that may not match predefined scenarios.

Adaptive models examine large datasets to identify hidden relationships between variables. They detect patterns that humans may overlook, such as subtle correlations between transaction frequency and account age, or links between device identifiers and suspicious behavior. These models also reduce false positives by recognizing legitimate variations that do not represent risk.

However, machine learning introduces challenges. Models must be explainable, particularly in regulated environments. Investigators must understand why an alert was triggered, what variables contributed to the outcome, and whether the model's reasoning aligns with regulatory expectations. Explainability ensures transparency, supports audibility, and prevents reliance on "black box" outputs.

Effective behavioral analytics combines automated detection with human expertise. Models highlight anomalies, but investigators interpret them using context, experience, and judgment. When used together, machine learning and human analysis create a robust detection environment capable of adapting to evolving threats.

Combining Behavioral Analytics with Transaction Monitoring

Behavioral analytics enhances traditional transaction monitoring by adding depth and context. While transaction monitoring focuses on individual events, behavioral analytics identifies patterns across time, channels, and entities. This combination creates a holistic detection framework.

For example, a transaction monitoring alert triggered by a large transfer becomes more meaningful when behavioral analytics shows that the customer has recently changed transaction types, expanded counterparty networks, or begun using new accounts. Conversely, an alert may be deprioritized if behavioral context shows that the transaction aligns with long-term patterns.

Behavioral analytics also improves investigations. Investigators can review timeline charts, activity heat maps, and behavioral summaries to understand how suspicious activity fits within broader behavioral trends. This context helps determine whether escalation, additional monitoring, or customer outreach is appropriate.

Using Behavioral Insights to Strengthen Controls

Behavioral insights not only support detection but also contribute to broader control enhancements. When analytics reveal recurring patterns associated with misconduct, institutions can adjust risk models, strengthen controls, and enhance preventive measures.

For example, if behavioral analytics shows increased misuse of dormant accounts, institutions may strengthen dormant account management processes. If analytics indicates that fraud attempts consistently involve specific transaction types, detection rules can be refined.

LINK ANALYSIS AND NETWORK MAPPING

Link analysis and network mapping are essential tools in modern financial crime investigations. Criminal activity rarely occurs in isolation; it is almost always the product of interactions between individuals, companies, accounts, and digital assets. Understanding these relationships helps investigators identify hidden connections, uncover coordinated activity, and build a more complete picture of how illicit schemes operate. Link analysis allows investigators to transform scattered data points into structured intelligence, revealing patterns that would be impossible to detect through manual review alone.

The Purpose of Link Analysis

Link analysis focuses on identifying connections - direct and indirect - between entities involved in financial activity. These entities may include customers, employees, vendors, bank accounts, corporate structures, digital wallets, phone numbers, email addresses, IP addresses, or physical locations. The core purpose is to understand how these entities interact and whether their relationships reflect legitimate business activity or potential misconduct.

Link analysis supports several objectives. It helps detect collusion between internal staff and external actors. It reveals whether suspicious transactions involving multiple accounts originate from a common source. It exposes complex ownership structures designed to hide ultimate beneficiaries. And it identifies networks that facilitate criminal conduct, including fraud rings, money laundering syndicates, and cyber-enabled schemes.

Through analyzing how entities relate to one another, investigators can trace the flow of money, influence, or information across networks and determine whether they align with known risk typologies.

Building Relationship Maps

Network mapping visualizes the connections uncovered through link analysis. Rather than reviewing text descriptions, investigators can see the structure of a network at a glance. Nodes represent entities, and edges represent relationships - financial transfers, shared addresses, ownership ties, or communication links. Visualization helps investigators understand complexity, identify central actors, and spot anomalies.

Constructing relationship maps requires accurate, structured data. Investigators pull information from internal systems, public sources, OSINT findings, transaction monitoring systems, and external databases. The quality of a network map depends entirely on the quality of the underlying data. Missing or incorrect data leads to incomplete or distorted networks, potentially obscuring important relationships.

Once the data is aggregated, mapping tools display relationships at varying levels of detail. Investigators can zoom out to observe general structures or zoom in to examine specific interactions. The dynamic nature of these tools allows investigators to refine maps as new data emerges, ensuring networks evolve alongside the investigation.

Identifying Key Nodes and Influencers

Within any network, certain nodes play more significant roles than others. These may be individuals who control multiple accounts, companies that serve as intermediaries, or digital wallets that receive funds from numerous sources. Identifying these key nodes is essential for understanding how networks operate and where influence or control resides.

Network mapping tools often provide metrics such as centrality scores, which measure how crucial a node is within the overall structure. For example, a node with high betweenness centrality may serve as a bridge between different parts of the network, indicating that it plays an important coordinating role. A node with many direct connections may be a hub of activity, potentially indicating a high-risk entity or a facilitator.

Key nodes help investigators prioritize their efforts. Focusing on central actors allows investigators to disrupt networks more effectively, understand the motivations behind the activity, and identify where further evidence is likely to be found.

Layered Structures and Concealed Relationships

Illicit networks often rely on layered structures to obscure relationships. Criminals use intermediaries, shell companies, nominee owners, or digital anonymity tools to create distance between themselves and their activities. Link analysis helps investigators peel back these layers by identifying indirect relationships and hidden paths.

For example, a suspicious transfer may appear to involve unrelated parties until investigators discover that both entities share a common director, address, or ultimate beneficiary. Network mapping reveals these indirect links visually, reducing the likelihood that important connections will be overlooked.

Layered networks are common in money laundering schemes. Funds may move through multiple accounts, jurisdictions, or asset types to disguise their origin. Link analysis reconstructs these paths, illustrating how value moves through the system and where it ultimately settles. Even when criminals use sophisticated techniques, mistakes - reused information, repeated patterns, or unmasked connections - often provide entry points for investigators.

Detecting Collusion and Coordinated Activity

Collusion typically involves multiple actors working together, often covertly, to conduct illicit activity. Link analysis is one of the most effective methods for detecting collusion because it highlights unusual or unexplained relationships between individuals, accounts, or entities.

For example, investigators may identify employees who appear unconnected but access the same accounts, approve transactions for the same customers, or share external contacts. In external fraud schemes, multiple customers may use the same IP address, physical address, or device. In cybercrime, multiple wallets may be controlled by the same entity despite appearing independent.

Patterns such as synchronized activity, shared resources, or repeated interactions between seemingly unrelated entities often indicate coordinated behavior. Network mapping illustrates these patterns clearly, allowing investigators to trace how groups operate and where control is centralized.

Integrating OSINT and Internal Data

Link analysis becomes powerful when internal data is integrated with external sources. Public information - corporate registry data, social media profiles, property records, leaked datasets, sanctions lists, and news articles - provides context that internal records alone cannot supply.

For example, internal data may show that a customer frequently receives transfers from multiple sources, but OSINT may reveal that those sources share a common beneficial owner or are part of the same informal network. Similarly, OSINT might show that a vendor is owned by a relative of an employee, suggesting undisclosed conflicts of interest.

Integrating multiple data types allows investigators to build more accurate and complete networks. Each data point adds dimension to the analysis, supporting stronger conclusions and better risk assessment.

Visualizing Transaction Flows

One of the most valuable applications of network mapping is the visualization of transaction flows. Instead of reviewing transactions in spreadsheets or narrative form, investigators can see how funds move across accounts, channels, or jurisdictions. Flows reveal direction, volume, and frequency - key indicators of laundering, fraud, or transfer schemes.

Visualization tools illustrate whether funds move in a circular pattern, pass through multiple intermediaries, or converge on a central account. These patterns provide insight into the network's purpose. Circular flows may indicate layering in money laundering. Convergent flows may suggest consolidation of illicit proceeds. Rapid outbound flows from new accounts may signal mule behavior.

Transaction flow analysis also helps investigators identify bottlenecks - points in the network where funds concentrate before being distributed. These bottlenecks often represent vulnerabilities in the criminal process and can guide intervention strategies.

Strengthening Investigative Decision-Making

Link analysis and network mapping support decision-making throughout the investigative lifecycle. At the beginning of an investigation, they help define scope, prioritize leads, and form initial hypotheses. As the investigation develops, they help identify new entities, clarify relationships, and validate or challenge assumptions. During case development, they provide visual evidence that can be shared with stakeholders, regulators, or law enforcement.

AI, MACHINE LEARNING, AND PREDICTIVE RISK MODELS

Artificial intelligence (AI) and machine learning have transformed the landscape of financial crime detection. Traditional rules-based systems remain useful, but they are limited by rigid structures and cannot easily adapt to new behaviors or emerging risks. Criminals evolve quickly, adjusting methods to avoid detection, exploiting weaknesses in monitoring systems, and using technology to operate across borders and platforms. AI and machine learning provide institutions with the ability to analyze large volumes of data, identify subtle patterns, and predict potential misconduct before it escalates. When implemented correctly, these models strengthen investigative capabilities, improve efficiency, and enhance an institution's ability to manage risk.

The Role of AI in Financial Crime Detection

In financial crime detection, AI enhances monitoring systems by identifying activity that does not fit established norms or rules. It examines data holistically, recognizing connections that may not be visible when transactions are reviewed in isolation.

AI supports both supervised and unsupervised learning. Supervised learning models use historical data to predict outcomes based on known examples, such as previous suspicious transactions or confirmed fraud cases. Unsupervised models do not rely on labeled data; instead, they identify unusual patterns or outliers within datasets. Both approaches contribute to stronger detection mechanisms by expanding the system's ability to identify risks.

Machine Learning as a Core Analytical Tool

Machine learning functions by examining large datasets and detecting complex patterns that traditional analytics cannot identify. Unlike static rules, machine learning models continuously adapt to new information. As more data becomes available, models refine their understanding of behaviors, relationships, and risk indicators.

In financial crime investigations, machine learning is particularly valuable for detecting anomalies. Anomaly detection models identify transactions or behaviors that deviate from expected patterns. These deviations may indicate fraud, collusion, sanctions evasion, or other misconduct. Models analyze multiple variables simultaneously - transaction size, location, timing, counterparties, and behavioral history - creating a multi-dimensional view of risk.

Classification models are also widely used. These models categorize transactions based on likelihood of risk, allowing institutions to prioritize alerts and allocate investigative resources more effectively. When combined with behavioral analytics, classification models provide a deeper understanding of whether certain actions represent legitimate customer behavior or potential misconduct.

Predictive Risk Models and Early Detection

Predictive risk models use historical data, behavioral indicators, and statistical analysis to anticipate future risks. These models do not simply detect suspicious activity after it occurs; they assess the likelihood that an entity will engage in misconduct. Predictive capabilities are particularly useful in areas such as insider trading, account takeover, mule activity, and early-stage fraud schemes.

Predictive risk modeling requires comprehensive datasets. Models examine long-term patterns, subtle correlations, device identifiers, communication behavior, and transaction sequences. When a customer exhibits characteristics similar to known high-risk profiles, the system may assign an elevated risk score, triggering closer monitoring or preventive measures.

In money laundering cases, predictive models can identify layering behaviors that precede large illicit transfers. In cyber-enabled fraud, models can detect the early signs of coordinated activity, such as repeated login attempts, unusual device clusters, or sudden changes in communication patterns. Predictive risk models serve as an early warning system, enabling institutions to respond before financial loss or regulatory exposure occurs.

Data Quality and Model Accuracy

AI and machine learning models are only as effective as the data they rely on. Poor-quality data leads to inaccurate predictions, high false positives, and unreliable outputs. Institutions must establish strong data governance practices, ensuring that inputs are clean, accurate, consistent, and complete.

Key pieces of data include customer information, transaction history, device identifiers, geolocation data, communication logs, and external risk indicators. When data sources conflict or contain gaps, models may misinterpret behavior or overlook important risk factors. Continuous validation and calibration are necessary to maintain accuracy.

Model accuracy also depends on diversity of data. If a model is trained only on a narrow set of examples, it may overfit to those patterns, failing to recognize broader typologies or emerging risks. Expanding training datasets, incorporating external information, and verifying outputs through human review help ensure that models remain robust and reliable.

Explainability and Regulatory Expectations

One of the primary challenges in deploying AI and machine learning within financial crime detection is ensuring explainability. Regulators expect institutions to understand how models work, why alerts are generated, and which variables influence outcomes. Black-box models that produce outputs without clarity cannot withstand regulatory scrutiny.

Explainability involves articulating the logic behind model predictions, documenting model development, and maintaining transparency around data sources. Institutions must be able to demonstrate that models operate consistently, fairly, and without unintended bias. Clear audit trails, detailed documentation, and periodic model reviews are essential.

Explainability also supports investigators. Analysts must understand why the system identified an activity as risky. When investigators have clarity, they can assess whether alerts require further action, identify gaps in the model's logic, and provide feedback that supports ongoing improvement.

Combining AI Outputs with Human Judgment

AI enhances investigative processes, but it does not replace professional judgment. Human investigators provide context, interpret ambiguous behavior, and decide when escalation is necessary. AI identifies patterns, but investigators determine significance. Human oversight ensures that models do not misinterpret legitimate behavior or overlook nuanced risks.

The most effective detection environments combine automated intelligence with human expertise. Analysts review AI-generated alerts, validate findings, and incorporate additional information that models cannot access, such as insights from interviews or historical case knowledge. This partnership strengthens decision-making and reduces the likelihood of errors.

AI also assists investigators by triaging low-risk cases, allowing human resources to focus on more complex or urgent matters. When AI prioritizes alerts, investigators can concentrate on cases requiring advanced analysis, improving efficiency and investigative quality.

Evolving Threats and Continuous Model Improvement

Financial crime evolves continuously, requiring models to adapt. Criminals monitor detection methods, identify weaknesses, and adjust tactics. AI systems must evolve at the same pace to remain effective. This requires continuous retraining, recalibration, and refinement.

Model improvement involves incorporating new data, reviewing false positives and false negatives, and analyzing emerging typologies. Institutions must track global trends, regulatory changes, and new fraud techniques, ensuring that models reflect current risks.

Continuous improvement also helps address bias or drift. Over time, models may produce outputs that deviate from expected standards, requiring corrective action. Regular reviews help detect these issues early, maintaining model integrity and compliance.

Strategic Integration of Predictive Models

Predictive risk models should support broader risk management strategies. They guide decisions about enhanced monitoring, customer due diligence, resource allocation, and strategic initiatives. When integrated effectively, predictive models improve operational resilience and enhance overall financial crime prevention.

CHAPTER 15

FOLLOWING THE MONEY

TRACING LAYERED AND OBSCURED TRANSACTIONS

Tracing layered and obscured transactions is one of the most challenging aspects of financial crime investigation. Criminals intentionally design transaction paths to frustrate detection, obscure the origin of funds, and create distance between themselves and the illicit proceeds. Effective tracing requires a methodical approach, detailed analysis, and a clear understanding of how funds move through different parts of the financial system. While criminals may attempt to conceal their activities, every transaction leaves a trace. The challenge is piecing together those traces into a coherent narrative that reveals intent, structure, and participants.

Understanding the Purpose of Layering

Layering is the stage of money laundering in which criminals attempt to conceal the origin of illicit funds by moving them through a series of complex transactions. These movements are often designed to break the audit trail, reduce transparency, or exploit gaps between institutions, products, or jurisdictions. Layering does not occur by accident; it is intentional, and its complexity is tailored to the criminal's knowledge of the financial system.

The purpose of layering is to disconnect the proceeds from their criminal source. This is typically achieved by passing funds through multiple accounts, converting them into different asset types, involving intermediaries, or moving funds across borders. Layering may take place slowly to avoid detection, or rapidly to exploit weaknesses in real-time monitoring systems. Regardless of timing, the goal is the same: to confuse the trail.

Recognizing Layering Techniques

Criminals use a variety of techniques to obscure transactions, often combining multiple strategies to maximize confusion. Understanding these methods helps investigators recognize red flags and reconstruct movement patterns.

One common method is structuring, where large amounts of money are broken into smaller transactions to avoid reporting thresholds. When repeated across multiple accounts or institutions, structuring becomes part of a larger layering plan.

Third-party accounts - operated by individuals who appear uninvolved in the crime - add another layer of concealment. These accounts may belong to family members, associates, or unwitting participants. Criminals exploit the trust and perceived legitimacy of these third parties to move funds without attracting attention.

Conversion into different forms of value is another technique. Funds may be moved from bank accounts into virtual assets, prepaid cards, commodities, or high-value goods. These conversions complicate tracing efforts because they create multiple transaction types and data sources.

Cross-border transfers remain one of the most effective means of obscuring funds. Differences in regulatory regimes, reporting standards, and data accessibility create opportunities for criminals to exploit gaps between jurisdictions.

Mapping Transaction Sequences

The foundation of tracing layered transactions is reconstructing the sequence of movements. Investigators must assemble transaction histories chronologically, identifying each step the funds take as they move through accounts, institutions, and asset types. This sequence forms the backbone of the investigative narrative.

Transaction mapping often begins with identifying the initial point where illicit funds enter the system. From there, investigators follow each transfer, withdrawal, conversion, or deposit that occurs downstream. Mapping involves reviewing bank statements, ledger entries, blockchain records, and internal system data. Each movement must be accounted for to determine whether it aligns with legitimate behavior or signals concealment.

Visualizing these sequences through flow charts or network diagrams helps investigators spot anomalies and recognize emerging patterns. While individual transactions may appear benign, the sequence as a whole often reveals a deliberate effort to obscure origin or ownership.

Identifying Anomalies and Inconsistencies

Layered transactions contain inconsistencies that alert investigators to potential misconduct. These inconsistencies may be subtle: sudden increases in account activity, unusual transaction timing, multiple transfers between related accounts, or patterns inconsistent with customer profiles.

Anomalies often stand out more clearly when viewed across time. For example, a business that typically processes small domestic payments may suddenly send multiple international transfers to unrelated entities. An individual with modest income may engage in rapid conversions of funds into virtual assets. A company with no operational footprint may receive large transfers that are quickly dispersed to other jurisdictions.

These anomalies do not prove wrongdoing, but they demonstrate behavior requiring further investigation. When combined with contextual information - customer documentation, ownership records, or OSINT findings - they contribute to a more comprehensive understanding of the transaction flow.

Using Multi-Source Data to Strengthen Tracing

Tracing layered transactions requires information from diverse sources. Internal bank records provide detailed transaction histories, but they often need to be supplemented with external data. Corporate registry filings may reveal connections between entities involved in transfers. Social media or public records may show relationships between individuals controlling accounts. Blockchain explorers may reveal patterns in virtual asset movements.

Integration of these data sources allows investigators to follow the full chain of events. Criminals rely on complexity to hide their activity, but complexity leaves traces - addresses reused across accounts, shared phone numbers, repeated patterns in transaction timings, or correlations between account activity and known events.

Investigators must approach data integration systematically, ensuring that each source is verified, contextualized, and accurately linked to the relevant part of the transaction sequence. This level of diligence prevents false assumptions and strengthens evidentiary quality.

Following the Money across Asset Types

One of the more sophisticated challenges in tracing obscured transactions is following funds across different asset types. Criminals frequently use conversion to complicate tracing efforts. Cash may be deposited and transferred into corporate accounts. Bank funds may move into cryptocurrency. Virtual assets may be exchanged for high-value goods. Commodities may be sold to generate legitimate-appearing proceeds.

Each asset type has its own record formats, data availability, and regulatory requirements. Tracing across these boundaries requires familiarity with multiple systems, including banking platforms, relevant analysis tools, corporate registries, customs data, and property records.

Investigators must identify the points at which funds change form. These conversion points often represent vulnerabilities for criminals because they require interactions with regulated entities, exchanges, or intermediaries who maintain records or are subject to reporting requirements.

Reconstructing Intent and Narrative

Tracing money is only part of the process. Investigators must also interpret what the movement of funds reveals about intent. Patterns of rapid transfers, circular flows, repeated use of offshore jurisdictions, or involvement of shell companies often point to a deliberate design rather than coincidence.

Reconstructing intent requires combining quantitative analysis - transaction flows, timing, patterns - with qualitative context such as statements made by individuals, corporate histories, or evidence from interviews. When investigators can articulate a coherent narrative of how and why funds were moved, the tracing becomes a powerful tool for legal and regulatory action.

Overcoming Obstacles and Incomplete Data

Even with strong systems, investigators often encounter incomplete or inconsistent data. Some jurisdictions limit access to banking information. Some asset types lack standardized reporting. Criminals may use privacy-enhancing tools or unregulated services. In these cases, investigators must rely on inference, indirect evidence, and triangulation.

Triangulation involves analyzing multiple lines of evidence to determine whether they point to the same conclusion. For example, if funds disappear into a jurisdiction with limited transparency but reappear in an account controlled by the same individual, the movement may be inferred even if direct records are scarce.

IDENTIFYING BENEFICIAL OWNERSHIP AND SHELL STRUCTURES

Identifying beneficial ownership is one of the most important and complex tasks in financial crime investigations. Criminals frequently rely on opaque corporate structures, legal intermediaries, and layers of formality to conceal their involvement in illicit activity. Shell companies, trusts, nominee directors, and offshore entities are used strategically to distance the criminal from the proceeds of wrongdoing. While corporate structuring can be legitimate, it becomes problematic when the arrangement serves no economic purpose other than to disguise control or ownership. Investigators must be skilled at identifying the real individuals behind corporate entities and understanding how each component contributes to the larger concealment strategy.

Understanding Beneficial Ownership

Beneficial ownership refers to the natural person who ultimately owns, controls, or benefits from an entity or arrangement, even when their name does not appear on official documents. Legal ownership and beneficial ownership may differ significantly. A person may appear as a director or shareholder on paper without exercising real control, while another individual - who is not listed - may direct the entity's decisions, access its accounts, or benefit from its transactions.

Determining beneficial ownership requires examining the difference between what is publicly declared and how the entity operates in practice. This includes reviewing patterns of decision-making, the flow of funds, relationships between associated companies, and the role of intermediaries. Beneficial ownership becomes especially relevant in cases involving money laundering, corruption, tax evasion, sanctions evasion, and large-scale fraud.

Characteristics of Shell and Front Companies

Shell companies are legal entities with little or no genuine business activity. They may not have employees, physical offices, or operational systems. Their purpose is often to provide a legal façade that criminals can use to move, store, or disguise illicit funds. Not all shell companies are illegal; some are created for legitimate reasons such as holding assets or facilitating mergers. However, in financial crime cases, shells are typically used for opacity.

Front companies, by contrast, have some operational activity but are used to hide illicit proceeds within legitimate operations. They may mix illegal funds with legitimate revenue, use business operations to launder money, or act as intermediaries between criminal actors and the financial system.

Common indicators of shell or front companies include nonexistent physical presence, the use of virtual offices shared with numerous unrelated entities, minimal or no online presence, and financial activity inconsistent with stated business operations. Understanding these characteristics helps investigators determine whether a company is legitimate or part of a concealment strategy.

Techniques Criminals Use to Hide Ownership

Criminals employ a range of techniques to obscure ownership. One common method is the use of nominee directors or shareholders. Nominees appear as formal owners but do not exercise actual control. They may be paid to serve as a figurehead, often without any knowledge of the company's true purpose. Nominees can include lawyers, accountants, or professional service providers operating in jurisdictions where such arrangements are common.

Another technique is layering ownership across multiple jurisdictions. A company in one country may be owned by a holding company in another, which in turn is owned by a trust or foundation in a third. Each jurisdiction may have different transparency requirements, making it difficult to trace ownership. These multi-layered structures are designed to exploit differences in reporting standards and legal frameworks.

Criminals also use bearer shares - ownership instruments that do not record the owner's name. Although many jurisdictions have banned or restricted bearer shares due to their abuse in money laundering, they still exist in some countries and continue to pose challenges for investigators.

Trusts further complicate ownership identification. They separate legal ownership (held by the trustee) from beneficial ownership (held by the beneficiary). While trusts can be legitimate, they also allow criminals to hide behind legal arrangements that lack clarity in public records.

Methods for Uncovering Beneficial Ownership

Effective identification of beneficial ownership relies on a combination of documentary review, data analysis, and contextual investigation. Corporate registries are a starting point, but they must be supplemented with additional sources because criminals rarely rely solely on official filings.

Investigators examine incorporation documents, shareholder registers, annual filings, and changes in ownership. Sudden or frequent changes in directors or shareholders can indicate attempts to obscure control. Shared addresses, repeated use of the same corporate service provider, or overlapping personnel across multiple entities may indicate coordinated ownership structures.

Public information is also useful. OSINT tools can identify relationships, shared connections, lifestyle indicators, and undisclosed business affiliations. Social media, professional directories, and online business listings can reveal links not visible in formal records.

Financial data provides another perspective. Tracing account activity, payment flows, and transaction patterns can reveal who truly exercises control. If an individual consistently authorizes transactions, communicates with financial institutions, or benefits from the entity's activities, that individual may be the true beneficial owner regardless of formal documentation.

The Role of Offshore Jurisdictions

Offshore jurisdictions play a significant role in obscured ownership. These jurisdictions may allow companies to be formed quickly with minimal disclosure requirements and limited public transparency. They often provide legal structures such as international business companies, trusts, and foundations designed to facilitate privacy.

While not all offshore activity is illicit, certain patterns raise concern. These include companies registered in well-known secrecy jurisdictions without a legitimate business rationale, ownership chains that circle back into high-risk jurisdictions, and structures used by individuals with no economic ties to the countries in which their companies are incorporated.

Investigators must approach offshore structures with caution but not with assumption. The key is understanding whether the structure has a genuine business purpose or exists solely to obscure ownership. Coordination with foreign authorities, mutual legal assistance mechanisms, and cross-border intelligence sharing may be necessary to obtain information unavailable in public sources.

Identifying Hidden Relationships and Control

Ultimately, identifying beneficial ownership requires uncovering hidden relationships. These relationships may be personal, financial, or operational. Criminals often rely on trusted associates - family members, close friends, or long-term business partners - to serve as intermediaries. They may instruct others to act on their behalf, exert influence without signing documents, or control accounts without appearing formally connected to them.

Investigators must look beyond names on paper. Behavior offers strong evidence of control. If a person routinely gives instructions to employees, approves payments, negotiates contracts, or uses assets owned by a company, that person may be the true beneficial owner. Consistent use of company funds for personal expenses is another strong indicator.

Patterns of communication can also provide insight. Emails, messaging records, shared digital accounts, and access logs can reveal who directs activities behind the scenes. These indicators help reconstruct the role individuals play within a structure.

Strengthening Investigative Conclusions

Beneficial ownership investigations require clear, evidence-based conclusions. Investigators must document findings thoroughly, explaining how ownership was identified, which sources were used, and how relationships were established. Transparency is essential, especially when findings support regulatory action or criminal proceedings.

CROSS-BORDER FLOWS AND MULTI-JURISDICTIONAL CHALLENGES

As financial systems become increasingly interconnected, criminals exploit differences between jurisdictions to move funds quickly, avoid detection, and take advantage of regulatory inconsistencies. Tracing money across borders is a complex task that requires technical skill, legal awareness, and persistent investigative effort. Each jurisdiction brings its own laws, reporting standards, banking practices, privacy rules, and record-keeping norms. These differences create challenges, but they also offer opportunities for investigators who understand how to interpret transaction flows within a global context.

The Nature of Cross-Border Movement

Cross-border movement of funds occurs for legitimate reasons - international trade, investment, remittances, and corporate operations - but it is also central to laundering, fraud, bribery, sanctions evasion, terrorist financing, and tax evasion. Criminals exploit international transfers because they create distance between the origin and destination of funds. Once money crosses a border, it often enters a regulatory environment with different transparency standards, making detection more difficult.

Some transfers involve a simple outbound transaction from one country to another. Others involve complex pathways: funds may pass through multiple accounts, correspondent banks, payment processors, cryptocurrency exchanges, or intermediary institutions in several jurisdictions. Each step introduces additional challenges for investigators, particularly when the movement involves high-risk countries or jurisdictions known for secrecy or weak enforcement.

Exploiting Jurisdictional Gaps

Multi-jurisdictional challenges arise from differences in legal frameworks. Some countries maintain robust reporting requirements, public registries, and transparent banking systems, while others allow companies to form easily with minimal disclosure. Criminals strategically select jurisdictions where transparency is low, or cooperation with foreign authorities is slow.

Layering often exploits these jurisdictional gaps. For instance, funds may originate in a country with strong oversight, flow through an offshore entity in a secrecy jurisdiction, and ultimately land in an account located in a permissive regulatory environment. Each transfer reduces the visibility of the original transaction and complicates efforts to trace the funds.

Correspondent banking adds additional complexity. When small banks in high-risk jurisdictions rely on larger banks for access to global markets, information about the underlying parties may not transfer fully. Criminals take advantage of this opacity, routing funds through correspondent accounts to conceal their true source or beneficiary.

Regulatory and Legal Constraints

Investigators face numerous legal challenges when dealing with cross-border flows. Privacy laws, bank secrecy legislation, and data protection rules vary widely. What is accessible in one country may be restricted in another. Some jurisdictions require formal court orders, diplomatic channels, or lengthy procedures before providing access to financial information.

Mutual legal assistance treaties (MLATs) facilitate information sharing between countries, but MLAT requests can be slow, bureaucratic, and highly dependent on political cooperation. In urgent cases, delays can undermine efforts to freeze or recover assets before they are moved further.

Informal cooperation channels - such as regulatory networks, financial intelligence units, and industry partnerships - can provide quicker access to insights, but these channels often have limitations. Investigators must balance legal compliance with investigative urgency, ensuring that information is obtained lawfully while still pursuing time-sensitive leads.

Challenges in Interpreting Foreign Records

Financial records differ significantly between jurisdictions. Some countries maintain detailed bank statements with consistent formatting, while others provide sparse information or rely on outdated systems. Languages, currency formats, reference codes, and documentation standards vary widely.

Investigators must understand how foreign institutions structure accounts, record transactions, and classify banking activity. Misinterpretation can lead to errors in tracing flows or misunderstandings about the purpose of a transaction. In some regions, businesses operate informally or use cash-intensive models, making financial records less precise.

Foreign corporate documents may also follow different conventions. Ownership disclosures may be limited, nominee arrangements accepted, or annual filings inconsistent. Understanding these nuances is essential when evaluating whether an entity is legitimate or part of a concealment strategy.

Following Digital Asset Movement across Borders

Cryptocurrency has intensified cross-border challenges. Digital assets move across jurisdictions without passing through traditional banking systems. Criminals exploit this feature to transfer value quickly and with fewer intermediaries. Although blockchain records are transparent, identifying the jurisdictional relevance of a wallet or exchange often requires OSINT, subpoenas, or cross-border cooperation.

Many crypto exchanges operate across multiple jurisdictions, each with different regulatory requirements. Some exchanges are strictly supervised, while others offer limited oversight. Criminals may route funds through exchanges in permissive jurisdictions, complicating tracing efforts. The global nature of digital assets requires investigators to understand the interaction between blockchain analytics, international regulation, and local compliance standards.

Multi-Jurisdictional Record Fragmentation

Cross-border financial activity often produces fragmented evidence. Bank statements may exist in one country, corporate filings in another, and transactional metadata in yet another. No single jurisdiction has the full picture.

Investigators must assemble evidence from multiple sources, linking disparate components into a coherent chain. This requires patience, coordination, and careful documentation. Fragmentation also increases the risk of missing key connections if investigators rely only on easily accessible data.

To overcome fragmentation, investigators create unified timelines, cross-reference data points, and use link analysis tools to integrate information. Every transaction must be understood both individually and in relation to the wider chain. The absence of a record in one jurisdiction may be explained by the presence of a correlating record in another.

Cultural, Operational, and Institutional Differences

Beyond legal variation, cultural and institutional differences impact investigations. Banking norms vary - some jurisdictions rely heavily on cash, others on digital transfers. Record-keeping practices range from highly digitalized systems to paper-based archives. In some countries, customer identification standards are rigorous; in others, they may be minimal or inconsistently enforced.

Institutional priorities also differ. Some authorities focus heavily on anti-money laundering compliance, while others prioritize tax collection or economic security. These differences influence response times, cooperation levels, and the completeness of shared information.

Investigators must remain aware of these differences and approach each jurisdiction with realistic expectations. A nuanced understanding of local practices helps avoid misinterpretations and supports more effective requests for information.

Strategies for Overcoming Multi-Jurisdictional Barriers

Effective cross-border investigation requires adaptability, intelligence-sharing partnerships, and use of both formal and informal channels. International bodies such as the Egmont Group facilitate cooperation between financial intelligence units.

Industry-led partnerships allow institutions to share typologies, trends, and risk indicators. Public–private collaborations often yield insights faster than formal legal processes.

Investigators should prioritize early evidence preservation. Once funds move across borders, they may be withdrawn, converted, or transferred to jurisdictions with limited cooperation. Acting quickly - obtaining internal records, issuing internal holds, and initiating information requests - is critical.

Using technology is also important. Advanced analytics tools help investigators trace flows across currencies, institutions, and asset classes. Visualization tools reveal patterns that textual records cannot. Blockchain analysis tools offer clarity in digital asset investigations, even when the movement spans numerous jurisdictions.

Developing a Coherent Investigative Narrative

Ultimately, tracing cross-border flows requires constructing a coherent narrative supported by evidence from multiple jurisdictions. Investigators must piece together records, explain differences between systems, and articulate how funds moved, why they moved, and who benefited.

ASSET RECOVERY AND RESTRAINT STRATEGIES

Asset recovery is a central objective in financial crime investigations. While understanding how illicit proceeds move is important, the ultimate aim is to restrain, seize, and return those assets to victims or the state. Criminal schemes often revolve around financial gain, so recovering assets not only restores losses but also disrupts criminal networks and removes the incentive for future wrongdoing. Effective recovery relies on early action, strategic planning, cooperation between agencies, and a thorough understanding of legal mechanisms across jurisdictions. Because criminals often disperse funds quickly and strategically, investigators must work with precision and urgency to preserve value before it is lost.

The Importance of Early Intervention

Early intervention is critical in asset recovery. Once criminals suspect they are under scrutiny, they frequently move funds into inaccessible jurisdictions, convert them into hard-to-trace assets, or use intermediaries to disperse them. Investigators who identify suspicious activity early can initiate restraint actions before assets disappear.

Timing is essential. As soon as investigators uncover evidence indicating that funds may represent the proceeds of crime, they should consider whether freezing or restraining those assets is warranted. Delay increases the risk that funds will be dissipated, especially in cases involving rapidly movable assets such as cryptocurrency, online payment platforms, or offshore accounts. Early intervention requires collaboration between legal, compliance, and investigative teams to ensure that decisions are made swiftly and in accordance with legal standards.

Legal Tools for Restraint and Recovery

Asset restraint and recovery rely on a range of legal tools. These include freezing orders, production orders, restraint orders, confiscation orders, and civil recovery proceedings. Each tool serves a different purpose and may be used at different stages of an investigation.

Freezing orders prevent individuals from moving or dissipating assets while an investigation is ongoing. They can apply to bank accounts, property, securities, and other forms of value. Restraint orders are typically broader and may cover multiple asset types, preventing any disposal or movement without authorization.

Confiscation orders generally follow a criminal conviction and allow the state to seize assets proven to be the proceeds of crime. Civil recovery mechanisms allow the state to recover assets without a criminal conviction when evidence shows that the assets are linked to unlawful conduct. These civil tools are particularly useful in cases where suspects reside abroad, are uncooperative, or where a criminal trial is not achievable.

Investigators must understand which legal mechanism is appropriate in a given situation and coordinate closely with legal counsel to ensure compliance with procedural requirements. Proper documentation, evidence preservation, and clear articulation of the link to criminal conduct are essential for obtaining legal orders.

Locating and Identifying Recoverable Assets

Locating assets requires a systematic approach. Criminals hide proceeds in a variety of forms—bank accounts, real estate, luxury goods, corporate structures, digital assets, and cash-intensive businesses. They may transfer assets to relatives, business partners, or shell companies to complicate recovery efforts. Effective asset tracing requires investigators to identify both the assets themselves and the individuals or entities who control them.

Financial records, corporate filings, transaction histories, property registries, and blockchain data provide insight into where assets may be held. OSINT sources help identify lifestyle indicators, undisclosed holdings, and relationships that reveal control over assets not recorded in a suspect's name. In some cases, indirect evidence - such as use of a property or consistent payment of expenses - may suggest beneficial ownership even when formal title remains elsewhere.

Investigators must also consider hidden value. Artwork, precious metals, luxury vehicles, and collectibles may hold significant worth but be overlooked in traditional reviews. Unusual expenditures can indicate where illicit funds have been converted into alternative asset types.

Cross-Border Recovery Challenges

Cross-border asset recovery presents additional complexities. Differences in legal frameworks, cooperation mechanisms, and court procedures can significantly affect the speed and success of recovery efforts. Some jurisdictions require extensive documentation to support foreign restraint orders; others may impose strict privacy laws that limit access to financial information.

Mutual legal assistance treaties facilitate cooperation between countries, but requests often move slowly and may require extensive translation, certification, or judicial review. When assets are located in multiple jurisdictions, investigators must coordinate efforts to avoid duplication, conflicting claims, or gaps in enforcement.

Despite these challenges, cross-border recovery is achievable with careful planning. Investigators should anticipate potential foreign involvement early, gather jurisdiction-specific intelligence, and prepare robust evidence packages. Collaboration with foreign regulators, financial intelligence units, and international partners increases the likelihood of successful enforcement.

Preserving Value During Recovery

Once assets are located and restrained, preserving their value becomes essential. Assets can lose value quickly if not managed properly. Perishable goods, volatile investments, and cryptocurrencies pose particular risks. Even real estate may deteriorate or require maintenance to retain value.

Institutions responsible for asset management must ensure that seized assets are stored, insured, and monitored appropriately. In some cases, liquidation may be necessary to prevent loss, provided it complies with legal requirements and preserves the interests of victims. Effective value preservation ensures that recovered assets remain usable and that legal orders can be executed without unnecessary loss.

Civil and Criminal Recovery Approaches

Asset recovery can follow criminal or civil pathways, each with advantages and limitations. Criminal recovery relies on proving that the suspect committed an offense. While powerful, this approach may be impractical in cases where suspects reside abroad, evidence is incomplete, or prosecution is unlikely.

Civil recovery focuses on the assets rather than the individual. Authorities must demonstrate that the property is connected to unlawful conduct, but they do not need to secure a criminal conviction. Civil recovery is valuable in cases involving politically exposed persons, foreign officials, or individuals who use complex corporate structures to avoid direct legal exposure.

Both approaches require strong evidentiary support. Investigators must gather records that demonstrate the link between assets and unlawful conduct, explain patterns of movement, and identify controlling individuals.

Recovering Digital Assets

Digital assets present unique recovery challenges. Cryptocurrencies move rapidly, exist outside traditional banking systems, and can be held in wallets controlled only by private keys.

However, blockchain transparency often provides investigators with powerful tracing opportunities. Once funds are linked to a specific wallet, investigators can track their movement and identify points where they intersect with regulated exchanges.

Recovering digital assets typically requires coordination with cryptocurrency platforms, legal requests to exchanges, and expert blockchain analysis. When keys are seized, law enforcement can transfer digital assets into controlled accounts to prevent unauthorized movement. The speed of intervention is critical.

PART IV

SECTOR-SPECIFIC FINANCIAL CRIME RISKS

CHAPTER 16

FINANCIAL INSTITUTIONS

BANKING SECTOR EXPOSURE AND COMMON TYPOLOGIES

THE BANKING sector sits at the center of global financial systems, serving as the primary gateway for legitimate commerce as well as a frequent target for abuse. Because banks process vast volumes of transactions, offer diverse products, and operate across multiple channels, they are exposed to a wide spectrum of financial crime risks. Criminals exploit weaknesses in internal controls, gaps in customer due diligence, and limitations in monitoring systems. Banks must understand how they are exposed and recognize the typologies most frequently used to exploit their infrastructure. This understanding forms the basis for effective prevention, timely detection, and credible reporting.

The Central Role of Banks in Financial Crime

Banks serve as the backbone of financial activity, providing services required for payments, savings, investments, lending, foreign exchange, and trade finance. These functions, while essential, also create opportunities for criminal misuse. When illicit funds enter the banking system, they gain legitimacy. Criminals rely on banks to store proceeds, move them across borders, convert them into other forms of value, or disguise ownership through corporate accounts. Because of this role, banks face regulatory expectations that exceed those placed on most other sectors.

Exposure increases with size, geographic presence, product diversity, and customer complexity. Large institutions often face the most significant challenges because they conduct business across multiple jurisdictions, serve high-risk customer segments, and manage extensive networks of correspondent relationships. Yet smaller institutions are not immune. Criminals may target smaller banks precisely because they assume controls are weaker or oversight is less sophisticated.

Customer Risk and Weak Onboarding

One of the banking sector's most consistent vulnerabilities is weak customer onboarding. When banks do not obtain accurate or complete information at account opening, the entire risk assessment process becomes flawed. Criminals exploit this by presenting misleading or incomplete information, using forged documents, or relying on intermediaries to open accounts.

Incomplete onboarding often leads to inadequate understanding of the customer's activities, allowing suspicious behavior to blend in with legitimate patterns. Shell companies, in particular, rely on weak onboarding processes. They may present plausible but vague business descriptions, use shared addresses, and offer little evidence of substantive activity. If banks fail to question these inconsistencies, they may inadvertently facilitate laundering, sanctions evasion, or fraud.

Customer risk also evolves. Legitimate customers may become compromised or engage in misconduct later. Banks must therefore continuously update their understanding of customer behavior, especially when transaction patterns diverge from initial expectations.

Transaction Typologies Exploiting the Banking System

Criminals use predictable methods to abuse banking channels. Understanding these typologies helps banks identify risk early.

Structuring is a common issue. Individuals deposit or transfer funds in small increments to avoid triggering reporting thresholds. Structuring often involves multiple accounts, cash-intensive businesses, or coordinated activity across several individuals. Banks with inadequate monitoring thresholds may miss this behavior.

Layering through rapid transfers is another frequent tactic. Funds move quickly between accounts, often across institutions or borders, to create confusion. When banks do not analyze the full flow of funds or fail to integrate cross-channel monitoring, these movements may appear unrelated, masking the underlying scheme.

Use of third-party intermediaries is also prevalent. Criminals often rely on friends, relatives, or coerced individuals to conduct transactions on their behalf. These "fronts" obscure the identity of the true controller and complicate attribution. Banks must identify when account behavior does not align with the known profile of the account holder, such as unusual volumes, inconsistent sources of funds, or activity that appears directed by others.

Corporate accounts present additional risks. High-risk entities may transact in patterns inconsistent with their stated business purpose. Misuse of trade finance instruments, false invoicing, and over- or under-valuation of goods are common in money laundering and sanctions evasion. Banks that rely solely on documentation without verifying authenticity are especially vulnerable to these typologies.

High-Risk Products and Services

Certain banking products inherently present higher exposure. Cross-border wire transfers move funds quickly and often involve counterparties with limited transparency. Without strong screening, banks may inadvertently process payments linked to high-risk jurisdictions or sanctioned parties.

Cash services also carry significant risk. Large cash deposits, especially when inconsistent with customer profiles, often indicate unreported income, criminal proceeds, or tax evasion. When branches fail to question unusual cash activity or lack systems to detect patterns across multiple locations, criminals exploit these gaps.

Correspondent banking introduces further complexity. When banks provide services to foreign banks, especially in high-risk regions, they may process transactions involving unknown underlying customers. Weak due diligence on respondent banks can expose institutions to significant laundering, terrorist financing, or sanctions-related risk.

Remote Channels and Digital Exposure

The growth of online banking, mobile payments, and remote onboarding has increased exposure to identity fraud, account takeovers, and synthetic identities. Criminals use compromised credentials, falsified documents, or automated bots to open accounts or initiate transactions. Because remote channels remove face-to-face interaction, banks must rely heavily on document verification, digital fingerprints, device intelligence, and behavioral analytics.

Rapid onboarding services offered by digital platforms attract legitimate customers seeking convenience but also appeal to criminals seeking quick access to the financial system. If controls focus only on document validation without examining behavioral patterns, institutions may miss signs of fraudulent account creation.

Internal Vulnerabilities

Banks also face exposure from within. Weak governance, inadequate oversight, and insufficient training contribute to risk. Inconsistent escalation procedures or poor communication between departments can allow suspicious activity to go unchallenged.

Employees may also engage in misconduct. Insider activity includes unauthorized account access, manipulation of records, or collusion with external actors. Banks must ensure strong access controls, audit logs, and segregation of duties to reduce internal risk.

Mule Accounts, Funnels, and Correspondent Banking Risks

Mule accounts, funnel activity, and correspondent banking relationships represent some of the highest-risk areas within financial institutions. Criminals exploit these mechanisms to move funds quickly, obscure their involvement, and exploit gaps in monitoring. Understanding these risks is essential for identifying suspicious behavior, protecting institutions from regulatory exposure, and disrupting illicit networks. Each of these typologies presents unique challenges, but they share a common feature: criminals rely on intermediaries or structural weaknesses to disguise transactions. Strong controls and informed investigative practices are essential for mitigating these threats.

MULE ACCOUNTS AND THEIR ROLE IN FINANCIAL CRIME

Mule accounts are accounts used to receive and transfer illicit funds on behalf of criminals. The individuals controlling these accounts are often unaware of the true purpose of the transactions, but in many cases, they knowingly participate for financial gain. Mules provide criminals with a temporary buffer between the proceeds of crime and the final destination of funds. Because mule accounts blend into normal banking operations, they can be difficult to detect without strong monitoring systems.

Mule activity typically follows identifiable patterns. Accounts may receive funds from multiple unrelated sources and quickly transfer them onward, often within minutes or hours. The account holder's profile may not align with the size, frequency, or purpose of the transactions. Students, the unemployed, or individuals facing financial hardship are frequently recruited, as they are more likely to accept offers that promise easy income. Criminal groups reach potential mules through social media, messaging platforms, job adverts, or personal networks.

Mule activity is common in cyber-enabled fraud, including romance scams, investment fraud, and phishing schemes. When victims transfer money, it is often first routed through mule accounts before being withdrawn as cash, moved to cryptocurrency exchanges, or transferred offshore. Because of this, mule accounts are essential intervention points. Early detection can disrupt entire fraud chains and prevent further losses.

Funnel Accounts and Rapid Consolidation Schemes

Funnel accounts are another high-risk typology. These accounts are used to consolidate funds from numerous geographic locations before dispersing them elsewhere. Criminal organizations use this technique to aggregate proceeds from widespread criminal activity - such as drug trafficking, human smuggling, or coordinated fraud - into a central pool.

Funnel activity typically involves cash deposits made in multiple branches, often spread across states or regions. Deposits are usually just below reporting thresholds and are followed by rapid electronic transfers or withdrawals. The deposits may be made by different individuals, none of whom appear connected to the account holder. This separation between depositors and account owners is deliberate, making it harder for institutions to trace the origins of funds.

Banks must recognize that funnel accounts rarely have legitimate business justification. A business with no broad geographic footprint should not receive cash deposits from distant regions. When such behavior appears, it signals possible money laundering or proceeds consolidation. Strong monitoring rules, combined with customer due diligence, help institutions determine whether activity is consistent with legitimate operations.

Risks Arising from Correspondent Banking

Correspondent banking plays a critical role in global financial systems, allowing banks in one jurisdiction to provide services to banks in another. While essential for cross-border payments and international commerce, correspondent banking presents significant risks. Criminals exploit correspondent relationships to move funds through layers of intermediaries, taking advantage of the fact that the correspondent bank may not have visibility into the underlying customers or transactions of the respondent bank.

This lack of visibility creates vulnerabilities. If a respondent bank has weak controls, inadequate customer due diligence, or exposure to high-risk clients, the correspondent bank may unknowingly process transactions linked to illicit activity. This creates regulatory and reputational risk. International enforcement actions have demonstrated that correspondent banks are held accountable when they fail to assess and manage risks associated with foreign banking partners.

Key risk factors include respondent banks located in high-risk jurisdictions, those with limited regulatory oversight, or those offering services such as foreign exchange, cash management, or remittances without strong compliance frameworks. Correspondent banks must evaluate whether their partners maintain effective anti-money laundering controls, understand their customer base, and monitor high-risk behaviors.

The Challenge of Limited Transparency

Limited transparency is one of the most significant challenges in both mule and correspondent banking risks. Mule accounts obscure the identity of the true beneficiary. Correspondent banking obscures the identity of the underlying customer. Criminals rely on this opacity to exploit the system.

Banks must remain alert to inconsistencies, incomplete information, and unusual customer behavior. Enhanced due diligence plays a critical role. When institutions understand who controls accounts, who benefits from transactions, and how funds move through networks, they are better positioned to identify suspicious patterns.

Technology also assists in addressing transparency gaps. Link analysis, behavioral analytics, device intelligence, and geo-location tools help detect inconsistencies that may signal mule behavior or respondent bank weaknesses. These tools complement human judgment by highlighting anomalies requiring deeper review.

Strengthening Controls and Monitoring Frameworks

Mitigating mule and funnel account risks requires strong controls at account opening, continuous monitoring, and rapid intervention. Banks should scrutinize account holders whose financial profiles do not align with observed activity. Sudden spikes in transaction volume, funds received from unrelated sources, or transfers that leave the account as quickly as they arrive are common warning signs.

For correspondent banking, institutions must implement clear onboarding standards for respondent banks, including assessments of regulatory environments, ownership structures, product offerings, and risk management frameworks. Ongoing reviews, periodic audits, and targeted monitoring of high-risk corridors help ensure that correspondent relationships do not expose institutions to hidden risks.

Banks must also maintain clear escalation pathways. When suspicious behavior is detected - whether involving a mule account or a respondent bank - institutions must respond quickly. This may involve freezing transactions, limiting account functionality, conducting enhanced reviews, or filing suspicious activity reports.

FINTECH, PAYMENT PLATFORMS, AND EMERGING VULNERABILITIES

Fintech companies and digital payment platforms have reshaped how financial services operate. They offer speed, convenience, and accessibility on a scale traditional institutions struggled to achieve. However, these innovations also create new exposures. Criminals exploit emerging technologies, gaps in regulatory coverage, and rapid onboarding processes to move illicit funds, commit fraud, and bypass traditional controls. Understanding the vulnerabilities inherent in fintech ecosystems is essential for investigators and compliance professionals who must assess risk in an environment defined by constant change.

The Appeal of Fintech to Criminal Actors

Fintech platforms combine rapid onboarding, frictionless payments, and user-friendly interfaces. These features are attractive to legitimate customers but equally appealing to criminals. With minimal documentation, individuals can create accounts, link payment methods, and send funds across platforms instantly. When fintech companies prioritize customer growth or market expansion over compliance maturity, controls may lag behind risk.

Speed amplifies exposure. In traditional banking, suspicious funds may remain within the system long enough for detection tools to flag them. In fintech platforms, funds can move through multiple accounts, transfer to cryptocurrencies, or be withdrawn within minutes. This immediacy reduces intervention opportunities and requires systems capable of near real-time analysis.

Some fintech firms operate across borders without fully integrating regulatory expectations from each jurisdiction. Criminals exploit regulatory arbitrage, choosing platforms with the least oversight or onboarding requirements. When companies offer services globally but compliance frameworks remain localized, gaps inevitably emerge.

Weaknesses in Digital Onboarding

Digital onboarding is central to fintech operations. It relies heavily on automated document verification, biometric checks, and database matching. While these technologies enhance convenience, they also create opportunities for misuse.

Identity fraud is a persistent challenge. Criminals use stolen identities, forged documents, or synthetic identities to create accounts. Synthetic identities -constructed from valid and fabricated information - are particularly difficult to detect. Once established, these identities serve as vehicles for money laundering, mule activity, and fraud.

Some fintech companies rely on superficial checks that validate documents but fail to identify behavioral inconsistencies. Automated systems may approve accounts that appear legitimate on paper but are controlled by criminal networks. Without robust behavioral analytics, fintech companies may overlook patterns inconsistent with genuine customer activity.

High-Risk Product Features

Certain fintech product features carry heightened exposure. Instant payments are especially vulnerable because they provide no opportunity to pause or review transactions before completion. Fraudulent transactions can be executed before victims or institutions realize what has occurred, making recovery difficult.

Peer-to-peer transfers also present risks. These platforms allow users to send funds using only email addresses, usernames, or phone numbers. Criminals exploit this anonymity, directing victims to send payments to mule accounts or creating chains of transfers that obscure tracing.

Prepaid cards and stored-value accounts are another high-risk product. These accounts often have low onboarding requirements and allow rapid spending, cross-border transfers, or withdrawals. Criminals use them to distribute proceeds from fraud schemes or to cash out illicit funds discreetly.

Buy-now-pay-later services introduce additional vulnerabilities. Fraudsters use stolen identities or compromised credentials to obtain goods without payment, reselling them for quick cash. Because these services are structured as consumer credit products, they may fall outside traditional monitoring frameworks.

Crypto-Enabled Fintech Activity

Many fintech innovations intersect with cryptocurrency services. Digital wallets, crypto exchanges, and tokenized payment systems expand opportunities for both legitimate and illicit use. Criminals exploit the speed of crypto transfers combined with the accessibility of fintech platforms to move funds with minimal friction.

Some fintechs integrate cryptocurrency without fully understanding blockchain-related risks. When platforms allow users to transfer funds between fiat and crypto environments without adequate monitoring, criminals can obscure the source of funds quickly. While blockchain transparency offers investigative advantages, fintech platforms must have the capability to interpret and act on that information.

Gaps in Governance and Compliance Maturity

Fintech companies vary widely in compliance maturity. Some operate with sophisticated governance frameworks, but many startups prioritize product development and rapid scaling over risk management. Compliance programs may be understaffed, under-resourced, or treated as secondary to commercial objectives.

Common weaknesses include inadequate monitoring rules, limited escalation pathways, and insufficient training for frontline employees. Some firms rely excessively on automated systems without integrating human oversight. As transaction volumes grow, these weaknesses amplify risk.

Because many fintechs lack long operational histories, their risk indicators may be poorly defined. They may also lack robust data governance structures, resulting in inconsistent or incomplete customer information. These gaps hinder accurate risk assessment and impair monitoring effectiveness.

Vulnerabilities in Third-Party Dependencies

Fintech platforms frequently rely on third-party service providers for key functions such as payment processing, identity verification, cloud hosting, and data analytics. While these partnerships enable rapid innovation, they also introduce risk. If a third-party provider has weak controls, the fintech platform becomes exposed to vulnerabilities outside its direct control.

Dependence on external identity verification services can also create blind spots. If verification errors occur - or if criminals learn to bypass the verification system - the fintech platform may unknowingly onboard high-risk customers.

Cloud-based systems present additional challenges. While cloud services provide scalability and flexibility, they require strong cybersecurity measures, access controls, and monitoring. If a fintech platform does not implement robust controls, it becomes vulnerable to account takeovers, credential theft, and data breaches.

Regulatory Challenges and Evolving Expectations

Regulatory frameworks have struggled to keep pace with fintech innovation. Some jurisdictions classify fintechs as banks; others treat them as payment institutions, lending platforms, or technology providers. These inconsistencies create uncertainty for both regulators and institutions, complicating compliance obligations.

Investigators working with fintech data must understand how regulatory expectations apply to each business model. Payment platforms, for example, may be subject to transaction monitoring requirements similar to traditional banks, while lending platforms may face obligations related to identity verification and fraud prevention.

Regulators increasingly expect fintechs to maintain strong anti-money laundering frameworks, conduct enhanced due diligence on high-risk customers, and report suspicious activity promptly. As enforcement actions become more frequent, compliance maturity is no longer optional.

INSIDER FRAUD AND GOVERNANCE WEAKNESSES

Insider fraud represents one of the most damaging threats to financial institutions. While external actors frequently draw attention, employees and internal stakeholders often have the greatest ability to exploit vulnerabilities. Insiders possess access to systems, customer information, transaction capabilities, and operational processes that external criminals struggle to penetrate. When governance structures are weak, oversight is inconsistent, or internal controls are poorly enforced, insiders find opportunities to commit fraud, facilitate external schemes, or undermine institutional integrity. Understanding how insider risks emerge - and how they can be mitigated - is essential for protecting financial institutions from financial loss, reputational harm, and regulatory action.

The Nature of Insider Risk

Insider fraud occurs when employees, contractors, or trusted partners misuse their access for personal gain or to support criminal activity. This can include unauthorized transactions, manipulation of records, theft of customer information, approval of fraudulent applications, or collaboration with external groups. Insiders may act alone or as part of a coordinated effort. In some cases, external criminals intentionally recruit or compromise employees, offering financial rewards, coercion, or blackmail to gain access to systems.

Motivations vary. Financial pressure, personal disputes, greed, or resentment toward the institution can influence behavior. Weak oversight, limited segregation of duties, and poor monitoring increase the likelihood of opportunistic misconduct. In high-pressure environments where performance metrics drive decision-making, employees may also manipulate processes to meet targets or conceal mistakes.

Insider risk is not limited to lower-level staff. Senior employees have broader access, deeper system knowledge, and authority to override controls. When individuals in governance roles participate in or ignore misconduct, risk multiplies. Institutions must therefore adopt a holistic approach that considers all levels of the organization.

Weaknesses in Governance Structures

Governance weaknesses contribute significantly to insider risk. Institutions that lack clear accountability, consistent oversight, or effective control frameworks are more vulnerable. When policies exist only on paper or are inconsistently enforced, insiders recognize that detection is unlikely.

Poor segregation of duties is a common weakness. When a single individual can initiate, approve, and reconcile transactions, opportunities for fraud increase dramatically. Similarly, when employees can create or modify customer records without checks, manipulate loan applications, or access sensitive data without monitoring, institutions become exposed to internal abuse.

Weak governance also manifests through inadequate reporting channels. If employees feel unable to report misconduct safely, fraudulent behavior may continue unchecked. In some institutions, a culture of silence or fear discourages whistleblowing. In others, management may fail to investigate red flags or treat allegations with the seriousness they deserve.

Another governance issue is insufficient oversight of third parties. Contractors, service providers, and temporary staff may have system access comparable to full-time employees but face fewer controls or lower scrutiny. Without proper onboarding, monitoring, and access restrictions, third-party insiders can significantly increase risk.

Abuse of System Access and Data

System access is a key vulnerability. Employees with legitimate access may misuse it to gather confidential information, adjust accounts, manipulate balances, or bypass controls. Access can be exploited to create unauthorized accounts, approve fraudulent transactions, or issue payments to personal accounts or accomplices.

Customer information is particularly valuable. Insiders may sell personal data to external criminals, enabling identity theft, phishing, account takeover, or loan fraud. Institutions that do not monitor system activity closely may fail to detect unusual access patterns, such as repeated retrieval of dormant accounts, excessive viewing of customer files, or access to areas unrelated to the employee's duties.

Improper access often goes unnoticed in environments with outdated access controls or where resources do not align with system complexity. Institutions must regularly review access rights, implement strict role-based permissions, and use monitoring tools capable of identifying abnormal system activity.

Collusion between Insiders and External Actors

Collusion between insiders and external criminals poses a serious threat. When employees act intentionally to assist external actors, the sophistication of schemes increases. Collusion can involve approving fraudulent loan applications, lifting red flags on suspicious transactions, providing early warnings of investigations, or deliberately weakening controls.

Criminal groups may target insiders specifically for their access. They may offer bribes, exploit personal vulnerabilities, or build relationships over time. In some cases, employees initiate the contact, offering their services to criminal networks. Institutions must recognize that collusion is often deliberate, strategic, and difficult to detect through traditional transactional monitoring alone.

Behavioral analytics can help identify patterns that suggest collusion. Examples include unusual working hours, repeated access to high-risk accounts, or interactions with external parties inconsistent with job responsibilities. Monitoring must extend beyond transactions to include user activity and access logs.

Lack of Effective Oversight and Audit

Internal audit and compliance functions serve as critical lines of defense. When these functions lack independence, resources, or authority, insider fraud is more likely to go undetected. Audits must assess not only formal compliance but also operational behavior, cultural indicators, and weaknesses in system controls.

Institutions that rely on outdated audit practices or infrequent reviews create opportunities for insiders to exploit gaps. Modern financial institutions require continuous auditing approaches supported by data analytics. This ensures that unusual patterns are detected in real time rather than months after misconduct occurs.

Oversight must also extend to senior leadership. Tone at the top matters. When leaders demonstrate ethical behavior, enforce policies, and support transparency, insider misconduct becomes less likely. Conversely, when leadership ignores red flags or prioritizes profit over integrity, governance erodes and insider fraud becomes easier to perpetrate.

Strengthening Internal Controls and Culture

Mitigating insider fraud requires strong controls, robust monitoring, and a culture of accountability. Institutions must implement access controls, segregation of duties, multi-factor authentication, and comprehensive monitoring of system activity. Technology plays an important role, but equally important is the human element.

Training helps employees understand the seriousness of insider risk and recognize early signs of misconduct. Clear reporting channels encourage internal reporting, while protections for whistleblowers ensure that individuals feel safe raising concerns.

CHAPTER 17

PUBLIC SECTOR AND PROCUREMENT

EMBEZZLEMENT, GHOST VENDORS, AND PROCUREMENT FRAUD

PUBLIC SECTOR procurement is particularly vulnerable to manipulation because it often involves large budgets, multiple layers of authorization, and broad discretion in awarding contracts. When oversight structures are weak or inconsistently applied, individuals can exploit procurement systems to divert funds, secure illegal advantages, or bypass competitive processes. Embezzlement, ghost vendors, and procurement fraud are among the most frequent and damaging forms of misconduct in this environment. They undermine public confidence, increase operational costs, distort service delivery, and often create long-lasting financial and institutional harm.

Embezzlement within Public Funds

Embezzlement in the public sector involves the unauthorized use of government funds, assets, or resources for personal benefit. It typically occurs when employees control financial processes or have access to accounting systems that allow them to manipulate records. In many cases, the misconduct is incremental rather than sudden. Individuals exploit gaps in reconciliation, rely on outdated procedures, or take advantage of the assumption that internal staff act in good faith.

The methods used to execute embezzlement vary widely. Some individuals manipulate payment instructions or redirect legitimate transactions to personal accounts. Others alter accounting entries to conceal unauthorized withdrawals or misappropriate physical assets by falsifying inventory records. Weak segregation of duties significantly increases risk because the same individual may initiate, authorize, and record transactions without oversight. Once a pattern is established and remains undiscovered, offenders often become more confident and expand their activities.

Detecting embezzlement requires consistent scrutiny of financial records, clear audit trails, and regular verification of balances by independent personnel. Anomalies such as unexplained adjustments, unusual timing of entries, or inconsistencies between financial data and operational activity often serve as early warning signs. Public sector entities that rely heavily on manual processes or tolerate informal workarounds face particular exposure because these environments reduce the likelihood of timely detection.

Ghost Vendors and False Supplier Schemes

Ghost vendors represent one of the most common procurement manipulation techniques in government environments. A ghost vendor is a fabricated or illegitimate supplier created to generate false invoices or receive payments for goods or services that were never delivered. These schemes can be orchestrated by insiders acting alone, by employees colluding with external actors, or by external parties who infiltrate vendor registration systems through forged documents.

In many cases, the creation of a ghost vendor begins with exploiting weaknesses in supplier onboarding. If verification procedures are superficial or inconsistent, offenders can register companies without valid identification, physical presence, or operational capability. Once the vendor is established, fabricated invoices are submitted, approved by insiders, and paid from public funds. Payments may be structured to avoid detection by staying below approval thresholds or disguised among legitimate vendors with similar names.

Some schemes go further by creating the appearance of legitimacy through forged delivery notes, fabricated service confirmations, or manipulated procurement documentation. In other instances, insiders modify existing vendor records by changing bank account information so that legitimate payments are diverted to fraudulent accounts. These schemes often remain undetected for extended periods, especially in organizations that do not regularly review vendor master data or compare procurement records with physical outcomes.

Preventing ghost vendor activity requires disciplined supplier onboarding, periodic validation of vendor information, segregation of duties in procurement and finance departments, and independent verification of delivered goods or completed services. Regular analytics on payment patterns, vendor concentration, and invoice characteristics also help identify suspicious suppliers that do not match operational requirements.

Procurement Fraud and Manipulated Contracting Processes

Procurement fraud encompasses a broad range of actions designed to influence contract awards, manipulate bidding processes, or distort pricing to benefit specific individuals or entities. In public sector environments, procurement fraud has far-reaching consequences because it not only causes financial losses but also affects service delivery, infrastructure quality, and long-term public trust.

One of the most common forms of procurement fraud involves manipulating competitive bidding. Offenders may structure tender requirements so narrowly that only a favored bidder qualifies, or they may design criteria that exclude capable competitors. Collusion between internal staff and suppliers is also prevalent. Insiders may leak confidential information, provide advance notice of tenders, or guide suppliers on how to structure bids. In some cases, multiple bidders coordinate to create the appearance of competition while ensuring a predetermined supplier is awarded the contract.

Invoice manipulation is another key component of procurement fraud. This includes inflating quantities, increasing prices without justification, or issuing multiple invoices for the same work. Fraudulent change orders can also be used to increase contract value after the initial award, allowing offenders to bypass competitive processes under the guise of unforeseen requirements.

Misrepresentation of contract performance is frequently used to hide operational failures. Contractors may be paid for incomplete work, substandard construction, or services that do not meet contractual specifications. Where monitoring mechanisms are weak, these deficiencies persist undetected, leading to inflated costs and reduced public service quality.

Procurement fraud is particularly challenging to identify because many of its indicators resemble legitimate administrative decisions. Investigators must examine the entire procurement life cycle, including planning, tendering, evaluation, contracting, performance monitoring, and payment processing. Irregularities often appear when documentation does not align with actual activity, when decision-making patterns favor specific suppliers repeatedly, or when cost deviations lack credible explanation.

The Importance of Institutional Integrity

Public sector procurement rests on the assumption that processes are impartial, competitive, and transparent. When embezzlement, ghost vendors, or procurement fraud infiltrate these systems, the damage extends beyond immediate financial loss. Public confidence erodes when citizens perceive that funds intended for essential services are misused, diverted, or exploited for personal enrichment. Over time, this distrust undermines institutional legitimacy and reduces willingness to comply with broader civic responsibilities.

Effective prevention requires more than procedural controls. It demands a culture of integrity supported by leadership, accountability, and consistent oversight. Employees must understand their responsibilities, recognize the consequences of misconduct, and feel confident in reporting concerns. Institutions must ensure that procurement systems are structured to minimize discretion, enforce transparent decision-making, and maintain comprehensive documentation at every stage.

INFLATED CONTRACTING AND KICKBACK STRUCTURES

Inflated contracting and kickback structures are among the most entrenched forms of public sector corruption. They distort procurement outcomes, waste public resources, and create systemic weaknesses that persist long after individual schemes are uncovered. These practices rely on manipulating contract values, engineering artificial costs, and creating covert financial arrangements that reward decision-makers or insiders for steering public funds toward favored contractors. Unlike simple fraud, inflated contracting schemes often blend legitimate activity with concealed misuse, making them harder to detect and more corrosive to institutional integrity.

How Inflated Contracting Emerges

Inflated contracting occurs when the price of goods or services is intentionally increased beyond fair market value. The inflated amount is not incidental; it is an engineered surcharge designed to generate profit for corrupt actors. This practice frequently appears in infrastructure projects, public works, health procurement, and defense contracts - areas where budgets are large, oversight may be stretched, and technical complexity can obscure manipulation.

The inflation may be introduced at any stage of procurement. In the planning phase, specifications may be written to require unnecessarily expensive materials. During tendering, eligibility criteria may be structured to favor suppliers known for inflated pricing. After contract award, amendments or change orders may be issued to increase value without competitive review. In some cases, contractors intentionally underbid to win the tender and later introduce inflated variations, relying on the expectation that public entities will approve additional funding to avoid project delays.

The core feature is that the price does not reflect genuine economic need. Instead, it is shaped by collusion between insiders and contractors who share a mutual understanding that inflated costs will generate compensatory benefits for those involved. This collusion may be subtle, relying on signals and established relationships rather than explicit agreements. It may also be facilitated by intermediaries who introduce contractors to officials in exchange for future benefits.

Mechanics of Kickback Arrangements

Kickback structures are financial arrangements where a contractor or supplier secretly returns part of the contract value to a public official or facilitator. These payments may be disguised as consulting fees, marketing expenses, success-based commissions, or subcontracting arrangements. The purpose is to reward the official for approving inflated contracts, overlooking deficiencies, or manipulating procedures to ensure a specific contractor receives the award.

Kickbacks are rarely paid directly. Offenders prefer indirect methods to avoid detection. Funds may flow through shell companies, third-party agents, or layers of subcontractors. Some schemes use cash withdrawals or offshore transfers to obscure the trail. In higher-risk environments, payments may take non-monetary forms such as gifts, travel, property, or employment opportunities for family members. The structure is designed to create distance between the official receiving the benefit and the funds used to finance it.

In many cases, kickbacks are not one-time events. They become part of a sustained relationship between officials and suppliers. Contractors who benefit from this arrangement often become repeat winners of public tenders, reinforcing the cycle and discouraging legitimate bidders from participating. The ongoing nature of these relationships makes them especially damaging, as they entrench a closed procurement environment where outcomes are predictable and competition is more symbolic than genuine.

Role of Documentation and Contract Manipulation

Inflated contracting schemes rely heavily on documentation that appears legitimate but is strategically framed to support improper decisions. Procurement files may include inflated cost estimates, technical justifications for premium pricing, or reports claiming specialized expertise that does not exist. Officials may approve supplier quotations without proper benchmarking or rely on market assessments conducted by parties connected to the contractor.

During contract execution, documentation becomes a tool to justify additional payments. Contractors may submit variation orders supported by exaggerated claims of unforeseen conditions or scope changes. Supervising officials may certify work that is incomplete or of lower quality. Inspection reports may be drafted to conceal deficiencies, enabling contractors to collect full payment despite failing to meet obligations.

The manipulation of documentation is particularly problematic because oversight bodies often rely on paper records to evaluate compliance. When documentation is structured to create an appearance of legitimacy, it becomes difficult to challenge decisions without independent technical assessments, site visits, or forensic reviews of communication patterns.

Influence Networks and Gatekeeper Roles

Inflated contracts rarely succeed without the involvement of individuals positioned at key decision points. These may include procurement officers, engineers, project managers, finance officials, or political appointees. Each actor plays a role that, intentionally or not, enables the scheme to progress.

Gatekeepers often control access to critical information such as tender timelines, pricing benchmarks, evaluation criteria, and internal assessments. Contractors seeking to secure inflated contracts may cultivate relationships with these individuals to gain insight into vulnerabilities. In some cases, influence extends beyond procurement personnel. Senior officials may intervene in processes, issuing directives that override technical recommendations or pressuring evaluation committees to select preferred suppliers.

These influence networks are sustained by a mix of personal relationships, political connections, and financial incentives. Because the parties involved often understand the risks, they communicate cautiously, relying on intermediaries or informal arrangements. Over time, these networks become embedded within institutional culture, making it difficult for new personnel to challenge established patterns.

Impact on Public Institutions

Inflated contracting and kickback schemes carry financial, operational, and reputational consequences. Public funds are diverted away from essential services, leading to reduced quality in infrastructure, healthcare delivery, education programs, and other critical areas. Projects funded with inflated budgets often remain unfinished or require additional funding to address deficiencies created by low-quality workmanship.

Operationally, inflated contracts distort planning and budgeting. Public entities may accept inflated costs as normal, making it difficult to establish accurate benchmarks. This normalization shifts the entire procurement environment upward, causing systemic inefficiency. Honest suppliers struggle to compete against inflated pricing structures supported by illicit payments, resulting in reduced participation and declining market competitiveness.

The reputational impact is equally serious. When inflated contracting becomes public knowledge, citizen trust deteriorates. Perception of corruption discourages investment, undermines government legitimacy, and fosters cynicism toward public governance. In extreme cases, inflated contracting becomes so pervasive that public institutions struggle to function effectively, as staff become reluctant to challenge misconduct for fear of retaliation.

Addressing and Preventing Inflated Contracting

Effective prevention requires strengthening procurement governance, improving transparency, and ensuring that oversight mechanisms are independent and adequately resourced. Benchmarking contract values against market prices, enforcing competitive tendering, and requiring justification for deviations are essential safeguards. Procurement committees should include members with technical expertise capable of assessing pricing and identifying anomalies. Internal audits must focus not only on compliance but on assessing whether economic value was achieved.

PEP-RELATED CORRUPTION AND INFLUENCE ABUSE

Politically exposed persons (PEPs) occupy positions of authority that grant them access to public resources, regulatory power, and decision-making influence. These roles are intended to serve the public interest, yet they can also create opportunities for corruption when individuals misuse their authority for personal benefit or to favor particular private actors. PEP-related corruption and influence abuse represent some of the most complex and impactful risks within the public sector. The consequences extend far beyond financial loss; they undermine governance, reduce institutional credibility, and weaken the framework that supports economic development and public trust.

Understanding PEP Exposure

PEPs are individuals who hold, or have recently held, senior public functions. Their official power places them in a position that can influence procurement, licensing, taxation, regulatory enforcement, infrastructure development, and national policy decisions. This influence extends not only to the PEP themselves but often to their close associates, family members, and intermediaries who may act on their behalf.

The risk associated with PEPs is not rooted in their status alone. It arises from the combination of authority, discretion, and limited oversight that often accompanies their roles. Many decisions made by senior officials involve judgment, interpretation, and the ability to shape outcomes. When these decisions are exploited to benefit private actors in exchange for money, assets, or political support, corruption becomes embedded in institutional processes.

Mechanisms of Influence Abuse

Influence abuse by PEPs occurs in various forms, each reflecting the particular powers associated with their office. One common mechanism involves directing public contracts to preferred suppliers in exchange for kickbacks or financial rewards. PEPs may apply pressure on procurement committees, override technical evaluations, or interfere with competitive bidding to ensure specific companies receive government contracts.

Licensing and regulatory approvals represent another channel for corruption. PEPs may influence the granting of permits, concessions, or regulatory exemptions that allow private actors to operate in sectors such as mining, telecommunications, pharmaceuticals, construction, or energy. In these cases, the value transferred is not always immediate. Some PEPs grant favorable regulatory treatment in exchange for future benefits such as political financing, stakes in private companies, or employment opportunities for associates.

Influence abuse also appears in public appointments. Senior officials may place allies in key positions within regulatory bodies, procurement offices, or state-owned enterprises. These appointments enable further misconduct because the individuals selected may be more willing to overlook irregularities or assist in facilitating improper transactions. In some environments, entire networks of PEPs and loyal appointees operate collectively to control the allocation of public resources.

Use of Intermediaries and Proxies

PEPs rarely engage directly in corrupt exchanges. They rely on intermediaries who act as buffers between the official and the commercial party. These intermediaries may be business associates, lawyers, relatives, political supporters, or trusted advisors. Their purpose is to negotiate terms, collect payments, and manage the flow of benefits. Because these intermediaries operate outside formal government structures, their activities are more difficult to trace.

Proxies also play a key role in concealing beneficial ownership. PEPs may hold assets through companies registered in the names of relatives or associates. They may also use proxy shareholders to hide stakes in entities that receive government contracts or benefit from regulatory privileges. This structure allows the PEP to profit from decisions while maintaining plausible distance from the transactions that generate those benefits.

Some proxies hold positions in sectors that interact frequently with the government, such as construction, import-export, or energy. Their businesses may experience rapid growth due to favorable treatment, but the true beneficiary is the PEP whose authority drives these advantages. In these cases, financial flows often appear legitimate unless thoroughly examined.

Offshore Structures and Asset Concealment

PEPs frequently use offshore jurisdictions to hide the proceeds of corruption. These jurisdictions offer privacy, low disclosure requirements, and limited cooperation with foreign authorities. Funds may be routed through a chain of companies, trusts, or foundations designed to obscure the connection to the PEP. In some cases, money is transferred using professional facilitators who create multi-layered ownership structures to prevent straightforward identification of beneficiaries.

Once proceeds are concealed offshore, they may be reintegrated into the global economy through real estate purchases, investment portfolios, luxury goods, or commercial enterprises. The reintegration process may appear legitimate because it is framed as foreign investment or income from offshore business ventures. Without investigative scrutiny, the connection between the assets and the original acts of corruption remains undetected.

Digital assets have also become a channel for PEP-related corruption. Because certain crypto platforms allow pseudonymous transfers, offenders can quickly move funds across borders without relying on the traditional banking system. Although these technologies offer new methods of concealment, the principles remain consistent: separation of the PEP from the financial flow and minimization of documentation that could expose their involvement.

State-Owned Enterprises as Vehicles for Corruption

State-owned enterprises (SOEs) often represent high-risk environments for PEP-related influence abuse. SOEs control significant budgets, manage critical infrastructure, and operate with a mix of commercial and public sector oversight. PEPs may influence SOEs to award inflated contracts, hire specific companies, or pursue projects that benefit private interests rather than public objectives.

Board appointments in SOEs are a common tool for influence. By placing loyal individuals in leadership positions, PEPs can exert control over procurement decisions, financial management, and strategic planning. These individuals may approve subsidies, grant exclusive supply agreements, or authorize transactions that channel public resources to companies linked to political actors.

Because SOEs sometimes operate with reduced transparency compared to central government bodies, misconduct may persist for extended periods before detection. Audits may be limited in scope, and internal oversight mechanisms may lack independence. This environment allows influence abuse to operate in the background of legitimate commercial activity.

Political Financing and Quid-Pro-Quo Arrangements

Political financing is another avenue through which corruption linked to PEPs occurs. Private actors may provide donations, sponsorships, or campaign support in exchange for favorable treatment. In some environments, political financing is used as a channel for disguised bribery, where funds are recorded as party support but are intended to influence official behavior.

PEPs may also use public resources to support their political influence. State contracts may be directed to businesses that later contribute to campaign activities or mobilize political support. These arrangements distort democratic processes by linking public expenditure with political loyalty rather than public value.

Investigative Challenges and Red Flags

Investigating PEP-related corruption is particularly challenging because the individuals involved understand oversight systems and have influence over institutions responsible for monitoring their behavior. Traditional indicators of corruption, such as unusual wealth or asset accumulation, may be difficult to assess because PEPs often have access to legitimate sources of income and complex financial arrangements.

However, certain patterns commonly emerge. Family members who acquire substantial assets without clear income, companies that receive repeated public contracts despite weak capacity, and intermediaries who hold stakes in sectors relevant to government decisions all raise concerns. Contracts awarded without competition, major infrastructure projects implemented through obscure partnerships, and sudden regulatory exemptions may also indicate abuse of influence.

CONTROLS, TRANSPARENCY, AND OVERSIGHT MECHANISMS

Public sector procurement depends on systems that protect public funds, support fair competition, and ensure that contracts are awarded and executed in the public interest. When controls are weak or inconsistently applied, corruption, inflated pricing, and misuse of authority become far more likely. Effective controls and oversight mechanisms create structural barriers that reduce opportunities for misconduct, increase accountability, and strengthen public confidence in government operations. Transparency complements these controls by ensuring that decisions, processes, and financial outcomes can be scrutinized both internally and externally.

Foundations of Strong Procurement Controls

Sound controls begin with a procurement framework that clearly defines roles, responsibilities, and stages of the purchasing process. A well-designed framework minimizes discretion, requires documentation at each stage, and separates functions so that no individual controls the entire procurement cycle. Segregation of duties is essential because it prevents the concentration of authority that often enables fraud. For example, the person who initiates a purchase should not be the same person who approves the vendor or authorizes payment.

Standardized procedures also play a critical role. When procurement activities follow consistent rules - such as competitive tendering, defined evaluation criteria, and documented justification for exceptions - opportunities for manipulation decrease. Standardization limits arbitrary decisions and forces officials to justify actions that deviate from established requirements. This reduces the influence of personal relationships and political pressure, which are frequent drivers of procurement misconduct.

Risk assessments strengthen control environments by identifying areas where vulnerabilities are most acute. High-value contracts, emergency procurement, specialized technical projects, and sectors with historical exposure to corruption should receive proportionately greater oversight. Institutions that regularly update risk assessments and adjust controls accordingly are better equipped to respond to emerging threats.

Transparency as a Preventive Tool

Transparency is one of the most powerful deterrents to corruption in public procurement. When processes are visible and decisions can be reviewed by stakeholders, misconduct becomes more difficult to conceal. Transparency does not mean publishing every operational detail; rather, it means ensuring that essential information is accessible, understandable, and complete.

Publishing tender notices, evaluation results, awarded contracts, and contract amendments increases public visibility. Civil society organizations, journalists, competing suppliers, and oversight bodies can use this information to identify irregularities that might otherwise go undetected. Transparency also provides legitimate suppliers with confidence that tendering processes are conducted fairly, encouraging wider participation and reducing dependency on insiders or politically connected entities.

Financial transparency further strengthens integrity. Clear disclosure of project budgets, payments made to contractors, and changes in contract value provides insight into whether public spending aligns with the original procurement objectives. When financial data is withheld or presented in a fragmented manner, oversight bodies struggle to detect discrepancies or assess whether public money is being used effectively.

Digital procurement platforms enhance transparency by centralizing information, reducing opportunities for document tampering, and allowing automatic tracking of procurement activities. These platforms allow real-time access to procurement documentation and reduce opportunities for informal interference. However, technology alone cannot replace governance; strong rules and consistent enforcement are required to ensure that digital tools are used effectively.

Oversight Bodies and Independent Review

Oversight mechanisms function best when they are independent, well-resourced, and empowered to act without interference. Internal audit units, inspector general offices, procurement regulatory authorities, and parliamentary committees all play important roles in monitoring procurement integrity. Each performs a different function, but collectively they form a multilayered defense.

Internal auditors evaluate compliance with rules and assess whether procurement decisions achieve value for money. Their work helps identify systemic weaknesses such as repetitive sole-source contracting, poor documentation, or patterns of supplier favoritism. However, internal audit effectiveness depends on independence from operational management and access to accurate, complete information.

External oversight is equally important. Supreme audit institutions, anti-corruption agencies, and legislative committees provide checks that extend beyond internal structures. They can investigate high-risk areas, examine procurement strategies, and review major public projects that carry significant exposure to corruption. Their independence is critical, as public sector corruption often involves individuals who are themselves in positions of authority.

Complaints mechanisms also support oversight. Suppliers, staff, and citizens must have channels through which they can report irregularities or challenge procurement decisions without fear of retaliation. When these mechanisms are functional, they serve as early warning systems that alert authorities to potential misconduct.

Strengthening Documentation and Data Integrity

Reliable documentation is the backbone of procurement integrity. Every stage - from planning to payment - should produce records that can be reviewed by oversight bodies. Inconsistent documentation, missing approvals, or unexplained amendments often indicate weaknesses or concealment efforts.

Contracts, technical specifications, evaluation reports, and change orders must be complete and stored in secure, accessible systems. Oversight bodies rely heavily on these documents to trace decisions, verify compliance, and evaluate whether outcomes match expectations. In environments where documentation is fragmented or vulnerable to manipulation, corruption thrives because investigators cannot reconstruct decision-making processes or verify claims made by contractors.

Data integrity is equally important. Procurement systems must protect against unauthorized changes, ensure that audit trails cannot be altered, and maintain records that reflect genuine activity. Digital signatures, time-stamping, and tamper-resistant storage support these objectives. Without strong data controls, procurement misconduct may be hidden behind fabricated entries, retroactive approvals, or altered records.

Monitoring Contract Execution

Controls must extend beyond contract award. Many procurement schemes occur during contract execution, where inflated fees, substituted materials, or incomplete work may escape scrutiny. Effective oversight therefore requires ongoing monitoring of performance against contractual obligations.

Technical verification is essential. Independent engineers, project managers, or inspectors must confirm that deliverables meet required standards. Their assessments should be documented thoroughly and compared against payment requests to ensure that funds are disbursed only for completed work. When monitoring is superficial or constrained by resource limitations, contractors may take advantage of the situation to reduce quality or inflate claims.

Financial monitoring is equally important. Payment schedules, price adjustments, and variation orders should be reviewed for consistency with contract terms. Significant deviations require documented justification and, where necessary, approval from higher authorities. Oversight bodies often identify issues in areas such as repeated change orders, unexplained cost escalation, or performance certifications that lack supporting evidence.

Building a Culture of Accountability

Controls and oversight mechanisms succeed only when supported by a culture that values integrity. Leadership must demonstrate commitment to ethical behavior, enforce consequences for misconduct, and support staff who identify risks or report concerns. Training programs help employees understand procurement rules, recognize manipulation techniques, and appreciate their role in safeguarding public funds.

A culture of accountability ensures that procedures are not treated as administrative obstacles but as essential components of public governance. When employees recognize that oversight enhances fairness, reduces risk, and strengthens public trust, they are more likely to adhere to rules and challenge irregularities.

CHAPTER 18

REAL ESTATE AND LUXURY GOODS

PROPERTY-BASED LAUNDERING AND TITLE LAYERING

REAL ESTATE remains one of the most attractive channels for laundering illicit funds. Property transactions involve significant monetary value, are often subject to limited scrutiny in comparison to financial products, and can be layered through complex ownership structures that obscure beneficial control. Criminal groups, corrupt officials, tax evaders, and professional facilitators exploit these characteristics to convert illicit proceeds into stable, high-value assets. Property-based laundering is not confined to luxury markets; it occurs in residential, commercial, and industrial sectors alike. The methods vary in sophistication, but all rely on the same principle: using real estate to store, disguise, or reintegrate illicit value while distancing the offender from the original proceeds.

Why Real Estate is Attractive for Laundering

Real estate offers several structural advantages that make it well suited for laundering. Property markets in many jurisdictions permit foreign buyers, cash purchases, and the use of legal entities to hold title without public disclosure of beneficial ownership. Even where regulations exist, enforcement may be weak, and compliance expectations vary widely between agents, lawyers, developers, and financial institutions. These inconsistencies create an environment in which illicit funds can enter the market with minimal resistance.

Properties also appreciate over time, providing both concealment and profit. Unlike assets that require active management or technical expertise, real estate is simple to hold and can generate legitimate rental income, enhancing the appearance of lawful wealth. Once a property is purchased with illicit proceeds, it becomes part of the legitimate economy, and subsequent transactions - even if financed with clean funds - reinforce the perception of legitimacy.

In many jurisdictions, real estate professionals are not subject to the same reporting obligations as financial institutions. This makes the sector vulnerable to manipulation by criminals who prefer environments with weaker oversight. Where due-diligence checks exist, they may be limited to identity verification rather than deep assessment of source of funds, especially when transactions are structured through intermediaries or corporate entities.

Methods of Property-Based Laundering

Property-based laundering occurs at different stages of the transaction cycle. The most direct method involves purchasing property outright with illicit funds. Offenders may use cash, bank transfers through lightly regulated intermediaries, or funds routed through shell companies. Cash purchases, while increasingly restricted in some jurisdictions, remain common in markets where cash reporting requirements are weak or poorly enforced.

Layering occurs when criminals use multiple transactions to distance illicit funds from their origin. A common approach involves purchasing property through a legal entity, then transferring ownership to another entity, often in a different jurisdiction. The property may be sold quickly, used as collateral for a loan, or gifted to an associate. Each transfer increases complexity and reduces the visibility of the original offender.

Professional facilitators play a major role in these schemes. Lawyers, accountants, realtors, and corporate service providers may assist in setting up ownership structures, managing funds, or conducting transactions. Some operate negligently by failing to question unusual arrangements; others actively participate by designing structures intended to evade scrutiny. Their involvement adds legitimacy to transactions and helps offenders bypass controls.

Title Layering and Ownership Obfuscation

Title layering refers to the strategic use of multiple ownership layers to obscure the identity of the person controlling a property. Criminals may use shell companies, trusts, partnerships, or nominee arrangements to separate legal ownership from beneficial ownership. Each additional layer complicates investigation and delays efforts to trace the underlying source of funds.

Shell companies are particularly common. They can be established in jurisdictions with minimal disclosure requirements, enabling criminals to conceal their identities behind corporate veils. These companies may appear legitimate on paper, complete with nominal directors and registered addresses, yet they exist primarily to hold and transfer property. Nominee directors or shareholders further obscure control by acting on behalf of the true owner.

Trusts are another tool used in title layering. In many jurisdictions, trust arrangements do not require public disclosure of beneficiaries. Criminals exploit this by placing property under the control of trustees who manage the asset while shielding the identity of the true beneficiary. When combined with offshore structures or legal professionals acting as trustees, these arrangements become extremely difficult to penetrate.

Layering often extends beyond ownership. Properties may be registered under company names in different jurisdictions, financed by offshore loans, or transferred between related entities to create a confusing web of transactions. These layers not only mask ownership but also legitimize the flow of funds. Each transaction appears ordinary on its own, but collectively they form a structure designed to hide illicit origins.

Use of Financing to Conceal Illicit Funds

Financing arrangements offer additional opportunities for concealment. Criminals may purchase a property with illicit funds and later obtain a mortgage from a legitimate financial institution. The mortgage payments are made with clean money, creating an impression that the property was acquired legitimately. This method blends dirty and clean funds in a way that complicates tracing.

In other situations, criminals use false or inflated loans between shell companies to justify large transfers of money. The property serves as security for the loan, giving the appearance of legitimate debt and repayment obligations. These financing structures create documentation that appears credible, reducing suspicion even when underlying transactions have no commercial basis.

Developers may also be involved in laundering schemes. Pre-construction purchases, bulk purchases of units, or investment into property development projects can be financed with illicit funds. These investments often appear as routine commercial activity, making them harder to identify as laundering. In some cases, criminals negotiate arrangements with developers who accept large payments without verifying source of funds.

Cross-Border Laundering Through Property Markets

Cross-border transactions amplify the challenges of property-based laundering. Criminals may purchase property in one country using funds transferred from accounts in another, routed through shell companies in a third. These multi-jurisdictional structures exploit differences in disclosure rules, regulatory capacity, and information-sharing agreements.

High-value real estate markets in global cities are especially attractive. They offer political stability, strong property rights, and opportunities to store wealth securely. Criminals may purchase luxury homes, commercial buildings, or investment apartments with little scrutiny. In some cities, foreign ownership is common, reducing the visibility of suspicious patterns. When combined with offshore ownership structures, these transactions become nearly indistinguishable from legitimate investment activity.

Challenges for Investigators and Regulators

Investigating property-based laundering is challenging because real estate transactions generate large volumes of documentation that appear legitimate. Purchase contracts, valuation reports, loan agreements, and title records rarely reveal the true purpose of the transaction. Identifying laundering requires looking beyond documents to understand financial flows, ownership patterns, and the economic rationale of decisions.

Regulators face additional challenges due to fragmented oversight. Real estate transactions may involve multiple parties - agents, lawyers, banks, developers - each with different regulatory obligations. Where oversight is weak or enforcement resources are limited, high-risk transactions pass through without adequate scrutiny.

Impact on Markets and Public Integrity

Property-based laundering distorts real estate markets by inflating prices, reducing affordability, and encouraging speculative activity. When illicit funds enter the market, they create artificial demand that disadvantages legitimate buyers. Over time, this can reshape neighborhoods, alter investment patterns, and reduce confidence in regulatory systems.

At a broader level, property laundering facilitates corruption, tax evasion, and organized crime by providing a secure method of storing illicit wealth. When criminals or corrupt officials can freely acquire and hold property, their influence grows and public trust declines. Preventing these schemes requires coordinated action across financial institutions, real estate professionals, regulators, and law enforcement.

FAST FLIPS, OVER-VALUATION, AND UNDER-VALUATION

Manipulation of property value is one of the most common methods used to disguise illicit funds in real estate markets. Offenders exploit weaknesses in valuation processes, market opacity, and the discretion afforded to appraisers and intermediaries. Fast flips, over-valuation, and under-valuation each distort the true economic position of the transaction and allow criminals to shift value in ways that support laundering, tax evasion, corruption, or fraud. These schemes can occur independently or as part of broader laundering structures, but their effect is the same: the creation of false market signals that conceal financial crime under the appearance of ordinary real estate activity.

Fast Flips as a Laundering Technique

Fast flips refer to the rapid purchase and resale of a property within a short period, often at an artificially inflated or deflated price. The core purpose is to move illicit funds, quickly, through multiple transactions to obscure their source and create a paper trail that appears legitimate.

In a typical scheme, a criminal buys a property with illicit funds and quickly resells it to an associate at a significantly higher price. The profit from the resale appears lawful, supported by formal contracts and recorded payments. Because property transfers create official documentation, the transaction gives the appearance of legitimate capital gain. The funds generated from the resale, now recorded as proceeds from property investment, can be deposited into financial institutions with less scrutiny.

Fast flips may also be used in reverse. A property is purchased at an inflated price by a complicit buyer, allowing the seller - who may be a corrupt official, a professional facilitator, or an entity linked to criminal groups - to justify sudden wealth. The inflated purchase provides a façade for income or asset growth that would otherwise attract suspicion. These transactions can be particularly effective when conducted through multiple intermediaries, giving the impression of unrelated market activity rather than coordinated manipulation.

The speed of the resale is a critical feature. By completing transactions within weeks or months, criminals limit the exposure of illicit funds to monitoring systems and disrupt the ability of authorities to detect unusual patterns. In markets with high transaction volumes, fast flips may blend into legitimate activity unless investigators examine the circumstances closely.

Over-Valuation as a Method of Concealment and Gain

Over-valuation occurs when a property is deliberately appraised at a value higher than its true market worth. This technique enables criminals to introduce larger sums of illicit money into the financial system under the guise of standard property transactions.

One common pattern involves collusion between the buyer, seller, and a compliant or negligent appraiser. The inflated valuation allows a buyer to obtain a mortgage or loan for an amount far exceeding the actual value of the property. The excess funds can then be extracted and moved through financial accounts as loan proceeds rather than criminal earnings. This approach not only launders money but also creates opportunities for mortgage fraud, particularly when the loan is later defaulted intentionally.

In public corruption cases, over-valuation is often used to transfer illicit benefits. A politically exposed person may sell a property at an inflated price to a favored contractor or an entity seeking influence. The inflated payment serves as a covert bribe disguised as a legitimate property purchase. Because real estate values can vary widely based on location, renovations, and market sentiment, inflated prices may not attract immediate suspicion, especially in markets with limited transparency.

Developers may also participate in over-valuation schemes. By artificially increasing the stated value of units in a development, they can attract illicit investors seeking opportunities to legitimize illicit funds. These inflated values can distort local markets and increase affordability problems for legitimate buyers.

Under-Valuation and the Concealment of Wealth

Under-valuation serves the opposite purpose: minimizing the declared value of a property to disguise wealth, evade taxes, or support illicit transfers. Offenders may record a property purchase at a significantly lower price than the true value, while transferring the remaining amount through unrecorded channels. These arrangements reduce the visibility of large cash movements and create a financial record that understates the buyer's assets.

Under-valuation is especially common in jurisdictions where property transfer taxes are high or where informal cash payments are culturally accepted. Criminals exploit this by negotiating off-the-books payments that leave no official trace, allowing them to hide both the origin and the scale of their financial resources. In corruption cases, under-valuation allows officials to acquire valuable property without declaring its true worth, avoiding scrutiny that might reveal disproportionate wealth.

In some schemes, under-valuation is used with intermediaries. A property is purchased cheaply from a vulnerable seller - sometimes through pressure or deceit - and later resold at full market price. The profit appears legitimate despite the initial exploitation. This practice harms both individuals and markets, contributing to distortions in land value and creating opportunities for compounding laundering schemes.

The Broader Impact on Real Estate Markets

Manipulating valuations undermines the integrity of property markets. Artificial pricing creates misleading signals for buyers, lenders, and policymakers. When fast flips, over-valuation, and under-valuation become widespread, they inflate bubbles, distort investment decisions, and reduce confidence in official price indices. These distortions make it difficult for legitimate investors to assess market conditions, weakening transparency and increasing volatility.

Financial institutions face increased risk as well. Inflated valuations lead to unsound lending decisions, while under-valued transactions expose banks to suspicious activity without sufficient documentation. In both cases, institutions may unknowingly support laundering schemes or suffer losses when manipulated properties fail to reflect true value.

Significance for Investigators and Compliance Professionals

Identifying valuation manipulation requires cross-checking financial flows, transaction timing, ownership links, and deviations from market norms. Patterns such as rapid resales, repeated involvement of the same intermediaries, unexplained price jumps, and transactions involving offshore entities often signal deeper issues. Because valuation practices involve professional judgment, investigations must consider not only the transaction itself but the context in which it occurs.

HIGH-VALUE GOODS, AUCTIONS, AND ART-MARKET ABUSE

High-value goods - including fine art, luxury collectibles, jewelry, rare vehicles, and antiquities - play a significant role in complex financial crime schemes. These markets attract illicit actors because they allow value to be transferred discreetly, assets to be moved across borders with minimal documentation, and ownership to be concealed behind intermediaries. Unlike traditional financial products, many high-value goods operate within markets that lack standardized pricing, routine due diligence, or consistent regulatory oversight. This combination of mobility, opacity, and flexibility makes the sector particularly vulnerable to laundering, tax evasion, and corruption.

Why High-Value Goods Appeal to Illicit Actors

High-value goods provide unique advantages for criminals seeking to store or transfer wealth. First, they are portable and easily moved across jurisdictions. A painting, piece of jewelry, or luxury watch can be transported more discreetly than cash or traditional financial assets. Second, valuation is highly subjective. Works of art, rare collectibles, and limited-edition items do not have fixed prices. Criminals exploit this subjectivity by engineering inflated or deflated valuations to disguise illicit transfers or justify unusual financial flows.

Third, these markets often rely on private sales and discretionary negotiation. Private transactions reduce visibility because they occur outside public auction houses and are less likely to require formal documentation. Even when records exist, they may not include the true beneficial owner, as intermediaries often act on behalf of unnamed buyers or sellers. This arrangement allows criminals to distance themselves from transactions and avoid linking the movement of assets to their identity.

Fourth, many high-value goods appreciate over time, providing both a store of value and a means of legitimizing illicit wealth. A criminal who purchases a painting with illicit proceeds may later sell it through a reputable dealer, presenting the profit as legitimate capital gain. This process converts dirty money into clean income while using the natural characteristics of the art market as a shield.

Auction Houses as Vectors for Risk

Auction houses, especially those dealing in fine art and rare collectibles, present unique vulnerabilities. Their role as intermediaries between anonymous buyers and sellers creates opportunities for illicit actors to participate in transactions without revealing their identity. While major auction houses have improved compliance practices in recent years, gaps remain.

Bidding can be conducted through agents, advisers, or shell companies, allowing criminals to mask their involvement. Funds may be deposited in advance of an auction without robust verification of origin, particularly when the buyer is represented by a well-known dealer. In some cases, auction houses accept large payments through complex financial channels, including offshore accounts, without detailed scrutiny of source of funds.

Auction prices also fluctuate widely based on demand, rarity, and reputation. Criminals exploit this variability to move large sums of money under the guise of legitimate art acquisition. For example, an associate may bid excessively on a piece of art owned by a criminal, effectively transferring illicit funds in the form of a winning auction payment. Because the transaction is recorded as a sale, the funds appear legitimate once they enter the seller's account.

The auction environment also enables layering. A criminal may purchase art in one jurisdiction, move it to a freeport facility in another, and later resell it through a private auction or dealer. Each step creates additional distance between the original illicit funds and the final proceeds.

Freeports and Storage Facilities

Freeports - secure storage facilities located near ports or airports - play an increasingly important role in high-value laundering schemes. These facilities offer long-term storage for art, gold, luxury goods, and other valuable items. Stored items may remain inside for years without undergoing customs clearance, creating an environment where assets can change hands without public disclosure.

Freeports operate with significant discretion. Ownership records are often limited, inspections may be infrequent, and transactions can occur within the facility without triggering cross-border reporting requirements. Criminals use freeports to conceal assets, avoid taxation, and transfer ownership through private contracts. Because the goods never officially enter or exit a country, authorities face challenges in identifying and tracing them.

Art Dealers, Galleries, and Private Brokers

Art dealers and galleries serve as intermediaries with substantial influence over valuation and documentation. They can introduce buyers to sellers, authenticate works, and manage transfers. However, their due-diligence obligations vary widely. In some jurisdictions, dealers are not required to verify beneficial ownership or assess the legitimacy of funds, creating opportunities for criminals to exploit weak compliance practices.

Private brokers play a similar role. They negotiate transactions, guide clients through acquisitions, and often manage purchases on behalf of anonymous buyers. Their involvement adds complexity because they may interact with auction houses, galleries, and storage facilities while providing little transparency about the true source of funds. The trust-based nature of these relationships enables laundering schemes to persist undetected, especially when brokers operate internationally.

Antiquities and Cultural Property

The trade in antiquities is particularly vulnerable due to weak provenance records, geopolitical conflict, and the involvement of multiple intermediaries. Looted artifacts are often smuggled out of their country of origin, laundered through false documentation, and sold to collectors who may not question the legitimacy of the item. Criminal networks exploit this sector because the lack of standardized records makes it difficult to trace the origins of objects. The illicit trade in antiquities not only funds organized crime and extremist groups but also contributes to the loss of cultural heritage.

Market Abuse and Manipulation

Manipulating market perception is another method of laundering within the luxury goods and art sectors. Criminals may engage in coordinated purchases to artificially increase the value of a particular artist's work. By creating the appearance of legitimate demand, they inflate the market price, allowing them to sell pieces at a higher value later. This manipulation can be conducted through shell companies, proxies, or complicit dealers, allowing offenders to transform illicit funds into legitimate gains.

Conversely, under-valued sales allow criminals to discreetly transfer wealth to associates. A buyer may acquire an item for a fraction of its true market value, effectively receiving a financial benefit that is concealed within a private sale. Because valuations are subjective, these discrepancies rarely attract scrutiny unless examined by specialists or regulators.

Risks for Institutions and Investigators

Institutions involved in high-value goods must understand the complex nature of these markets. Investigators face challenges because records may be incomplete, pricing is subjective, and intermediaries operate across borders. Effective detection relies on assessing transaction patterns, examining linked entities, and evaluating whether valuations align with market norms.

DETECTION METHODS AND COMPLIANCE EXPECTATIONS

Detecting financial crime in real estate and luxury goods markets requires a disciplined approach that goes beyond routine verification. These sectors operate through complex transactions, discretionary valuations, and intermediaries who often play significant roles in facilitating purchases. Effective detection depends on identifying patterns that indicate manipulation, recognizing structures designed to obscure beneficial ownership, and understanding the behavioral and financial signals associated with high-risk activity. Compliance frameworks must therefore be structured to manage these unique risks while ensuring that legitimate commerce is not hindered.

Understanding Transaction Context and Economic Purpose

One of the most important detection methods involves evaluating the economic rationale behind a transaction. Real estate acquisitions or purchases of high-value goods should align with the buyer's profile, income sources, and lawful business activities. When the financial behavior of a client appears inconsistent with their stated background, the risk of financial crime increases.

Compliance teams must examine the broader context of a transaction rather than relying solely on surface-level documentation. Sudden interest in high-value properties, unexplained cash purchases, or repeated acquisitions of luxury goods by individuals with limited verifiable income may indicate attempts to launder illicit funds. Similarly, transactions that lack clear commercial justification - for example, purchasing artwork at prices significantly above market benchmarks - require closer scrutiny.

Reviewing transaction timing is also critical. Patterns such as rapid purchases and resales, abrupt changes in ownership structures, or transfers that coincide with known legal events affecting a client can signal attempts to conceal assets or distance funds from their origin.

Beneficial Ownership Identification

Real estate and luxury goods sectors are frequently exploited by criminals who conceal their identity behind legal entities, nominees, or intermediaries. Effective detection therefore hinges on establishing the true beneficial owner. Compliance expectations require that institutions identify not only the legal owner but also the individual who ultimately controls or benefits from the asset.

This process may involve reviewing corporate structures, analyzing shareholder records, assessing trustee arrangements, and verifying whether declared owners have legitimate control over the entity. In cases where multiple layers of companies or offshore jurisdictions are involved, enhanced due diligence becomes essential. Any reluctance to disclose ownership information, use of professional intermediaries without clear justification, or reliance on opaque structures should be treated as red flags requiring further investigation.

Beneficial ownership identification also extends to understanding the source of funds. Institutions must assess whether funds used for purchases are consistent with the beneficial owner's legitimate income and whether they originate from transparent, traceable channels. Payments routed through multiple third parties, offshore accounts, or newly formed companies warrant additional scrutiny.

Valuation Analysis and Market Comparisons

Given that real estate and luxury goods markets often lack standardized pricing, valuation analysis plays a central role in detection. Transactions that deviate significantly from market norms - either through inflated or deflated pricing - may indicate laundering, fraud, or disguised transfers of value.

Compliance teams should compare proposed transaction values with independent market data, recent comparable sales, and professional appraisal reports. When valuations appear inconsistent or lack credible justification, institutions must investigate further. This includes examining whether the appraiser is independent, qualified, and free from conflicts of interest.

In the luxury goods sector, specialists or external experts may be needed to assess authenticity, provenance, and market value. Suspicious disparity between stated value and known market ranges often signals an attempt to manipulate the appearance of wealth or to justify questionable financial flows.

Monitoring Intermediaries and Third Parties

Intermediaries are frequently involved in high-risk sectors, including real estate agents, lawyers, brokers, developers, consultants, and art dealers. Because these individuals can act on behalf of clients, compliance expectations require institutions to assess their role, independence, and potential exposure to conflict.

Institutions should review whether the intermediary has a legitimate relationship with the client and whether their involvement aligns with the nature of the transaction. Multiple intermediaries, especially those operating across jurisdictions, may indicate attempts to obscure beneficial ownership or add unnecessary layers to avoid detection. Payments made to or through intermediaries require particular caution, especially when funds are transferred to unrelated third parties or when invoices lack detailed descriptions.

Cross-Border Activity and Source of Wealth Verification

Cross-border transactions introduce additional risks due to differences in regulatory regimes, beneficial ownership standards, and financial transparency. Compliance teams must pay special attention to property purchases or luxury acquisitions involving buyers from high-risk jurisdictions, countries with strict secrecy laws, or regions with known corruption concerns.

Verification of source of wealth becomes essential in such cases. Institutions must obtain credible evidence that the client's wealth was generated through legitimate means. This may include tax records, business financials, audited statements, or independently verified documentation. Vague descriptions such as "investment income" or "family wealth" without supporting detail should not be accepted.

Use of Technology and Data Analytics

Technology enhances detection capabilities by identifying unusual transaction patterns and connections between entities. Data analytics can reveal repeated involvement of the same intermediaries, clustering of high-value purchases linked to specific addresses, or patterns of rapid resales that resemble laundering cycles. Systems that integrate public records, property registries, trade databases, and sanctions lists can identify risks that would be difficult to detect manually.

However, technology must complement - not replace - professional judgment. Automated alerts are only useful when paired with trained compliance staff capable of interpreting anomalies and assessing whether they reflect genuine risk.

CHAPTER 19

CASINOS AND GAMING ENVIRONMENTS

MONEY LAUNDERING TYPOLOGIES: CHIP PASSING, SLOT CYCLING, JUNKETS

CASINOS and GAMING venues are attractive environments for laundering because they combine large financial flows, high customer anonymity, and complex operational structures. The movement of chips, tokens, and credits can create the appearance of legitimate gambling activity while concealing illicit origins. Criminals exploit these characteristics through specific typologies, including chip passing, slot cycling, and the misuse of junket systems. Each technique exploits a different part of the gaming ecosystem, yet all aim to convert dirty money into funds that appear legitimate.

Chip Passing as a Concealment Method

Chip passing is one of the most common laundering practices in brick-and-mortar casinos. The typology is simple in structure yet effective when executed with minimal scrutiny. A criminal enters a casino with illicit cash, buys chips, then transfers them to another individual - often an associate or a complicit actor. The second individual redeems the chips, presenting the funds as gambling winnings or gaming proceeds.

This method separates the person introducing illicit funds from the person redeeming them. By doing so, it weakens the transactional link that would otherwise reveal suspicious behavior. Chip passing typically occurs in environments where floor surveillance is limited, or where staff are unable to identify coordinated behavior between guests. In many cases, the parties act as ordinary players, engaging in minimal betting to avoid drawing attention before completing the chip transfer.

Chip passing also appears in more elaborate schemes. Criminal groups may rotate multiple individuals through a casino, each holding chips purchased by a central figure. Chips may be passed at gaming tables, in restrooms, or even outside the casino - through private arrangements facilitated by intermediaries. When gaming staff are unfamiliar with the players or when identification is not required for chip redemption, these transactions become more difficult to detect.

The primary risk factor is the separation of chip purchase and chip redemption. When the person cashing out cannot be reasonably connected to the original purchase, the transaction warrants heightened scrutiny.

Slot Cycling and Machine-Based Laundering

Slot machines offer another avenue for laundering through a method commonly called slot cycling. This involves inserting illicit cash into slot machines, conducting minimal gaming activity, and then cashing out the remaining credits. The ticket or payout slip generated by the machine is then presented at the cashier window or redeemed through automated kiosks.

Slot cycling creates an appearance of legitimate gambling losses and winnings. Because slot machines record play electronically, the payout ticket indicates gaming activity - even though the player may have wagered only a small fraction of the inserted cash. Many casinos permit significant redemption amounts without requiring extensive identification, especially where regulatory thresholds for reporting are weak or where on-site monitoring is limited.

Criminals favor slot cycling for several reasons. It requires no interaction with staff, occurs in crowded areas where oversight is more challenging, and leaves behind digital records that appear legitimate at first glance. Some offenders use multiple machines simultaneously or move between machines to avoid drawing attention. Others break large sums into smaller amounts to stay below reporting thresholds or to reduce the appearance of unusual play patterns.

More sophisticated variations involve structuring deposits across multiple visits or coordinating activity among several individuals acting on behalf of a criminal organization. These cycles can produce convincing records of gameplay while quickly converting illicit cash into casino credit or payout tickets, which can then be redeemed or transferred.

Junkets and High-Value Laundering Risks

Junkets present a more complex and higher-risk laundering typology, particularly in regions where casinos rely heavily on VIP programs. Junkets are organized groups of high-stakes players brought to casinos by promoters who arrange travel, accommodation, and credit. The financial arrangements within these programs create opportunities for laundering, especially when credit is issued directly by junket operators rather than by the casino.

One common risk is the commingling of funds. Junket promoters may pool money from various individuals, mixing legitimate capital with illicit proceeds. These combined funds are then used to purchase chips or establish credit for VIP players.

When winnings are paid out, the funds appear to originate from legitimate gaming activity rather than from criminal sources.

Another risk arises when junket operators act as financial intermediaries. They may facilitate currency exchange, manage player accounts, and settle debts across borders. This creates a layer of separation between the casino and the players' financial activity. Criminal organizations exploit this structure to move money internationally under the cover of junket operations, bypassing conventional banking controls.

Junkets have also been associated with underground banking systems. In some regions, junket promoters maintain networks capable of transferring large sums between countries without formal banking channels. These networks may be used to repay gambling credit, settle criminal obligations, or reintegrate illicit funds into legitimate financial systems. Because junket arrangements vary widely between jurisdictions, regulatory oversight is inconsistent, leaving significant gaps that can be exploited.

Operational Behaviors and Common Risk Indicators

Across chip passing, slot cycling, and junket abuse, several behavioral patterns commonly emerge. Players who spend little time gambling yet conduct large chip purchases, individuals who avoid placing meaningful wagers, and groups that appear coordinated in their movements often present elevated risk. Unusual redemption patterns - such as cashing out frequently, avoiding table play, or redeeming chips purchased by others - also warrant attention.

Complex junket arrangements involving opaque financial flows, offshore accounts, or unexplained credit issuance must be treated as high-risk. Casinos that do not verify the financial background of VIP players or rely heavily on third-party organizers are particularly exposed.

ONLINE GAMING (IGAMING) AND CROSS-BORDER RISKS

The rapid growth of online gaming has transformed the gambling industry, expanding access to millions of players across multiple jurisdictions. While this expansion has created legitimate economic opportunities, it has also introduced new risks for financial crime. Online casinos, sports-betting platforms, and digital gaming environments allow players to move funds electronically, convert money into gaming credits, and execute cross-border transactions with minimal friction. These characteristics make iGaming an attractive channel for laundering, especially when platforms operate across regulatory boundaries or in jurisdictions with inconsistent oversight.

Digital Wallets and the Movement of Funds

Online gaming platforms typically rely on digital wallets, prepaid accounts, and linked payment services that allow players to deposit, withdraw, and transfer funds with ease. Criminals exploit these features by using multiple payment methods, including bank transfers, credit cards, e-money, and cryptocurrency, to obscure the origin of funds.

A common typology involves depositing funds into an iGaming account, wagering minimally or not at all, and then withdrawing the remaining balance as "gaming winnings." Because withdrawals often appear as payouts from a regulated gaming platform, they are perceived as lower risk by financial institutions unless supported by additional analysis. This method allows criminals to convert illicit proceeds into funds that appear to be derived from gambling activity.

In some cases, criminals use multiple accounts to move funds between player wallets. Transfers between accounts - especially when structured as peer-to-peer in-game transactions - can mask the source of funds and create the impression of legitimate social gaming behavior. This becomes more complex when accounts are registered in different jurisdictions or operated through VPNs that obscure the player's true location.

Anonymity and Identity Challenges

Identity verification remains a major challenge in online gaming. Many platforms allow players to register with minimal documentation, particularly when they offer free-to-play modes or operate without strong regulatory requirements. Criminals take advantage of this by creating multiple accounts, using false credentials, or leveraging stolen identities purchased through illicit marketplaces.

The challenge intensifies when offshore iGaming platforms accept players from countries where they are not licensed. These platforms may not follow rigorous Know-Your-Player (KYP) requirements, enabling criminals to bypass domestic AML safeguards. Because player activity is distributed across multiple platforms and jurisdictions, it becomes difficult for authorities to monitor patterns or identify coordinated laundering schemes.

Even when identification is required, criminals use technological tools to obscure their identity. VPNs, proxy servers, and anonymization software can disguise IP addresses, making it appear as though a player is located in a different region. This prevents gaming operators from accurately applying jurisdictional controls or identifying prohibited activity.

Cross-Border Transactions and Regulatory Arbitrage

Online gaming platforms routinely process international payments, making cross-border movement of funds a core feature of the industry rather than an exception. This creates fertile ground for regulatory arbitrage - where criminals exploit mismatches between the regulatory standards of different jurisdictions.

A common pattern involves depositing illicit funds into a platform licensed in a lightly regulated jurisdiction and then withdrawing the funds to a bank account located in a stricter jurisdiction. Because the withdrawal originates from a licensed operator, financial institutions may apply less scrutiny to the transaction. Criminals further complicate detection by routing funds through multiple platforms or converting balances into different currencies.

Some platforms also allow payments in digital assets, including cryptocurrencies. These payments can be processed instantly, across borders, and without reliance on traditional financial institutions. While many operators have implemented controls, gaps remain - particularly with offshore casinos that accept crypto deposits without robust due diligence. Once cryptocurrency is converted into gaming credits and then withdrawn, tracing its origin becomes significantly more difficult.

Gaming Credits, Bonuses, and Incentive Abuse

iGaming operators frequently use bonuses, credits, and promotional incentives to attract players. These features create opportunities for criminals to manipulate account balances in ways that support laundering.

For example, a criminal may deposit illicit funds, claim a bonus, wager minimally, and withdraw the combined balance. This allows the account to generate gains unrelated to real gameplay, disguising the movement of funds behind promotional structures. Some criminals coordinate with accomplices to trade bonuses or exploit loopholes across multiple accounts, amplifying the volume of transactions while avoiding genuine risk-taking.

In platforms that support peer-to-peer gaming - such as online poker - players may collaborate to intentionally lose to an accomplice, transferring value under the guise of standard gameplay. This technique mirrors chip passing in physical casinos but occurs digitally, often with fewer constraints and more limited monitoring capabilities.

Convergence with Other Crime Types

Online gaming is increasingly intersecting with cybercrime, fraud, and identity theft. Criminals use compromised payment cards, synthetic identities, and phishing schemes to fund gaming accounts. Once the funds are inside the platform, they can be layered, transferred, or withdrawn before the fraud is detected. This convergence complicates detection because gaming operators may see only the transaction activity - while the underlying financial crime originates elsewhere.

Organized crime groups also use iGaming platforms to move funds between countries, settle debts, or distribute proceeds among members. The lack of physical interaction and the speed of digital transfers allow these groups to operate with reduced visibility.

Operational Red Flags and Emerging Threats

Several indicators commonly signal high-risk activity in online gaming environments. These include rapid deposits and withdrawals with little gameplay, multiple accounts linked to the same device or payment method, cross-border transfers that lack economic justification, and significant activity routed through VPNs or anonymizing services. Unusual betting patterns, coordinated play between multiple accounts, and use of high-risk payment channels also warrant concern.

KNOW-YOUR-PLAYER (KYP) AND SURVEILLANCE TECHNIQUES

Casinos and gaming operators face unique challenges when assessing player risk. Unlike traditional financial institutions, gaming venues handle large volumes of cash, rapid transactions, and a wide range of player behaviors that may or may not indicate illicit intent. Know-Your-Player (KYP) frameworks and surveillance techniques are therefore essential components of an effective anti-money laundering program. These measures allow operators to understand who their players are, how they behave, and whether their activity is consistent with legitimate gameplay or reflects attempts to conceal illicit funds.

Purpose of KYP in Gaming Environments

KYP extends beyond basic identity verification. Its objective is to create a comprehensive understanding of a player's typical behavior, financial capacity, source of funds, and reason for engaging in high-value gaming activity. Casinos and online platforms must be able to explain not only who the player is but whether their pattern of play aligns with their profile.

Because gaming allows rapid conversion of cash into chips, tickets, or credits, KYP helps operators identify anomalies early. When a player consistently wagers below expected levels, redeems chips without meaningful play, or uses multiple payment methods without clear rationale, enhanced scrutiny becomes necessary. KYP also assists in identifying whether a player may be acting on behalf of someone else - a common concern in chip passing, junket activity, and online account misuse.

In environments with VIP programs, KYP becomes even more critical. High-value clients often receive special treatment, access to credit, and concierge services. Without strong controls, these privileges can mask suspicious financial activity. Understanding the background, wealth sources, and business interests of VIP players is therefore essential to prevent misuse of the casino's financial infrastructure.

Identity Verification and Player Onboarding

Effective KYP begins with rigorous identity verification. Casinos must ensure that each player's identity is authentic, current, and supported by credible documents. For online gaming platforms, this includes verifying government-issued identification, assessing device fingerprints, validating payment methods, and confirming that the player is operating from a permitted jurisdiction.

Identification alone, however, is insufficient. Operators should assess the economic profile of players engaging in significant gaming activity. This may involve reviewing available information on occupation, financial background, and source of funds. Discrepancies - such as a player with modest declared income engaging in high-stakes gaming - warrant further inquiry.

In jurisdictions where anonymous or low-information gaming is allowed, operators must still apply risk-based measures. Even if initial identity documents are not required for low-level transactions, thresholds should trigger more comprehensive checks. The challenge for operators is balancing accessibility with the responsibility to identify and mitigate risk.

Behavioral Monitoring and Player Profiling

The core of KYP lies in ongoing behavioral monitoring. Casinos maintain detailed records of play, including buy-ins, wagers, chip exchanges, credit usage, cash-outs, and time spent on the gaming floor. Surveillance teams analyze this information to identify patterns that deviate from normal play.

For example, players who purchase large amounts of chips but avoid placing significant wagers may be attempting to launder funds through chip redemption. Similarly, individuals who frequently exchange chips, bounce between tables without a consistent gaming strategy, or cash out repeatedly in short intervals may be attempting to create the appearance of legitimate play.

Online gaming platforms track deposit behavior, device data, IP addresses, session frequency, and betting patterns. Numerous accounts using the same device, repeated failed identity checks, or the use of anonymizing tools may indicate suspicious activity. Sudden changes in play behavior - such as a historically low-value player making large deposits or engaging in high-stakes bets - also require review.

Behavioral monitoring is not intended to judge the quality of play but to identify financial patterns inconsistent with ordinary gaming behavior. This distinction is essential to avoid profiling legitimate players while focusing on activities that may indicate risk.

Casino Floor Surveillance and Technology Integration

Physical casinos rely heavily on surveillance systems to complement KYP. High-definition cameras, table monitors, and digital recording systems provide a comprehensive view of player movements, chip exchanges, and interactions. Surveillance professionals analyze footage to detect coordinated behavior, collusion, or chip passing.

Advanced casinos integrate surveillance data with transaction logs to create a holistic view of player activity. When a player buys chips at one table, moves to another, and later redeems chips in a pattern that appears unusual, systems can flag the behavior for review. Real-time monitoring tools allow surveillance teams to intervene promptly when potential risks arise.

Facial recognition technology is also emerging as a key tool. When used responsibly and within regulatory limits, it helps identify banned players, monitor high-risk individuals, and detect those who attempt to enter a property under false identities. This technology also assists in linking activities across multiple visits, enabling long-term risk assessment.

Online Surveillance and Data Analytics

Digital gaming platforms rely on analytics to monitor player behavior. Algorithms assess transaction velocity, gaming duration, payment methods, and geographical patterns. When gaming activity is inconsistent with a player's historic profile, or when multiple accounts exhibit coordinated behavior, systems can automatically flag the activity for investigation.

Data analytics also help detect structured deposits, rapid withdrawals, and unusual win-loss ratios. Because online environments provide detailed digital footprints, operators can identify suspicious patterns faster than in physical casinos - provided they have robust systems in place.

Integration of KYP with AML Decision-Making

KYP and surveillance findings feed directly into AML decision processes. When operators identify potential risk, they must apply enhanced due diligence, restrict player activity, or file suspicious transaction reports. Effective integration ensures that early detection leads to timely intervention rather than delayed action.

AML CONTROLS, RISK INDICATORS, AND CASE STUDIES

Effective anti-money laundering (AML) controls in casinos and gaming environments require a combination of strong internal systems, trained staff, and an operational culture that prioritizes integrity. Gaming venues manage continuous streams of cash, digital payments, chips, credits, and player interactions. These elements create a dynamic environment where illicit funds can blend into legitimate gaming activity unless robust controls are in place. Strong AML frameworks provide the structure needed to detect unusual behavior, mitigate risk, and ensure that gaming operators meet regulatory obligations.

Core AML Controls in Gaming Operations

AML controls begin with a structured risk assessment that identifies where vulnerabilities exist within gaming products, payment channels, and customer segments. This assessment guides the development of procedures that dictate how players are onboarded, monitored, and reviewed. A risk-based approach ensures that higher-risk players and activities receive proportionately higher scrutiny.

One of the most important controls is transaction monitoring. Casinos must maintain systems that track chip purchases, exchanges, cash-ins, cash-outs, and credit play. These systems should link financial activity to an identifiable player profile. When activity deviates from expected patterns, alerts must be generated for review. High-quality monitoring systems distinguish between ordinary gaming behavior and transactions that may indicate layering or structuring.

Another essential control is the enforcement of thresholds. Casinos must identify when a player reaches reporting limits for cash transactions or chip exchanges. Threshold-based triggers for due diligence, source-of-funds reviews, and reporting obligations ensure that large movements of money are not ignored. Controls must apply equally across table games, slot machines, and digital platforms.

Staff training is also critical. Employees must understand common laundering typologies, know how to recognize suspicious behavior, and feel empowered to escalate concerns. Training cannot be a one-time exercise; it requires continuous reinforcement to keep pace with emerging risks. Surveillance teams, cage staff, dealers, and online operations personnel all play distinct roles and must receive role-specific guidance.

Record-keeping underpins all AML processes. Casinos must maintain detailed records of player identification, transactions, suspicious activity reports, and internal reviews. Strong documentation ensures that operators can demonstrate compliance during regulatory examinations and support investigations when necessary.

Key Risk Indicators in Casinos and iGaming

Consistent identification of suspicious behavior depends on recognizing indicators that commonly accompany laundering attempts. One significant indicator is minimal play. When a player buys chips or deposits funds but wagers very little before cashing out, the activity suggests a desire to convert funds rather than participate in gaming. This pattern appears in both physical casinos and online platforms.

Another indicator is the use of multiple accounts or identities. Criminals may register several accounts to spread transactions, avoid thresholds, or coordinate play. In physical venues, similar risks appear when multiple individuals appear to operate together, share chips, or alternate between tables without meaningful gaming behavior.

Unusual payment methods also raise concern. The use of prepaid cards, large numbers of small transactions, transfers from unrelated third parties, or deposits in foreign currencies without clear justification may point to attempts to obscure the source of funds. In online gaming, the use of VPNs, anonymized payment channels, or frequent changes in IP address is another warning sign.

Excessive movement of chips is a prominent risk factor in physical casinos. Chip passing, rapid chip exchanges, or redemptions by individuals who did not purchase the chips merit immediate attention. In digital environments, rapid deposit-and-withdraw patterns, disproportionate bonus exploitation, and repeated player-to-player transfers warrant further review.

High-risk jurisdictions also play a role. Transactions linked to countries with weak AML controls, high corruption risk, or known criminal networks must be scrutinized. Cross-border movement of funds into gaming accounts is not inherently suspicious, but when combined with irregular behavior, it strengthens the risk profile.

Case Studies

One such case involved a criminal organization using a major casino to convert drug proceeds into legitimate funds. Members purchased large amounts of chips with cash, placed minimal bets at low-risk tables, and cashed out using checks issued by the casino. The checks were deposited into bank accounts as gaming winnings. The scheme operated for months before surveillance identified frequent chip exchanges between the same group of individuals.

Another case involved misuse of online gaming accounts. A network of players based in multiple countries used online poker platforms to transfer funds by intentionally losing to one another.

Because online poker involves direct competition between players, these losses provided a discreet means of transferring value. Funds deposited through illicit channels were withdrawn as legitimate winnings by accomplices, making detection difficult until coordinated account patterns were flagged by the platform's analytics team.

A further example concerned a junket operator who commingled legitimate client funds with proceeds from illegal gambling operations. By extending credit to VIP players and settling accounts through offshore transfers, the junket facilitated the movement of large sums without triggering banking controls. When regulators identified inconsistencies in reported player activity, they initiated an investigation that uncovered widespread financial misconduct.

Strengthening AML Integrity in Gaming

The effectiveness of AML safeguards depends on the alignment of systems, staff, and leadership. Operators must integrate monitoring tools with strong governance and clear procedures for escalation. Coordination between compliance teams, surveillance units, and gaming operations ensures that risk indicators are promptly reviewed. Continuous improvement, driven by regulatory updates and emerging typologies, is critical in an environment where criminal methods evolve rapidly.

CHAPTER 20

CRYPTOCURRENCY AND DIGITAL ASSETS

CRYPTO ECOSYSTEM

THE CRYPTOCURRENCY ECOSYSTEM has expanded rapidly in recent years, creating new opportunities for legitimate financial innovation while simultaneously presenting significant risks for money laundering and illicit finance. Digital assets operate across decentralized networks with high transaction speed, global accessibility, and varying levels of anonymity. This environment enables criminals to move funds quickly, exploit regulatory gaps, and obscure the origin of illicit proceeds. Understanding how exchanges, decentralized finance (DeFi) platforms, and peer-to-peer (P2P) markets function is essential for identifying vulnerabilities and implementing effective controls.

Centralized Exchanges and Their Risk Exposure

Centralized cryptocurrency exchanges act as gateways between traditional financial systems and blockchain networks. They allow users to convert fiat currency into digital assets and vice versa. Because of this role, exchanges are a primary entry and exit point for laundering schemes. Criminals often use exchanges to cash out stolen funds, purchase cryptocurrencies with illicit proceeds, or distribute funds across multiple wallets.

Some exchanges operate in strict regulatory environments and apply comprehensive Know-Your-Customer (KYC) and AML controls. These platforms require identity verification, monitor transactions, and report suspicious activity. However, others - particularly those based offshore - may apply minimal oversight or intentionally design their platforms to avoid regulatory scrutiny. Criminals gravitate toward these unregulated exchanges because they provide anonymity and limited data retention.

A common laundering tactic involves "exchange-hopping," where funds are transferred between multiple exchanges in quick succession. This creates layers of transactions that complicate tracing and reduces the visibility of the origin of funds. Criminals may also use multiple exchange accounts registered under false identities, stolen identities, or synthetic profiles. When combined with the speed of transfers, these factors create significant challenges for investigators.

Decentralized Finance (DeFi) and Protocol-Based Risks

DeFi platforms operate without centralized intermediaries. They rely on smart contracts - self-executing code deployed on the blockchain - to manage lending, trading, asset swaps, and yield farming. While DeFi enables innovation and offers transparent access to financial services, its decentralized structure introduces vulnerabilities that criminals exploit.

Many DeFi platforms do not require identity verification. Anyone with a crypto wallet can interact with protocols anonymously. This anonymity, combined with the ability to execute high-value transfers instantly, makes DeFi attractive for laundering. Criminals frequently use DeFi liquidity pools, decentralized exchanges (DEXs), and automated market makers to obscure transaction flows.

One common method is "chain-hopping," where funds are rapidly moved across multiple blockchains using decentralized bridges or swap protocols. This creates a trail that spans several networks, making it harder to trace the original source. Another method involves using lending protocols to deposit illicit funds as collateral and borrow other assets, effectively transforming tainted funds into assets with a new transaction history.

Flash loans - a DeFi innovation - also create risks. A flash loan allows a user to borrow large sums without collateral, provided the loan is repaid within the same transaction block. Criminals have used flash loans to exploit vulnerabilities in smart contracts, steal assets from protocols, and quickly distribute stolen funds across multiple wallets.

The absence of centralized oversight in DeFi means there is no compliance team to intervene, no customer service to identify suspicious patterns, and no entity responsible for performing AML checks. This creates a challenging environment for enforcement, particularly when protocols are designed to operate autonomously.

P2P Markets and Informal Crypto Trading

Peer-to-peer markets facilitate direct transfers between users without using an exchange order book. These markets are especially prominent in jurisdictions with financial restrictions, limited banking access, or high inflation. P2P platforms enable users to negotiate prices, choose preferred payment methods, and connect with buyers or sellers directly.

Criminals exploit P2P markets because the transactions often occur outside of traditional banking channels. Buyers and sellers may use cash deposits, gift cards, mobile payments, or foreign accounts, making it difficult to verify the source of funds. Some P2P platforms have limited KYC controls, allowing users to create multiple accounts and conduct high-volume transactions with minimal oversight.

In many laundering schemes, P2P traders act as informal money exchangers. They receive illicit funds in one form - often fiat currency or compromised bank transfers - and convert them into cryptocurrency, or vice versa. Some operate organized networks where multiple traders coordinate to move funds across borders without detection. These groups can conduct hundreds of small transactions, each below regulatory thresholds, making monitoring more difficult.

Because P2P platforms rely on marketplace ratings and social trust, criminals may build reputational legitimacy over time. Once they appear credible, they can conduct larger transactions without attracting attention.

Cross-Ecosystem Laundering Flows

Criminals often combine centralized exchanges, DeFi protocols, and P2P markets to increase complexity and reduce traceability. A typical scheme might begin with funds sent to an unregulated exchange, followed by transfers to multiple wallets, movement through decentralized swaps, and conversion to stablecoins before being cashed out through P2P brokers.

Each step adds distance between the illicit source and the final withdrawal, making the entire flow harder to trace - especially when criminals use privacy-focused coins or mixing tools as additional layers.

Implications for Investigators and Compliance Professionals

Understanding how these ecosystems interact is essential for detecting suspicious activity. Compliance teams must examine transaction patterns across chains, identify wallets linked to known illicit activity, and assess whether customer behavior aligns with legitimate economic purpose. Cross-platform monitoring, blockchain analytics, and international cooperation play crucial roles in addressing the unique risks posed by digital assets.

MIXERS, TUMBLERS, AND OBFUSCATION TOOLS

As cryptocurrency adoption increases, criminals continue to exploit technologies that obscure transaction history and disguise the origin of funds. Mixers, tumblers, and other obfuscation tools are central to this effort. These services disrupt blockchain transparency by breaking the link between the sender and receiver, making tracing more difficult for investigators. While the underlying technology can sometimes be used for privacy-enhancing purposes, criminals frequently use it to introduce deliberate opacity into laundering schemes.

Purpose and Function of Mixing Services

Mixing services - also known as tumblers - operate by pooling cryptocurrency from numerous users and redistributing the funds in a manner that obscures the original transaction paths. A user sends cryptocurrency to the mixer, which combines it with assets from other participants. The service then returns an equivalent amount, minus a service fee, to a new wallet chosen by the user. Because the outbound transactions originate from a pooled fund rather than directly from the user's wallet, blockchain analysis becomes significantly more challenging.

Mixers rely on the high transaction volume within their pools to break the traceable link between inputs and outputs. The more participants a mixer has, the harder it becomes to determine which outgoing funds correspond to which incoming transaction. Some mixers incorporate additional randomness - varying the size, timing, and distribution of payouts - to further hinder forensic analysis.

Criminals use mixers to remove traces of illicit origins after hacks, ransomware attacks, darknet market activity, and fraud schemes. For example, stolen funds may first be fragmented across multiple wallets before entering a mixer, creating several layers of complexity prior to output.

Decentralized Mixers and Protocol-Based Obfuscation

Traditional mixers are centralized services controlled by an operator. However, the ecosystem has evolved toward decentralized, autonomous mixers built on smart contracts. These decentralized mixers remove human intermediaries and allow users to deposit and withdraw funds anonymously through a protocol rather than a business entity.

One of the most well-known models involves smart contracts that accept fixed-denomination deposits. After a mandatory waiting period, the user can withdraw their funds to an unrelated address. Because the pool contains numerous deposits of identical value, it becomes difficult to match any specific withdrawal with a particular deposit. Decentralized mixers are particularly challenging for investigators because they lack a central operator to subpoena, shut down, or force into compliance.

These tools have been heavily exploited in major cybercrime incidents. Some ransomware groups rely on decentralized mixers as their primary laundering method, routing payments through protocols that intentionally avoid keeping user records. Additionally, decentralized environments enable cross-chain mixing, where funds are exchanged between blockchains in a manner designed to break traceability across networks.

Obfuscation through Chain-Hopping and Cross-Asset Conversion

Not all obfuscation requires dedicated mixing services. Criminals frequently use chain-hopping - rapid transfers between multiple cryptocurrencies - to complicate investigative efforts. Moving from Bitcoin to a privacy coin, then back to a mainstream cryptocurrency, creates a fragmented trail that spans multiple blockchain networks. Each conversion introduces additional data points that investigators must reconcile.

Cross-chain bridges and decentralized exchanges facilitate these conversions without requiring KYC verification. Criminals may route funds through a series of swaps that ultimately lead to assets with less transparent transaction histories.

Privacy-focused cryptocurrencies add another layer of difficulty. Coins with built-in obfuscation features - such as shielded transactions, private addresses, or zero-knowledge proofs - allow users to conduct transfers without publicly visible balances or transaction details. When illicit funds enter these ecosystems, visibility drops sharply.

Fogging Tools and Wallet-Level Obfuscation

Beyond mixers and chain-hopping, criminals use wallet-level obfuscation tools to create misleading transaction patterns. Some wallets automate splitting transactions across hundreds of micro-addresses, each sending small amounts to new locations. Others allow users to generate new addresses for every transaction, making it more difficult to link activity to a single user.

CoinJoin protocols also facilitate group-based mixing. These allow multiple users to pool their transactions into a single joint transfer, which is then redistributed. The final outputs make it difficult to attribute which portion of the transaction belongs to whom. While CoinJoin is presented as a privacy feature, criminals regularly use it to conceal illicit activity.

Identifying Obfuscation Techniques in Investigations

Although mixers and obfuscation tools complicate blockchain analysis, investigators have developed methods to identify their use. Certain transaction patterns, wallet addresses, and behavioral characteristics are strongly associated with mixing services. These include:

- Transactions entering large pools with recognizable mixing signatures
- Fragmented deposits split into uniform-sized transactions
- Immediate transfers into privacy coins following illicit activity
- Repeated use of cross-chain bridges without economic justification

Forensic blockchain platforms maintain databases of known mixer addresses, enabling investigators to flag suspicious flows quickly. While obfuscation reduces visibility, it rarely eliminates all traces. Analysts often compare timing, transaction amounts, and wallet clustering to identify underlying relationships that mixers attempt to hide.

AML Implications for Institutions

Financial institutions, crypto exchanges, and digital asset service providers must implement monitoring tools capable of identifying when clients interact with mixing services. Many regulated exchanges now block transactions linked to mixers or require enhanced due diligence before processing them.

Institutions must also maintain policies that prohibit facilitating transfers to known obfuscation services. Customer behavior that indicates deliberate avoidance of transparency - such as repeated attempts to access blacklisted mixers - should trigger enhanced review or account restrictions.

NFT EXPLOITATION AND DIGITAL ASSET MANIPULATION

Non-fungible tokens (NFTs) have introduced a new form of digital ownership, enabling the buying and selling of unique digital assets ranging from artwork and collectibles to virtual land and in-game items. While NFTs offer innovative use cases, they also create opportunities for financial crime due to their subjective value, limited regulatory oversight, and the ease with which they can be transferred across borders. Criminals exploit these characteristics to launder money, manipulate prices, and hide the movement of funds within digital ecosystems.

Why NFTs are Attractive for Illicit Finance

NFTs appeal to criminals for several structural reasons. First, they lack standardized pricing. The value of an NFT often depends on rarity, creator reputation, and market sentiment. Because prices are subjective, criminals can justify unusually high or low purchase amounts without attracting immediate scrutiny. This ambiguity allows illicit value to be transferred under the guise of legitimate art or digital asset transactions.

Second, NFT marketplaces operate globally and allow users to transact pseudonymously. Wallets can be created without personal information, and transactions are typically recorded only on the blockchain, not tied to verified identities. This makes it difficult for investigators to determine who is behind a transaction or whether multiple wallets are controlled by the same person.

Third, NFTs can be moved instantly between wallets without intermediaries, reducing oversight and limiting opportunities for detection. Criminals use this capability to transfer high-value assets across jurisdictions with minimal traceable ties to the individuals involved.

Wash Trading and Price Manipulation

One of the most common forms of NFT misuse is wash trading - a practice where the same individual buys and sells an asset using different wallets under their control. The purpose is to inflate the perceived value of the NFT, create a false sense of market demand, or launder illicit funds.

For example, a criminal may purchase an NFT from themselves at a high price using illicit proceeds. Because blockchain transactions do not reveal personal identities, observers see a legitimate sale at a premium price. The seller wallet - also controlled by the criminal - receives funds that appear to come from a genuine buyer. This method effectively converts illicit money into clean proceeds under the appearance of successful digital asset trading.

Wash trading also enables price inflation, allowing criminals to manipulate the market value of specific projects. By generating a history of high-priced sales, criminals can mislead legitimate buyers and later sell the NFT to unsuspecting investors at inflated prices. Artificially created price histories make detection difficult unless investigators analyze wallet relationships and behavioral patterns.

Rug Pulls and Fraudulent NFT Projects

NFTs have also been exploited through fraudulent projects commonly known as rug pulls. In these schemes, developers promote a new NFT collection with promises of future utility, community benefits, or integration into gaming environments. Once the project generates significant sales, the creators disappear, leaving buyers with worthless digital assets.

While rug pulls primarily involve consumer fraud, they often intertwine with laundering techniques. Criminals may use project funds to move illicit assets or route stolen money through multiple wallets associated with the project before abandoning it. Because many NFT projects are created by anonymous teams, accountability is limited, and stolen funds are difficult to recover.

Use of NFTs in Broader Laundering Chains

NFTs can also be embedded within larger laundering schemes that combine several digital tools. For instance, criminals may purchase an NFT with cryptocurrency obtained through illicit activity, transfer the NFT to another wallet, and then resell it on a different marketplace. This sequence creates multiple layers of transactions, each adding distance between the original illicit funds and the final proceeds.

Offenders may also use cross-chain bridges to move NFTs between networks, making it more difficult to track the asset's provenance. Some marketplaces allow NFTs to be fractionalized, meaning ownership is split across multiple tokens. This fragmentation introduces additional complexity and allows criminals to disperse illicit value across numerous wallets or participants.

Gaming, Metaverse, and Virtual World Vulnerabilities

NFTs are increasingly integrated into virtual worlds and blockchain-based games. Players can own digital land, in-game items, and character assets represented as NFTs. Criminals exploit these systems by purchasing high-value items with illicit funds and later selling them to unsuspecting players, effectively converting tainted cryptocurrency into clean proceeds.

Virtual worlds also enable peer-to-peer transfers of NFTs without oversight. Criminals may move assets through multiple avatars or accounts, creating a complex network of transactions that resemble genuine gameplay. Because these environments often lack strong AML controls, they present high-risk channels for laundering and value transfer.

Red Flags and Detection Challenges

Identifying NFT-based financial crime requires a deep understanding of wallet behavior, marketplace activity, and blockchain patterns. Several indicators can signal suspicious activity. These include significant price jumps without market justification, repeated sales of the same NFT between linked wallets, rapid transfers of NFTs following high-value purchases, and sudden spikes in trading activity centered on a single collection.

Marketplaces must also pay close attention to users who transact at volumes inconsistent with their profiles, frequently buy NFTs with minimal artistic or commercial value, or attempt to move funds immediately following suspicious purchases. While blockchain transparency provides valuable data, the pseudonymous nature of wallets complicates attribution unless investigators use advanced analytics or obtain information through regulatory processes.

Compliance and Market Responsibilities

As NFTs continue to grow in popularity, regulatory expectations are increasing. Marketplaces must adopt risk-based approaches that include customer due diligence, transaction monitoring, and reporting mechanisms. Failure to implement these controls leaves platforms vulnerable to exploitation and regulatory intervention.

REGULATORY BLIND SPOTS AND FORENSIC TOOLS

Cryptocurrency and digital asset markets evolve faster than most regulatory frameworks can adapt. This rapid development creates blind spots that criminals exploit, from unregistered exchanges and decentralized platforms to anonymity-enhancing tools and cross-border loopholes. To counter these risks, investigators and compliance teams rely on increasingly sophisticated forensic tools that analyze blockchain activity and reveal hidden patterns. Understanding the gaps and the available technological solutions is essential for building an effective response to financial crime in the digital asset sector.

Gaps in Global Regulatory Coverage

One of the most significant blind spots arises from inconsistent regulation across jurisdictions. Some countries have adopted strict licensing requirements for digital asset service providers, while others permit exchanges to operate with minimal oversight. Criminals exploit these disparities by routing funds through regions where AML controls are weak, reporting requirements are limited, or enforcement resources are insufficient.

Another gap stems from the decentralized nature of many services. DeFi protocols, decentralized exchanges, autonomous mixers, and on-chain lending platforms often operate without a legal entity responsible for compliance. Because these systems run on code rather than through a centralized organization, regulators struggle to apply traditional requirements such as KYC, reporting rules, or internal controls. This creates environments where large sums of money can move without any human-driven oversight.

Peer-to-peer trading represents another blind spot. P2P platforms allow direct transfers between buyers and sellers, often using informal payment methods. Some platforms advertise themselves as “no KYC” services, attracting users seeking anonymity. These unregulated markets can handle significant volumes and frequently serve as entry points for illicit funds. Regulatory frameworks that focus solely on centralized entities overlook these informal channels.

Privacy-focused cryptocurrencies also challenge oversight. Coins with built-in privacy features offer limited transaction visibility by design, reducing the effectiveness of blockchain analysis. While these assets represent only a portion of the market, their ability to conceal balances and transaction flows makes them appealing to illicit actors who wish to bypass transparency requirements.

Challenges of Attribution and Identity

Even when blockchain data is fully visible, the pseudonymity of digital wallets remains a major regulatory challenge. Wallet addresses do not inherently reveal the identity of the owner. When criminals use multiple wallets, false identities, or stolen credentials, linking transactions to a specific individual becomes extremely difficult. Mixers, obfuscation tools, and rapid cross-chain swaps further complicate attribution.

Regulators increasingly expect exchanges and other service providers to collect and verify customer information. However, gaps remain when users transact entirely on-chain or through services that do not require identity verification. This lack of clear ownership records limits the ability of authorities to identify beneficial owners and track cross-border financial flows.

Forensic Tools and Blockchain Analytics

Despite these challenges, blockchain's transparency provides powerful opportunities for forensic analysis. Specialized analytics platforms have emerged that trace flows of funds, cluster related wallet addresses, identify patterns associated with illicit activity, and monitor transactions in real time. These tools help investigators map out complex laundering schemes that attempt to mask movement across multiple wallets or chains.

Forensic tools use a combination of transaction graph analysis, behavioral heuristics, and machine-learning models to identify relationships between wallets. For example, analysts can detect when multiple wallets belong to the same user by observing withdrawal patterns, transaction timing, or shared network characteristics. Even when funds pass through mixers or privacy-enhancing tools, forensic methods can identify entry and exit points, providing investigators with key leads.

Real-time monitoring tools alert compliance teams to suspicious transactions by comparing wallet activity to known typologies. These signals include sudden spikes in transaction volume, repeated interactions with high-risk services, or transfers involving wallets associated with prior criminal activity. Exchanges use this information to block or freeze transactions, conduct enhanced due diligence, and report suspicious activity to authorities.

Cross-Chain and Multi-Asset Forensics

One of the most important advancements in blockchain forensics involves tracking funds across multiple blockchains. Criminals often move assets between chains to reduce traceability. Modern forensic platforms now integrate data from various networks - Bitcoin, Ethereum, stablecoins, privacy coins, and other digital assets - to construct a unified view of laundering pathways.

Cross-chain analysis reveals when assets are swapped through decentralized bridges, converted into different tokens, or passed through smart contracts designed to obscure origin. Investigators can identify patterns such as rapid asset transformation, repeated use of the same bridges, or transfers between wallets that regularly engage in obfuscation behavior.

Stablecoins have become a favored asset in laundering chains because they are pegged to fiat values and supported widely across exchanges. Forensic tools track stablecoins closely, focusing on accounts that rapidly move funds through multiple chains without an economic rationale.

Data Sharing and International Cooperation

Given the global nature of digital assets, no single regulator or institution can mitigate risks alone. Effective oversight requires cooperation between exchanges, law enforcement agencies, financial intelligence units, and blockchain analytics firms. Shared databases of high-risk wallets, cross-border information exchange, and coordinated investigations have become standard components of modern AML efforts in the digital asset space.

Industry alliances and working groups contribute to the development of best practices and improve visibility into emerging threats. Some jurisdictions also require exchanges to implement the "travel rule," mandating that sender and receiver information accompany cross-platform transfers. While not universally adopted, this requirement enhances transparency and strengthens attribution.

Adapting to Rapid Technological Change

The pace of innovation in digital assets demands that regulators continuously update their frameworks. New asset types, evolving smart contract designs, and emerging financial products require fresh approaches to oversight. Regulatory strategies must balance risk mitigation with support for legitimate innovation, ensuring that financial crime controls evolve alongside market developments.

Forensic capabilities must also expand. As criminals adopt more sophisticated methods, analytics tools must analyze larger datasets, detect new typologies, and integrate advanced technology such as artificial intelligence. A proactive approach - supported by strong governance and cross-sector collaboration - is essential to ensure that regulators, investigators, and compliance teams remain effective in an increasingly complex digital landscape.

CHAPTER 21

NON-FINANCIAL BUSINESSES AND PROFESSIONS (DNFBPS)

GATEKEEPER RISKS: LAWYERS, ACCOUNTANTS, TCSPS

Designated Non-Financial Businesses and Professions (DNFBPs) play a crucial role in the global financial system because they sit close to the creation, management, and movement of wealth. Lawyers, accountants, and trust and company service providers (TCSPs) act as intermediaries between clients and financial institutions, helping structure transactions, establish legal entities, resolve tax matters, and conduct mergers or asset transfers. While most professionals operate with integrity, their legitimate functions can be misused by criminals seeking to obscure ownership, disguise illicit sources of funds, or create complex structures that impede detection. This intersection between professional expertise and financial activity creates significant gatekeeper risks.

Why Professional Gatekeepers are Targeted

Criminals target gatekeepers because of the specialized knowledge these professionals possess. Lawyers understand legal frameworks, corporate formation rules, contractual structures, and litigation strategies. Accountants can manage financial statements, tax filings, and asset valuations. TCSPs can set up companies, trusts, foundations, partnerships, and nominee arrangements in jurisdictions around the world. These capabilities allow gatekeepers to design structures that appear legitimate, comply superficially with regulatory requirements, and create distance between the criminal and the money.

Gatekeepers also provide credibility. When a respected professional handles a transaction or vouches for a client's arrangements, banks and counterparties may be less inclined to question unusual features. Criminals rely on this credibility to minimize scrutiny, especially when dealing with cross-border transactions or complex legal entities. This is why professional enablers often appear in major corruption, fraud, and laundering cases - they act as the bridge between illicit money and the regulated financial sector.

Another factor is confidentiality. Professional-client privilege protects certain communications, particularly for lawyers. While this privilege does not extend to knowingly facilitating crime, it provides a layer of privacy that criminals may try to exploit. Additionally, many professional services involve legitimate confidentiality, making it harder for authorities to detect misuse until damage has already been done.

Lawyers and Legal-Structure Risks

Lawyers can inadvertently or deliberately facilitate laundering through various services. Some of the highest-risk activities include establishing companies or trusts, holding client funds in escrow accounts, engaging in property transactions, or drafting complex contractual arrangements that obscure true ownership.

Client accounts are particularly vulnerable because criminals can transfer funds into or through a lawyer's trust account, making the movement appear legitimate. These accounts are designed to hold funds temporarily for legal purposes, but they may also be used to layer illicit proceeds. In property transactions, lawyers may facilitate purchases on behalf of clients without fully verifying source of funds, enabling criminals to embed illicit money into real estate markets.

Legal professionals may also create shell companies, draft nominee agreements, or design multi-jurisdictional corporate structures that shield beneficial owners. When these services are provided without adequate due diligence, they create significant blind spots for financial institutions and regulators.

Accountants and Financial Manipulation Risks

Accountants play a central role in verifying financial information, preparing statements, and ensuring compliance with tax obligations. Criminals seek their support to manipulate financial records, disguise fraudulent revenue, or justify unexplained wealth.

In some schemes, accountants prepare misleading financial statements that present illicit proceeds as legitimate business earnings. These statements support loan applications, investment activity, tax filings, or cross-border transfers. Criminals may also use accountants to establish and manage companies that serve as vehicles for laundering, filing tax returns that show fabricated income streams.

Tax advisory services present additional risks. Accountants may assist clients in moving funds offshore, structuring assets to avoid detection, or exploiting treaty arrangements to minimize disclosure. While tax planning is legitimate, the boundary between lawful tax minimization and illicit concealment can be exploited easily when professionals do not apply strong ethical standards.

TCSPs and Ownership Obscuration

TCSPs create and administer legal structures such as corporations, partnerships, trusts, and foundations. Their services are frequently used in cross-border transactions and asset protection arrangements. Criminals exploit these capabilities to hide beneficial ownership, move illicit funds into opaque vehicles, or build structures that mask the origin of assets.

TCSPs often operate in jurisdictions with favorable corporate secrecy laws. They may set up companies with minimal information requirements, appoint nominee directors, or manage accounts on behalf of absentee owners. When combined with offshore jurisdictions, these services create multiple layers of anonymity that hinder investigations.

In some cases, TCSPs not only establish entities but also control their operation, manage bank account access, and facilitate transfers. This level of involvement can make them central figures in laundering schemes, whether knowingly or through negligence.

Vulnerabilities Arising from Professional Autonomy

Gatekeepers often operate in highly autonomous environments. Professional judgment determines how much due diligence is applied, how clients are screened, and how unusual activity is assessed. When professionals prioritize client relationships, profit motives, or competitive pressures over compliance, the risk of facilitating illicit finance increases.

Regulation of DNFBPs varies significantly across jurisdictions. In some countries, lawyers and accountants are subject to strong AML requirements; in others, their obligations are limited or poorly enforced. These inconsistencies allow criminals to seek out professionals in lenient jurisdictions and use them as entry points into the global financial system.

Mitigating Gatekeeper Risks

Effective mitigation requires strong internal controls, ethical standards, and a culture of accountability within professional firms. Professionals must conduct thorough client due diligence, verify beneficial ownership, and understand the economic purpose of the services they provide. Suspicious activity reporting should be applied consistently, even when the client relationship is long-standing.

STRUCTURING ILLICIT DEALS AND LAUNDERING MECHANISMS

Professionals within the DNFBP sector are often involved in the structuring of complex transactions. While most of this work is legitimate, the same tools used to facilitate lawful business can be exploited to conceal illicit assets or disguise criminal proceeds. Lawyers, accountants, and TCSPs are well positioned to design multilayered arrangements that can obscure beneficial ownership, move funds across borders, and create structures that make tracing difficult for authorities. Understanding these mechanisms is essential for identifying how illicit deals are engineered and where vulnerabilities lie.

Use of Legal Entities to Conceal Ownership

One of the most common mechanisms involves the creation of layered corporate structures. Criminals often request multiple companies in different jurisdictions, each holding shares in another entity. These entities may include international business companies, limited partnerships, foundations, or special purpose vehicles. When combined, they create distance between the beneficial owner and the assets.

TCSPs frequently assist in forming these entities and appointing nominee directors or shareholders. Nominees act as front figures, allowing criminals to avoid public association with the company. While nominee services can be legitimate, misuse occurs when professionals fail to determine the true controlling party. When these entities interact with financial institutions, the absence of clear ownership records becomes a significant vulnerability.

Trusts are another vehicle commonly used to hide beneficial ownership. Criminals may establish discretionary trusts in secrecy jurisdictions, appoint a professional trustee, and then transfer assets into the structure. Because trusts separate legal ownership from beneficial enjoyment, tracing asset control becomes difficult. Some professionals further obscure this by establishing a series of trusts in different jurisdictions with interconnected beneficiaries, making it nearly impossible to determine who ultimately exercises control.

Complex Contractual Arrangements

Illicit deals often rely on carefully crafted contracts that create the appearance of legitimate business transactions. Lawyers may draft consulting agreements, service contracts, licensing arrangements, or loan documents that mask the true purpose of a payment. Criminals may use these contracts to justify large transfers from one entity to another, even when no real service is provided.

For example, a company controlled by a criminal group may issue a contract for "strategic advisory services" to an offshore entity. Funds are transferred under the contract, appearing legitimate, but in reality they represent proceeds of corruption or fraud being moved through corporate accounts. Without rigorous review, banks may accept these transactions because they are supported by professional documentation.

False invoicing is a recurrent theme across laundering schemes. Accountants may assist in preparing invoices that inflate the cost of goods or services, enabling criminals to justify large payments. These invoices are then matched with financial statements, creating a consistent but fraudulent narrative. When used across multiple jurisdictions, false invoicing becomes a sophisticated method of moving funds disguised as business expenses.

Real Estate as a Laundering Mechanism

Real estate is a favored asset class for laundering due to its stability, perceived legitimacy, and potential for appreciation. Professionals help structure transactions through escrow arrangements, layered ownership, or corporate acquisitions that hide the true purchaser.

In many schemes, criminals establish an offshore company and use it to purchase property. The company's director may be a nominee or a professional intermediary, obscuring the true owner. Accountants may prepare financial records showing legitimate income sources, allowing the property purchase to appear lawful. Lawyers may facilitate the transaction through client trust accounts, which can act as temporary holding vehicles.

Structuring also involves property flipping. A criminal may purchase real estate through one entity and then sell it to another entity they control at an inflated price. The artificial profit created by the resale gives the impression of legitimate capital gains. Professionals involved in drafting agreements or managing corporate structures may inadvertently facilitate these moves if they fail to question unusual aspects of the transaction.

Use of Intermediaries and Third Parties

Criminals often engage intermediaries to further distance themselves from illicit funds. These intermediaries may serve as company directors, shareholders, trustees, or authorized signatories. In some cases, they are professionals paid to act as representatives; in others, they are unaware of the criminal nature of the activity.

Intermediaries are also used to open bank accounts, sign contracts, or conduct transactions. When banks review documentation, the involvement of reputable professionals can mask the underlying risks. This is why professional facilitation plays such a prominent role in large-scale financial crime: intermediaries give credibility to structures designed to conceal.

Complex deals often involve multiple intermediaries across different countries. Funds may pass through law firm trust accounts, accounting firms, or company service providers before reaching their final destination. Each step adds a layer of distance and complexity, complicating investigative efforts.

Manipulation of Lending and Investment Structures

Criminals exploit lending mechanisms by creating loan agreements between related entities. A criminal-owned offshore company may "lend" money to a domestic entity, allowing illicit funds to enter the formal financial system as loan proceeds. Repayments from the domestic entity are then routed to accounts controlled by the criminal or reinvested in legitimate businesses.

Criminals may inject illicit funds into venture capital structures, hedge funds, or private trusts. Because these investments appear to involve standard financial instruments, they may draw less scrutiny. Professionals involved in structuring these investments play a key role in facilitating or detecting misuse.

Cross-Border Transactions and Jurisdictional Arbitrage

The global reach of DNFBPs enables criminals to exploit jurisdictional inconsistencies. Lawyers or TCSPs in one jurisdiction may establish entities governed by the laws of another, where corporate transparency is limited. Accountants may assist in routing funds through tax-neutral environments before repatriation. These cross-border strategies are designed to exploit weak regulatory points and create confusion about which jurisdiction holds authority.

REAL-WORLD TYPOLOGIES AND PROFESSIONAL FACILITATION

The involvement of professional intermediaries in financial crime is a recurring theme across major global cases. Lawyers, accountants, and trust and company service providers are often positioned at the center of illicit schemes because they possess the expertise needed to structure transactions, manage corporate entities, and navigate multiple legal systems. While most professionals operate ethically, certain typologies reveal how illicit networks exploit their skills - sometimes knowingly, and sometimes through negligence or inadequate controls. Understanding these real-world patterns is critical to recognizing warning signs and preventing abuse.

Use of Professionals in Large-Scale Corruption Schemes

Corruption cases frequently involve extensive use of professional facilitators to move illicit wealth across jurisdictions. A common pattern involves a public official receiving bribes in exchange for contracts or political influence. The official cannot openly receive the funds, so professionals create entities or trust arrangements to hold the assets discreetly.

In one widely known case, networks of offshore companies were created by advisors to channel funds from state-owned enterprises into accounts controlled by corrupt officials. Lawyers drafted the corporate documents, nominee directors were appointed through TCSPs, and accountants produced financial statements to present the appearance of legitimate business activity. By distributing activities across multiple jurisdictions, the facilitators ensured that no single authority had full visibility of the scheme.

Property purchases are often embedded within these structures. Corrupt officials frequently use professionals to acquire real estate under corporate names, allowing them to enjoy the property without linking it to their identity. Lawyers arrange the transactions, TCSPs serve as shareholders of the purchasing entity, and accountants provide supporting financial records. Without strong controls, these arrangements can go unnoticed for years.

Trade-Based Laundering and False Invoicing

Trade-based money laundering often requires professional assistance to execute at scale. Criminals manipulate invoices, shipping documentation, and accounting records to disguise illicit transfers as legitimate trade flows. Accountants play a central role in preparing financial statements that support falsified invoices or inflated shipping costs.

In one typology, a criminal network establishes a series of import-export companies. Professionals then prepare documentation showing artificially inflated values for goods. Banks and customs officials see plausible documentation, while the inflated invoices justify the movement of significant funds across borders. Lawyers may draft the commercial agreements used to justify the trade activity, and TCSPs may set up the companies involved, allowing the scheme to persist with minimal scrutiny.

Another variation involves under-invoicing, where goods are declared below value so that criminals can shift funds through separate channels. Professionals maintain the corporate records, manage accounts, and maintain the appearance of compliance, even when trade volumes significantly exceed the company's legitimate capacity.

Professional Facilitation in Tax Evasion Schemes

Professionals are frequently involved in facilitating tax evasion through complex offshore arrangements. These schemes often rely on multi-layered corporate structures, trusts, or foundations located in secrecy jurisdictions. Lawyers may propose asset-protection structures that also serve to conceal wealth. Accountants prepare financial statements that show minimal taxable income, and TCSPs administer entities with little understanding of the true beneficial owner.

In some cases, high-net-worth individuals rely on professionals to establish residency in favorable tax jurisdictions while maintaining substantial activity elsewhere. Advisors draft contracts, restructure ownership, and manage the client's affairs through proxy entities. While some practices are legitimate tax planning, others cross the line into concealing assets and avoiding disclosure requirements.

Prominent global leaks - such as the Panama Papers and similar disclosures - demonstrate how extensive networks of professionals can be involved in creating shell companies, opening accounts, and moving funds for clients whose wealth has unclear origins.

Use of Trust Accounts and Escrow Facilities

Professional trust accounts are frequently abused because they offer a temporary holding place for funds that appear to be associated with legitimate legal transactions. Criminals may deposit illicit money into a lawyer's trust account under the pretext of a property deal or business transaction. Once inside the account, the funds gain legitimacy due to the professional's involvement.

Professionals who do not monitor their trust accounts carefully may unknowingly facilitate layering. Funds may move through several trust accounts before being released to a final destination, creating the appearance of lawful transfers. This typology highlights the importance of strict oversight of client accounts and strong internal controls within professional firms.

Facilitation of Corporate Hijacking and Fraud

In certain fraud schemes, professionals help criminals establish entities used to deceive investors or creditors. For example, a fraudster may hire a reputable accounting firm to prepare financial statements for a newly formed company. The statements inflate revenue or misrepresent assets to attract investment. Lawyers may create the corporate structure, open bank accounts, and draft shareholder agreements. TCSPs may provide nominee directors to give the appearance of legitimacy.

When these companies collapse - often after substantial investor losses - investigators discover that professionals played a role in enabling the scheme, whether knowingly or through insufficient due diligence.

Coordinated Laundering Through Networks of Professionals

Some sophisticated criminal groups operate across multiple countries and rely on dozens of professionals at once. One law firm may set up corporate structures, an accounting firm may manage books, and a TCSP may administer trusts and nominee arrangements. Funds move across several layers of entities, each supported by credible documentation prepared by professionals.

These networks create barriers for investigators. Documents appear legitimate, transactions are structured to comply with minimal local requirements, and professionals often operate under strict confidentiality norms. Only when authorities obtain access to multiple jurisdictions does the full pattern emerge.

Importance of Professional Integrity

Professional facilitation is not inevitable. Most issues arise when professionals lack adequate due diligence processes, rely too heavily on client representations, or prioritize commercial interests over ethical obligations. Strong internal controls, compliance training, and clear escalation procedures significantly reduce the likelihood of involvement in illicit activity.

REGULATORY EXPECTATIONS AND CONTROL ENHANCEMENTS

Regulators increasingly recognize that the financial system's integrity depends not only on traditional financial institutions but also on designated non-financial businesses and professions. Lawyers, accountants, and trust and company service providers occupy critical positions in transactions that shape global commerce. Because these professionals can either strengthen or weaken safeguards against illicit finance, regulators have developed expectations and control requirements designed to address the risks inherent in their work. Effective compliance frameworks protect both the profession and the wider economy.

Expanding Regulatory Responsibility for DNFBPs

Many jurisdictions now require DNFBPs to implement AML programs similar to those used by banks. These obligations typically include customer due diligence, beneficial ownership verification, record-keeping, ongoing monitoring, and suspicious transaction reporting. Regulators expect professionals to apply these measures even when services are advisory or administrative rather than transactional.

A central regulatory expectation is risk-based due diligence. Professionals must understand the nature of the services they provide, the risks those services carry, and the profile of their clients. This assessment must guide the depth of checks performed. High-risk services - such as incorporation in secrecy jurisdictions, trust formation, or cross-border transactions - require enhanced due diligence and ongoing monitoring.

Regulators also emphasize the importance of identifying politically exposed persons (PEPs) and high-risk public officials. DNFBPs must screen clients and beneficial owners, evaluate potential corruption exposure, and implement controls to prevent misuse of professional services by individuals seeking to conceal illicit wealth. These expectations are aligned with broader global efforts to combat corruption and financial crime.

Beneficial Ownership Transparency

One of the most significant areas of regulatory focus is beneficial ownership. Regulators expect DNFBPs to identify the real individuals who ultimately control companies, trusts, foundations, or other legal structures. This includes identifying persons behind nominee arrangements, offshore entities, and layered corporate structures.

Jurisdictions are increasingly establishing beneficial ownership registries. Professionals responsible for company formation or administration must collect accurate information and submit it to these registries. Regulators expect DNFBPs to maintain updated records and challenge clients when ownership information appears inconsistent, incomplete, or intentionally opaque.

Beneficial ownership transparency reduces the opportunity for criminals to hide behind front companies or complex structures. Regulators view DNFBPs as essential participants in ensuring this transparency is achieved and maintained.

Monitoring Professional Trust Accounts

Because trust and client accounts can be misused to layer illicit funds, regulators expect strong internal controls and oversight of these accounts. Professionals must ensure that funds held in trust correspond to legitimate legal or business activities. Clear audit trails, reconciliation procedures, and segregation of client funds are mandatory features of compliant trust account management.

Regulators also expect professionals to identify unusual patterns within trust accounts. Large cash deposits, frequent transfers from unrelated third parties, or funds that do not align with the stated purpose of the transaction must be investigated. When suspicious activity is identified, professionals are obligated to file reports with the appropriate financial intelligence unit.

Suspicious Transaction Reporting Obligations

Suspicious transaction reporting is a central expectation for DNFBPs. Professionals must recognize indicators of illicit behavior and escalate concerns promptly. Examples include clients who avoid providing information, insist on unnecessary secrecy, request complex structures without a legitimate rationale, or exhibit behavior that suggests attempts to disguise beneficial ownership or source of funds.

Regulators expect reporting obligations to be applied consistently and without regard to client relationship pressures. Even long-standing clients must be subject to scrutiny when their actions deviate from established patterns. Failure to report suspicious activity can result in severe regulatory consequences for both the individual and the firm.

Internal Governance and Compliance Culture

Regulators stress the importance of strong internal governance. Firms must designate compliance officers, establish internal reporting lines, develop written AML policies, and ensure staff are trained to recognize risks. Compliance must be integrated into the firm's culture rather than treated as a procedural obligation.

Training is a key expectation. Staff must understand AML regulations, ethical requirements, red flags associated with professional services, and the importance of documenting decisions. Regulators expect firms to provide refresher training and ensure staff understand emerging trends and typologies.

Regulatory inspections often focus on whether firms can demonstrate that their controls operate effectively. This includes reviewing client files, monitoring documentation, and evaluating whether firms take corrective action when deficiencies are identified. Strong documentation is essential for demonstrating compliance during inspections.

Cross-Border Cooperation and International Standards

Because DNFBPs frequently operate in multiple jurisdictions, regulators emphasize alignment with international standards, particularly those established by the Financial Action Task Force (FATF). Professionals must understand cross-border risks, including differing corporate transparency rules, inconsistent beneficial ownership regulations, and varying levels of enforcement across jurisdictions.

Regulators expect DNFBPs to apply enhanced scrutiny when clients or services involve high-risk jurisdictions. This includes assessing the legitimacy of offshore companies, the purpose of cross-border transfers, and the source of funds from foreign clients. International cooperation is essential, as information-sharing mechanisms between authorities help identify misuse of professional services.

Strengthening Controls Through Technology

Regulators increasingly encourage DNFBPs to adopt technology that enhances risk detection. Tools that conduct automated screening, monitor transactions, and verify beneficial ownership can strengthen compliance frameworks. Electronic document verification, digital KYC systems, and analytics platforms help professionals identify inconsistencies, perform faster risk assessments, and maintain audit trails.

Technology, however, is not a substitute for professional judgment. Regulators expect firms to combine automated tools with human oversight. Effective controls require both accurate data and informed analysis.

Building a Strong Professional Defense Against Abuse

Ultimately, regulators expect DNFBPs to act not only as service providers but as gatekeepers who protect the financial system from abuse. Firms must demonstrate ethical responsibility, apply controls rigorously, and challenge clients when necessary. By strengthening governance, improving transparency, and enhancing professional accountability, DNFBPs can significantly reduce opportunities for illicit finance.

CHAPTER 22

CHARITIES AND NON-PROFITS

MISUSE FOR TERRORIST FINANCING AND DIVERSION SCHEMES

Charities and non-profit organizations (NPOs) play an essential role in humanitarian relief, social development, education, health programs, and community support. Their presence in high-risk regions and conflict zones often places them on the front lines of crises where government institutions have limited reach. Unfortunately, these same characteristics make NPOs vulnerable to exploitation by terrorist organizations seeking to divert funds, conceal financial flows, and present a façade of legitimacy. The misuse of charitable platforms for terrorist financing poses a significant threat to both global security and the credibility of the non-profit sector.

Why Charities are Targeted by Terrorist Networks

Terrorist organizations often face barriers when attempting to move money through formal financial institutions. Charities, however, operate on a model of trust, public goodwill, and humanitarian mandate. This allows them to receive donations, deploy funds internationally, and operate in environments where oversight is difficult. Terrorist groups exploit these conditions to raise, store, and channel money under the cover of legitimate charitable activity.

In many cases, the public perception of charities as benevolent entities reduces scrutiny from donors and, at times, regulators. Terrorist networks use this trust to mask fundraising efforts, portraying financial requests as urgent humanitarian appeals or religious obligations. Funds are then diverted to support recruitment, training, propaganda, or armed operations.

In conflict regions, charities may also be the only actors able to move supplies across borders or into controlled territories. Terrorist groups exploit this operational necessity by imposing "taxes," demanding bribes, or coercing organizations into handing over a portion of their funds or resources.

Diversion through Front Organizations

One of the most common typologies involves the creation or infiltration of front charities. A terrorist organization may establish a charity that appears to conduct legitimate work but uses donations for operational purposes. These front entities often register with minimal oversight, use emotionally compelling narratives to attract donors, and distribute limited aid to maintain credibility. The bulk of funds, however, are diverted.

In other cases, legitimate charities may be infiltrated by individuals sympathetic to extremist causes. These insiders can manipulate procurement, accounting, and program delivery to divert a portion of funds. Diversion may occur through inflated invoices, fraudulent supplier arrangements, or "ghost beneficiaries" who do not exist. Because donors and oversight bodies rely heavily on self-reporting, discrepancies may remain hidden without external audits.

Terrorist groups may also use charities as conduits to transfer funds across borders. Donations are collected in one jurisdiction, transferred to a partner organization abroad, and then partially or fully diverted. The cross-border nature of these transfers increases complexity for investigators and exposes gaps in regulatory coordination.

Misuse of Cash-Based Operations

Many charities operate in regions where banking systems are underdeveloped or inaccessible due to conflict. As a result, they rely heavily on cash to distribute salaries, purchase supplies, or deliver humanitarian aid. Cash-based operations are inherently vulnerable because they lack the traceability and auditability of digital transactions.

Terrorist networks exploit this by intercepting cash shipments, imposing control over distribution points, or infiltrating local staff responsible for managing cash. In some cases, armed groups force charities to pay "access fees" or protection payments to operate in contested areas. These funds are then used to finance extremist activities.

Cash couriers may also be used to transport funds under the pretext of aid delivery. A courier may claim to be transporting emergency relief money, but a portion of those funds is intentionally set aside for terrorist operations. Without strict monitoring and reconciliation procedures, such schemes can continue undetected.

Abuse of Remittance Channels and Informal Systems

Some charities rely on informal value transfer systems, especially in regions lacking reliable banking infrastructure. Systems such as hawala can be used legitimately, but they also enable anonymous transfers. Terrorist groups exploit informal channels to move funds that have been raised under charitable pretenses. By disguising transfers as humanitarian payments, they obscure the origin and destination of funds.

Additionally, some charities unintentionally finance terrorism through relationships with local implementing partners. These partners may operate in remote or high-risk areas where direct oversight is difficult. If the partner organization has ties to extremist groups, funds intended for aid programs can be diverted for illicit purposes.

Fundraising Through Religious and Community Networks

Religious donations, community fundraising drives, and humanitarian campaigns can be exploited for terrorist financing. Extremist groups often use social, cultural, or religious networks to solicit donations that appear to support legitimate causes. The emotional appeal of charitable giving can mask illicit intentions, especially when fundraisers use language that resonates with sympathetic communities.

In some cases, extremist narratives are embedded within charitable appeals. Funds collected during religious gatherings, holiday events, or community initiatives may be partially redirected to support extremist operations. This misuse damages community trust and places legitimate religious institutions at risk of reputational harm.

Indicators of Terrorist Abuse in the NPO Sector

Several behavioral patterns may indicate misuse of charitable platforms. These include organizations with limited track records receiving unusually large donations, vague or unverifiable program descriptions, inconsistent financial reporting, or high volumes of cash withdrawals. Sudden changes in leadership, unverified implementing partners, and activities in high-risk regions without adequate risk mitigation frameworks also warrant scrutiny.

Additionally, charities that conduct minimal on-the-ground operations despite significant fundraising activity present clear red flags. Transactions involving regions under terrorist control, unusual procurement patterns, or repeated use of intermediaries with unclear credentials should prompt further review.

Protecting the Sector from Abuse

Charities can mitigate risks by implementing strong governance structures, conducting due diligence on donors and partners, and maintaining transparent financial records. Independent audits, board oversight, and strict controls on cash distribution strengthen integrity. International coordination between regulators, financial institutions, and humanitarian organizations further reduces opportunities for extremist groups to infiltrate the sector.

RISKS IN HUMANITARIAN AND RELIGIOUS ORGANIZATIONS

Humanitarian and religious organizations play a vital role in providing aid, social support, education, and community services. Because they often operate in vulnerable regions and maintain deep ties with local populations, they serve as essential lifelines during crises. However, these same strengths expose them to significant financial crime risks. Their presence in high-risk areas, reliance on decentralized networks, and sometimes limited internal oversight make them susceptible to exploitation by criminal groups, corrupt actors, and extremist organizations. Understanding these risks is crucial for safeguarding the integrity of the charitable sector.

Operational Environments with Elevated Risk

Humanitarian organizations frequently work in conflict zones, disaster-stricken locations, or areas with weak government institutions. In such environments, formal banking systems may be unreliable or inaccessible. Organizations often rely on cash distribution, informal money transfer channels, or local intermediaries to carry out their operations. These conditions create significant vulnerabilities.

Armed groups or criminal networks may exert control over certain regions, forcing aid organizations to negotiate access. These interactions expose charities to extortion, forced payments, or diversion of supplies. In some cases, aid deliveries must pass through multiple checkpoints where local authorities or armed factions impose informal taxes or seize goods. While the priority is to deliver aid, the obligation to maintain neutrality often conflicts with the risk of inadvertently supporting illicit actors.

Additionally, limited infrastructure in remote areas can make oversight difficult. Field teams may operate with minimal supervision, allowing opportunities for internal fraud or misappropriation. Weak documentation, inconsistent reporting, and reliance on manual processes further complicate accountability.

Risks Unique to Religious Organizations

Religious organizations hold a position of trust within communities, which makes them effective channels for charitable giving. Their deep social networks, international reach, and established community relationships contribute to strong fundraising capabilities. However, these features can also be exploited by actors seeking to mask illicit financial activity.

Religious donations, including tithes, zakat, offerings, or communal charity, often involve significant cash flows. Cash-based giving is inherently difficult to trace, and in many faith communities, giving anonymously is culturally accepted. This creates an environment where illicit funds can be introduced without scrutiny.

Some religious institutions operate across borders, supporting missions, educational programs, and humanitarian campaigns. When funds move through informal networks or across multiple countries, gaps in oversight can emerge. Individuals within these networks may exploit these gaps to divert funds or support extremist causes. While the majority of religious organizations operate with integrity, a small number may be influenced or infiltrated by individuals promoting extremist agendas.

Mismanagement and Internal Governance Issues

Many humanitarian and religious organizations face internal governance challenges that increase exposure to financial crime. Smaller organizations may lack formal compliance functions, audit capabilities, or standardized financial controls. Inadequate segregation of duties, insufficient board oversight, and a lack of documented procedures can enable misuse of funds by insiders.

Mismanagement does not always involve malicious intent; it can stem from limited resources or insufficient training.

However, weak governance creates openings that illicit actors can exploit. Fraud schemes involving fictitious beneficiaries, inflated expenses, false reporting, or ghost employees often arise in environments where oversight is minimal.

In religious institutions, leadership structures may be informal or hierarchical, with decision-making concentrated among a few individuals. This centralization can make it difficult to challenge suspicious activity or detect misappropriation. When internal controls rely heavily on trust rather than documented processes, vulnerabilities become more pronounced.

Risks Linked to Local Partners and Implementing Agencies

Humanitarian operations frequently require collaboration with local partners, field agents, or subcontractors. These partnerships are essential for reaching remote areas, navigating cultural dynamics, and delivering aid efficiently. However, local partners may lack strong governance frameworks or may have undisclosed affiliations with political, criminal, or extremist groups.

Diversion can occur through manipulated procurement processes, favoritism toward certain suppliers, or inflated pricing. Equipment and supplies intended for beneficiaries may be siphoned off by corrupt partners, reducing the impact of aid programs. In regions with active conflict, local partners may be coerced to relinquish part of their resources to armed groups in exchange for safe passage.

Verification of beneficiaries also presents challenges. In some contexts, lists of recipients are created locally with little independent validation. Criminal groups may infiltrate these processes, adding fictitious names or prioritizing supporters, thereby diverting aid while maintaining the appearance of legitimate distribution.

Cross-Border Funding and Global Networks

Both humanitarian and religious organizations receive funding from international donors. These cross-border flows can introduce additional complexity, especially when funds pass through multiple financial institutions or jurisdictions before reaching their intended destination. Donor organizations typically expect rapid deployment of funds, which may lead to reduced scrutiny or reliance on expedited procedures.

Some religious organizations maintain global networks that collect donations in one country and distribute them abroad. These networks sometimes rely on informal transfer mechanisms, especially when operating in high-risk regions. While often used for legitimate purposes, informal systems can conceal the movement of funds, complicating audit trails and increasing exposure to misuse.

Humanitarian organizations also face pressure to deploy aid quickly, especially during emergencies. Rapid disbursement can lead to relaxed controls, increased cash usage, and reduced verification—all of which raise the risk of diversion.

Balancing Aid Delivery with Risk Management

Humanitarian and religious organizations often face a difficult balance: delivering life-saving aid while implementing strong financial controls. Excessive regulation or intrusive oversight can hinder operations, especially in volatile environments. Conversely, weak controls expose organizations to financial crime, reputational damage, and potential sanctions.

To manage these tensions, organizations must adopt risk-based approaches that consider the specific environments in which they operate. This includes training field staff, strengthening partner vetting, improving financial documentation, and employing technology where feasible. Effective communication between headquarters and field teams is essential for maintaining oversight without obstructing aid delivery.

GOVERNANCE FAILURES AND EXPLOITABLE WEAKNESSES

Charities and non-profit organizations depend heavily on public trust. Their ability to raise funds, operate in sensitive environments, and deliver critical services relies on confidence that resources are managed responsibly and ethically. When governance structures are weak, gaps emerge that allow financial crime, corruption, and diversion of funds to occur. These weaknesses not only compromise organizational integrity but also threaten the safety of beneficiaries and undermine public confidence in the entire sector. Understanding governance failures is essential to preventing abuse and strengthening the resilience of non-profits.

Insufficient Board Oversight and Strategic Direction

A strong, independent board is one of the most important safeguards within a charity. Boards provide strategic oversight, set ethical standards, and ensure accountability. However, many organizations suffer from boards that are either too passive or overly dependent on executive leadership. When board members lack expertise, fail to challenge management decisions, or have limited involvement in financial oversight, the organization becomes vulnerable.

In smaller charities, the board may consist of volunteers with limited time or formal training in governance. This can result in weak scrutiny of budgets, insufficient review of risk assessments, or lack of attention to internal audit findings. In some cases, board members may defer entirely to the founder or CEO, creating an unhealthy concentration of authority. Without balanced governance, questionable financial decisions or inappropriate relationships with donors and suppliers may go unchallenged.

Concentration of Power in Senior Leadership

Governance failures often arise when too much control rests with a single individual or a small leadership group. Some organizations are built around charismatic founders who have significant influence over fundraising, programming, and financial management. While founder-led models can drive innovation, they become risky when checks and balances are absent.

Concentrated power can result in unilateral decision-making, inadequate financial controls, and the ability to override established procedures. Executives may authorize payments without proper documentation, select vendors without competitive bidding, or approve partnerships lacking due diligence. When staff fear challenging leadership or reporting concerns, governance failures escalate.

In some cases, senior leaders may have personal or political affiliations that create conflicts of interest. Without clear policies to address such conflicts, decision-making may be compromised, leading to favoritism, misuse of funds, or alignment with high-risk networks.

Weak Internal Controls and Financial Management

Robust financial controls are essential for preventing misuse of funds. Many governance failures stem from inadequate internal controls, poorly maintained records, or insufficient segregation of financial duties. When the same individual is responsible for approving expenditures, managing bank accounts, and reconciling financial records, opportunities for fraud increase significantly.

Weak controls become especially risky in organizations with high cash usage or decentralized operations. In humanitarian contexts, field offices may manage large cash distributions with limited oversight. Without documented procedures, clear spending limits, or regular reconciliation, field teams may unintentionally or deliberately misuse funds. Fraud schemes may involve fictitious vendors, inflated procurement costs, or reimbursement of expenses that were never incurred.

Limited technological capacity further exacerbates control weaknesses. Organizations relying on manual record-keeping, paper receipts, or informal tracking systems are more likely to face discrepancies that go unnoticed until financial audits reveal significant gaps.

Inadequate Partner Vetting and Oversight

Many charities rely on local implementing partners to deliver programs in regions where they lack direct access. While partnerships can enhance reach and cultural understanding, they introduce substantial governance risk. Weak partner vetting allows organizations with poor governance or illicit affiliations to gain access to donor funds.

Exploitable weaknesses emerge when organizations fail to verify the legitimacy, capacity, or integrity of local partners. Without thorough background checks, operational assessments, or financial vetting, charities may unknowingly fund organizations connected to political groups, criminal networks, or extremist entities. These risks intensify in high-conflict regions where local actors are difficult to monitor.

Once partnerships are established, inadequate oversight - such as infrequent site visits, incomplete financial reviews, or lack of performance monitoring -permits diversion, fraud, or manipulation of beneficiary lists. Some partners may engage in double billing, falsifying documents, or redirecting supplies to unauthorized recipients.

Poor Transparency and Reporting Practices

Transparency is a cornerstone of good governance. When organizations fail to publish accurate financial statements, disclose conflicts of interest, or explain how funds are allocated, they create opportunities for misuse. Donors and regulators rely on transparent reporting to assess performance and detect irregularities. Insufficient reporting conceals weaknesses and makes it easier for illicit actors to operate without scrutiny.

In some organizations, reporting practices are inconsistent across departments or geographic locations. Field offices may submit delayed or incomplete financial records, while headquarters may lack standardized formats for reporting. These inconsistencies create blind spots that can be exploited.

Lack of Risk Management Frameworks

Effective governance requires structured risk management, including identifying risks, assessing likelihood and impact, and developing mitigation strategies. Many charities lack formal risk registers, scenario planning, or crisis management procedures. Without these tools, organizations are ill-equipped to anticipate financial crime risks, especially when expanding into new regions or launching new programs.

Risk management failures often result from limited resources or insufficient expertise. However, the absence of a structured framework leaves organizations dependent on individual judgment rather than systematic controls.

Cultural and Organizational Barriers

Governance weaknesses are sometimes rooted in organizational culture. A culture that prioritizes mission above compliance may inadvertently encourage shortcuts, especially during emergencies. Staff may believe that rigid controls slow down aid delivery, leading them to bypass procedures. While speed is important, neglecting controls invites significant risk.

Additionally, organizations with hierarchical cultures may discourage whistleblowing or open communication. When employees fear retaliation or lack confidence in internal reporting mechanisms, governance failures remain hidden.

MONITORING, TRANSPARENCY, AND COMPLIANCE MEASURES

Strong monitoring frameworks and transparent reporting practices are essential for safeguarding charities and non-profit organizations from financial crime risks. These measures ensure that donor funds are used appropriately, programs achieve their intended impact, and the organization maintains the trust of beneficiaries, regulators, and the public. Effective compliance frameworks do not hinder humanitarian work; rather, they strengthen operational integrity and help organizations function responsibly in complex environments.

Building Robust Monitoring Systems

Monitoring is the backbone of accountability in non-profit operations. A well-structured monitoring system enables organizations to track financial flows, oversee program implementation, and detect anomalies before they escalate into significant issues. For many charities, monitoring must occur at both the headquarters and field levels, requiring coordination across departments and geographic regions.

Operational monitoring involves verifying that activities are carried out as planned and that program objectives align with donor expectations. Financial monitoring focuses on ensuring that expenditures match approved budgets and are supported by documented evidence. In high-risk areas where cash usage is common, organizations must implement controls that reconcile funds quickly and accurately. Field teams should be required to maintain detailed records, including receipts, beneficiary lists, and distribution logs, even when operating under challenging conditions.

Remote monitoring can also play a critical role, especially in conflict zones or inaccessible areas. Tools such as satellite imagery, mobile reporting platforms, and third-party verification can supplement physical oversight. While these methods cannot fully replace on-the-ground checks, they enhance visibility and reduce opportunities for diversion or misreporting.

Importance of Transparent Reporting

Transparency is essential for maintaining public confidence in the non-profit sector. Donors, regulators, and beneficiaries rely on clear reporting to understand how funds are allocated and what results have been achieved. Transparent reporting also deters misuse by signaling that financial activity is subject to scrutiny.

Organizations should publish annual reports, audited financial statements, and clear descriptions of programs and achievements. These documents must be detailed enough to demonstrate accountability but written in a manner that is accessible to the general public. Transparency extends beyond financial statements to include procurement policies, governance practices, conflict-of-interest procedures, and partner selection criteria.

For donors, visibility into administrative costs, project expenditures, and the distribution of resources across programs is critical. When donors see inconsistencies, vague explanations, or significant unexplained variances, trust erodes. Transparent reporting provides assurance that funds are being managed responsibly and that processes support organizational integrity.

Implementing Effective Compliance Frameworks

Compliance frameworks in charities must address the unique challenges faced by the sector. These frameworks should include controls for financial management, partner due diligence, conflict-of-interest management, anti-corruption policies, and anti-money laundering measures. Compliance should be embedded into daily operations rather than treated as an administrative burden.

One key component is clear delineation of roles and responsibilities. Staff involved in procurement, finance, program delivery, and partner coordination must understand their obligations. Segregation of duties is essential to minimize risks. For example, the individual approving expenditures should not be the same person reconciling accounts or managing procurement processes.

Another important component is consistent screening. Charities must screen donors, partners, suppliers, and staff against sanctions lists, terrorism databases, and high-risk indicators. This screening helps prevent resources from flowing to illicit actors, especially in regions where extremist groups exert influence. Screening systems should be updated regularly and integrated into onboarding processes for all relevant parties.

Anti-fraud policies also play a critical role. Staff should be trained to recognize signs of fraud, misconduct, or diversion. Clear reporting channels - supported by whistleblower protections - encourage individuals to raise concerns without fear of retaliation. Internal investigations must be conducted objectively, with appropriate documentation and escalation procedures.

Strengthening Due Diligence on Partners

Because many non-profits rely on local implementing partners, due diligence must be thorough and consistent. Organizations should assess a partner's governance structure, financial history, operational capacity, and reputation within the community. Site visits, interviews, financial reviews, and reference checks can help determine whether a partner operates responsibly.

Due diligence is not a one-time exercise. Ongoing monitoring is necessary to ensure that partners continue to meet expectations. This includes reviewing financial reports, verifying program results, and monitoring adherence to contractual requirements. When concerns arise, organizations must be willing to suspend partnerships or implement enhanced oversight.

Leveraging Technology for Oversight and Efficiency

Technology can significantly strengthen compliance measures when used appropriately. Digital accounting systems, mobile data collection tools, and electronic document management solutions reduce the likelihood of manipulation and increase the timeliness of reporting. Automated alerts can detect unusual transactions, while centralized databases ensure consistency across field offices.

Data dashboards give leadership real-time visibility into program performance and financial flows. This enables faster identification of risks and more informed decision-making. Technology also enhances auditability: records are easier to retrieve, inconsistencies are easier to identify, and large datasets can be analyzed for trends that indicate potential misuse.

However, technology is not a replacement for sound judgment. Compliance frameworks must combine digital tools with human oversight. Staff must be trained to interpret data, respond to red flags, and maintain rigorous standards.

Cultivating a Culture of Accountability

At the heart of strong compliance lies organizational culture. Culture determines whether staff feel responsible for safeguarding donor resources and whether ethical standards are upheld consistently. Leaders play an essential role in shaping this environment by emphasizing transparency, reinforcing controls, and modeling ethical behavior.

Training programs should emphasize not only procedures but also values. Staff must understand why controls exist and how they contribute to the integrity of operations. When organizations foster open communication, encourage staff to raise concerns, and respond promptly to issues, they create a culture where risks are identified early and managed effectively.

Ensuring Long-Term Sector Integrity

Effective monitoring, transparency, and compliance measures strengthen the resilience of charities and non-profits. These systems help prevent misuse, protect beneficiaries, and preserve donor confidence. By aligning governance with strong oversight and ethical principles, organizations can continue to operate in challenging environments while maintaining the trust essential to fulfilling their mission.

CONCLUSION

FINANCIAL CRIME continues to evolve in scale, sophistication, and impact, and institutions must recognize that conventional approaches are no longer sufficient to address the risks they face. This book has emphasized that financial crime is not a single event or isolated act. It is a systemic threat shaped by human behavior, technological advancement, regulatory weaknesses, professional facilitation, and interconnected criminal networks. Practitioners must therefore rely on structured reasoning, evidence-based methods, and a clear understanding of how illicit activity manifests across different sectors.

A central theme throughout the chapters is that effective investigation depends on clarity. When professionals understand how offenders think, how systems fail, and how financial structures can be misused, they are better equipped to interpret complex patterns and distinguish genuine misconduct from legitimate behavior. Precision in analysis reduces uncertainty, strengthens decision-making, and protects institutions from both under-reaction and over-reaction. The responsibility of investigators extends beyond simply identifying anomalies; it includes interpreting intent, assessing context, and considering the broader implications of each finding.

Another key message is the importance of organizational resilience. Controls, governance, and oversight cannot remain static. Institutions must continuously revise their frameworks to address emerging risks, ensure transparency, and build cultures that support ethical conduct. Technology plays an important role, but it cannot replace professional judgment. Automated tools enhance detection, but well-trained staff, informed leadership, and strong lines of accountability determine whether systems function effectively in practice.

This book also highlighted the broader consequences of financial crime. Beyond immediate financial losses, these offenses distort markets, damage public confidence, weaken governance, and undermine national and international security. Understanding these impacts reinforces why proactive prevention, comprehensive investigations, and timely reporting are essential to protecting societies and maintaining the integrity of global financial systems.

As financial crime continues to adapt, so must the professionals responsible for combating it. The knowledge and frameworks presented in this book aim to support that effort by providing practitioners with practical guidance rooted in real-world conditions. The goal is not simply to respond to individual cases but to strengthen long-term capacity, promote sound judgment, and encourage disciplined practice across all stages of risk management and investigation.

www.ingramcontent.com/pod-product-compliance
Lightning Source LLC
LaVergne TN
LVHW051054210926
848486LV00002B/105

* 9 7 8 1 9 9 8 3 7 6 0 9 4 *